FRANCE BEFORE 1789

France before 1789

THE UNRAVELING OF AN
ABSOLUTIST REGIME

Jon Elster

PRINCETON UNIVERSITY PRESS

PRINCETON & OXFORD

Requests for permission to reproduce material from this work
should be sent to permissions@press.princeton.edu

Published by Princeton University Press
41 William Street, Princeton, New Jersey 08540
6 Oxford Street, Woodstock, Oxfordshire OX20 1TR

press.princeton.edu

Library of Congress Cataloging-in-Publication Data

Names: Elster, Jon, 1940– author.
Title: France before 1789 : the unraveling of an absolutist regime / Jon Elster.
Description: Princeton : Princeton University Press, [2020] | Includes bibliographical
    references and index.
Identifiers: LCCN 2019038091 (print) | LCCN 2019038092 (ebook) | ISBN 9780691149813
    (hardback) | ISBN 9780691200927 (ebook)
Subjects: LCSH: Social groups—France—History—18th century. | Social psychology—
    France—History—18th century. | Political psychology—France—History—18th century. |
    France—Social conditions—18th century. | France—Politics and government—18th century.
Classification: LCC HN425 .E47 2020 (print) | LCC HN425 (ebook) | DDC 302.0944–dc23
LC record available at https://lccn.loc.gov/2019038091
LC ebook record available at https://lccn.loc.gov/2019038092

British Library Cataloging-in-Publication Data is available

Editorial: Rob Tempio and Matt Rohal
Production Editorial: Kathleen Cioffi
Jacket Design: Pamela L. Schnitter
Production: Erin Suydam and Danielle Amatucci
Publicity: Alyssa Sanford and Katie Lewis
Copyeditor: Jay Boggis

Jacket art: The First and Second Estate (nobles and clergy) ride on the back of the Third,
the peasants, 1789. Color engraving. / Musée de la Ville de Paris, Musée Carnavalet, Paris,
France / Photo credit: Erich Lessing / Art Resource, NY

This book has been composed in Miller

Printed on acid-free paper. ∞

Printed in the United States of America

10 9 8 7 6 5 4 3 2 1

For Hilde

CONTENTS

Preface · ix

CHAPTER 1	Introduction	1
	The Nature of the Ancien Régime	1
	Mechanisms: The Importance of Choice	8
	Mechanisms: Interaction	20
CHAPTER 2	The Psychology of the Main Social Groups: Motivations	32
	Interest	32
	Reason	35
	Passion	39
	The Nobility of the Robe	59
	The Peasantry	60
	Seigneurial Justice	88
	The Urban Populations	91
	The Clergy	95
CHAPTER 3	The Psychology of the Main Social Groups: Information and Beliefs	102
	Top-Down Beliefs	102
	Bottom-Up Beliefs	118
	Horizontal Belief Formation	131
CHAPTER 4	The Royal Government and the Courts	139
	Unwritten Constraints	139
	The Tools of Government	154

Discretionary Tools — 161

Revenues and Spending — 170

Necker Cause of the Revolution? — 173

The Legal System — 178

CHAPTER 5   Deliberating Bodies — 188

The Estates-General (1302–1614) — 188

The Main Provincial Estates — 200

The Provincial Estates and the Parlements — 206

CHAPTER 6   Conclusion — 214

The Limits of Our Knowledge — 214

Exemptions and Exceptions — 216

Scarcity, Urgency, and Uncertainty — 217

Injustice and Norm Violations — 219

Conspiracy Theories and Agency-Bias — 221

Passive Resistance — 223

Second Best? — 227

Wars, Taxes, and Loans — 229

Tocqueville — 231

Appendix: Bibliographical Overview · 235

References · 245

Index · 259

THIS BOOK BEGAN as a background chapter in a book comparing the making of the American constitution (1787) and the French constitution (1791). It turned out that the understanding of each of these processes required a substantive presentation not only of the events triggering them, but also of the psychological and institutional aspects of, respectively, the American colonies and the *ancien régime*. As the two background chapters swelled in length, I decided to publish them separately. The present volume will be followed by a study of *America before 1787: The Unraveling of a Colonial Regime*. The comparison between the two constituent assemblies will be the topic of a book on *1787 and 1789: The Making of Two Constitutions*. Strictly speaking, the title of the present volume is a bit misleading, since the discussion of many crucial events in 1787 and 1788 is postponed to volume 3. However, I do cite sayings and events from the last two years before the Revolution to illustrate permanent features of the old regime.

The original background chapters were quite selective. I focused on aspects of the pre-constitutional systems that would prove relevant for the understanding of the constitution-making processes, while ignoring some aspects that would normally have their place in a free-standing monograph such as the present one. In transforming the chapter into a book, I have taken account of more dimensions of the *ancien régime*, although the weights I give them are still shaped by their relevance for constitution-making. For instance, the details I present in chapter 5 about the voting systems in the Estates-General before 1789 and in the provincial Estates would probably be excessive in a presentation of the *ancien régime*, but are important for understanding its transformation and breakdown. In this respect, I believe I follow Tocqueville. In *The Ancien Régime and the French Revolution*, the portrait of the regime is always harnessed to the end of understanding the revolution

Tocqueville's great book has guided me in other ways as well. Like him, I focus on social and political psychology (chapters 2–3) and on institutional analysis (chapters 4–5). To some extent, this book can be read as a long footnote to Tocqueville, spelling out in more detail his broad and general analyses, and occasionally disagreeing with them. Tocqueville relied on his intuitive knowledge of the *ancien régime* and on his deep understanding of human nature. While I cannot claim to equal him in either respect, I can benefit from developments in the social sciences and the accumulation of factual knowledge that have taken place since his time. I am, in fact, a social scientist and not an historian.

The book is also programmatic, as an attempt to practice *the union of history and psychology*, which are, in my opinion, the two main pillars of the social sciences. That history can learn from psychology is obvious. That psychology can learn from history is less obvious, but no less true, as shown by a great book by Paul Veyne, *Le pain et le cirque*. Tocqueville and Veyne are the founders of the union I am trying to practice. *Philosophy*, too, can make important contributions. I shall draw extensively upon Aristotle, Seneca, Montaigne, Locke, Hume, and John Stuart Mill.

The book is written in three layers. The first is the main text, where I summarize my main claims and suggestions. The second consists of the footnotes where I cite my sources. The third consists of the footnotes where I pursue some theoretical issues in more detail. (Some footnotes serve both functions.) Hence the footnotes are intended to bridge the gap between two scholarly communities, by pointing social scientists to new explananda and historians to new explanations.

In the Appendix, I discuss the main writings by contemporaries and historians that I rely on. (Some readers may want to look at these summaries first.) I would never have been able to master this material and complete this book if I had been limited to books I own and to physical libraries. The coming of the Internet, with digitized and often searchable versions of obscure publications, has made it possible to compress into a few years work that in the past might have required a decade. Google, Internet Archive, and Galllica, among others, perform an invaluable public service in making recondite and sometimes virtually *introuvable* texts available to scholars with a one-click. In the References, texts available in open access on-line are starred.

On the basis of a very rough draft of chapter 2, Arlette Jouanna encouraged me to persist in my efforts to understand the *ancien régime*. Without her support, this book might not have seen the light of day. Once I had completed a full draft, I asked Stephen Holmes, Bernard Manin, Julian Swann, and Timothy Tackett to join me for a two-day book workshop at the Collège de France. While they, too, were overall encouraging, they asked acute questions and made telling criticisms that forced me to reorganize the basic structure of the book and rewrite pretty much every page. I am sure I have not responded to all their objections, and equally sure that the changes they triggered made the book immeasurably better, and spared me from many embarrassing mistakes. They have my deepest gratitude. At Yale University, Hélène Landemore organized a book workshop that helped me get some key issues into better focus. Comments by two readers for Princeton University Press also provided useful suggestions. Finally, I want to thank the Collège de France for financial support of the first workshop, and to acknowledge travel support for Timothy Tackett and Julian Swann from, respectively, the University of California at Irvine and Birkbeck College, London.

Unless an English source is cited, translations from French are mine.

FRANCE BEFORE 1789

CHAPTER ONE

Introduction

The Nature of the Ancien Régime

The French *ancien régime* was exceedingly complex, at all levels. In agriculture, which occupied at least 80 percent of the population, almost each piece of land was subject to an immense variety of formal and informal burdens, duties, and rights, which varied from province to province,[1] from one village to its neighbor, and from one family to another. Trade and, indirectly, production were hampered by internal tolls.[2] Citizens paid a number of direct and indirect taxes, which also varied across regions and were subject to numerous exemptions as well as to arbitrary methods of assessment and collection.[3] Because the French kings were in constant need of money for their many wars, taxes often had to be supplemented by

---

1. I shall often use the term "province" loosely, to cover three subdivisions of the kingdom: the *généralités*, which collected taxes; the *gouvernements*, which had a mainly military function; and the *intendances*, which were an administrative unit. For an overview of their changing and overlapping functions and borders, see Barbiche (2012), pp. 365–374, 331–332, 383–932. The clergy was divided into fourteen to sixteen ecclesiastical provinces, which elected delegates to its quinquennial assemblies and bore little relation to the other partitions.

2. Many examples in AP 18, 303–13. The minister of Louis XVI, Necker (1784–1785, vol. 2 pp. 172–173), said that the complexity of the toll system was such that only one or two men in each generation mastered it completely. Although it is impossible to determine the importance of the profitable ventures that *were not undertaken* because of high transaction costs, the grievance books suggest that it was considerable (Shapiro and Markoff (1998), p. 273). As I document in chapter 2, direct taxes, too, could blunt the incentive to produce and to trade.

3. Esmonin (1913) is a masterful study. Blaufarb (2010) presents an impressive documentation of "two and a half centuries struggle against exemptions from the *taille*" in Provence.

loans (often in the form of government bonds), the interest on which was paid irregularly if at all. The offices in the legal system were the private property of those who held them, creating a large space for arbitrary or self-interested decisions. The courts were also engaged in a constant tug-of-war, even a "kind of civil war,"[4] with the king, one of many reasons why a literal reading of the idea of an "absolute" monarchy is meaningless.[5] The kings had absolute power only in the small circle of their family and the Court, where they often exercised it tyrannically. If someone contradicted them, they often responded by turning their back on their interlocutor. The decisions taken by the king's council in Paris were executed in the provinces by officials who often behaved as petty tyrants. The division of the population in three orders—clergy, nobility, and commoners—with many-layered subdivisions generated an intense struggle for *préséance* or rank that could paralyze decision-making. In Paris (after 1682 at Versailles, 21 kilometers west of Paris), the royal court was not only a financial drain, but also a hotbed of intrigues where ministers came and went on the basis of the whims of the king, his mistresses, his entourage, and, under Louis XVI, his wife. The kings were also obsessed with the private lives of the citizens and established a *cabinet noir* that could open their letters, a system people exploited to make false statements about their enemies. The kings also used, to an extent unparalleled elsewhere in Western Europe, the tool of exiling those who for some reason displeased them to their landed properties or to towns distant from Paris.

The purpose of this book is to present the main features of this prodigiously complex social system. In doing so, I shall try to go beyond formal institutions to show how they worked in practice. Like Tocqueville, but with more examples, I shall cite many contemporary texts that illuminate the perverse and sometimes pathological effects of the system. Although the presentation of many examples does not transform anecdotes into a law-like regularity, they do indicate that we are dealing with a robust *mechanism* rather than an idiosyncratic event.[6] I shall not hide, however, that some episodes and anecdotes are included, in part, for their sheer entertainment value. This procedure has also a more substantive justification, since *wit* (*esprit*) was a dominant value in the French elite. Wit could

---

4. An expression used by a *syndic* from Languedoc who assisted at a *lit de justice* in Paris in 1756 (Jouanna 2014 d, p. 582).

5. When I refer to the Royal Court at Versailles, I spell "Court" with a capital C. When I refer to the various judicial bodies, I use lower-case spelling.

6. For expositions of the idea of mechanism on which I rely, see Elster (1999), chap. 1; Elster (2011); and Elster (2015a), chap. 2.

ruin the career of the target of a *bon mot* and promote, but also occasionally ruin, that of the person who displayed it.

In chapter 5, I shall go back to 1302, to study the origin and further development of the institution of the Estates-General and other representative bodies. Most of the discussion will focus, however, on the seventeenth and eighteenth centuries: the emergence of absolute monarchy during the reign of Louis XIII, its stabilization under Louis XIV, and its increasing brittleness under his two successors.

We have to ask, obviously, whether the *ancien régime*, which for many purposes can be defined as the period from the beginning of the personal reign of Louis XIV in 1661 to the 1789 Revolution, has sufficient internal coherence and continuity to count as *one* regime.[7] Repeating some earlier remarks, and anticipating on later chapters, some important features that remained more or less the same are the following.

Continuity

Individuals, institutions such as the Church, and the government were obsessed (the word is not too strong) with keeping their financial affairs away from the light of publicity.

Members of all social orders were obsessed (again, the word is not too strong) with rank or *préséance*.

Because of its constant wars and the inefficient tax system, the government was obsessed (again, the word is not too strong) with the need for money, a fact that induced a short time-horizon which never left any breathing space to reform the administration.

Individual agents, too, were rarely in a position to pursue their long-term interest.

Many public offices were de jure the personal property of the office-holder and his family, while others approximated the same status de facto, creating a patrimonial system that prevented the emergence of a rational bureaucracy.

The separation of powers was never complete, since the kings had their own "retained justice" (*justice retenue*) that allowed them to take any legal case out of the ordinary courts to be judged by a royal official or a special royal court.

---

7. In a Volume 2, I shall also ask to what extent the American colonies from 1629 to the Revolution can be counted as one, coherent regime.

This mechanism, which allowed the administration to be judge in the cases brought against it, was reproduced at a local level in the form of seigneurial justice.

In a system that was both inefficient and inequitable, nobles, the Church, and privileged commoners were exempt from the main property tax (*taille*).

Taxes were supplemented by the issuing of government bonds, at interest and reimbursement schedules that were at the intersection of social, economic, and political conflicts.

The psychology of the kings often prevented them, for reasons I discuss in chapter 4, from appointing competent advisers or listening to their advice.

The kings also had at their disposal informal tools of oppression and control, such as exile, imprisonment without a court order, and the opening of private letters.

At the same time, inevitably, there were some more or less sharp discontinuities.

Change

Living standards increased; in the eighteenth century, barring the cruel years of 1709–10, few people died of hunger.

The tax system was reformed, introducing new direct taxes from which no one was exempt as well as indirect taxes that came to be a more important source of revenue than direct taxes.

There was less state violence and less popular violence, but increased violence by the private armies of tax farmers.

There was substantial increase in the power of the *intendants*

The century-long exclusion of nobles from the government ended around 1760.

The half-century-long exclusion of the courts (*parlements*) from politics ended in 1715.

The *justice retenue* became less important under Louis XV and Louis XVI.

The desacralization of the kings went hand in hand with a decline in religious fervor, both facts being arguably causes, or effects, or constitutive, of the Enlightenment.

In the decades before 1789, one observed a quiet revolt of the parish priests against the upper clergy, who had completely dominated them in the past.

Overall, the regime became less harsh, a fact that Tocqueville used to explain its downfall (chapter 2).

In some ways, the continuity dominates the change. To be sure, in accounting for the Revolution of 1789, recent events, such as the near-bankruptcy of the public finances in 1788 and near-starvation in parts of the countryside in 1789, often have more explanatory power than the more distant past. Yet the impact of these dramatic circumstances was always mediated by dispositions that had been shaped over centuries, be it the concern of the Parisian bourgeoisie over the payment of interest on governmental bonds, the obsession of people in the towns with the price of bread, the tendency of the courts to refuse to register royal edicts, or peasant fears of hoarders and speculators.

Yet the regime fell in 1789, not in 1750 or 1715. As suggested by the subtitle of the present book, the cumulative impact of the changes made it increasing brittle and vulnerable. Drawing on Tocqueville's two main works, we can move beyond descriptive enumeration and ask the *causal* question of stability versus instability. In *Democracy in America*, Tocqueville argued for the stability of American democracy by presenting it as what Marc Bloch, referring to medieval agriculture, called "un admirable engrenage," a set of wonderfully interlocking parts. As Tocqueville wrote, '[d]esires proportion themselves to means. Needs, ideas, and sentiments follow from one another. Leveling is complete; democratic society has finally found its footing [*est enfin assise*]."[8] In a draft manuscript, he drew a contrast between this stable American society, in which "everything hangs together" (*tout s'enchaîne*) and the unstable European societies, in which there is "confusion in the intellectual world, opinions are not in harmony with tastes nor interests with ideas."[9] In another draft he notes that "Laws act on mores and mores on laws. Wherever these two things do not support each other mutually there is unrest, division, revolution."[10]

Almost certainly, the last phrase refers to the 1789 Revolution. Although his book on the *ancien régime* does not contain explicit theoretical statements similar to those I just quoted, it does propose some destabilizing mechanisms. In a succinct statement from the notes for the unfinished second volume, Tocqueville writes that "Men had developed

8. Tocqueville (2004a), p. 739; see also Bloch (1999), p. 99; and Elster (2009a), chap. 6.

9. Tocqueville (1992), p. 940. This passage is not included in Tocqueville (2001).

10. Tocqueville (2010), vol. 1, p. 111.

to the point where they had a clearer sense of what they lacked and suffered more from it, even though the sum total of their suffering was much smaller than before. Their sensitivity had grown far faster than their relief. *This was true of the grievances of liberty and equality as well as of money.*"[11]

The "grievance of liberty"—the removal of one form of oppression makes the remaining ones more acutely felt—will concern me in chapter 2.[12] The "grievance of money" is spelled out as follows:

> Poor management of public finances, which had long been only a public ill, now became for countless families a private calamity. In 1789, the state owed nearly 600 million to its creditors, nearly all of whom were debtors themselves and who, as one financier said at the time, found, in their grievances against the government, partners in everyone who suffered as they did from the fecklessness of the state. Note, moreover, that as the number of malcontents of this sort grew, so did their irritation, because the urge to speculate, the passion to get rich, and the taste for comfort spread along with the growth of business and *made such evils seem unbearable to the very same people who, thirty years earlier, would have endured them without complaint.*[13]

The "grievance of equality," finally, can be stated in terms of the sociological theory of status incongruence, according to which increased equality in one dimension causes inequality *in other dimensions* to appear as more and more intolerable. If status barriers to occupational choice remain constant or even became more rigid (as happened in 1781 for access to high military office), while economic conditions are becoming more equal, rich commoners will feel increasingly frustrated.[14]

11. Tocqueville (2004b), p. 1071; my italics. This passage is not included in the English translation (Tocqueville 2001) of the notes for the second volume.

12. Contrary to the influential interpretation of Davies (1962), this "Tocqueville effect" is *not* due to anticipations rising faster than actual developments. While Tocqueville (1987, pp. 75–76) mentions this mechanism in his analysis of the 1848 Revolution, he does not cite it in his writings on the 1789 Revolution.

13. Tocqueville (2011), p. 159; my italics.

14. Commenting on Athenian politics in the fifth century BCE, Walcot (1978), p. 64, writes that "perhaps democracy actually intensified rather than reduced feelings of envy: the very fact that all citizens were equal as voters in the assembly simply may have made some that much more aware of their inequality in birth or wealth or even good luck." Whereas Tocqueville (as I read him) found the source of incongruence in increased economic equality, Walcot locates it in increased political equality. In both cases, objective improvement may have led to subjective discontent.

Among other destabilizing mechanisms, Tocqueville emphasizes particularly the *homogenizing of society*:

> When the bourgeois had thus been isolated from the noble, and the peasant from the noble and bourgeois, and when, by a similar process within each class, there emerged distinct small groups almost as isolated from one another as the classes were, it became clear that the whole society had been reduced to a homogeneous mass with nothing to hold its parts together. *Nothing was left that could obstruct the government, nor anything that could shore it up.* Thus, the princely magnificence of the whole edifice *could collapse all at once*, in the blink of an eye, the moment the society that served as its foundation began to tremble.[15]

The first two sentences suggest that the measures taken by the kings to weaken any opposition undermined the royal authority, because organic solidarity was transformed into a mechanical similarity that did not leave the king anyone to call on in times of crisis. The last sentence suggests an analogy with a house of cards. If placed in a turbulent environment its collapse is inevitable, but the timing and the force of the particular gust of wind that brings it down is unpredictable. Although retroactive statements about inevitability are often affected by hindsight bias, Tocqueville had a good track record in predicting revolutions *before* they occurred. His accurate predictions of the 1830 and 1848 Revolutions[16] lend credibility to his retrodiction of the events of 1789.

My book is less ambitious than Tocqueville's. I do not have a concluding chapter titled "How the revolution emerged naturally from the foregoing," because I think there was more contingency than he allowed for. My aim is to help us see the events as intelligible in the light of widely applicable *mechanisms*, not as uniquely determined in the light of general *laws*.

---

15. Tocqueville (2011), p. 124; my italics. He may have been inspired by the words spoken to Napoleon by the poet François Andrieux: "On ne s'appuie que sur ce qui résiste" ("You can lean only against what offers resistance"). In 1648, one of the leaders of the *Fronde*, the magistrate Broussel, used a vivid metaphor to make the same point: "One does not destroy the authority of the kings by combating its excesses, but, on the contrary, *one supports it by resisting it*, just as in an edifice the flying buttresses support the mass, while seeming to resist it" (cited after Aubertin 1880, p. 212; my italics).

16. For 1830, see the letter to his brother Edouard and his sister Alexandrine of May 6, 1830 (Tocqueville (1998), p.67). For 1848, see his speech on January 27, 1848 in the National Assembly, partly reproduced in Tocqueville (1987), pp. 13–15.

Mechanisms: The Importance of Choice

The argument of the book is driven by two concerns: the quest for *causality* and the quest for *agency* (methodological individualism).[17] Jointly, these concerns imply a focus on *choice* as the key explanatory variable. A negative implication is that the mere *effect* of an institution cannot serve to explain it. It may well be true that this or that institution of the *ancien régime* served as a safety valve by keeping discontent at manageable levels, but that fact does not explain why it exists. Tocqueville, who mostly adhered to the principles of methodological individualism (without indicating that he had *any* methodology), violated them when he wrote that after the last Estates-General in 1614, the last before the Revolution,

> The . . . desire to escape the tutelage of the estates led to the attribution to the *parlements* of most of their political prerogatives. . . . There was *a need* to appear to provide new guarantees in place of those that had been eliminated because the French, who will put up rather patiently with absolute power as long as it is not oppressive, never like the sight of it, and it is always wise to raise some apparent barriers in front of it, barriers that cannot stop it but nevertheless hide it a little.[18]

As an historical analysis of the *origins* of the politicized *parlements*, this statement is sheer fantasy. As a comment on the *effects* of the politicization it may or may not be true (see chapter 4), but it is not absurd.

While compelling as a first principle, methodological individualism is often too demanding in practice. We rarely have the documentary evidence that we would need to identify the beliefs and motivations of, say, each peasant in an insurrection or each magistrate in a judicial strike. Nor can we assume that an occasional explicit statement by an agent is reliable and representative. It is also difficult to consistently avoid the cardinal sin of inferring mental states from the actions they are supposed to explain. Historians are forced to triangulate many sources to impute motivations and beliefs. When drawing on their work, I cannot but trust their intimate knowledge that comes from a lifetime in the archives.

To this caveat, I shall add another one. Beliefs and desires are intrinsically hard to identify with precision, for three reasons stated by James Madison in *The Federalist* # 37. First, there is *indistinctness of the object*: it

---

17. The remarks in this section are more fully developed in Elster (2015a) and in Elster (forthcoming).

18. Tocqueville (2011), p. 100; my italics. The flaw in the argument is the assumption that needs generate their own satisfaction.

is not always clear whether the agents possessed stable beliefs and desires that they used as premises for action. A riot that is cut short because the participants go home for dinner (chapter 2) probably did not stem from a deep and strong conviction. Did the French peasantry really "believe" in rumors about an impending tax on children? Second, there is *imperfection of the organ of conception*: "The faculties of the mind itself have never yet been distinguished and defined, with satisfactory precision, by all the efforts of the most acute and metaphysical philosophers" (Madison). How can we determine whether a reform triggered a *desire* for more reforms or a *belief* that more reforms were imminent? Can we tell for sure whether an act of aggression was motivated by anger, by envy, or by hatred? Finally, there is *inadequateness of the vehicle of ideas*: "no language is so copious as to supply words and phrases for every complex idea, or so correct as not to include many equivocally denoting different ideas" (Madison). In his journal, the bookseller Hardy is constantly struggling to find the words for the exact degree of credibility of the rumors he is reporting. In other words, there may not be a fact of the matter; even if there is, we may not be able to grasp it; even if we could, we may not be able to state it unambiguously. As Hegel notes somewhere, language always says both more and less than what the speaker or writer intended. Yet as Eliot's Sweeney says, "I gotta use words when I talk to you."

The focus on choices—their antecedents and their consequences—puts me in a different camp from many historians of the *ancien régime*. I shall pay little attention to the intellectual and cultural preconditions, or alleged preconditions, of the Revolution. The influence of the Enlightenment on political events and social movements was possibly strong, but it was certainly diffuse, often too diffuse to provide a causal, individual-level explanation of specific choices and decisions. Although, as I said, desacralization of the king and decline in religious fervor coincided with the Enlightenment, the causal relations are opaque. Depending on one's definitions, desacralization and decline in religious fervor may even be *constitutive* of the Enlightenment.

When parish priests deserted en masse to the third estate in June 1789, when soldiers refused orders to shoot on the people in July 1789, and when women intruded on the privacy of the royal couple in October 1789, they certainly exhibited lack of the traditional deference towards their superiors. Yet the actions of the parish priests may have been due mainly to the fact that for the first time in the history of the Estates-General they formed a majority of the clergy, those of the soldiers to the unwise decisions of the July conspirators, and those of the women to the popular attitude towards

Marie-Antoinette. I shall cover these events in Volume 3. Here, I am only suggesting that these specific facts, *demonstrable independently of the events they are intended to explain* (at least in part), are more probative than more diffuse and general tendencies.

The relevance of *discourse analysis* is limited in a context where the vast majority of the people was illiterate. We do not know to what extent discontent percolated down from the educated elites or, on the contrary, whether popular unrest provided the ferment for more articulate statements by lawyers and wealthy commoners. There is more evidence about intra-elite discourse. We may, for instance, follow the semantic transformations of terms like "credit" from the sixteenth century to the eighteenth, reflecting the changing relations between the monarchs and the nobles.[19] Yet it is only these relations that have causal efficacy, not their verbal expressions.

For many social scientists, the privileged form of choice is *rational* choice. While often useful, rational-choice explanations of behavior cannot, in my opinion, claim any privilege, except on the (irrelevant) grounds that they lend themselves to mathematical modeling. Let me first state the standard rational-choice model of action and then generalize it. The standard model and the general model involve many of the same variables: *desires* (preferences, motivations), *beliefs*, and *information*. The general model also introduces *emotions*.

The basic elements of the standard rational-choice model are shown in Figure 1.1. The arrows stand both for causal relations and for optimality relations. The desire, for instance, is both what makes the action optimal and what causes it. A rational choice is the joint product of the agent's desires and her well-informed beliefs: doing as well as (she rationally believes) she can. For the beliefs to be rational, she has to collect an optimal amount—not too little, nor too much—of information, and then process it rationally in light of prior, more general beliefs. In this model, there is *no room for motivated belief formation*—it excludes a direct causal influence of desires on beliefs.[20]

19. Jouanna (1989), chap. 3; Smith (1997).
20. An example: to form a rational belief about the weather some time hence, you can look out of the window or consult the forecast, in either case drawing on prior beliefs about the reliability of these sources. If it is important for you to know how the weather will turn out, you might check the forecast, and check two forecasts if it is very important; if your motive is idle curiosity, looking out of the window is good enough. (However, if it is extremely important, you might want to check so many forecasts that by the time you have formed your belief the time for action has passed.) This fact opens for an indirect causal influence of desires on beliefs, mediated by information-gathering. The information loop

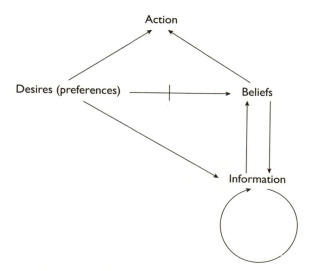

FIGURE 1.1. The standard model of rational choice.

The standard model of rational choice can obviously explain a great many actions. To take an example from chapter 2, since peasants knew from experience that prompt payment of taxes in a given year would lead to higher impositions in the next year, they rationally procrastinated in paying, even if they had to pay a fine for late payment. Knowing that the *cabinet noir* would open and read their correspondence, many high-placed individuals took rational precautions, Turgot by sending his mail by private courier, Madame de Sévigné by using pseudonyms when referring to the royal household, and Saint-Simon by including only anodyne matters (chapter 3). Bondholders rationally demanded higher interest rates for risky loans (chapter 4). Such examples could be multiplied indefinitely.

Game theory—which ought really to be named "the theory of interdependent decisions"—is a special case of rational-choice theory. It arises when each of two or several agents need to form rational expectations about what the others will do, in order to respond optimally to their choices. In an early treatment, Nicolas de Montmort provided a numerical example that seems to lead to an infinite regress of "I think that he thinks that I think . . . ," and added, "Such questions are very simple, but I believe they are unsolvable. If that is the case, it is a great pity, for this problem often arises in ordinary life, as when each of two people who have some business

reflects the fact that the search may provide decisive information early on so that there is no need to persist.

together wants to adjust his behavior to that of the other."[21] Some game theorists claim that this insolvability has since been overcome, since the idea of an *equilibrium*, in which each agent chooses the best response to the best-response choices of all others, allows one to short-circuit the infinite regress. However, in Montmort's example, this "solution" requires the agents to use a chance-wheel that assigns calculable probabilities to each of the possible responses (I simplify), a requirement that makes the "solution" devoid of empirical interest. In my view, this is also the case for many of the other solution concepts that game theorists have proposed. Be this as it may, for my purposes in this book the relevant question is whether agents can be assumed to *know each other's preferences*. In a two-person game involving the provision of a public good, for instance, each agent may not know whether the other prefers mutual cooperation over being the unilateral non-cooperator. There may be two equilibria, one good (mutual cooperation) and one bad (mutual non-cooperation), but if the agents do not know each other's preferences none of the equilibria will stand out as *the* solution. In chapter 2, I suggest that some of the perverse features of *préséance* can be understood in this perspective.

When the rational-choice model fails, it is either because of *indeterminacy*—the model does not tell the agent what to do—or because of *irrationality*—the agent does not do what the model tells her to do.

Indeterminacy arises largely because of uncertainty. Because of the unreliable flow of *information* to the royal government, rational belief formation about the capacity of the economy was virtually impossible (chapter 3). Conversely, because the government shrouded both its revenues and expenses in secrecy, other agents, such as the *parlements*, had no basis for forming a rational judgment about the need for new taxes (chapter 4). In fact, the government itself often did not know the size of its debt (chapter 3). Also, as we shall see, game-theoretic situations can generate uncertainty, for instance if agents are unable to predict whether others agents are likely to cooperate.

Irrationality arises when the processing of information is subject to either a "cold" (unmotivated) bias or a "hot" (motivated) bias. Cold bias is a recent, revolutionary idea developed by psychologists and behavioral economists over the last half-century.[22] They have demonstrated by experiments and field studies that both the ancient and classical moralists (see below) were wrong when implicitly *assuming that irrationality*

21. Montmort (1713), p. 406.
22. For an incomplete overview, see Elster (2015a), chapter 15.

was always due to passion. Zero-sum mercantilist policies, such as those advocated by Colbert (chapter 3), may be due to a cold cognitive bias.[23] Although I cannot cite specific instances, I am confident that officials in the *ancien régime* (as officials everywhere) were occasionally subject to the sunk-cost fallacy (throwing good money after bad) or to the recency effect (paying more attention to new information than to older, equally relevant data).

I shall understand hot bias mainly as emotional bias, although it can also have other sources.[24] When emotion shapes cognition, it can do so in two main ways. First, as La Fontaine wrote, "Each believes easily what he fears and what he hopes." The second half of that phrase refers to garden-variety wishful thinking, such as the belief of the peasantry that a temporary relief from a tax would be a permanent one or that relief from one tax implied the relief from all others (chapter 2). The first half of the phrase is more puzzling: why would people form beliefs that are both unsupported by evidence (as in wishful thinking) *and* are contrary to what they would like to be true? John Stuart Mill proposed an ambiguous answer: "[T]he most common case of [Bias] is that in which we are biased by our wishes; but the liability is almost as great to the undue adoption of a conclusion which is disagreeable to us as of one which is agreeable, if it be of a nature to *bring into action any of the stronger passions*. . . . Indeed, it is a psychological law, deducible from the most general laws of the mental constitution of man, that any strong passion *renders us credulous as to the existence of objects suitable to excite it*."[25] I leave it to readers to sort out the relation between the two statements I have italicized. Independent of "general laws," however, the existence of fear-based rumors (chapter 3) provides indisputable proof that we easily believe what we fear. Social psychologists have also found that fear induces both *stronger risk-aversion* (compared to the agent's non-emotional state) and *more pessimistic risk-assessments* (compared to those of a neutral observer).[26]

Anger and, more conjecturally, enthusiasm have the opposite effects on both dimensions.[27] It follows that when we observe agents engaging in highly risky behavior—magistrates ordering officials not to execute a

23. Kemp (2007).

24. Loewenstein (1996) argues that "visceral factors" more generally, including emotions as well as pain and hunger, can also bias cognition. In chapter 2 I discuss how *the transmutation of hunger into anger* can enter into the explanation of subsistence rebellions.

25. Mill (1846), V. 1; see also Thagard and Nussbaum (2014).

26. Lerner and Keltner (2001).

27. For anger, see ibid. For enthusiasm, Jennifer Lerner (personal communication) confirms my hunch. It might be hard, however, to demonstrate it in the laboratory.

royal edict (chapter 4) or urban consumers pillaging bakeries for bread (chapter 3)—the explanation may either be a cognitive one (underestimating the risk) or a motivational one (assessing the risk correctly and accepting it). In the first case, the appropriate term may be *foolhardiness*; in the second, *courage*. In practice, as Madison warned, we may not be able to tell.

Emotions can also shape cognition by their *urgency*, by which I mean a desire to act sooner rather than later. (A more vivid term is "inaction-aversion.") Although this tendency can be rational in the face of an acute danger or need, it is also observed in situations where there would be nothing to lose and possibly something to gain from taking the time to gather more information. In *On Anger* (I. xi), Seneca asked:

> How else did Fabius restore the broken forces of the state but by knowing how to loiter, to put off, and to wait—*things of which angry men know nothing*? The state, which was standing then in the utmost extremity, had surely perished if Fabius had ventured to do all that anger prompted. But he took into consideration the well-being of the state, and, estimating strength, of which nothing now could be lost without the loss of all, he *buried all thought of resentment and revenge* and was concerned only with expediency and the fitting opportunity; he *conquered anger* before he conquered Hannibal (my italics).

In the *ancien régime*, urgency on the part of the government was mainly a rational response to the constant need for money to fund wars, pay creditors, and pay for luxury at the Court. By contrast, crowds provide examples of urgency-caused *irrationality*, when they attack alleged malefactors on the basis of suspicions without taking the time to verify them. There was but a short step from an accusation to a conviction that it was justified (chapter 3). The suspicions and the anger they generated were, in turn, shaped by the tendency to believe what one fears.

Figure 1.2 shows how emotions can be integrated in a more general model of choice,[28] which deviates from the standard model in two ways. On the one hand, the general model *contrasts* with the standard model in allowing for a causal influence from desires to beliefs. In belief formation, causality and optimality can diverge. On the other hand, the general model *expands* the standard model in allowing for a causal influence from beliefs to desires, mediated by emotions. In the standard model, desires are the unmoved movers in the machinery of action, whereas the general model

---

28. More general, but still a simplification that omits many causal links. For a fuller model, see Elster (forthcoming).

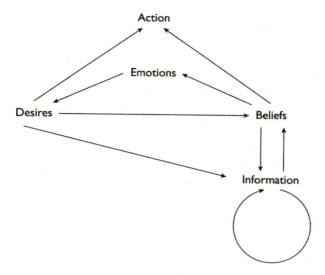

FIGURE 1.2. A general model of choice.

allows us to go a step further back in the causal chain. In the formation of desires, the question of optimality and causality diverging from each other does not arise, since the notion of an optimal desire is not well defined.

Emotions are triggered by beliefs, but can be reinforced by *perceptions*. *Reading* in the tax documents the list of duties levied by tax officials may cause anger, but *seeing* the "black-robed counselors" in the streets may turn the anger into fury (chapter 2). In this book, I refer to beliefs as a shorthand for both cognitions and perceptions as causes of emotion. Emotions differ among each other mainly by *the beliefs that trigger them* and by *the desires for action they trigger*. To illustrate, consider the difference between (what Descartes called) anger and indignation. A feels anger when he believes that B has harmed him unjustly, and indignation when he believes that B has harmed a third person C unjustly. Both anger and indignation make A want to harm B, but experiments confirm the intuition that third-party punishments will be substantially weaker than second-party ones.

In these experiments, carried out by Ernst Fehr and his cooperators, the intensity of anger and indignation is measured by how much the subjects are willing to harm themselves in order to harm the target of their emotion.[29] In the *ancien régime*, harming another person in anger could be risky or costly; leaders of rebellions were often executed. Indignation,

29. Se Fehr and Fischbacher (2004). Harm to oneself is measured by the amount of monetary loss a subject incurs. For instance, the experimental protocol might be that in

expressed as speaking truth to power (chapter 3), did not impose any material harm on the targets, whether it was the king or his officials, but if expressed publicly it might undermine, or be thought to undermine, their legitimacy. Criticizing the regime in public could, however, involve punishment of the critic, but mainly in the form of censorship, exile, or imprisonment (chapter 4). In the eighteenth century, these reactions were sometimes seen as badges of honor rather than as punishments.[30]

Anger also differs from *hatred*, in that the former rests on the belief that the target person performed a bad *action* while the latter rests on the belief that he or she has a bad *character*. According to Aristotle, these two emotions also differ in their desires for action: an angry person wants his offender to suffer, while a person who feels hatred wants the other person to disappear from the face of the earth. *Contempt*, too, is based on beliefs about character, triggering avoidance behavior. One can propose similar characterizations in terms of *triggering beliefs* and *triggered actions* for most of the twenty-odd emotions that can be robustly distinguished from each other. Whereas I believe most of them are found in all societies, the situations that trigger them vary immensely. What is shameful in one society, such as obesity, can be a source of pride and envy in another.

The main emotions I discuss in this book are negative: fear, anxiety, envy, anger, indignation, resentment, hatred, disappointment, shame, and contempt. Sometimes a reform can trigger a positive emotion of *hope* that more reforms will be coming (and disappointment when they are not). I shall discuss such episodes in Volume 3. Below I shall also point to some paradoxical emotional reactions, as when the discovery that a fear was groundless triggered anger rather than relief, and that a reform made people more dissatisfied rather than less. Moreover, I shall discuss mechanisms by which the non-emotional state of *hunger* was transmuted into anger.

For the ancient moralists, *reason* was the antonym of passion (or emotion). They never defined, however, what they meant by reason. Did they refer to any *dispassionate* motivation, or did they also require reason to be *disinterested*? Modern writers, notably the French moralists of the seventeenth century and the authors of *The Federalist Papers*, were more explicit. Instead of the dyad reason-passion, they proposed a triad:

---

order to cause an offender to lose two monetary units (MU), the agent will have to suffer a cost of one MU.

30. In 1771, Hardy, vol. 2, p. 51, reports that the *Premier President* of the *parlement* of Paris as well as several other magistrates were upset for not having received *lettres de cachet* sending them into exile.

reason-interest-passion. Reason and interest are both dispassionate, but only reason is also disinterested. As I shall use this triad of motivations to characterize the agents of the *ancien régime*, I need to say a bit more about each of them.

Reason, as I understand it here, is the rational pursuit of the long-term public good.[31] It is not merely a matter of efficiency or raison d'état, at least if one holds (as I do) that social justice is part of the conception of the public good. I shall devote considerable space to the question whether officials from the king downward were concerned with the welfare of the French and not merely with the glory of France (and their own).

Interest is the pursuit of the good of a proper subset of society, be it a group or an individual. In this book, I consider mainly material interests, while noting (chapter 4) that an interest in salvation could also be motivating. As many moralists have observed,[32] the pursuit of *long-term* interest may mimic or simulate the pursuit of the public interest, since people are sometimes willing to cooperate in situations that invite free-riding if—but only if—they expect that others will reciprocate. An example from Hume shows the difficulty:

> Your corn is ripe [in August]; mine will be so [in September]. It is profitable for us both, that I should labour with you [in August], and that you should aid me [in September]. I have no kindness for you, and know you have as little for me. I will not, therefore, take any pains upon your account; and should I labour with you upon my own account, in expectation of a return, I know I should be disappointed, and that I should in vain depend upon your gratitude. Here then I leave you to labour alone: You treat me in the same manner. The seasons change; and both of us lose our harvests for want of mutual confidence and security.[33]

There exists, however, a solution in terms of long-term self-interest that, in terms of the example, can be spelled out as follows: I have an incentive to cooperate with you in August 2020, because I know that your desire to receive my cooperation in August 2021 will make you keep your promise to help me in September 2020. When fighting factions of

31. For normative purposes, this seems like an appropriate definition. For explanatory purposes, one may omit the requirement of rationality. As Kant noted, *enthusiasm* can inspire the pursuit of the general good while also subverting the choice of the best means to that end (Elster forthcoming b).

32. Elster (2004)

33. Hume (1978), pp. 520–521. I have substituted "August" and "September" for Hume's "today" and "tomorrow."

magistrates or of nobles kept a temporary truce during the harvest,[34] they may have been acting under "the shadow of the future." While long-term thinking can thus mimic reason's efficiency dimension, it cannot mimic the social justice dimension in the case of orphans, the elderly, the disabled, or the very poor—those who cannot reciprocate for any assistance they might receive. Even when reciprocation would have been feasible—one peasant abstaining from denouncing his neighbors to the tax collector in the expectation that they will do the same—the short time horizon induced by acute material scarcity could make denunciation rational for self-interested agents.[35] Moreover, nobody could be certain that their neighbor would abide by the tacit contract, even if all might have been willing to do so were they confident about the others.

Passion, or emotion, is the pursuit of goals motivated by episodic or standing emotions, some of which I have enumerated. Often, an emotion triggers only an *action tendency* that never leads to a full-blown action, because the tendency is counterbalanced by another emotion, by self-interest, by social norms, or by moral norms. The action tendency may also remain unfulfilled because the emotion runs out of steam (many emotions have a "short half-life"). Some repressive actions by the monarchy, whether against the peasantry (chapter 2) or against subversive writers (chapter 4), subsided after a short while. Sometimes, the government counted on this mechanism, when it imposed an edict by force on the first day of the judicial vacations, hoping that tempers would cool over the summer (chapter 4).

Above, I have followed a tradition initiated by Aristotle, which focuses on the effects of emotions on *action*. I shall also pay attention to another tradition, initiated by Seneca and continued by La Rochefoucauld, which focuses on the effects of emotion on *other mental states*, which may or may not then become precursors of action. Seneca wrote, "Those whom they injure, they also hate." A French proverb says, "Who has offended can never forgive." These and many other reactions are due to the insidious operation of *amour-propre*, self-love, or egocentricity. An institution to

34. Bercé (1974), p. 257.

35. In this book, I shall never refer to *pure time preferences*, that is, a preference for an early reward over a later reward *merely* because it arrives earlier. While possibly important, the impact of this factor is intangible. Instead I focus on time preferences induced by necessity. Suppose I have the choice between catching fish in the stream with my hands and making a net that will enable me to catch many more fish. If I cannot catch fish while making the net, however, the opportunity cost of making the net may be so high that I cannot afford it. In other words, taking one step backward to enable two steps forward is not an option if the agent cannot survive the temporary retreat.

which I belong must be an important one since *I* belong to it. (The magistrates in the *parlements* were massively subject to this institutional pridefulness.) My opinion must be correct since it is *mine*. While *amour-propre* is universal—nobody likes to be contradicted—the nobility of the *ancien régime* exhibited it to an unusual degree, as demonstrated and denounced by Pascal, La Rochefoucauld, Pierre Nicole, and La Bruyère. In later chapters I provide cases in which *disagreements were taken as insults*, with a chilling effect on discussions.

There are variations in *intensity* both within and across emotions. Envy has to be stronger when it causes an agent to harm himself in order to harm another person ("black envy") than when it merely causes him to harm the other at no cost to himself ("white envy"). As noted, for a given offense the emotion aroused in the person who has been offended is stronger—and induces a more severe punishment—than the emotion the same action arouses in a third-party observer. It is more difficult to compare the intensity of different emotions when they are triggered by different actions. I suggest, however, that by and large, *emotions of interaction* are stronger, and induce more radical behavior, than *emotions of comparison,* just as "having power over someone" is more consequential than "having more power than someone." In one sense, these comparisons are meaningless. "Having *a bit* of power over someone" can obviously be *less* consequential than "having *a lot* more power than someone." I shall not try to address this question in the abstract, but only make the factual claim that in the relations between the bourgeoisie and the nobility in the *ancien régime*, the bourgeoisie's *resentment of contempt* was stronger than the *envy of privileges* that Tocqueville, for instance, emphasized. Face-to-face contempt leaves deeper marks than "envy at a distance." For the nobles, having power over their tenants, in the form of seigneurial justice, was more important than enjoying tax exemptions. Within the comparison-based emotions, horizontal jealousies among towns and provinces seem to have mattered more than vertical envy between classes.

I have been writing as if the relation between a cognitive antecedent and the triggering of an emotion, as well as the relation between the emotion and the subsequent action, are always one-to-one. I believe that another person deliberately hurt me, I get angry, and I retaliate. While this pattern is frequently observed, the relations can also be one-many.[36] Consider for instance Tocqueville's claim that the tax exemptions of the nobles generated envy in the bourgeoisie. These might also, however, have generated

36. Elster (2011).

anger towards the king for granting and maintaining these exemptions, just as a child that is not offered the ice cream her sister received may react to the injustice of their parents rather than against the better fortune of her sibling. To be sure, the offended party might experience both emotions—anger towards one agent *and* envy towards another. In 1789 fear of brigands co-existed with anger towards those who were believed to have sent them on their way. In other cases, people might experience two emotions towards the *same* agent. Thus if an autocratic ruler enacts strong repressive measures, he might induce both fear and hatred in the public, the former triggering compliance and the latter rebellion. The net effect can go either way. Commenting on the persecution of heretics under Henry VIII, Hume writes that "those severe executions which in another disposition of men's minds, would have sufficed to suppress [the new doctrine], now served only to diffuse it the more among the people, and to inspire them with horror against the unrelenting persecutors."[37] As we shall see (chapter 3), the persecution of Protestants under Louis XIV illustrates the same effect.

Mechanisms: Interaction

Explanations of social phenomena need *micro-foundations*. In the previous section I have attempted to sketch what they might be. However, even if *per impossibile* we could decipher the motivations and beliefs of all individuals, we would need to supplement the micro-foundations with the *interaction mechanisms* that explain the workings of the social system at a larger scale. In this book, the two main ways in which actions by individuals coalesce to yield outcomes that could not have been brought about by any one of them are *social movements* and the activities of formal *decision-making bodies*. As shown by the relation between the crowds in Paris and the *parlement*,[38] the two processes can influence or shape each other.

The dynamics of social movements depend not on any given motivation of the participants, but on the *motivational mix*. It also depends on a range of factual *beliefs*. Since these movements are forms of collective action, they raise the free-rider problem: why do participants choose to engage in risky or costly actions when the personal benefits from *their* participation is, in most cases, vanishingly small? Why not stay on the

---

37. Hume (1983), vol. 3, p. 217.

38. Felix (1999), p. 404. During the Revolution, the relation between rebellions in the countryside and the decisions by the Constituent Assembly exhibited the same two-way causality (Elster 2007). I shall return to this process in Volume 3, notably when considering the decisions on the night of August 4, 1789.

sidelines and let others take the risks or incur the costs? If everybody thinks along those lines, however, they will all stay on the sidelines. As we shall see shortly, the free-rider problem is not the only obstacle to collective action.

Some individuals may perhaps initiate or join a social movement because they hope to emerge as leaders if it succeeds, but such cases, if they exist at all, seem rare.[39] It is safe to say that in the *ancien régime* nobody joined a social movement to get a private good of this kind. People were mobilized for a *collective good*—lower prices, higher wages, abolition of unjust institutions or practices—from which all would benefit, whether they were leaders, followers, or bystanders. The question then, to repeat, is why not everybody were bystanders (a somewhat incongruous idea).

Since material *interest* is always directed towards private goods or the avoidance of private harms, it might seem that we can rule it out as a motivation. Modern theories of collective action allow for it, however, in the form of selective benefits to participants or selective punishment of non-participants. To explain why workers join trade unions, for instance, one can cite the facts that some of the union dues go to fund summer camps for members and that non-members will be denied the wage increases negotiated by the union. Once again, I do not see anything like this happening in the *ancien régime*. In any case, the movement that leads to the formation of a union or a comparable organization cannot itself rely on these motivations. Also, social movements in the *ancien régime* did not lead to durable organizations or associations: they would have been crushed.

It might seem more accurate to say that the social movements were *ephemeral*, either crushed or dissolved when their demands were met, yet this perspective is also somewhat anachronistic. Most movements were crushed, and few demands were met, but the movements had a *nuisance value* that caused authorities and property-owners to try not to trigger them. In preindustrial England, urban food riots caused by the high prices of bread invariably ended in failure—producing nothing but "a few ruined mills and victims on the gallows," as the historian of these movements writes.[40] Yet by virtue of their nuisance value the rebellions had a long-term success in making the government and the propertied classes behave

39. See Elster (2016) for criticism of authors who impute this motivation to *all* participants in collective action.

40. Thompson (1971), p. 120. He also asks (ibid.) whether the revolts "would have continued over so many scores, indeed hundreds of years, if they had consistently failed to achieve their objectives." This explanation, while not impossible, assumes an improbable degree of intergenerational solidarity.

more moderately than they would have done otherwise. I believe the same mechanism was at work in preindustrial France. In times of hunger, the privileged might provide relief to the poor, not out of humanitarian concerns, but for fear of riots (chapter 2).

I am not implying that the participants in these movements *believed* that their cause was hopeless. In some cases, they may not have cared about the prospects of success, since they "had only one death to die."[41] In other cases, the movement was sustained by the wishful belief that the king would respond to their protestations by abolishing the abuses (chapter 2). In still other cases, they may at least have counted on personal impunity, by the mechanism of safety in numbers (see below). Also, in some cases the risk of punishment for participation may have been dominated by the risk of ostracism for non-participation (see below).

On this background, let me sketch a stylized "snowball model" of how social movements may originate, develop, or perhaps fail. Its purpose is not to provide explanations of actual movements, but to offer some of the nuts and bolts that can enter into such explanations.

I shall assume that at least some participants are moved by their perception of a public good—abolition of abuses, social justice, reducing high prices created by speculators and hoarders—that they want to bring about. I do not imply that they are moved by *reason*, defined earlier as a disinterested *and dispassionate* concern for the public good. On the contrary, their belief that the status quo is unjust triggers *anger*, which induces a higher propensity for risk-taking behavior, as explained earlier.[42] By virtue of the strength of their motivation these individuals act as *first movers*. They may be saints, heroes, or just slightly mad. As Tocqueville noted, "the same energy that impels a man to rebel in a violent way against a common error almost always carrie[s] him beyond the bounds of reason."[43]

To pursue this line of argument, I shall rely on a typology of norms that I have developed elsewhere,[44] distinguishing among *moral norms*, *quasi-moral norms*, and *social norms*. Moral norms are *unconditional*, in the sense that their force does not depend on what other people do. This

---

41. Nicolas (2008), p. 423.

42. By and large, few social movements in the *ancien régime* were led by persons who were not personally affected by the injustice, and thus would have been moved by indignation rather than by anger. As I note below, however, in some cases we observe what appears as *disinterested solidarity* of the parish priests with their flock, based on third-party indignation rather than on second-party anger.

43. Tocqueville (2004a), p. 701.

44. Elster (2015a), chap. 5; Elster (2017); Elster (2018).

is the motivation of first movers. Quasi-moral norms are *conditional*, in the sense that their force depends on the agent *observing* what others are doing.[45] Social norms, too, are conditional, in the sense that their force depends on the agent *knowing that she is being observed* by others.[46] Apart from the first movers, who follow moral norms, most other participants are motivated by quasi-moral and social norms, or, in the words of Yves-Marie Bercé, by "*solidarity and fear*."[47]

The Madisonian caveats stated above obviously apply to this typology. In many cases we cannot tell what motivates the participants in collective action. In fact, the agents themselves may not always have had a clear idea, but simply gathered "weapons in hand, without knowing why."[48] In a crowded situation where everyone is both observing and being observed, it may be impossible or meaningless—there may not be a "fact of the matter"—to distinguish quasi-moral from social norms. Yet one fact seems clear: solidarity cannot be the sole motivation—what would it mean to feel solidarity with other agents also motivated only by solidarity? Some of the agents towards whom one shows solidarity must have initiated or joined the movement for other reasons.

These reasons may be moral norms, as just explained, but joining a movement can also have more complex antecedents. Drawing on the work of Thomas Schelling, Mark Granovetter observes that individuals may have different thresholds for the number of previous joiners required to trigger their own participation.[49] Thus in addition to first movers we may

---

45. I call them *quasi*-moral rather than moral because they *justify non-cooperative responses* to the non-cooperative behavior of others.

46. To illustrate the distinction, consider the limitation of water consumption in times of shortage. Those who follow the moral norm of doing what would be best if everyone did the same ("everyday Kantianism") would limit their consumption accordingly. In Bogotá, under the imaginative mayorship of Antanas Mockus, people followed a quasi-moral norm when reducing their consumption of water. Although individual monitoring was not feasible, the aggregate water consumption in the city was shown on TV, so that people could observe whether others were for the most part complying. It appears that enough people did so to sustain the conditional cooperation, saying to themselves, "Since other people are cutting down on their consumption, it's only fair that I should do so as well." Social norms, finally, can cause house-owners to refrain from filling their swimming pool or watering their lawns out of fear of their neighbors shaming them.

47. Bercé (1974), p. 459. In the movement of the *tard-avisés* (late-comers) in the late sixteenth century, "those who did not respond to a first convocation to an assembly received a second and more urgent one, where threats of arson and destruction of their possessions replaced the initial promises" (ibid., p. 264). For other forms of ostracism of violators of communal solidarity, see Markoff (1996), p. 262.

48. Bercé (1974), p. 229.

49. Granovetter (1978).

distinguish between *early joiners* and *late joiners*. Granovetter's model can be supplemented by a more elaborate analysis of the motives for joining than the one he provides. Some people motivated by quasi-moral norms may feel the pull of fairness when relatively few others have joined,[50] whereas others feel an obligation to join only at later stages. Similarly, some people motivated by social norms may feel uncomfortable if they are shamed by only a few joiners, whereas for others massive social pressure may be required. Finally, the level of risk-aversion may determine the time of entry into the movement, since (for a given repressive force) the risk for any protester of being arrested or punished goes down with the number of protesters (safety in numbers).

The *snowball mechanism* arises because the low-threshold joiners increase the size of the movement and thus create the conditions for high-threshold individuals to join. This was Granovetter's fundamental insight. To his analysis, we can add a *cross-over effect*: the influx of people with one motivation may create the threshold level required for people with other motivations to join. When some join because they are afraid of being shamed, they may trigger the quasi-moral norm of fairness in others. Those who join because they are motivated by a norm of fairness can create the conditions for risk-averse individuals to join as well. It can also happen that the movement runs out of steam, because the first movers do not attract any joiners, or too few to create a momentum.[51] Finally, if participants have emotional motivations, the fact that emotions have a short half-life may cause the movement to *unravel* when risk-aversion gets the upper hand. Often peasant uprisings flare up and spend themselves like flames in dry grass (chapter 3). Urban crowds may stop rioting when it is time for dinner (chapter 2).

Turning now to the role of *beliefs* in social movements, consider first the beliefs that potential participants have about each other. In the analysis above, I made the simplifying assumption that (apart from first movers) individuals will join a movement on the basis of their observation of what others *have done* (or are doing). However, their beliefs about what others *will do* may be just as important.[52] In a state of *pluralistic ignorance*—a

---

50. Another Madisonian caveat: when quasi-moral norms have a *very low* threshold, they are hard to distinguish empirically from moral norms.

51. If there are ten first movers, who then attract twenty others, while forty is the lowest threshold for the rest of the population, the movement will not grow in size beyond thirty.

52. Rule (1989), p. 47, argues that the threshold "model is probably less informative when would-be participants have various sources of information about each other's potential for riotous behavior, apart from actually observing such behavior directly. On the other hand, where actual behavior on the spot is the best or only way for would-be participants

phenomenon first conceptualized by Tocqueville[53]—*each person* may believe, falsely, that she is the *only one* (or one of the few) to be willing to join a movement. As a result, all stay home and nothing happens. The fact that nobody turns out confirms their (false) belief. By the nature of the case, it is hard to tell how often pluralistic ignorance prevents people from rebelling, but I believe it must be a frequent occurrence, not least because the authorities often work to keep people ignorant. In an early intuition of pluralistic ignorance, Seneca wrote, "A proposal was once made in the senate to distinguish slaves from free men by their dress; it then became apparent how great would be the impending danger *if our slaves should begin to count our number*" (*On Clemency* XXIV; my italics). In the *ancien régime*, as in autocracies everywhere, spontaneous assemblies above a certain size were forbidden.

Beliefs in the form of *rumors* (see chapter 3) were a vital piece in the machinery of social movements. The object of the rumor could be the hoarding of grain, the approach of brigands or of soldiers,[54] an impending tax reform that would justify the refusal to pay taxes, the kidnapping of children, or the deliberate starving of the people to reduce the size of the population.[55] The rumors might be circulated for their entertainment value, as one may watch horror movies without believing in their reality. Even when they were taken seriously and used as premises for action, their source might be a hawker offering sensationalist rumors to attract buyers, an egocentric trying to make himself important, or just somebody trying to stir up trouble. Also, as noted earlier, the step from accusation to conviction might be short. Many hesitated to express disbelief in the rumor, lest they be accused of cowardice or complicity with the authorities. Sometimes, in Lefebvre's succinct formulation, "the people scared itself" (*se faisait peur à lui-même*), as in an episode from 1703 when "the tocsin would sound; each village would send a runner to neighboring villages and ask for their help; detachments arriving to help would be taken for enemies and, without further ado one would announce that the harm is done."[56]

---

to gauge the extent of support their own riotous action might have—that is, in a situation of . . . pluralistic ignorance—threshold processes appear more likely to matter."

53. Tocqueville (2004a), p. 758. In chapter 2 I discuss how he applied the idea to the obsession with *préséance* in the *ancien régime*.

54. Referring to the events in the summer of 1789, Lefebvre (1988), p. 46, writes that "for a long time, there had been no difference between brigands and soldiers," both being seen as predators on the peasant communities.

55. In philosophical terminology these were *intensional objects*, which did not necessarily have any existence outside the mind of the believers.

56. Lefebvre (1988), p. 75; my italics.

The propagation and especially the magnification of rumors remain ill-understood. Hans Christian Andersen's story in which one feather turns into five hens in the telling and retelling does not exaggerate the multiplying effect in the transmission of rumor,[57] but the mechanisms are hard to nail down. Montaigne, who was both an observer of the devastating effects of rumor during the wars of religion and an acute psychologist, offered what may have been the first analysis, relying on the tendency of the purveyors of rumors to *fill in gaps* in the narrative:

> The distance is greater from nothing to the minutest thing than it is from the minutest thing to the biggest. Now when the first people who drank their fill from the original oddity come to spread their tale abroad, they can tell by the opposition which they arouse what it is that others find it difficult to accept; they then stop up the chinks with some false piece of oakum. . . . At first the individual error creates the public one: then, in its turn, the public error creates the individual one. And so it passes from hand to hand, the whole fabric is padded out and reshaped, so that the most far-off witness is better informed about it than the closest one, and the last to be told more convinced than the first. It is a natural progression. For whoever believes anything reckons that it is a work of charity to convince someone else of it; and to do this he is not afraid to add, out of his own invention, whatever his story needs to overcome the resistance.[58]

A rough impression is that rumors inspired by anger or fear were more frequent than those inspired by hope.[59] The object of anger-inspired rumors could be some flagrant injustice, such as hoarding of grain to raise prices and starve the people. The object of fear-inspired rumors could be the arrival of brigands, as in the Great Fear of 1789. In that episode, *fear of brigands co-existed with anger* towards those who had hired or

---

57. After the insurrection of workers in Paris in June 1848, two men who were observed sitting by the side of a country road in Normandy became ten, three hundred, six hundred in the telling and retelling, until finally one could hear that three thousand "levelers" (*partageux*) were looting, burning, and massacring. Thirty thousand soldiers were sent out to counter the threat. An investigation revealed that one of the two was mentally ill and that the other was his father, who was taking care of him (Lefebvre 1988, pp. 76–77).

58. Montaigne (1991), p. 1162; see also Shibutani (1966), p. 37 on the urge to "complete the incomplete."

59. The only quantitative study known to me (Knapp 1944) found that of 1,089 war-related rumors gathered in the United States in September 1942, 65 percent had their origin in anger, 25 percent in fear, and only 2 percent in hope (mostly "pipe-dreams").

commissioned them.[60] The object of hope-inspired rumors was usually an impending alleviation of the burdens of the people. My impression—again a very rough one—is that hope-inspired rumors were for the most part pipe-dreams and not used as premises for action, an exception being the tendency to refuse to pay taxes that people thought were about to be abolished anyway. Anger and fear were more likely to inspire rumors that could trigger violent action.

I turn now to the second interaction mechanism at work in the *ancien régime*, the activities of formal decision-making bodies (chapter 5). These include the meetings of the upper clergy every five years, the irregular meetings of the Estates-General, the regular meetings every year, two years, or three years of the provincial Estates, and the ongoing activities of the magistrates in the *parlements*, interrupted only by the judicial vacations. At the local level, there were innumerable village assemblies. Concerning the *parlements*, I limit myself for now to their political activities, that is to their protestations (remonstrances) to royal edicts. Their judicial functions will concern me in chapter 4.

Strictly speaking, almost by definition no bodies in an absolute monarchy could possess *hard* decision-making competence, in the sense of being capable of imposing decisions that could not be overruled by the king and that might even constrain his behavior.[61] They might not even be masters of their own decision-making rules, as shown by the meta-decision by the finance minister Bertin in 1762 that henceforward decisions by the unruly Estates of Brittany would no longer require the unanimous agreement of all three estates, but that two of them would be able to outvote a third (see chapter 5). Yet the deliberating bodies of the *ancien régime* were far from being sham bodies, such as parliaments under most Communist regimes.

As in many other cases of collective decision-making, deliberating bodies in the *ancien régime* proceeded by voting, arguing, and bargaining.[62]

All these bodies, or sections of them, voted on proposals in votes that could be very close. In the assembly of the clergy in 1755, "the bishops were divided over the issue whether a refusal to accept the bull Unigenitus was a mortal sin or merely a sin in a serious matter. 16 bishops were of the first

---

60. Lefebvre (1988), p. 270. To repeat, these were intensional objects only.

61. The clergy could and did refuse communion to the kings, as happened to Louis XV as a result of his flagrant adulteries. Even an "absolute" monarch could not command communion.

62. For the relations among these three modes of interaction, see Elster (2013), chap. 1.

opinion and 17 of the second."[63] Although the *parlements* aimed for unanimity in their decisions, consensus was achieved only because "those who had opted for the least popular proposal had an opportunity to adhere to one of the others, a process that was repeated until unanimity had been achieved."[64] As I document in chapter 4, the initial votes could be close. In one dramatic decision in 1764, the *parlement* of Brittany refused by 13 votes to 12 to register without protestations (*purement et simplement*) a royal declaration.[65] However, even though we may have the *numbers of votes* pro and con, we rarely have the *names of the voters*, as strict adherence to methodological individualism would require.

The Estates-General, unlike the provincial Estates, never adopted a system of voting by estates, by which each of them would cast a vote and then reach a decision by majority or unanimity. Yet within each estate, the votes of the various provincial deputations were aggregated by majority rule to yield an opinion. Strangely (for us), the vote of an estate figured only as an output of its internal deliberation, never as an input to a vote by the Estates-General. In this respect, the Estates-General differed from other nested political systems, such as the Continental Congress where the vote of a state deputation was both the output of its internal votes and an input to the voting of the larger body.[66] One reason why the Estates-General never developed voting rules *by* estates was the indeterminacy of voting *within* each estate, since there were competing proposals for how to define the voting subunits of each estate (chapter 5).

From the records available to us (that is, known to me) it is hard to assess the importance of *arguing* (persuasion without the use of threats or promises). Georges Picot seems too sanguine when he refers, with regard to the Estates-General of 1560, to an "[i]nevitable effect of deliberation among men: how bad their plans and how terrible their passions might be, it substitutes moral force for material force and the power of reasoning for violence."[67] One can assume, nevertheless, that as in assemblies everywhere, arguing sometimes led to the elimination of a proposal when

63. Bernis (1903), vol. 1, p. 325. He adds that "this division scandalized the public and weakened considerably the force of the clergy, which consists mainly in its union."

64. Swann (2017), p. 176.

65. Félix (1999), p. 331. He raises the possibility that if the *Premier Président*, who was the king's man in the *parlement*, had not been absent because his daughter was sick, French history might have taken a different course.

66. Elster (2014).

67. Picot (1888), vol. 2, p. 171. The kernel of truth in this claim is that deliberation creates an incentive for the interlocutors to *appear* to appeal to reason, thus generating "the civilizing force of hypocrisy."

shown to be Pareto-inferior (not preferred by anyone) to another proposal. Also, as in assemblies everywhere, some participants must have been sensitive to arguments ad hominem, in the sense in which Locke used that expression: "to press a man with consequences drawn from his own principles or concessions,"[68] to which we may add consequences drawn from his past behavior. These remarks apply equally to the deliberations of the *parlements*.

With respect to *bargaining*, we can go beyond these generalities. In the Estates-General and in the provincial Estates, the three estates negotiated not only with each other, but also with the royal government, demanding concessions on a number of issues in exchange for consent to taxation (chapter 5). In fact, they could bargain with each other about which demands to make when bargaining with the king,[69] much as industry unions bargain with each other about which collective demands to make when bargaining with the employers' union.[70] The main issue was always the allocation of the tax burden.[71] Because the Estates-General were an assembly of provinces as much as an assembly of estates, bargaining over taxation also took place among the former.[72] Overall, the process was skewed in favor of the kings, by virtue of their stronger bargaining power. They could dismiss the deputies, close the doors to their meeting rooms, or refuse to pay their costs.

Even more important, when the kings made concessions to the Estates-General, the latter had no permanent machinery that could enforce a tax strike if the kings did not keep their promises, which they virtually never did. "One cannot find in our whole history a single king who scrupulously limited taxation to what the Estates-General had authorized."[73] The provincial Estates were more successful in bargaining with the government over their "free gift," although it is hard to nail down the exact sources of their bargaining power (chapter 5). Also, the clergy could hold the kings to their promises by virtue of the fact that its assemblies met regularly, at five-year intervals, and could refuse the free gift if the king had not kept the promises he made to the previous assembly.[74] As in the example

68. Locke (1979), p. 686.

69. Picot (1888), vol. 3, pp. 20–21. Masselin (1835) has many examples from the Estates of 1484.

70. For the relation between labor-labor bargaining and capital-labor bargaining, see Elster (1989), chap. 4.

71. For a summary see Picot (1888), vol.5, pp. 33–44.

72. Ibid., vol. 1, p. 381.

73. Ibid., vol. 5, p. 139.

74. Maury (1879), p. 766.

adapted from Hume, the promises were enforceable because of *repeated* and *open-ended* interactions at *fixed dates* relatively *close in time*.

In some cases (chapter 4) the government negotiated with the *parlement* of Paris before issuing its edicts, to ensure that they would be registered without remonstrances, but it is not clear whether this was a regular or an occasional process. Since the *Premier Président*, unlike the other magistrates, was directly beholden to the king, he had the opportunity to act as a mediator by informing the king about what was acceptable to the *parlement* and vice versa. These remarks do not apply, however, to the period between 1673 and 1715, when the *parlements* were largely reduced to rubber-stamping bodies, or to the period between 1771 and 1774 when they briefly lost many of their powers. They apply to some extent, but not fully, to the period between 1715 and 1750, when the *parlements* could make remonstrances, but not publish them. The reemergence of the courts after 1750 as powerful political bodies occurred after the regular publication of their protestations against royal edicts created a two-way *interaction between courts and crowds,* mainly in Paris. In the struggles between the king and the *parlements,* publication now conferred a valuable bargaining tool on the latter (chapter 4).

The resistance of the *parlements* to the royal government was limited by collective action problems *within* and *between* the courts. Before the magistrates in a *parlement* were sent into exile, they received *lettres de cachet* in the early hours of the morning and were given the choice between compliance and resistance. Since each would be unaware of the choices of the others, they might comply even though they would have resisted if assured that others would resist too (chapter 4). Another collective action problem—known by game theorists as "The Battle of the Sexes"—arose when problems of *préséance* made the magistrates reluctant to confer the presidency to one among themselves in cases where the normal president recused himself (chapter 2).[75] The same situation could arise among the *parlements,* when the provincial courts were reluctant to let Paris take the lead in a common front (the *union des classes*), against the king.

---

75. This situation arises when there are several arrangements that are Pareto-superior (preferred by everybody) to the status quo, each of which brings special benefits to one of the agents. In a multi-lingual society it may be in everybody's interest to have one official language, but disagreement over which language to choose may prevent any of them from being selected. In this example (as in the *ancien régime*), prestige may matter more than material interest. Strictly speaking, therefore, it is inaccurate to say that all would have preferred to have any language chosen as the official one rather than none. A solution, briefly discussed in chapter 2, would have been to choose the official language by lot.

I conclude this Introduction by noting that two-way interaction between courts and crowds was mainly an urban phenomenon. Social movements in the countryside must have shaped the deliberations of provincial *parlements* and Estates, but with some exceptions (see chapter 5) these bodies did not use public opinion as a resonance board in their struggles with the royal administration. A two-way interaction between Paris and the countryside was not established until the summer of 1789. By contrast, in the last forty years before the Revolution the publicly stated opposition of the *parlement* of Paris to Louis XV and to Louis XVI contributed decisively to the undermining of royal authority. In one of the many counterfactual questions that arise in any discussion of the demise of the *ancien régime*, we can ask whether it might have survived if Louis XVI had not resurrected the *parlements* when he succeeded to the throne in 1774.

CHAPTER TWO

The Psychology of the Main Social Groups

MOTIVATIONS

IN THIS CHAPTER and the following, I consider the mental precursors and causes of action—motivations and beliefs—of the main categories of agents in the *ancien régime*.

Interest

Much of the time, the actors of the old regime were moved by their material *interest*. Peasants tried to shift the tax burdens onto other villagers; the *seigneur* protected them from exploitation by the state so that they could afford to pay their dues to him; artisans fought for higher wages and cheaper bread; magistrates refused to register fiscal legislation that would hurt their income; officials granted tax exemptions and other favors to one another.

Often, the interest had a short time horizon. Many peasants were opposed to a wise ordinance of 1669, which restricted the exploitation of the forests in the interest of future generations.[1] Also, it was "hard for the poor, in bad years, to let the fallow remain completely unproductive. Land at rest is the future of the harvest, but the necessities of the present are imperative."[2] Short leases reduced the incentive of many peasants to invest

1. Nicolas (2008), p. 637.
2. Saint-Jacob (1960), p. 263.

in improvements whose fruits would only materialize later.[3] In bad years, they had to sell their crop just after the harvest when prices were at their lowest.[4] Only rich peasants could afford to wait to sell their grain until just before the next harvest, when it would command higher prices.[5]

The royal government was always short of money and rarely able to take a long-term perspective, carrying act-utilitarianism to an extreme by disregarding the disincentive effects on the economic agents of its own actions. Bercé describes the mindset of the tax officials in the following terms: "The exorbitant costs of tax collection seemed justified as long as the immediate cash inflow was assured. The speed of the levies, 'the acceleration of the monies,' as one said, took priority over the yield."[6] As a counterpart of this urgency, repression was rarely sustained over time: "to avoid it, it was enough to avoid the rigor of the moment."[7] The great rationalizer Colbert tried but failed to replace the "maxims of confusion," where everything was constantly done and undone,[8] by "maxims of order." The handling of loans and government bonds was no more rational. Because the government could not make credible promises of interest payment or reimbursement, it often had to offer high interest rates to attract investors. From time to time, notably in 1661 and 1715, the government then established special courts (*Chambres de Justice*) to confiscate the "usurious" profits, thus further undermining its credibility.[9] Financiers were unpopular: "one held

3. Turgot (1844), vol. 1, p. 518; Lefebvre (1924), p. 263–264. Young (1974), vol. 1, p. 51 writes, "Give a man the secure possession of a bleak rock and he will turn it into a garden; give him a nine years lease of a garden and he will convert it into a desert." Also ibid., p. 88: "the magic of property turns sand into gold." Land owned by the Church could not be legally leased for more than nine years, or sometimes three years, a rule that created an incentive for the lessee to make hay while the sun shines by exhausting the land (Le Duc 1881, pp. 235–236). By one estimate (Plongeron 1974, p.172), about 10 percent of agricultural land was owned by the Church. Although most leases attached to a benefice expired automatically with the death of its holder, thus generating uncertainty and blunting the incentive to maintain and improve the land, some "enlightened benefice-holders obtained the privilege of granting 27-year leases that did not expire by their death or resignation" (Marion 1923, p. 31). Another obstacle was that nobody had an incentive to improve land held in common (Lefebvre 1924, p. 86), reflecting the maxim "What's everybody's business is nobody's business." The same comment applies to overgrazing (Saint-Jacob 1960, p. 373).

4. Nicolas (2008), p. 401.

5. Lefebvre (1924), pp. 246, 250.

6. Bercé (1974), p. 96. He refers to the period before 1660, but the description seems valid for the old regime as a whole; see the descriptions by Boisguilbert and Vauban that I cite below of the wasteful confiscations of property in lieu of tax payment.

7. Ibid., p. 558.

8. Lavissse (1989), p. 166;

9. Dessert (1984), chs. XI and XII; Marion (1927), pp. 72–77.

their usurious practice against them . . . without considering the fact that the absolute respect for commitments was the only way . . . to avoid these usurious practices."[10]

To save money, the state regularly paid its bills and debts too late, as a matter of policy.[11] In fact, on several occasions the government created intermediate bodies between paymasters and bondholders, only "for the purpose of delaying payment."[12] In the entire period of the old regime, the ministry of Calonne (1784–1788) was the only one that kept its promise to pay bondholders on a regular schedule.[13] Individuals shared the habit of late payments. Since peasants knew that any signs of affluence would cause them to be taxed more heavily the next year, and that paying taxes on time was one of these signs, it was in their interest to procrastinate, even if they had to pay a fine for late payment.[14] Nobles, too, tended to delay paying their taxes, sometimes in the hope that they might receive a tax amnesty, as had happened in 1717, but also because "the prejudices of the nobles made them view prompt payment as shameful and bourgeois. . . . One could almost measure the degree of nobility of a person by the amount of his tax arrears."[15] The nobles also knew that if their property was seized and put up for sale to cover their arrears, people would be reluctant to purchase it.[16]

10. Marion (1927), p. 67; see also ibid., p. 147. His book illustrates abundantly the chicanery of the financial institutions in their dealings with the citizens. For the holders of government bonds, receiving their interest was like pulling teeth. The procrastinations forced the government to offer higher rates of interests on new loans (Lüthy 2005, p. 477).

11. Marion (1927), p. 361–362; Gomel (1892), vol.1, p. 262.

12. Claeys (2011), p. 453.

13. To do so, however, it took out more loans to create a sinking fund—a chimerical project in the absence of a real surplus (Marion 1927, p. 364; Slater 2018, p. 78).

14. Boisguilbert (1707), p. 28; Marion (1927), p. 5; Saint-Jacob (1960), p. 529; Marion (1910), p. 12. Other effects included disincentives to the creation of wealth (Vauban 2007, p. 767; Goubert 2013, p. 107) and incentives to hide one's wealth (Boisguilbert 1707, pp. 28, 32, 123; Marion 1910, pp. 8, 236; Marion 1927, p. 167). These abuses were still rampant in 1779, when the Abbé de Véri denounced the iniquity and inefficiency of taxation in the Berri (Lavergne 1879, pp. 42–44). As in the America described by Tocqueville (2004a), p. 204, the rich could also have a motive to hide their wealth, for fear of the people rather than of the tax collector (Bercé 1974, p. 626). In 1667, the city of Dijon banned the performance of plays, because they "would make the king's ministers think that we are not so worn-out that we cannot think of joy" (cited after Lavisse 1989, p. 250). As we shall see, the government as well as individuals sometimes practiced the opposite policy, pretending to have wealth they did not in fact possess, in order to create "confidence."

15. Marion (1891), p. 66.

16. Ibid., p. 156; Argenson, vol. 6, p.164; Kwass (2000), p. 198; see also the entry "Séquestre" in Marion (1923) and the discussion in chapter 6.

Reason

Except for the last few remarks, these comments on the motivation of state agents and citizens have focused on *interest*. As in all times and places, this motivation shaped action powerfully, but it was far from the only one. One can neither deny the existence of public-spirited individuals moved by *reason* nor measure their importance. I can only cite some examples. Vauban, Boisguilbert, Fénélon, Turgot, and Malesherbes, all of whom I cite in chapter 3, stood out in their concern for the public good. Of the two institutions that were often decried as tyrannical or arbitrary, the royal *intendants* and the *parlements*, the former sometimes acted in a disinterested manner, whereas the latter were more concerned with a *reputation for disinterestedness*.[17] Some of the remarks I make here are supplemented by analyses in chapters 3 and 4.

The royal *intendants* were authorized to enforce justice in a local community by using their power of discretionary taxation (*taxe d'office*) of influential villagers (*coqs de paroisse*) or of local officials who had managed to change the tax rolls in their favor.[18] Although this power was explicitly limited to increase taxes, Esmonin argues that over time it came to be used to diminish them as well, thus recreating the arbitrary favoritism it was supposed to curb.[19] One *intendant* claimed to protect the integrity of the village by maintaining the archaic institute of *mainmorte* that prevented cultivators from selling their land. He argued that it offered a defense against the destructive agrarian individualism that threatened to transfer ownership to town residents and transform the tillers of the land into a rural proletariat.[20] In late eighteenth century

---

17. Elster (2009b), Conclusion.

18. Marion (1910), p. 6, together with the contemporary texts he cites on pp. 188, 190. Esmonin (1913), pp. 339–348, has a full discussion, with examples from Normandy. For an example from the Limousin, see Bercé (1974), pp. 160–61.

19. Esmonin (1913), pp. 345–48. His negative assessment (shared by Gomel 1892, vol. 1, p. 384) can be held up against that of Turgot (1844, vol.1, p. 456), who asserts that in the towns the *taxe d'office* by the intendant could obviate conspiracies while in the countryside it could make up for the ignorance and incompetence of the tax collectors. Marion (1910), p.7. also praises the system, but adds that it was used only exceptionally. To my knowledge, there is no systematic study of this practice. In Burgundy, the intermediary commission of the provincial Estates (the *élus*) could impose *cotes d'office* that were also supposed to prevent the wealthy from using their influence to avoid paying their fair share of taxes (Swann 2003, pp. 198–199). Toward the end of the *ancien régime*, there were complaints that the *élus* used this discretionary power to punish what they perceived as disrespectful behavior (ibid., p. 396).

20. Saint-Jacob (1960), pp. 423–424; also Markoff (1996), pp. 76–77. Véri (1930,

Burgundy, the *intendant* often tried to protect the peasants from "the aggressiveness of a *seigneurie* that the *parlement* supported with all its forces."[21] At the same time, he supported the village community against the provincial Estates when they tried to transform communal land into individually held plots.[22]

It is not clear how often the *intendants* behaved in this way, nor why they would do so. As the king's representatives, they were supposed to promote the greatness of France, not the welfare of the French—to maximize the net product of the kingdom, not to maintain the village as a safety net.[23] The official line was that there was no conflict between these two goals. In a speech Calonne made as *intendant* in Metz, he said that "As a general rule, the laborers and the wage earners are an accessory to the main body, the farmers. It is therefore not necessary to worry about their lot while that of the farmers is being improved. It is an inexorable principle that by increasing the production and output in an area, the welfare of all the inhabitants of that area is thereby increased, irrespective of their condition and status. The adjustment is automatic and to doubt it in the slightest would be to indicate an ignorance of the natural order."[24]

We meet the same argument in a memoir defending the edict of 1771 authorizing land owners to abolish the *vaine pâture* (common grazing on the fields after the harvest): "It will be said that large owners will make a considerable profit; this is the big objection, but it can be turned against those who make it: they will make a considerable profit, hence there will be improvements of the land and increase in foodstuff: that is the general and public good."[25] Against these Panglossian statements we may cite one made in 1767 by the former finance minister Bertin: "The difficulty is to decide between the preferential treatment (*faveur*) which

---

pp. 238–229) reports his astonishment at being told that an old peasant had said he *preferred being unable* to sell his land. Although Véri's initial presumption was in favor of the unrestricted freedom of commerce advocated by his friend Turgot, after hearing the story he concluded that "one should not always judge particular cases on the basis of general maxims." Workers, too, had an ambiguous attitude towards corporate structures, which could be seen either as constraints or as protections (Nicolas 2008, p. 527).

21. Saint-Jacob (1960), p. 483.

22. Ibid., pp. 517–518.

23. For some observations on the conflict between these two maximands, see Argenson vol. 2, p. 254; Marion (1927), p. 311–312; Jouanna (1989), p. 236; Pillorget and Pillorget (1995), pp. 784, 1173; Petitfils (2008), p. 490.

24. Cited after Rozental (1956), p. 59.

25. Cited after Lefebvre (1924), p. 89 note 1.

this suffering part of humanity deserves and the greater advantage of agriculture."[26] I shall return to the question of the disinterestedness of the *intendants*.

The *parlements* were regularly accused of self-serving behavior. They often rejected fiscal legislation that hurt the interests of their members. They were also obsessed with their institutional interests as a body. As noted in the Introduction, their *amour-propre* made them inflate the importance of the body in which they served. When they did occasionally object to tax increases even when these would not affect them personally,[27] they may have been motivated by their desire for popularity rather than by the public good.[28] To exclude that possibility one would have to identify financial remonstrances that were (i) not financially self-serving and (ii) not published. After 1753, it seems that these protestations were regularly printed and circulated.[29] The editor of the remonstrances of the *parlement* of Paris reports that of forty-six that were submitted to the king between 1715 and 1753, thirty-three remained unpublished.[30] In the subset of that subset that deals with taxes, the *parlements* "were above all concerned with defending the interests of its members,

26. Cited after Bloch (1930), p. 524. For other statements of this tension, see Lefebvre (1924), pp. 37, 72.

27. Egret (1970), p. 108.

28. Cardinal de Bernis (1980), p. 379 wrote that the badly paid and overworked judge "will naturally seek to compensate by reputation what he cannot hope to get by making a fortune, and this reputation is never more brilliant than when he can make his company resist the Court, notably in cases that interest religion or the welfare of the people." See also Argenson, vol. 5, pp. 427–428; Egret (1970) p. 132; Véri (1928), p. 293; Pillorget and Pillorget (1995), p. 487. Swann (1995), p. 169; and Swann (1997), pp. 329–333, offer a more nuanced picture, but do not provide data that would allow for a quantitative assessment of the relative importance of self-interest and disinterestedness. Flammermont (1888–1898), vol. 1, p. ii provides striking evidence for the lack of concern of the *parlements* for the public good: even though Louis XIV in his edict of 1673 authorized them to make remonstrances after registering the edicts, they never used this right even though they "might have caused the modification of badly conceived legislative dispositions." The remonstrances in 1714 concerning the papal bull *Unigenitus* was the only exception.

29. Kwass (2000), pp. 171–172; Rocquain (1878), p. 172. According to Félix (1999), p. 65, this change occurred after a victorious pamphlet war of the clergy against the government: "The magistrates had learned that for opposition to the government to succeed, it needed a support in the public opinion. The *parlements* thus adopted the habit of publishing their remonstrances." In 1763, Louis XV issued several edicts banning publication of the remonstrances (Barbier, vol. 8, pp. 100–104), but to no effect.

30. Flammermont (1888–1898), vol.1, p. xcv. Among the thirteen published ones, only two dealt with financial issues (devaluation of the coinage), and none with taxes. It is not clear from his text whether the published remonstrances were printed at the time they were made or at a later date. Argenson, vol. 6, p. 419 reports a remonstrance from 1751 that was printed against the king's command.

land-owners and office-holders, and only additionally (*par surcroît*) with the interests of the Parisian bourgeoisie, which enjoyed privileges from which the magistrates benefited, with the interests of consumers in general, of the poor (*le pauvre peuple*), and of commerce and industry."[31] Of the two unpublished cases he cites that involved the interests of the poor, only one from May 18, 1722 can really be said to do so, and even that one may have been inspired mainly by the interests of the Parisian bourgeoisie. Altogether, then, the evidence for any altruism that was *inconspicuous at the time* is almost nil.[32]

According to Jean Egret, "the major criticism the [*parlements*] made of the administrative monarchy" was that "under the name of the *intendant* one had established the anonymous despotism of the clerks" or, as Voltaire called it, "an absolute power in the fourth or fifth hand."[33] In a remonstrance from 1775, Malesherbes expresses this criticism forcefully and eloquently, arguing that "each man of the people is obliged on a daily basis to suffer the whims, the arrogance, even the insults of the henchmen of the tax farmer."[34] While there is no doubt that Malesherbes was indeed concerned with the welfare of the people, his fellow magistrates may have been more concerned with their own situation.[35] When the *parlement* of Bordeaux took steps to alleviate the effects of a bad harvest, its concern was that hungry citizens might disturb public order, not that they might starve.[36] Although it is impossible to make quantitative assessments in these matters, I believe that Malesherbes knew what he was talking about when he wrote to Turgot that "As to our magistrates in the *parlement*, almost all have a vice in common, which in my opinion is the worst of all—the indomitable habits of subtlety and falsity, which, combined with their easy resort to a despotic tone, make it impossible to deal with them."[37]

Many of the remonstrances are in fact masterpieces of unctuous doublespeak.[38] "The courts did not openly question the royal authority under

---

31. Flammermont (1888–1898), vol.1, p. lxxvii; see also ibid., p. xxii.

32. "The more glittering the deed the more I subtract from its moral worth, because of the suspicion aroused in me that it was exposed more for glitter than for goodness; goods displayed are already halfway to being sold" (Montaigne 1991, pp. 1157–1158).

33. Egret (1970), pp. 116, 132.

34. Malesherbes (2008), p. 166.

35. Marion (1891), p. 82.

36. Doyle (1974), pp. 204–205.

37. Cited after Grosclaude (1961), p. 293 note.

38. Malesherbes is a rare exception; see the irreverent and ironical remonstrance cited in Egret (1970), p. 104, telling the king that he hopes he can offer the people something better than "a narrow exemption from dues that are known to be impossible to collect."

Louis XV: they appeared to proclaim absolutism and to respect it, but they immediately added reservations, hesitations, and interpretations that tended towards nothing less than to distort or even annul it."[39] Sometimes, they claimed to know his duty better than he did. In 1771, even one of the king's lawyers did not hesitate to object to the suppression of the *parlements* by stating that if he did not refuse to register the edict "the king himself, when he comes round from his bedazzlement (*évanouisssement*), will be the first to blame him for his infidelity."[40] The upper clergy often exhibited the same tendency to false subtleties and evasiveness, wrapped up in unction. Saint-Simon describes its reactions to the papal bull *Unigenitus* in 1714: "Among those who accepted the [bull], there was not even a glimmer of unanimity. . . . The problem was to find *some means for receiving the words and rejecting the sense.*"[41] In the assemblies of the clergy (chapter 5), "the eloquence conserved some of the forms of the pulpit; it was deployed with that pedantic fulness and emphatic solemnity which strike us today as obscure and ridiculous. Far from making irreverent attacks on the royal power, the deputies lavished it with adulations while resisting its will."[42]

Passion

I shall now turn at greater length to the role of *passion* in the agents of the *ancien régime*. The passions were mostly negative, triggered by a violation of a perceived right or by an attempt to claim or enforce a right that was

---

Esmonin (1913), p. 23, cites a similar vacuous elimination of non-collectible taxes, but views it more favorably as "a precious encouragement" for the people.

39. Antoine (1970), p. 574.

40. Hardy, vol. 2, p. 311; see also the letter to Louis XV by the *chambre des comptes* of Aix in ibid., p. 397, urging him to rule by the scales of justice and not by the scepter and admonishing him: "Sire, the extent of your power must frighten yourself." In1771, the magistrates in the *parlement* of Dijon sent a letter to Louis XV essentially telling him that he would "praise them one day" for disobeying him (Swann 2017, p. 373).

41. Saint-Simon, vol. 25, p. 132; my italics. The reports (ibid., vol. 24, pp.107–119) of his discussions of the same topic with the Jesuit confessor of Louis XIV, Père Le Tellier, are hilariously funny.

42. Maury (1879), p. 795. He adds that "the cassock and the tonsure are unfortunately not an armor that protects men against ambitious and vindictive passions; they merely lend them an appearance of holiness that *deceives even those who feel them* by making them believe that they are always acting for the glory of God" (my italics). As always, the line between deception and self-deception is hard to draw. It can be difficult to tell when speakers and writers were themselves caught up in the pervasive tear-jerking (*larmoyant*) sentimentality of the late eighteenth century (Reddy 2001, chap. 5) and when they merely used sentimental language to deflect criticism. I defer a fuller discussion to Volume 3.

perceived as illegitimate. They could take the forms of anger, indignation, resentment, hatred, and contempt. Although emotions often expressed themselves in the language of justice and injustice, they were frequently rooted in social rather than in moral norms, as the next several paragraphs will illustrate.

In the old regime, the norm of *préséance* pervaded most social groups,[43] even the peasantry.[44] The word is usually translated as 'rank," "pre-eminence," "precedence," or "priority," but these terms do not convey the intensity of the emotions invested in the arrangements of seating, order of convocation, place in a procession, order of salutation, order of speaking, and other situations in which individuals had to be treated differentially in space or time.[45] Saint-Simon's obsession with *préséance* was extreme even for his time and probably detracted from his political efficacy, but in less extreme form the concern for rank was pervasive. La Bruyère conveys well this atmosphere of competition and rivalry:

> There is a certain thing which has never yet been seen under the canopy of heaven, and, in all likelihood, never will be: it is a small town without various parties, where all the families are united and all relations visit one another without reserve, where a marriage does not engender a civil war, where there are no disputes about precedence at the offertory, the carrying of the censer, or the giving of a cake to the church to be consecrated and distributed during mass, as well as about processions and funerals: where gossiping, falsehoods, and slandering are banished; where the *bailli* and the president of the court, the *élus* and the *assesseurs* are on speaking terms together; where the dean is well with the canons, the canons do not disdain the choristers, and the choristers bear with the singing-boys.[46]

43. The most sophisticated treatment (Cosandey 2016) is limited to conflicts within the nobility, thus ignoring *préséance* conflicts within each of the other two estates and among the estates.

44. Goubert (2008), p. 277, comments: "In a certain manner, the 'I desire to be treated as distinguished' (*Je veux qu'on me distingue*) of a marquis in Molière would not have been out of place in the countryside."

45. Cosandey (2016), pp. 173–180, shows in great detail how each spatial dimension generated its own norms of *préséance*: *above* took precedence over *below*, *in front of* over *behind*, and *to the right of* over *to the left of*. These dimensions were themselves hierarchically ordered, so that being *in front of on the left* took precedence over *being behind on the right*. Temporally, *earlier* took precedent over *later*. These might refer to either to the date of birth, to the creation of (say) a duchy, or to a precedent.

46. La Bruyère (1881), 5.50.

Conflicts of *préséance* took place within each of the three estates as well as among them. When individuals were ranked on several dimensions that did not produce isomorphic orderings, or when different precedents suggested different priorities, the outcome could be *violence* (especially before the reign of Louis XIV), an ingenious *compromise, paralysis, or withdrawal*. Examples follow.

Violence

In extreme cases, the conflict ended with one claimant to *préséance* killing the other. "Pierre Benoist, a notable from Limoges, was so upset that Petiot, a royal official, had been seated ahead of him at a wedding in 1649, that after the festivities he shot him in the back."[47]

In churches, "pre-eminence was usually marked by the right to a pew, to display arms in the interior and to a tomb niche,"[48] all of which were scarce goods. "Pews were commonly tied to specific plots of land. Problems arose when a purchaser of property of lower social status than his neighbours proceeded to sit in a position that suggested he was of higher rank . . . . The smashing of the offending pew was an all too frequent demonstration of public animosity, the retaliation for which might even spill over into the streets of the capital."[49]

A conflict over whose arms should be placed in a church window was resolved by a temporary compromise in which the two families took turns, until "after mass on the Sunday after Easter 1587 [the head of one family] was killed as he left the church."[50]

Compromise

"When a conflict of *préséance* [in the convocation to the Estates-General of 1576] arose between four barons and four lords from

---

47. Carroll (2006), p. 67

48. Ibid., p. 68.

49. Ibid., p. 73. Villagers, too, might destroy or burn pews as symbols of a hated domination (Nicholas 2008, pp. 301–302). Hunting privileges had the same dual position. Horizontally, they "were a major source of feuds" among the nobles (Carroll 2006, p. 63). Vertically, they served to demarcate them from commoners (Nicolas 2008, p. 291). As I note below, the presence and number of gallows on the land of a *seigneurie* also provided grounds for both horizontal and vertical differentiation.

50. Carroll (2006), pp. 68–69.

Périgord, one went so far as to have their names written in a circle on the list of convocation, so as not to ruffle sensitivities."[51]

Officers sometimes took turns to command so that nobody would be offended, with a serious loss of efficiency as a result.[52]

Rotation might not be sufficient, however, for who should serve first? In the assembly of nobles that met in 1649, that problem was solved by choosing the president for the first day by lot.[53]

In the assembly of notables that met in 1671, nobles and magistrates both claimed precedence over the other group. The proceedings were paralyzed until "an ingenious disposition of the seats made it possible to place the two on the same level."[54]

At a session in 1770 of the *Cours de Pairs*, a meeting of the *parlement* of Paris augmented by the peers of the kingdom, a conflict arose over whether the lay peers or the peers of the church should speak first; "it was decided that in the future one should only take account of the date of creation of the peerage."[55]

When it was feared that a high-ranked noble might, against the opposition of other nobles, "pretend to *préséance*" in a provincial assembly, he solved the problem by seating himself according to his age.[56]

When both the parish in which a deceased priest had resided and the chapter to which he had belonged claimed the right to bury him, someone proposed the Solomonic compromise of cutting his body in two and give one part to each claimant.[57]

Saint-Simon recounts that when two coaches carrying noble ladies met before a narrow vault and both refused to yield, the conflict was

51. Soule (1968), p. 44. Saint-Simon, vol. 29, p. 202, recounts a similar episode 150 years later, when nobles "all signed in a circle to banish all differences."

52. Petitfils (2014a), p. 348; Pillorget and Pillorget (1995), p. 504; Lavissse (1989), p. 576; Bertière (1990), p. 240; Cénat (2015), pp. 124–125. In the eighteenth century, alternation in offices became a means of multiplying them and selling them to generate revenue. Often, however, existing occupiers of the offices bought the newly created ones.

53. Jouanna (1989), p. 268.

54. Pillorget and Pillorget (1995), p. 147. The disposition can be seen in a contemporary print, accessible at http://gallica.bnf.fr/ark:/12148/btv1b8401776x/f1.item.

55. Hardy, vol. 1, p. 647.

56. Véri (1930), p. 233.

57. Ibid., p. 481. In the end, the parish priest "conceded the *préséance* to the canon" (ibid.). For another Solomonic compromise between the *noblesse de robe* and the *noblesse d'épée*, see Petitfils (2013), p. 445.

resolved by both coaches squeezing by, "at the expense of the small shops along the walls" of the vault.[58]

At a more exalted level, Marie-Antoinette and (the later) Louis XVI were married twice, first in Vienna and then in Versailles, "to avoid privileging one of the two involved parties."[59]

When the archbishop of Paris came to the royal chapel for investiture, he wanted the cross carried before him, which was unacceptable for the royal chaplain. "The solution adopted in 1747 was to allow the cross, but to put a note in the registers of the Order that this was 'without prejudice' to the conflicting claims."[60]

Paralysis

Groups that had objective interests in common might fail to promote them because of questions of *préséance*.

Lefebvre affirms that in Valenciennes, the local nobility was perfectly positioned to take the lead in agricultural reform. "It would have not cost it anything to assume the social role assigned to it; on the contrary, any improvement would increase its income as it possessed two thirds of the land. Yet it was above all concerned with imposing respect for the *préséances* and showing its jealousy and distrust of the *intendant*."[61]

Goubert affirms that all the inhabitants of the Beauvaisis were "mindful of precise distinctions and a punctilious hierarchy; ... their title, their place in the church, their rank in the processions were among their most important concerns. ... In the cities, where quarrels of *préséance* were not limited to the bourgeoisie, this attitude reached its most acute degree: the struggles among the communities did not only express professional rivalries, but also rivalries of *amour-propre*. These struggles ranked among the causes that *blocked ... any kind of awareness of common interests*."[62]

58. Saint-Simon, vol. 18, p. 124.

59. Bertières (2002), p. 21. The choice of Vienna for the first marriage was not made by lot, however.

60. McManners (1998), pp. 34–35; see ibid., pp. 429, 476, for similar cases. The belief that one could prevent an exception from becoming a precedent was probably illusory, and possibly known to be so, in which case the compromise was merely a form of face-saving for the defeated party. For another face-saving compromise, see Carroll (2006), p. 74.

61. Lefebvre (1924), p. 223.

62. Goubert (2008), pp. 277–278; my italics. In a footnote, he argues that this claim of a lack of class consciousness is not undermined by the occasional strikes in the *ancien*

Saint-Simon recounts how a majority in the *parlement* could be unable to block the king's will because of questions of *préséance*. Since the *Premiers Présidents* who would normally preside over the session often abstained themselves in such cases, for reasons of self-interest, the remaining members might not be able to agree on the presidency: "In this conflict, where nobody wants to yield, nobody can preside, and for lack of a president the session is adjourned. They all know what they have to lose from this dispute, but *pride prevails over reason and over the general interest of the corporation.*"[63]

Even more important, the claim of the Paris *parlement* to have *préséance* over the provincial courts was a recurrent obstacle to the solidarity of the "union des classes."[64]

At the meeting of the Estates-General in 1484, some provinces "preferred to lose irrevocably the authority of the Estates by abdicating their full freedom of choice, to the benefit of the [royal] council, rather than seeing the power shared with Normandy and Burgundy."[65]

When the archbishop of Sens tried, from 1756 to 1770, to unite two collegiate churches to his cathedral, his efforts failed because of the opposition of his canons: "By the proposed merger, the dignitaries of the two alien foundations would assume places in the choir subordinate, it is true, to the metropolitan [cathedral] dignitaries, but in advance of ordinary canons—this, they said, was 'revolting'. The archbishop sardonically replied that their pride had cost them 450 livres a year each, a 50 percent rise of income thrown away."[66]

Tocqueville claimed that the isolation of the guilds and professions from each other was due mainly to a reluctance to take the first

---

régime, which were punctual, local, brutal, and ineffective. Lavisse (1989), pp. 296–297, provides other examples of the mutual jealousy of the corporations, leading to litigation that could last for a century.

63. Saint-Simon, vol. 25, p. 318–919; my italics. He claims that the Court deliberately encouraged these conflicts.

64. Swann (1995), pp. 164, 246.

65. Picot (1888), vol. 2, p. 11. He refers to their motivation as "the double passion for honor and wealth" (ibid., p. 10), that is, for *préséance* and money. As noted, the system of cross-voting prevented similar conflicts among the estates (while perhaps generating conflicts among the provinces).

66. McManners (1998), vol. 1, p. 404. He notes, however that "as 1789 drew nearer . . . , bishops and canons drew together in a conservative alliance; their rivalry had been a luxury of privilege to be abandoned when both were threatened from below," by the parish priests (ibid., p. 430).

step, a fear of being inferior rather than a desire to be superior. "Each of them clung to his own particular status only because others distinguished themselves by theirs, but all were ready to meld into a single mass, provided that no one else could claim any advantage for himself or rise above the common level."[67]

Tocqueville's comment can be spelled out in game-theoretic terms. Each guild or profession would have been willing to give up its claims to precedence provided that the others did so too, but none would unilaterally take the first step. This preference order reflects that of an Assurance Game, which differs from the better-known Prisoner's Dilemma in which the insistence on precedence would be a *dominant strategy*, to be followed regardless of what other groups do. This interpretation may also apply to the comments by Julian Swann on struggles over *préséance* in the provincial Estates of Burgundy, in which he takes exception to the common claim that they were frivolous and pointless: "These struggles were vital to those involved precisely because the Estates were a vibrant and important institution, offering the perfect stage upon which to fight the battles for precedence that were central to the society and culture of the *ancien régime*. . . . All of those present were well aware that their colleagues had no choice but to defend their respective rights and privileges."[68] Like Tocqueville's statement, Swann's can be read as stating that the system was a *bad equilibrium*: although collectively disastrous, nobody had an incentive to deviate from it unilaterally. As we shall see, however, provincial nobles did to some extent abstain from quarrels among themselves.[69]

Withdrawal

If victory in a contest of *préséance* seemed unlikely and defeat would be unacceptably humiliating, withdrawing often seemed the best solution.

> In a conflict among four princes under Charles IX in 1570, described in great detail by Fanny Cosandey, the Duke of Nevers finally withdrew from the celebration of the king's marriage and forbade his wife from attending.[70]

---

67. Tocqueville (2011), pp. 91–92.

68. Swann (2003), p. 64.

69. Yet nobles often quarreled about who among themselves should be allowed to take seat in the provincial Estates where these existed (Pélaquier 2014 a, p. 45, Swann 2003, p. 68, Rébillon 1932, pp. 87–104).

70. Cosandey (2016), pp. 133–140.

At the other end of the social spectrum, "If one corporation was granted priority over another in the general assembly of notables, the losing group would refuse to attend. It would rather turn its back on public affairs altogether than suffer what it regarded as an affront to its dignity. The wigmakers' guild in the town of La Flèche decided 'to express by these means its justified pain at the award of priority to the bakers.'"[71]

Saint-Simon tells the story about how the Duc d'Orléans, as regent, backed down from a confrontation with the *parlement* by abstaining from participating in a process where the magistrates demanded to march on the right, with the regent on the left.[72]

He also tells how a marriage contract failed to be signed because the Duchess of Orléans did not want to sign after the wives of the royal princes.[73]

When Madame Palatine wanted to travel to the wedding of her daughter to a prince from another royal family, the trip was cancelled because of disagreement over the seating arrangements.[74]

At the opening of the Estates of Provence on December 31, 1787, the deputies from the third estate of Marseille protested against the *préséance* of the deputies from Arles, based on precedents giving Arles *préséance* in odd years and Marseilles in even years. The deputies from Marseille affirmed, not without reason, that the quasi-totality of the session would take place in 1788. Having exposed their grievance, they withdrew from the Estates.[75]

When the *maréchaux de France* were outmaneuvered by the *ducs et pairs* in the competition for the front seats in a funeral of the *maréchal* d'Estrées in 1737, they stayed away from the funeral of another *maréchal* in 1744.[76]

---

71. Tocqueville (2011), pp. 90–91.
72. Saint-Simon, vol. 25, p. 179.
73. Saint-Simon, vol. 19, pp. 64–65; see also ibid., pp. 66–67, 103.
74. Palatine (1985), p. 266.
75. Cubells (1987), p. 16. She affirms nevertheless that as a sign of the "ideological revolution" the "conflicts of *préséance* . . . had lost their power to mobilize the spirits" (ibid., p. 20), as illustrated by the example from p. 11 of her book that I cited earlier. The observation by McManners (1998), vol. 1, p. 430, cited in note 66 above suggests (what may or may not be) a different explanation, in terms of social conflicts overwhelming the symbolic ones.
76. Luynes (1860–1865), vol. 1, pp. 436–437; vol. 6, p. 138. In this case, the withdrawal followed defeat rather than being undertaken to preempt defeat.

At the quinquennial or decennial meetings of the Church, the
archbishop of Lyon was rarely present, because his "claim to
supremacy roused general suspicion."[77]

"As neither [the bishop of Mâcon nor the bishop of Auxerre] wished
to recognize the preeminence of the other, the governor [of
Burgundy] came up with an ingenious solution at the [provincial]
Estates of 1682, permitting them to alternate precedence from
one day to the next. Any relief was short-lived. At the assembly of
1694, . . . neither bishop entered the Estates for ten days because
of their continuing rivalry."[78]

An enmity due to a conflict of *préséance* might prevent the parties
from attending mass together, since this would amount to a public
act of reconciliation. "Those who took communion while they
harboured rancour in their heart put their salvation at peril. To
avoid contact with one's enemy one had to *avoid the parish church
altogether*."[79]

Consider now more specifically the psychology of the nobles. It is common to differentiate among them by two distinctions: provincial nobles
versus Court nobles (grandees) and sword nobles (*noblesse d'épée*) versus the legal *noblesse de robe*. Nobles of any of these categories might or
might not be *seigneurs*, that is, in possession of a fief. Younger sons of
nobles often did not possess a fief. (Conversely, a *seigneur* might be a commoner, that is, a member of the third estate.) In addition, the nobility of
old extraction tended to draw a sharp line separating them from the newly
ennobled, especially from the very recent nobles who could not transmit
nobility to their children.

Cardinal Bernis proposed four criteria—military or legislative profession, ancestry of the lineage, reputation, and power—and a hierarchy of
nine ranks within the order of the nobility. Among the newly ennobled,
he ranked the grounds of their elevation into the nobility in the following
order: military service, service in the magistracy, wholesale trade, literary achievements, achievements in the visual arts, useful achievements in
agriculture and navigation, and finally money.[80] "At least a century was

77. McManners (1998), vol. 1, p. 188.

78. Swann (2003), p. 62, cites this as one of several ecclesiastical conflicts over *préséance* among the clergy in Burgundy. As noted above, violence was also an alternative when
rotation failed to satisfy the parties.

79. Carroll (2006), p. 68; my italics.

80. Bernis (1980), pp. 165–167. There are many such catalogues. Bluche (1986b), p. 79,
cites the eighteenth-century genealogist Chérin, who distinguished five criteria: the age of the

needed to clean a commoner from the rust of his origin."[81] The accretion of noble status over time was matched by the dilution of the old nobility. When fifty-eight nobles in the electoral district of Beauvais met to elect their deputies to the Estates-General in 1789, only ten came from families that were noble two hundred years earlier. Among the others, more than half descended from wealthy textile families.[82]

A biographer of Henri IV writes that in the baroque age, conventionally defined as the period 1589–1661, the upper French nobility was characterized by the "hypersensitivity, intolerance, aggressiveness, cruelty, discouragement, impotence" of its members.[83] A generation earlier, discouragement and impotence had been less prominent. During the wars of religion, the nobles were engaged in a real struggle for power, based on what they saw as their "duty to rebel."[84] A generation later, aggressiveness and cruelty had waned in importance, as Louis XIV and his ministers cleverly defanged the nobles and relegated them to a largely ceremonial function. Under the last Valois kings (before 1589), "the most trusted remedy to prevent indiscipline from affecting the *grands seigneurs* was to call them to the Court and keep them close."[85] The nobles marked their discontent with the king by leaving the Court for their *terres* (landed properties).[86] After 1661 the nobles stayed on their *terres* only when forced into exile by the king (or if they could not afford the expenses at the Court). I shall return to this extraordinary tool of governance.

Hypersensitivity and intolerance persisted throughout the *ancien régime*, although in abated form.[87] I have already noted the obsession

---

lineage, services to the king, positions, alliances, and possessions. Vauban (2007), pp. 246–247 lists, without ranking them, thirteen "services to the king" that justify ennoblement. One that is worth mentioning is ennobling "a merchant who has gained 200,000 *écus* in legitimate trade, *on condition of pursuing the same trade during his whole life*" (my italics). Usually, nobility was *lost* by trading; Vauban proposed that it could be *lost by not trading*. To encourage trade, Richelieu promised nobility to commoners who had maintained a ship of roughly 800 cubic meters for five years (Pillorget and Pillorget 1995, p. 336), but did not require them to do so in the future.

81. Bernis (1980), p. 169.
82. Goubert (2013), p. 221.
83. Babelon (1982), p. 11.
84. Jouanna (1989).
85. Ibid., p. 84.
86. Ibid., p. 108.
87. "Louis XIV managed to pacify . . . these hypersensitive (*écorchés-vifs*) grandees, so touchy about the smallest marks of honor" (Jouanna 1989, pp. 396–397) There was, however, considerable regional variation. Nobles in Brittany stood out as exceptionally unruly

with *préséance*. The nobility could not tolerate the intrusive harassment by fiscal agents who wanted to verify their tax payments, as if the word of a noble were not sufficient.[88] Even after nobles began to pay some direct taxes, they insisted on being on separate tax rolls, so as not to be confused with the commoners.[89] Members of the warrior nobility deliberately refused to undertake the legal education that was required to achieve high office, and ostensibly showed off their ignorance in order to differentiate themselves from the legal nobility.[90] As a consequence, they did not find a place in the complex financial and administrative hierarchies of the absolute monarchy.[91] Saint-Simon, who advocated a regime where the nobility

---

(Marion 1898; Marion 1891, chap. 6). In 1753, some nobles in that province addressed a memoir to the king demanding the exclusion from the provincial estates of all whose nobility was posterior to 1453, because of the "annoyance of seeing people whose fathers [*sic*] were crawling in the dust take the floor and prevail over the true nobility" (Marion 1891, pp. 193–194). Private violence was also more prevalent than elsewhere (Carroll 2006, p. 65, citing a treatise from 1606). The nobles in Brittany remained turbulent to the end, when they refused to send deputies to the Estates-General in 1789.

88. Jouanna (1989), pp. 114, 269. In the period she discusses, the nobles were for the most part not subject to direct taxes, except (in some parts of France) if they possessed "villein land" of commoner origin (*terre roturière*). Yet they paid indirect taxes, notably the *gabelle* (salt tax). In the eighteenth century, nobles were just as opposed to inspections and verifications, but for more mundane reasons that they shared with other taxpayers (Marion 1927, pp. 168–169).

89. Tocqueville (2011) p, 85; Lefebvre (1924), p. 174; Marion (1891), p. 43; Kwass (2000), p. 164. Both honor and material self-interest might dictate this demand (Markoff 1996, p. 170–71).

90. Referring to the Court nobles, La Bruyère (1881, 9.24) writes that they neglect "to become acquainted not only with the interests of their princes and with public affairs, but with their own, while they do not know how to govern a household or a family, boast of this very ignorance, and are impoverished and ruled by their agents." Referring to the provincial nobles, Goubert (2013), pp. 214–221, emphasizes their vanity and incompetence. Like their peasants, they ended up with heavy debts that often forced them to sell off parts of their land. Jouanna (1989), pp. 96–98, affirms, however, that "the greatest lineages had amazing capacities for regeneration," adding that "in the present state of knowledge it would be hazardous to make an overall assessment." Chaussinand-Nogaret (1985), p. 63, who makes fine-grained distinctions among the provincial nobles, affirms that below a certain level of income, they were "unemployable for lack of money and education, marooned by prejudice in inability to redeploy themselves."

91. Jouanna (1989), pp. 44–45, 64; Chaussinand-Nogaret (1985), pp. 105–111. To this *negative self-selection*, Louis XIV added *negative selection*, by deliberately excluding members of the upper nobility from his Council (Pillorget and Pillorget, 1995, p. 687), not because of their incompetence but because of his vivid memory of the turbulence the nobles had created during his minority. (For the same reason, he deeply distrusted the *parlements*.) This quasi-banishment endured until about 1760. (It is possible, but would be hard to verify, that the negative self-selection was *caused* by the negative selection, through a sour-grapes mechanism.) Moreover, because the nobles were by and large not allowed

would occupy all the important posts, acknowledged that "for some time one will not be able to do without the magistrates as officials of finance; they have created a gibberish (*grimoire*) that only they can understand until it has been cleaned up by authority and effort and made accessible to the sword nobility."[92]

Arlette Jouanna has analyzed the mindset behind this self-destructive behavior, a quasi-biological belief that nobility stemmed from inborn character traits, and could not be grounded in skills acquired by training or justified by military accomplishments. It could be *revealed*, though, by such achievements. "In the sixteenth century, gentlemen made the cycle of novels *Amadis de Gaule* their bedside book. On almost each page, one finds stories about children of nobles abducted at birth and brought up among peasants, who suddenly revealed their quality by some extraordinary action."[93] To be sure, biology had to be supplemented by social mobility, since otherwise wars and infertility would ultimately have extinguished the nobility.[94] Yet, Bernis noted, fresh nobility had to prove itself through time, at least over two or three generations. The belief in the magical effect of the sheer passage of time created a cult of ancestry that permeated the nobility as whole.[95] Catching a venereal disease from a

---

to engage in trade, they were often unable to amass the fortune needed to buy an office (Bercé 1974, pp. 119, 131). On the motives behind this ban on engaging in trade, see Zeller (1957) as well as Dravasa (1965), pp.158–182. Even when the ban on (wholesale) trade was lifted in 1701, many nobles were so reluctant to use the opportunity that the edict was reissued several times (Chaussinand-Nogaret 1985, p. 92). It also seems that the nobles, even though sometimes addicted to dueling, were highly risk-averse in economic matters. Neither Richelieu nor Colbert succeeded in interesting them in overseas trade. "Suspecting a fiscal operation, one distrusted any government initiative in economic matters" (Pillorget and Pillorget 1995, p.773; see also p. 343). Not until after 1770 did they begin "to be massively involved in great overseas trading companies" (Chaussinand-Nogaret 1985, p. 95).

92. Saint-Simon, vol. 27, p. 18: see also ibid., p. 9 for an implacable diagnosis of the nobles. Jouanna (1977), pp. 205–206, notes that some nobles saw the introduction of Roman law as a deliberate effort to reserve legal office for the "technicians" formed by the universities.

93. Jouanna (1989), p. 23; also Jouanna (1977), p. 26.

94. Jouanna (1989), p. 24.

95. An extreme case was observed in 1768, when the noble delegates to the provincial Estates of Languedoc were required to have 400 years of nobility in the paternal line, as the result of a "gradual move from *having* to *being*" (Pélaquier 2014 a, p. 45). The belief may not have been purely magical, but due to a proto-Lamarckian belief in the transmissibility of acquired characteristics (Jouanna 1977, p. 40; Devyer 1970, pp. 164–175). In his *Traité de la Noblesse*, La Roque (1678, Préface) wrote that "There are in the seeds (*sémences*) I do not know which force, and I do not know which principle, that transfers and continues the propensities (*inclinations*) of the fathers to their descendants." In Languedoc only a

duchess, as did the son of Madame de Sévigné in 1680, was more accept-able than getting it from a prostitute, "as if the pain was less acute, the evil less bothersome, and the offense to God smaller."[96] Writing in 1830, Stendhal captured the attitude of the Marquise de la Mole by observing that "having had ancestors who had gone to the Crusades was the only advantage she appreciated."[97] The Crusades were also the holy grail for the nobility of *A la recherche du temps perdu*.

The ideology of the nobles harbored a deep ambiguity, however, in their attitude towards the martial arts. "One was never able to decide whether competence in bearing arms derived from a particular virtue inherited by blood, a virtue belonging to the race of nobles, or whether one had to work to acquire or to improve this competence."[98] Montaigne described two responses to this dilemma, counting either on raw courage or on secrecy:

[A]s I myself know from experience [fencing] is an art which has raised the hearts of some above their natural measure; yet that is not really valour since it draws its support from skill and has some other foundation than itself. The honour of combat consists in rivalry of heart not of expertise; that is why I have seen some of my friends who are past masters in that exercise *choosing for their duels weapons which deprived them of the means of exploiting their advantage* and which depend entirely on fortune and steadfastness, so that nobody could attribute their victory to their fencing rather than to their valour. When I was a boy noblemen rejected a reputation for fencing as being

---

single degree of nobility was required in the maternal line, reflecting perhaps the tendency for nobles to marry the daughters of rich commoners who had recently been ennobled, or perhaps the belief that there were no that maternal "seeds" to be transferred, since women only serve as the channel for the male seed (Jouanna 1977, p. 45). At the same time, there was a common requirement of "four quarters" of nobility (including two grandmothers) for civil or military office.

96. Sévigné, vol. 2, p. 868. Her son did not go so far in investing rank with physical significance as the Abbé de Polignac who, being surprised by rain while walking with the king in his gardens at Marly, responded to his solicitude by saying that "it's nothing; the rain at Marly does not wet you (*ne mouille pas*)" (Saint-Simon, vol. 13, p. 216). He was the subject of much ridicule. When the aged Duchess of Chaulnes, famous for her wit, took a twenty-five-year old financier as her lover, she quipped that "for a bourgeois, a duchess is never more than thirty years old" (editorial Introduction to Deffand 1866, p. li).

97. Stendhal (1952), p. 442.

98. Brioist, Drévillon, and Serna (2008), p. 50. They assimilate (ibid., pp. 106, 119) fencing to equitation and to dance, without asserting, however, that excellence in these activities was also supposed to be inborn.

an insult; *they learned to fence in secret* as some cunning craft which *derogated* from true inborn virtue.[99]

The idea that some activities derogated from the status of a noble could, as in this case, be a matter of customs and social norms, based on quasi-biological racist beliefs. As noted earlier, the ban on engaging in retail trade was a *legal* norm. However, as also noted, *wholesale* trade was allowed. There was also a legal norm proscribing nobles from personally conducting agricultural operations, but an exemption was made for *small-scale* operations, defined by a maximum number of ploughs that could be used. It is difficult (for me) to see how retail trade or large-scale agriculture could derogate from virtue. Conversely, it does not seem that the contempt of nobles for formal education stemmed from a belief that their inborn virtue sufficed for conducting matters of state, or for maintaining their estates. To reconstruct a coherent mind-set may be a vain effort.[100]

The cult of ancestry went together with contempt for the less well born, as will be illustrated by a famous episode at the Estates-General in 1614 and a no less famous passage from the *Memoirs* of Saint-Simon that I shall cite at some length.

At the Estates-General of 1614, a deputy from the third estate made a sly remark that younger brothers sometimes had to rebuild the houses that their elders had left in ruin. The nobility reacted with the utmost anger: "there was no fraternity between the nobility and the third estate; they did not want to be called brothers by the sons of cobblers; there was as much difference between them as between the master and his valet."[101] On the order of the king (that is, the queen regent), two deputies from the third estate had to apologize to the nobility.

In his obsession with *préséance*, ancestry, and legitimacy, Saint-Simon was slightly mad and not wholly representative of the nobility. Yet in a less intense form, the emotions expressed in the passage I shall cite were those of many nobles. The event that triggered them was a *lit de justice* (a solemn session of the *parlement*, presided by the king) in 1718, in which the role of governor of Louis XV was taken from the Duc de Maine, one of two illegitimate sons of Louis XIV, and given to the Duc de Bourbon,

99. Montaigne (1991), pp. 790–791; my italics. See also Brioist, Drévillon, and Serna (2008), pp. 120–128, on "Courage and skill."

100. Jouanna (1977), p. 16. For an example of contradictory attitudes towards acquired versus transmitted qualities, see Brioist, Drévillon, and Serna (2008), pp. 127–128.

101. Rapine (1651), pp. 153, 155. Sieyès cites the address the nobility made to the king on this occasion as an appendix to his *Essay on Privileges.*

third in the legitimate succession to the throne. Saint-Simon was hostile not only to these sons, whom he referred as "the bastards," but also to the magistrates who had supported their claims. Upon hearing the decree being read, he wrote,

I was dying with joy. I was so oppressed that I feared I should swoon; my heart dilated to excess, and no longer found room to beat. The violence I did myself, in order to let nothing escape me, was infinite; and, nevertheless, this torment was delicious. I compared the years and the time of servitude; the grievous days, when dragged at the tail of the Parliamentary car as a victim, I had served as a triumph for the bastards; the various steps by which they had mounted to the summit above our heads; I compared them, I say, to this court of justice and of rule, to this frightful fall which, at the same time, raised us by the force of the shock. . . . I thanked myself that it was through me this had been brought about. . . . I had triumphed, I was revenged; I swam in my vengeance; I enjoyed the full accomplishment of the most vehement and the continuous desires of all my life. I was tempted to fling away all thought and care. Nevertheless, I did not fail to listen to this vivifying reading (every note of which sounded upon my heart as the bow upon an instrument), or to examine, at the same time, the impressions it made upon every one. . . . During the registration, I gently passed my eyes over the whole assembly, and though I constantly constrained them, I could not resist the temptation to indemnify myself upon the *Premier Président* [of the *parlement*]; I perseveringly overwhelmed him, therefore, a hundred different times during the sitting, with my hard-hitting regards. Insult, contempt, disdain, triumph, were darted at him from my eyes, and pierced him to the very marrow; often he lowered his eyes when he caught my gaze; once or twice he raised his upon me, and I took pleasure in annoying him by sly but malicious smiles which completed his vexation. I bathed myself in his rage, and amused myself by making him feel it. I sometimes played with him by pointing him out to my two neighbors when he could perceive this movement; in a word, I pressed upon him without mercy, as heavily as I could.[102]

At the Court, the fear of *ridicule* could be paralyzing. Saint-Simon says about a lady at the Court that she was a "bewitching Siren, against

---

102. Saint-Simon, vol. 35, p. 236 (translation from Internet). I do not know of any comparable acknowledgement of the delights of *hubris*.

whom the only defense was to flee her. . . . No one could deliver ridicule as elegantly and cruelly, even when there was none."[103] La Bruyère, another close observer, wrote: "However able the great at Court may be, and whatever skill they may possess in appearing what they are not, and in not appearing what they are, they cannot conceal their malice and their inclination to make fun of other people, and often to render a person ridiculous who is not really so." For "a person of intelligence . . . , the dangerous inclination of a courtier to ridicule anyone [would induce] him to be very reserved."[104] For the less careful, the effects of ridicule could be dramatic. In prerevolutionary Paris, a young officer, wealthy but not noble, tried to gate-crash a ball at Versailles. "He was treated so severely that in his despair over the ridicule with which he was covered, at a time when ridicule was the worst of all evils, he killed himself when he came back to Paris. . . . The Duc de Luynes told his daughters on the day they were to be presented at the Court, 'Remember, in this country vices do not matter, but ridicule kills.'"[105] Horace Walpole observed that "designing men . . . have no weapon against good men [such as Malesherbes and Turgot] but ridicule."[106] The weapon could also be wielded against fools, as in Molière's play *Le méchant*, "Fools are on earth to keep us all amused," later cited by Madame de Merteuil in *Les liaisons dangereuses* and used by the diarist d'Argenson to characterize the outlook of his brother and the Comte de Maurepas, subsequently principal minister of Louis XVI.[107] Perhaps, for these cynics, to be good *was* to be a fool.

In the words of Joseph Droz, an acute early commentator on the *ancien régime* and a first-hand observer of its fall, it rested on "a *cascade of contempt*, which descended from rank to rank and which did not stop at the

103. Saint-Simon, vol. 3, p. 174.

104. La Bruyère (1881), 10.26. The Court was a minefield. "If a courtier be not continually upon his guard against the snares laid for him to make him ridiculous, he will, with all his sagacity, be amazed to find himself duped by people far less intelligent than he is" (ibid., 9.88). Saint-Simon tells many stories of this kind (e.g., vol. 6, pp. 42–43; vol. 15, p. 449). Maria Theresa (Mercy-Argenteau 1874, vol. 1, p. 197) admonishes Marie-Antoinette that if she continues to make fun of people just to please five or six of her coterie, honest people from whose company she would benefit will stay away from her. Mercy-Argenteau also comments on her tendency to "take part in the small pleasantries that are sometimes directed towards old people or towards those who have some remarkable facial disfigurement" (ibid., p. 327). The spirit of spiteful or malicious wit is well and alive in France today; only in that country, I believe, could one publish a 1150-page *Bouquin des méchancetés*, a *Book of Malicious Sayings* (Testu 2014).

105. Boigne (1999), vol. 1, pp. 73–74.

106. Walpole (1913), p. 30.

107. D'Argenson, vol. 5, p. 86.

third estate; the judge in a small court held the merchant in a disdain that the latter rendered to the artisan."[108] Similarly, one might characterize it as resting on a *cascade of préséance*, which involved a related hierarchy, but was based on different psychological mechanisms. In the sources, I find no trace of contempt in those who claimed *préséance* over members of inferior groups in the hierarchy, as long as the latter accepted their place. There are no indications of the haughtiness, disdain, *morgue,* and (in the original Greek sense) *hubris.*[109] I leave these questions here, hoping that a Proust will be forthcoming to do them justice.

Ridiculing others often went hand in hand with showing off one's wit (*esprit*). The Cardinal de Retz "never resisted the pleasure of a *bon mot* . . . , disregarding the hurt he inflicted and the likely resentment of the victim."[110] The seventeenth-century rake Bussy-Rabutin lost *two* friends, when he commented on the first's pursuit of the second, a lady with bad teeth: "Doesn't he see her teeth, and, worse, doesn't he smell them? I have always thought that love can make you blind, but I did not yet know that it can also make you catch a cold."[111] According to Cardinal Bernis, in the mid-eighteenth century "the mode of wit . . . was like an epidemic sickness." At an early stage in his career he sought a meeting with the principal minister of Louis XV, Cardinal Fleury, to solicit a post. Since Bernis was suspected of being more of a courtier than a priest and Fleury had strict criteria, he refused by saying, "Not while I am alive." Bernis replied, taking his reverence, "I shall wait."[112] (Fleury was eighty-eight years old at the time.) That *bon mot* made his reputation. In this case, the deployment of wit was not zero-sum. In other cases, one made one's reputation by destroying that of another, sometimes by bestowing praise that all except its object perceived as excessive (*persiflage*).[113] "A word could kill even if

---

108. Droz (1860) vol. 1, p, 81; my italics. Tocqueville held Droz (1773–1850) in high esteem (Jardin 1988 p. 484). In the Conclusion below I briefly discuss some possible influences of Droz on Tocqueville; for a more extensive discussion see Elster (2006).

109. As Fisher (1992), p. 11, shows, the Greek notion should be understood as behavior designed to produce shame, albeit not to bring about behavior modification: "It is from the absence of any motive, good or bad, apart from the pleasure of insulting, that one deduces that this is indeed hubris." The psychology of contempt is more complex and often involves avoidance behavior rather than deliberate humiliation.

110. Bertière (1990), p. 113.

111. Letter to (his cousin) Madame de Sévigné, August 17, 1654.

112. Bernis (1980), pp. 122–123.

113. Saint-Simon, vol. 2, pp. 195, 396; Hardy, vol. 1, p. 192–193. I assume that the age-old tactic of damning with *faint* praise was also used.

the rapiers were blunted."[114] La Bruyère commented that "persons who injure the reputation or position of others for the sake of a *bon mot* deserve to be punished with ignominy;"[115] instead they were rewarded.

The irresistible temptation of a *bon mot* could even override the interest of the witty speaker. Madame de Grignan, the daughter of Madame de Sévigné, married her son to the daughter of a rich tax farmer, justifying the misalliance by saying that "from time to time, the best lands need some manure. She took infinite pleasure in this *bon mot*. . . . Saint-Amans [the father of her daughter-in-law], who was ready to do everything to relieve their debts, finally heard about it and was so offended that he turned off the faucet."[116] After the death of Louis XV, someone told M. Le Gallick, the head of the Compagnie de Saint-Sulpice, "The king died of smallpox (*la petite vérole*)," to which he replied, "there is nothing small about the great." La *grande vérole* is syphilis. The *bon mot* caused him to lose his position.[117]

In the absence of wit, at least an exquisite politeness was required. Commenting on his meetings with several French *grand seigneurs* in 1787, Arthur Young would "praise them for equanimity but condemn them for insipidity. All vigour of thought seems so excluded from expression, that *characters of ability and inanity meet nearly on a par*: tame and elegant, uninteresting and polite, the mingled mass of communicated ideas has *powers neither to offend nor instruct;* where there is much polish of character there is little argument; and if you neither argue nor discuss, what is conversation?"[118] Although Young does not say so, there may have been a social norm against saying anything that could "offend" even if it did "instruct."[119] Madame Palatine wrote that at the Court, "[o]ne makes

114. Apostolidès (1981), pp. 53–54.

115. La Bruyère (1881), 9.80. For examples of *bon mots* with devastating effects, see Saint-Simon, vol. 1, pp. 250, 268.

116. Saint-Simon, vol. 12, p. 289. Duchêne (1985), pp. 270–271, doubts that she took pleasure in her *bon mot*. For my purposes, what matters is that Saint-Simon found the attribution credible.

117. Musset (1828), pp. 246–247.

118. Young (1794), vol. 1, pp. 26–27; my italics. Lüthy (1998), p. 16, refers to a "clarity whose criterion is elegance and good taste rather than truth." Stendhal (2006), p. 153, expands the analysis by an insightful comment that "[a]lthough one did not suspect it, this extreme politeness had completely destroyed the energy of the rich classes of the nation. There only remained the personal courage that has its source in extreme vanity, which politeness tends to stimulate and continually magnify in the hearts."

119. On the aversion in the elites of the old regime to being contradicted, see the hilarious comments by Malesherbes cited in Grosclaude (1961), p. 288, as well as Lavisse (1989), p. 246.

fun of people who like to talk and to reason, hence there is no agreeable conversation."[120]

The hypersensitivity of the nobles in some settings can be contrasted with their insensitivity in others. Tocqueville cites "Mme Duchâtelet, who, according to Voltaire's secretary, was quite comfortable disrobing in front of her servants, in view of the absence of incontrovertible proof that valets were men."[121] Mercy-Argenteau cites an episode from 1770, when the young Marie-Antoinette witnessed an accident in which the postilion of her coach fell off his horse and was severely injured. When she tried to console his brother and brother-in-law, who were both coach drivers, "one tried to reassure her by telling her that people in the stables were hard-hearted"[122] and thus incapable of feeling and suffering. I am not sure Tocqueville gets the contrast exactly right when he asserts that the "lord who lived on his estate usually displayed a certain familiar bonhomie toward his peasants, but his insolence toward the bourgeois, his neighbors, was almost without limit."[123] Like valets and coach drivers, peasants were usually *beneath contempt*.

The psychology of the Court nobles could be very different from that of the provincial nobles. Among the chief characteristics of the latter were a norm of *equality* among themselves, a norm of *independence* both from the Great and from the monarch, a norm of *préséance* over the bourgeoisie, and a norm of *supremacy* over the local peasantry.

In the assemblies of provincial nobles in 1649 (mentioned above) and 1651, equality of presiding, seating, and signing the final document was the norm.[124] On one occasion in 1651, it was decided that "nobody should leave the assembly during its sitting and that the vote of those who left it should be suppressed,"[125] lest they seek directives from the princes about how to vote. *The egalitarianism could strengthen the order as a whole*, if it

---

120. Palatine (1985), p. 235; see also Palatine (1989), p. 194.

121. Tocqueville (2011), p. 162. The words the secretary used in his memoirs were that "great ladies regarded their lackeys only as automata." I shall return to other examples of this attitude.

122. Mercy-Argenteau (1874), vol. 1, p. 108; see also ibid., p. 346 for another example of indifference toward the injuries of a groom. We cannot tell whether it was due to lack of empathy or to lack of sympathy.

123. Tocqueville (2011), p. 86. In *Democracy in America*, Tocqueville (2004a, p. 658) got it right: citing some callous remarks by Mme de Sévigné about "hanging as a diversion," he comments that she "had no clear idea of what it meant to suffer when one was not a noble." Another example of her throwaway callousness is a remark in a letter to her daughter of January 5, 1676 (vol. 2, p. 13), recounting how the soldiers quartered near her home in Brittany "amuse themselves by theft, and the other day roasted a small child on the spit."

124. Pernot (2012), p. 248.

125. Jouanna (1989), p. 267.

allowed natural leaders to emerge.[126] In Brittany, all nobles, not only their elected representatives, had the right to attend. Moreover, "[o]nly age served to give precedence in ceremonies and deputations."[127] When the provincial Estates of Provence met in 1787, for the first time since 1639, the assembly of nobles "decided that from then on the nobles should walk behind their *syndics* in order of age and without feudal distinctions. This small revolution put an end to the *préséance* of the marchionesses. . . . All nobles, all who were enfeoffed, were equal in dignity: only the superiority of white hair was admitted. It is an example of *very clear affirmation of class consciousness*."[128] In the Estates of Burgundy, "as befitting a social class that, whatever the social and economic realities, preached the virtues of equality, the chamber of the nobility had none of the elaborate quarrels about precedence and seating arrangements that so obsessed the clergy."[129]

In the chaotic minority of Louis XIV, the question of the independence of provincial nobles from the king was less salient. In the eighteenth century, however, they sometimes engaged in fierce resistance to Versailles. In particular, the unruly and obstructionist behavior of the nobles in Brittany at meetings of the provincial estates almost defies belief.[130] Although the governor of the province from 1753 to 1768, the Duc d'Aiguillon, tried to reduce the *independence of the nobility* by undercutting the *equality of the nobles*, he had only a mixed success.[131]

As noted, issues of *préséance* could arise in all social groups. To the extent that the provincial nobility was of recent origin, one might expect the issue to be especially salient. For the upstart, it was vital to distinguish himself from his origins, a need that was reinforced by the contempt in which he was held by the old families. Whereas an old family could afford to attach little importance to the particle *de* that preceded the family name, the fresh nobility or would-be nobles would insist on using it (or inventing it) to demarcate themselves.[132]

Finally, many provincial nobles clung to their supremacy over the peasantry in matters that did not have an immediate economic importance.

126. Ibid., p. 268.
127. Rébillon (1932), p. 85.
128. Cubells (1987), p. 11; see also p. 15.
129. Swann (2003), p. 67, adding, however, that "despite the theory of noble equality and the superficially democratic flavour of their assembly, [the position of permanent *élu* between the sessions of the Estates] was not a post open to all"; see also ibid., p. 121.
130. Rébillon (1932), pp. 164–182. The picturesque and sometimes hilarious descriptions in Marion (1891), chap. 6; and Marion (1898) are perhaps to be taken with a grain of salt.
131. Egret (1970), p. 165; Marion (1898), pp. 506–510; Rébillon (1932), pp. 67–72.
132. Goubert (2013), pp. 206–207.

This would notably be true of the nobles who were too poor to have a house in a nearby town, and for whom life revolved around their manor or castle. The *seigneur* usually had a bench reserved for himself and his family in the church, a privilege that the peasantry sometimes opposed by stealing the bench and burning it.[133] In Burgundy, the *seigneur* confiscated a vineyard from a peasant who had not paid homage on the day of his marriage.[134] Sometimes, the *seigneur* forbade dancing in the village when there had been a death in his family.[135] When there was a dance, he had the right to "the first dance." The *ius primae noctis* never existed, but its persistence as a fantasy is revealing.[136] Finally, probably most important, the right of the *seigneur* to act as a judge, even in his own cause, "conferred life to the *seigneurie* to which the domain gave a body."[137] In 1670, the magistrate Guillaume de Lamoignon defended seigneurial justice by arguing that "nothing distinguishes [the *seigneurs*] more from the other subjects of the king."[138] Seigneurial justice could also serve to differentiate *among* nobles. A duke could erect eight gallows on his land, a count six, and a baron four.[139]

The Nobility of the Robe

The psychology of the *noblesse de robe* is important for the understanding of the *parlements*. I discuss their behavior later, but some observations can be made here. The decisions of the magistrates were often motivated by their financial interests, but perhaps even more by their pridefulness and vanity, transmuted into a sense of honor.[140] They approved the arbi-

---

133. Nicolas (2008), p. 302; Bercé (1974), p. 432.

134. Saint-Jacob (1960), p. 246.

135. Nicolas (2008), p. 709.

136. Boureau (1995), p. 14.

137. "fait la vitalité de la seigneurie à qui le domaine donne le corps" (Saint-Jacob 1960, pp. 58–59).

138. Lavisse (1989), p. 270; see also Barbier, vol. 4, p. 372. Esmonin (1913), p. 196, says that tax exemption was the most important distinguishing feature, yet, I conjecture, the *power over others* conferred by seigneurial justice was more gratifying for the amour-propre of the nobles than a mere *superiority over others* (see chapter 1). In the *pays de taille réelle*, where taxes (and tax exemptions) followed the land rather than the person, there was not the same shame attached to paying the *taille*. The establishment of a cadaster proposed by finance minister Bertin in 1763 may have been motivated by a desire to attenuate this distinction in *pays de taille personnelle* as well (Félix 1999, p. 268).

139. Marion (1923), p. 243.

140. The observation by Petitfils (2014b), p. 577, that honor "served as a smokescreen for the pridefulness (*orgueil*) of the grandees" probably applies to the magistrates as well.

trary *taille*, from which they were exempt, but were moved to protest against proposals to create a cadaster that would have affected them. Yet, François Bluche argues, material interests cannot fully explain their skirmishes with the finance ministers in the second half of the eighteenth century: "The violence of this reactionary opposition is not explained merely by the nobiliary sentiments of its leaders. Their sense of unity (*esprit de corps*) is masked by the heat of the fight, the ardor of the polemic, *the pleasure of confronting the power to the point of making it stagger*. If they had been the cold and witting depositories of privilege, even the most anachronistic ones, our magistrates would have been monsters. Quite to the contrary, *the audacity of the parliamentary opposition is explained by passion*."[141] In addition, as I shall discuss later, the remonstrances of the magistrates were often inspired by their desire for popularity. As I noted, there is little tangible evidence that they were also moved by reason, as distinct from interest and passion.

The Peasantry

I now turn to the moral emotions of the peasantry of the old regime. To understand them, we must consider the vagaries of nature, the forms of surplus extraction, and subjective feelings of injustice.

I shall first present a rough overview of the state of France in 1745, constructed by the minister of finance Orry from the responses of the *intendants* to a questionnaire he had sent out.[142] The regions are classified into five categories: well-off (*à l'aise*), can live (*vivent*), some can live, some are poor (*les uns vivent, les autres sont pauvres*), poor (*pauvreté*), and miserable (*misère*). There does not seem to be strong correlation between the levels of welfare and the presence or absence of provincial assemblies or *états* (not shown on the map).[143]

The French peasantry could see their standard of living attacked by a number of natural causes: bad weather (one hail storm could wipe out

141. Bluche (1986b), p. 96; my italics.
142. The map is taken from Dainville (1952). In addition to asking the intendants about the size of the population and the productive capacities of the province, Orry asked them to inform him "as exactly and as secretly as possible" about the quantities of silver objects in the possession of private individuals. Astonishingly, he also asked them to spread rumors about impending increases in the entry fee and in recruitment to the militia and to report back to him how the inhabitants responded. The rumors about conscription elicited mostly negative responses, causing in some cases young men to flee or to enroll in the regular army (Lecuyer 1981).
143. The main provinces with such estates were Brittany to the extreme West, Burgundy in the Center, and Languedoc to the Southeast. See chapter 5 for details.

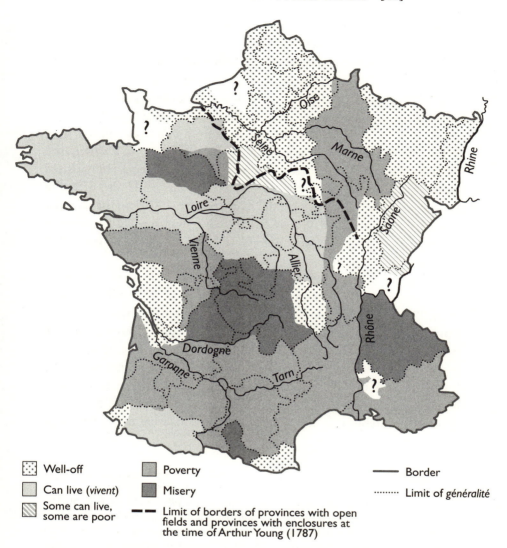

FIGURE 2.1. Conditions of the people in the eighteenth century. After the inquiry by Orry (1743). *Source*: Redrawn from Dainville (1952).

the grape harvest for several years), foot-and-mouth disease (which could wipe out the major part of a herd), and disease (plague and smallpox). It is also likely, although controversial, that a "little ice age" from 1550 to 1700 or beyond affected living conditions. In the following I focus on man-made causes, but one should keep in mind their interaction with natural ones. Bercé writes that "while lack of food made people vulnerable to contagion, the latter paralyzed trade and contributed to the high price of food."[144] Saint-Jacob writes that in the crisis of 1747–1749, "there were three facts that nobody forgot: foot-and-mouth disease, taxes, and high prices of grain. The illness seems to have been the most serious. No livestock, no cultivation."[145] Moreover, some "natural" causes were sustained by deliberate human action. Many *seigneurs* kept pigeons, mostly for their meat and eggs, to the great annoyance of the peasants as the birds ate the seed grain. According to a grievance book from 1789, two pigeons with their small ones consumed as much grain as one man.[146] In Flanders, the peasants "constantly requested, always in vain, that [pigeons] be enclosed from the sowing season to the harvest."[147] Pigeons could also dirty the water cisterns, which were essential in dry country.[148] When the *seigneur* hunted, the horses could also do damage. Since hunting was a monopoly of the *seigneur*, peasants were not allowed to shoot the small game that ravaged their fields.[149]

The previous paragraph enumerated some natural or natural-cum-social causes why the *gross* product of the land was less than it could have been. There were also purely social causes at work. Transaction costs—stamp taxes and internal tariffs—could deter people from engaging in mutually profitable ventures. The fear that any sign of affluence might trigger higher taxes could deter the investments that create wealth, such as the purchase of cattle or improvements on the land. Short leases on land also created a disincentive for improvements. Although it is impossible to quantify profitable activities that for such reasons were not undertaken,

144. Bercé (1974), p. 26; see also Le Roy Ladurie (1966), pp. 530–531; Pillorget (1975), pp. 315–317.

145. Saint-Jacob (1960), p. 299; see also p. 503 for the 1780s. Cattle were needed for manure, for ploughing, and for milk. They were vulnerable not only to disease, but also, in spite of many attempts to ban the practice, to seizure by tax authorities. The passive resistance of neighbors who refused to take care of the seized cattle (Bercé 1974, p. 353) was perhaps more effective than any edict. In any case, there might be nothing to seize: many peasants were reluctant to buy cattle because, as a visible sign of wealth, they could trigger increased taxes (Bouisguilbert 1707, pp. 35, 132; Vauban 2007, pp. 767, 774).

146. Levillain-Hubert (2001), p. 33. On p. 34 she reproduces a contemporary drawing of a women sowing grains and surrounded by pigeons. In a text from 1622, a specialist in financial matters enumerates the fate of the first handfuls of seed grain: the first for God, the second for the birds (presumably pigeons), the third for the *cens*, the fourth for the tithe, and the fifth for the taxes (Walter 1963, p. 229). "If the laborer really considered for whom he was sowing, he would not sow."

147. Lefebvre (1924), p. 135.

148. Saint-Jacob (1960), p. 529.

149. Ibid., p. 281.

the grievance books of 1789 show that people were aware of the stifling effects of the innumerable regulations.[150]

I now turn to the mechanisms of surplus extraction that determine the *net* product left for the peasantry. For any society, one can define the *maximal attainable inequality* (of income or consumption), subject to a subsistence constraint, and the *inequality extraction ratio* which is the ratio of actual inequality to this maximum.[151] If the ratio is 100 percent, a small upper class receives the whole national product minus what is needed for the subsistence of the producers. If the ratio exceeds 100 percent, the economy will not sustain itself. This may have been the case for the Spanish colonies in America. In most societies, however, the ratio is well below 100 percent. In contemporary France, for instance, it is about 32 percent. In England and Wales in 1759, it was 55 percent. In France in 1788, it was 76 percent, comparable to the Roman Empire in 14 A.D., Holland in 1561, and Peru in 1876.[152] Because of the uncertainty surrounding the raw data behind these calculations, the numbers must be taken as rough approximations only. They suggest a harshness of surplus extraction in the old regime that we can also infer from qualitative findings. Most strikingly, Esmonin argues that Louis XIV adopted the ideology that he was the real owner of all property in his kingdom, so that "when he taxes he is only taking part of his own property. . . . He had no scruples raising the *taille* to the highest level the taxpayers could support."[153] Although "everybody agreed on the need to limit taxes and not oppress the subjects . . . , the main reason was fear: 'Who presses the udder too hard, says Bossuet, to extract milk by heating and tormenting it, will make butter. Who presses men too hard, will excite rebellions and seditions'"[154]

---

150. At the same time, as noted, they were sometimes opposed to regulations that were in the long-term public interest, such as the 1669 forest ordinance. Other complaints about regulations may also have been due to a short-term perspective.

151. This paragraph summarizes findings from Milanovic, Lindert, and Williamson (2011).

152. In England and Wales in 1688, it was 57 percent. For France, the authors only give the data for 1788. An extrapolation nevertheless suggests the rough accuracy of the estimates by Sully as reported by George Carew (see Appendix).

153. Esmonin (1913), pp. 9, 13. Also Saint-Simon, vol. 20, pp. 172–173: "what he left to [his subjects], he did as a sheer favor" (*pure grâce*). It seems likely, however, that this attitude was Colbert's rather than the king's.

154. Esmonin (1913), p. 8, paraphrasing *Proverbs* 30:33 that Bossuet (1836, p. 293) is citing. The king, in fact, faced multiple constraints. If the people were squeezed too hard, not only might they rebel, but their health might be affected and hence their ability as farmers and as soldiers might suffer. Since harsh extractions in a given year would mostly affect the *fighting ability* of future soldiers many years later, the urgent monetary needs of

The king was constrained, however, by rival forms of surplus extraction. The French peasant paid not only taxes to the state, but also rents and other dues to the *seigneur*, and tithe to the church. Adding them all up there might be little left, especially if we also take account of indirect taxes, some of them levied on stipulated rather than on actual consumption, and of the high level of indebtedness of many peasants.[155] In the Beauvaisis, the "semi-misery" of the peasants was due to "the cascade of takings (*prélèvements*) and the accumulation of stakeholders who descended on their gross income."[156] From Burgundy, Saint-Jacob cites a contemporary complaint that after paying taxes and rent (not counting the tithe), the peasant could only work one day a week for himself.[157] In a grievance book from Burgundy in 1789 we read that "when the peasant has paid the seigneurial rent, the king's taxes, and provincial taxes [still not counting the tithe], he is at most left with a quarter of the income from his land."[158] In one village in the mid-eighteenth century with a gross income of 11,000 livres, "the clergy took 2,500, the *seigneur* 1,900, and direct royal taxation 1,975. In another, . . . with a gross income of 24,000 livres, the corresponding figures were 4,700, 4,150 and 4,230."[159] Assuming, conservatively, that indirect taxes equaled the direct ones, these extractions left about 25 percent for the villagers.

Each of the extracting agents might on some occasions protect the peasantry against the extractions of the others.[160] Fearing for his tithe, the parish priest might protect his flock against the *seigneurie*, even when

---

the kings would easily override this consideration. For most of the *ancien régime*, French recruits were in fact considerably shorter than those of Sweden and England (Komlos 2003), suggesting malnutrition. Harsh extractions in a given year could affect the *productive ability* of farmers and thus the tax base in the immediately following years, but it seems that even a future that close was often too remote to affect decisions.

155. On debts, see Goubert (2013), pp. 183–189; Le Roy Ladurie (1966), pp. 487–489, 595–600. By and large, the lenders do not seem to have been usurers, but local notables with some cash at hand. When they charged high interest, it was probably (as in the case of loans to the government) because of the high risk of default. An exception was the systematic exploitation of cultivators by lawyers and notaries in the east of France, who turned the smallest debts into lawsuits that ruined the peasants (Nicolas 2008, pp. 655–664; Ado 1996, pp. 68–70).

156. Goubert (2013), p. 180.

157. Saint-Jacob (1960), p. 139.

158. Ibid., p. 507.

159. McManners (1998), vol.1, pp. 95–96.

160. For analytical purposes, we may count the loss of a source of income as an extraction. When the administration denied peasants their traditional access to the forests, the local notables, who feared for their rent, were lukewarm in support of the royal policy (Nicolas 2008, p. 648). See also comments above on pigeons and game.

the latter was an abbey.[161] Saint-Jacob states that in Burgundy, "the *seigneurie* at all times tried to fight against external taxation to protect its own."[162] According to Follain, the provincial estates in Burgundy, Brittany, and Languedoc "protected taxpayers against the royal fisc only to allow other authorities and appetites to maintain themselves."[163] Bercé writes that when a nobleman in Auvergne forbade his peasants to pay the *taille*, the royal Council "ordered that 'the fruits of his villages should be seized and sold to pay the outstanding taxes . . . , which took priority over the rent claimed by the [*seigneur*].' The antagonism of the debts is here clearly stated."[164] Jouanna refers similarly to "a direct antagonism" of the *taille* and the rent, adding that "it was not rare for nobles to ring the church bells when the fiscal agents arrived, and to have their peasants meet them armed with hayforks, sticks, or muskets."[165]

Solidarity with the peasants against other predators was often a matter of self-interest, directly or indirectly. The less they were exploited by others, the more an agent could extract from them. Lower taxes allowed for higher rents.[166] The tithe was not adjustable upwards in the same way, but it could be collected more rigorously if taxes were lowered (or were collected less rigorously). After 1789, it was commonly argued that the peasantry would not benefit from the abolition of the tithe, since the rent would automatically be increased by an equal amount.[167] In the parts of

161. Nicolas (2008), pp. 268–269.

162. Saint-Jacob (1960), p. 126 note 9; see also Boisguilbert (1707), p. 22; Esmonin (1913), p. 51; Lavisse (1989), p. 172.

163. Follain (2008), p. 72.

164. Bercé (1974), p. 130.

165. Jouanna (1989), p. 252; also pp. 359–360.

166. Conversely, higher taxes made for lower rents. In his discussion of the *taille*, Locke (1953), pp. 207–208, writes that the "inhabitants of free towns that have land in the country perswade them selves that they nor their land pay not, because 'tis the pore tenant that pays, but yet according to the increase of their taxes their rents decrease." The hint at self-deception is worth noting.

167. "From 1789 onwards, one of the favorite arguments of the counterrevolutionaries [against the abolition of the tithe] was that it would not benefit the peasants, given that the major part of their land was not their property and that the owners were in a hurry to raise the leases in proportion to the suppressed dues" (Lefebvre 1924, p. 406). Sieyès (AP 8, p. 387) makes the same argument, but was accused by contemporaries (cited by Bastid 1970, pp. 82–85) and by historians (Lefebvre 1963, p. 151) of acting out of self-interest, as he was a tithe-holder himself. The charge seems unjustified, given that in *What Is the Third Estate* Sieyès made the same argument with regard to the *taille*, in which he had no personal interest: "It is worth pointing out that the abolition of the hearth tax (*taille*) will be very advantageous to the privileged orders in monetary terms if it is agreed, as seems likely, to replace it by a general subvention. . . . In regions in which the hearth-tax falls upon a person, it is very well

France where taxation followed the land and not the person, a noble who possessed villein land shared the interests of the people in low taxes.[168]

The seigneurial protection of the peasants against high taxes was also a condition for the rents to be seen as acceptable—it was the price of protection. When, after 1660, the tax collection became more orderly and less predatory, "the protection by the nobles through their credit [at Court] or their force became useless. At the same time, their local demands became less bearable. If denunciations of seigneurial violence begin at this time, it is not, to be sure, because it had not existed earlier, but because there had been no idea of complaining about it nor any power to resist it. We are dealing with a psychological shift. The couple protection-dues is broken, *their tacit contractual relation comes to an end*, because the means and the occasions for exercising the seigneurial protection have disappeared."[169] Below I shall discuss how the violation of a social contract could fuel sentiments of injustice. First, however, I consider the acute everyday concerns that could also motivate riots or insurrections.[170]

Hardships can generate social unrest. Among the 8,528 incidents of violence that Jean Nicolas found in all of France between 1660 and 1789, 1,497 were due to a subsistence crisis. (A large proportion were in 1788–1789.) In his study of insurrections in Aquitaine between 1590 and 1715, Bercé found 31 riots against the high price of bread, compared to 42 against soldiers living on the land and plundering the village, 63 against the collection of direct taxes, and 109 against the collection of indirect taxes. Now, hunger is not an emotion. Its immediate action tendency

---

known that, at bottom, the tax is paid by the landowner. The farmer, told by the landowner that he will take responsibility for the payment of his tax, simply pays higher proportional rent" (Sieyès 1789, p. 125). The validity of these arguments depends on the form of rent paid by the peasants. They are valid for sharecropping, but not for a fixed monetary rent, which, as noted below, was the "sore of the *seigneurie*" (see Saint-Jacob 1960, p. 123, for these and other regimes in Burgundy). However, "by the law of March 11, 1791, the abolition of the tithe did in fact profit the owner of the land: the farmer owned him the sum in money, the sharecropper as a proportion of the harvest" (Albert Soboul, marginal note to Jaurès 1968, p. 469).

168. Bercé (1974), p. 144.

169. Ibid., p. 131, my italics; see also pp. 691, 695.

170. In their discussion of the insurrection in Paris in August 1648, Pillorget and Pillorget (1995), pp. 489–493, make a partly similar distinction. A movement "oriented towards norms," which concern problems of everyday life, may (as in 1789) or not (as in 1648) turn into a movement "oriented towards values," which concern matters of principle. They also make the important suggestion that a panic that turns out to be based on false rumors may trigger anger towards those deemed responsible for triggering it, as if "the crowd was furious for having been afraid [and] unleashed its anger on the person or persons whom they deemed responsible for the panic." Similar reactions were observed in 1789 (Ado 1996, pp. 130, 133). I consider this mechanism further below and in Volume 3.

is to obtain food, if necessary by force,[171] but violence against persons is not a primary aim. Yet a subsistence crisis can also, as a secondary effect, induce emotions, which can trigger attack on persons over and above what is needed to get at food. (French terms for a riot are *émeute* and *émotion*.) As Bercé remarks, "the hunt for those who starve the people (*les affameurs*) had a reassuring function. Calamities from heaven are too horrible to imagine, one prefers to discover a responsible in flesh and blood, to hunt out the authors of the catastrophe. The riot responds to the need to find human causes for an impersonal disaster."[172] Nicolas finds that beyond the immediate lootings, "in one out of two [subsistence incidents] the public attacked the supposed authors of the penury."[173] While some of these imputations were probably justified,[174] others were not.[175] One cannot assess the proportion of cases in which they were.[176]

171. In an entry from 1750, Argenson, vol. 6, p. 181, cites approvingly reforms intended to bring beggars back to their village, commenting that by this project "one will banish mendacity from the kingdom, without, however, reducing poverty, which is extreme, but *the poor will die of hunger patiently.*" I read the words I have italicized as implying that a wandering beggar might pose a threat to others, e.g., by forcing a peasant to take him in and feed him lest his house be set on fire (Lefebvre 1988, p. 40). Back in his village, he would be less dangerous.

172. Bercé (1974), p. 547. This *agency bias* (Elster 2015 a, pp. 167–169), further discussed below, has been consistently observed in studies of famines in the old regime (Kaplan 1982, p.63 and *passim*; Lefebvre 1988, p. 47). In most cases, the commonly used phrase "starving the people" (*affamer le peuple*) should be taken in the sense of acting with a callous indifference to the welfare of the people (e.g., Kaplan 1982, p. 34). Exceptionally, it might mean acting with the deliberate goal of making the people worse off, in one alleged case because it was thought that France was too populated and that "one had to make some perish from misery" (Narbonne 1866, p. 144). Whether true or, as is more likely, not, this belief would trigger a more virulent anger than the belief that the elites simply did not care about the people. To illustrate, if A tells a malicious lie about B to prevent B from getting a position that A also covets, B's anger upon learning this fact will be stronger than what he feels upon learning that A did not bother to write a letter of recommendation for B for a position that A does not covet.

173. Nicolas (2008), p. 339.

174. Lefebvre (1924), pp. 246, 250; Saint-Jacob (1960), pp. 178, 195, 298, 300; Bercé (1974), p. 544.

175. A humorous imputation not intended to be taken seriously may nevertheless illuminate the agency bias. When a provincial canon, "given to good cheer and [with] a figure to match," spent some time in Paris, "'Take care not to add a name to the martyrology,' wrote a colleague, 'all that is needed is for the fishwives to take one look at you and decide that you are the cause of the high price of bread'" (McManners 1998, vol. 1, p. 422).

176. One should in any case distinguish causal from moral responsibility. Hoarders may be causally responsible for high prices, yet not be blamable. Adam Smith (1976, vol. 2, p. 35) wrote that "If [the merchant who holds stocks of grain during a famine] judges right, instead of hurting the great body of the people, he renders them a most important service. By making them feel the inconveniencies of a dearth somewhat earlier than they otherwise

I have emphasized that the peasantry was exposed to *multiple forms* of surplus extraction. This fact also generated *more frequent encounters* with the different oppressors, each of them reinforcing the subjective misery generated by the others.[177] Tocqueville captures the situation in a passage whose psychological acumen and literary power justify quoting it at some length:

> I ask you to imagine the French peasant of the eighteenth century, or even the peasant you know today, for he remains forever the same: his condition has changed, but not his state of mind. See him as he is depicted in the sources I have cited, so passionately in love with the land that he uses all his savings to purchase more, no matter what the price. To acquire this new land he must first pay a fee, not to the government but to other nearby landowners, who have as little influence over public affairs and are almost as powerless as he. When at last he gets the land he wants, he plants his heart in it along with his seed. This little corner of the earth that he can call his own fills him with pride and independence. Yet now the same neighbors arrive to take him away from his field and force him to work somewhere else for no pay. Should he try to protect his harvest from their wild game, these same neighbors stop him. They await him at the river crossing to demand that he pay a toll. He encounters them again at the market, where they sell him the right to sell his own produce. And when he returns home and wants to put the remainder of his grain to his own use—grain that he planted with his own hands and watched grow with his own eyes—he cannot do so unless he sends it to be milled in mills and baked in ovens owned by these same men. Part of the income of his small farm goes to paying them rent, and that rent is perpetual and irredeemable.

---

might do, he prevents their feeling them afterwards so severely as they certainly would do, if the cheapness of price encouraged them to consume faster than suited the real scarcity of the season. When the scarcity is real, the best thing that can be done for the people is to divide the inconveniencies of it as equally as possible." Young (1794), vol. 1, p. 493, wrote that "The multitude NEVER have to complain of speculators; they are ALWAYS greatly indebted to them"; see also Arrow (1982) on hoarding as a cause of intertemporal smoothing of consumption. Referring to the obsession with the provision of grain in the mid-seventeenth century, Lavisse (1989), p. 195, wrote that "Later, people came to understand that these suspicions and precautions aggravate or create the evil one wanted to banish, but it takes a long time to get used to reasoning about the fear of dying from hunger." Yet people living on the brink of starvation might act on their short-term needs rather than on their long-term interest. Also, the benefits from speculative hoarding depend on the hoarders forming correct anticipations about future scarcity (Ravallion 1987).

177. In technical language, their impact is not additive. For another case in which the impact of each encounter depends on the number of others, see Elster (2015a), pp. 242–243.

No matter what he does, he encounters these vexatious neighbors along his path, interfering with his pleasure, impeding his work, eating his produce. And when he has finished with them, others, clad in black, arrive and take the lion's share of his harvest. Imagine this man's condition, needs, character, and passions, and calculate if you can the wealth of hatred and envy that he has stored up in his heart.[178]

I now turn to the peasant conceptions of injustice, which had horizontal as well as vertical dimensions.

The main horizontal issue was the allotment of tax payments, notably of the *taille*, within and among the collectivities.[179] (A secondary issue, discussed later, was the selection of soldiers for the militia.) The government first determined the total tax revenue it wanted to be collected. This global amount was then the object of 4 successive allotments: among the 30 or so *généralités*, among their 4–15 subunits (*élections*), within each of these among 50 to 150 parishes, and finally among the couple of hundred (sometimes much less) households of the parish.[180] These numbers are approximate, but the order of magnitude seems right.[181] The total number of parishes was about 40,000.[182]

---

178. Tocqueville (2011), pp. 37–38.

179. Kwass (2000), chap. 3, has an extensive discussion of "petitions and the clamor for justice" in the allotment of the *vingtième* and the *capitation*, two direct taxes that even the privileged were supposed to pay. From his examples, as well as from those provided by Marion (1891), I form a strong impression that these demands were mostly self-serving. Individuals and groups could shop around, as it were, for some aspect of their situation in which they were treated less favorably than a suitably chosen reference group, including their own situation in the past. Injustices in the allotment of the *taille*, by contrast, was widely criticized by all observers, except for the *parlements* which benefited from the litigation to which they gave rise (Marion 1910, p. 6).

180. For a more fine-grained case study, see Bercé (1974), pp. 71–77.

181. See Dupont-Ferrier (1930). For simplicity, I ignore the differences in tax assessments between the *pays d'élection* that are described in the text and the *pays d'état*, in which the provincial Estates first negotiated the tax with the government and then decided on the allotment of taxes across dioceses, which decided on the allocation among parishes. The former covered three-fourths of the territory and paid five-sixths of the taxes (Marion 1927, p. 37).

182. The vast number of parishes, most of them poorly documented, makes it difficult to generalize about life in the villages. Even the scholars on whom I rely most, who spent their lives in the archives, were constrained by the haphazard survival or destruction of documents as well as by the need to limit themselves to one region. The best quantitative analyses, those of Shapiro and Markoff (1998), are limited to the 1789 grievance books, which are not necessarily representative of the *ancien régime* as a whole. Also, by the nature of the documents they do not provide hard data about population size, the level of taxation, the nature and amount of rents, and many other things one would want to know. See also chapter 6.

The officials of the old regime made several efforts to create an equitable tax system, in which individuals and communities would be taxed according to their productive capacities. In 1707, Vauban proposed a progressive land tax, from 5 to 10 percent, exempting no one and paid in kind. It was only briefly and partially implemented and would probably not have worked as a permanent solution.[183] Around the same time. Boisguilbert proposed a tax reform that would eliminate the need for officials who had discretionary powers of assessment and collection. In 1716, the finance minister, the Duc de Noailles, sent a revealing circular letter to the *intendants* asking them to gather the information needed to create a fair tax system, but to do so in an underhand manner. It is worth citing it at some length:

> The main object of the project we are sending you is to obtain for the people a beginning of relief through an equality in the allotment of taxes to which one has paid little attention. At the same time, we would like to gather an exact knowledge of the strength of the provinces and the capacities of the subjects of the King in order to establish a just and, if possible, unchanging schedule of taxation. You will understand that you might have to overcome obstacles created by those who, having been favored until now . . . will view as an ill for themselves what will be a source of good for others. It is above all necessary to *avoid that they fathom our plan to obtain an exact count.* . . . . It is therefore very necessary that you and the commissioners you might employ act so that, *without letting it be understood* that you have any other end than the equitable taxation within each parish, you can give an exact account to the Council of all its parts, both with respect to properties and to persons, so as later to establish an exact balance among the parishes in each *élection* and among the *élections* in each *généralité*.[184]

The shady practices Noailles wanted to get rid of were common. In 1636, a leader of a peasant movement in Charente complained that the "*élus* [tax officers in the *élection*] established their schedule so as to relieve the parishes where they possess property or which have bought their favor."[185] In 1663, Colbert tried to eliminate the *élus*, arguing that "there

---

183. See the survey of obstacles and objections in Touzery (2007), p. 738. A small-scale version of Vauban's proposal (a 2 percent land tax) was sought to be implemented in 1725, but failed because of obstruction by tax-exempt individuals and groups (Marion 1910, pp. 78–81).

184. The circular is reproduced in Marion (1910), p. 136; my italics. The admonition to proceed in secret is repeated several more times.

185. Bercé (1974), p. 385; the full text is in ibid., pp. 746–749. These "*élus*" were in fact

was nothing more harmful to the people than the multiplication of tax officers, up to twenty-two or twenty-three in each *élection*, who not only lived at the expense of the people but even caused an infinity of disorders by the reliefs and rebates that, for various interested reasons, they give to the rich."[186] To dismiss them, however, the king would have to reimburse them for their offices—a short-term cost that weighed more than the long-term benefits. Although Colbert was apparently willing to abolish their offices without compensation, Louis XIV was not.[187] He could, and did, however, take their powers away from them.

Noailles's letter reflects a probably well-founded fear that if the local notables were to find out that a reassignment of taxes across *élections* and *généralités* was being planned, they would be able to sabotage it. More generally, any attempt by the administration to gather information about property holdings was invariably perceived as the first step towards a general tax increase. The word "cadaster" was a hated one in *all* ranks of society.[188] In some cases the suspicion may have been justified,[189] but in other cases the goal of the government may only have been to create a uniform and impartial tax system, which would inevitably be at the expense of the rich while benefiting or at least not harming the poor.[190] The desire for *equality* were probably not inspired by the motive of *equity*, but rather by *efficiency: lever mieux pour percevoir plus* (tax better to collect more).[191] Esmonin claims that the unequal allocation of the *taille* hurt the royal treasury, since much of the tax burden was diverted to those unable to pay ("*non-valeurs*").[192]

---

not elected, but officials who had bought their office. They should not be confused with the *élus* in the provincial Estates of Burgundy (chapter 5).

186. Esmonin (1913), p. 116, note 2.

187. Lavisse (1989), p. 324.

188. Nicolas (2008), pp. 221–222; Saint-Jacob (1960), pp. 169, 334, 510; Marion (1927), p. 229; Claeys (2011), pp. 463–464. The idea of a "verification" (of the declarations of income and property) was no less hated (Flammermont 1888–1898, vol. 3, p. xxv; Marion 1891, p. 54; Marion 1927, pp. 168–169; Faure 1961, p. 203; Saint-Jacob 1960, pp. 330–331). The *pays d'états* had cadasters, as had the Limousin (as the only *pays d'élection*). Although the lack of a cadaster may have *protected individuals from the government*, it also *interfered with private transactions* by making it more difficult for would-be borrowers to use their land as collateral for loans (Félix 1999, pp. 436–437).

189. The Duc de Noailles (Marion 1910, p. 136) admits that this may have been the case in the past, notably during wars.

190. In addition to the efforts by the Duc de Noailles and Colbert cited earlier, one may point to a circular from 1741 by the finance minister Orry (in Marion 1910, p. 349).

191. Félix (1999), p. 279.

192. Esmonin (1913), pp. 151–152.

In his circular, Noailles affirms that "balance" or equality was desirable at three levels: among the *élections*, among the parishes, and among the taxpayers. It seems unlikely that ordinary people would be aware of unbalanced or unjust allotment of taxes across the *élections*. In his survey of peasant movements in 1636, Bercé find that "criticism of the *mode of allotment of the tax* . . . concerns inequalities of the tax base, be it at the level of the division among parishes or in the calculation of the quota of individual taxpayers."[193] Concerning the first criticism, he offers the example from Charente that I cited earlier. I have not come across any other cases of this kind, and I would not expect there to be many.[194] Because of the generally poor communications, the horizon of the peasants did not stretch much beyond the village.[195] Concerning the second criticism, Bercé writes that "one feared the influence of the rich on the establishment of the tax rolls. 'The five or six richest in each parish pay almost nothing.' They were present at the making of the rolls, and put pressure on the tax collectors. They were the creditors of many peasants, they had bought offices or fiefs, they had sharecroppers, tenants, servants."[196] In Burgundy, "the '*coqs de village*' [influential peasants] succeed in evading the taxes they should normally pay. No region is an exception to this practice. Tax collectors, tax assessors, local officials try to reduce their personal quotas. Farmers [property managers of a *seigneur*] are particularly aggressive."[197] In Normandy, "tax collectors gave free rein to their passions or their interests, as long as they did not have to fear reprisals [by the villagers] or punishment [by the authorities]."[198] Because the task of the collectors was burdensome (they could go to prison when they did not fill their quota), they sometimes overcharged the villagers who had elected them, with the result that some villagers abstained from showing up at the electoral assemblies.[199]

193. Bercé (1974), p. 385.

194. However, Boisguilbert (1707), p. 22, notes an interesting relation between intra-parish and inter-parish allocations: if an influential villager could persuade the *intendant* to reduce the quota for his parish, the tax collector might in return reduce his tax assessment. I suspect this may have been a common practice.

195. Saint-Jacob (1960), p. 78; Lefebvre (1924), pp. 230–237; Meuvret (1988), p. 48. Saint-Jacob (1960), pp. 323–324, states, however, that from the mid eighteenth century the improved network of roads in Burgundy created a network of common opinions. Because "the villages know each other better," uprisings "become more rational than spontaneous; this evolution of the peasant mentality is fraught with consequences."

196. Bercé (1974), p. 385.

197. Saint-Jacob (1960), p. 124, see also p. 187.

198. Esmonin (1913), p. 354.

199. Ibid., p. 355. This fact might explain why villagers were sometimes fined for not attending (Badeau 1878, pp. 33–34; Follain 2008, pp. 252–253). This conjecture receives

A recurrent pattern was the granting by the elites of privileges and exemptions to one another. John Locke writes that in Normandy, the *taille* "lights heaviest on the poor & lower sort of people, the richer sort befreinding & easeing one an other."[200] Goubert cites an example in which an individual A asks another person B for an exemption from military service for a third person C, a demand that B grants in exchange for an exemption from the *taille* for a fourth person D, a close relative of B's wife.[201] Esmonin cites several examples from Normandy of the mutual granting of tax exemptions within the elite.[202]

Some of the inequalities and the resentment they generated might be tempered by two equalizing mechanisms.[203] First, until it was abolished by Turgot in 1775, a "solidarity constraint" authorized the tax collector to force the richest inhabitants of the village to make up for a deficit in the targeted amount of taxes. Bercé writes that "even though the solidarity was detested by the opinion, it had the merit of correcting the injustices of tax allotment, by fetching the money where it was to be found."[204] Second, as I noted earlier, the *intendant* could use his discretionary power to tax the *coqs de village* as well as officials. Although rare in the seventeenth century,[205] the practice seems to have become general towards the end of the old regime.[206] As I also noted, it was often abused.

For a peasant, a tax exemption for someone *in his village* might trigger a personal feeling of injustice. In much of France, however, tax exemptions for property in a village were often given to absentee owners (*forains*). The *taille* could be levied as *taille réelle* or as *taille personnelle*. In the first regime, which, broadly speaking, existed in the provinces that had their

---

some confirmation from an ordinance in Champagne which decreed that the ordinary fine for non-attendance, five livres, was raised to twenty livres when the assembly elected the tax collector (Badeau 1878, p. 34). See also Esmonin (1913), p. 171–172.

200. Locke (1953), p. 148.

201. Goubert (2008), p. 210.

202. Esmonin (1913), pp. 157, 159, 251.

203. Pillorget (1975), p. 62, notes that in Provence "fear of popular anger, threat of a riot" might also serve as a "counterweight."

204. Bercé (1974), p. 103. It is puzzling that a measure correcting an injustice should be detested. The answer may lie in the fact that in many cases *all* inhabitants of the village, and not only the richest ones, were jointly responsible for the tax deficit (ibid., p. 566). Also, like the "*taxe d'office*," the practice could easily be abused (Esmonin 1913, pp. 497–499). Turgot (1844, vol. 2, pp. 377–378) persuaded the king to abolish the system because it treated the more affluent villagers unjustly.

205. Bercé (1974), p. 93, estimates that the revenue from this tax represented 4.7 percent of total tax income.

206. Lavisse (1989), p. 889.

own elected Estates (*pays d'états*), the tax was assessed on the property, regardless of where the owner resided. Tax allotments might be inequitable across communities, but were more likely to be equitable within each of them.[207] In the second regime, the tax was assessed on the owner, in principle on all his property, but in practice mainly on what he owned where he lived.

This second regime, which had a much greater potential for abuse and arbitrary impositions, entered into a complex system of incentives that caused people to leave the countryside for the towns. These included the hopes (1) of not being taxed for their property outside their place of residence, (2) of avoiding the burdensome task of tax collection,[208] (3) of avoiding the solidarity constraint, and (4) of buying a municipal office that carried with it exemption from the *taille*.[209] Its most glaring injustice was that land that was exempt from taxation because its owner lived elsewhere was nevertheless counted as part of the tax basis for the village. Each time someone left the village for the town (while retaining his land) or a *forain* bought a property, the others had to pay the tax in his stead.[210] Although by the nature of the case absentee owners could not be the target of face-to-face hostility, as a group they were detested. Yet "efforts [to restrict their rights] proved to be vain, since no royal legislation supported the wishes of the villagers."[211] Demands to replace the *taille personnelle* with the *taille réelle* were common,[212] but led to nothing, perhaps because a replacement would have required the creation of the feared cadasters.

The tithe could also generate horizontal forms of injustice. I have only come across one discussion of this issue, by John McManners, whom I shall cite at some length:

207. Follain (2008), p. 82, who explains the inequality across communities as due to the difficulty of modifying allotments in a zero-sum situation; see also Bercé (1974), p. 74, and Pillorget (1975), pp. 113–114. As noted in the text, between-community inequality would be less likely to generate perceptions of injustice than within-community inequality, except, perhaps, in the case of a neighboring parish.

208. Marion (1910), p. 16, asserts that the exemption from collecting the *taille* was more sought after than the exemption from paying it.

209. On these incentives and the inequalities they created, see Tocqueville (2011), p. 87; Saint-Jacob (1960), pp. 85, 124-125, 227, 423; Bercé (1974), pp. 22, 83; Follain (2008), p. 325; Esmonin (1913), p. 286.

210. Nicolas (2008), p. 202; Follain (2008), p. 325; Saint-Jacob (1960), p. 124. In a regime of *taille réelle*, the *forains* paid the ordinary *taille* on the land but—relying on a quid pro quo argument—might object to paying the taxes (*taille négociale*) used to fund village activities from which he did not benefit (Pillorget 1975, p. 71).

211. Saint-Jacob (1960), p. 85.

212. Bercé (1974), p. 393; Saint-Jacob (1960), pp. 303, 512.

The tithe was inevitably hated. It was all the more grudgingly paid when the peasant made comparisons. If he paid the tithe at a high rate, he would compare his burden with the lighter burden borne by others. Of a group of thirty-six parishes in Champagne, twenty-one paid a global sum equal to one third of all State taxation level, but four paid fully two-thirds of the total exactions of the Crown—an enormous disparity. The peasants were narrowly confined, physically and intellectually, within the boundaries of their village community, but where paying out was concerned, they knew when they were being unequally treated. In Brittany, where tithe in adjoining parishes could vary from one tenth to one thirty-sixth, this was a general complaint in the [grievance books]. That of the village of Comblessac asked for some reduction in its one-twelfth, "seeing that the parishes around owe it only on the fiftieth or [thirty-sixth] sheaf, and their land is better than ours."213

I do not know of any behavioral manifestations of resentment generated by unequal tithing. According to Jean Nicolas, reactions to unfair tithing (of which unequal tithing is but one species) took the forms of "cheating and litigating rather than acts of group violence."214 Among the forty-five tithe-related riots in his data base, most occurred in protests against external tithe-holders or against paying the tithe on new agricultural products not covered by custom. He cites no cases of riots due to unequal tithing, perhaps because it did not generate a well-defined adversary. Yet the perception of unequal tithing may well have contributed to a powerful if diffuse feeling in the peasantry of being subject to arbitrary and exploitative extractions. The feeling must have been reinforced when peasants "paid a tithe on potatoes, then another one on the pigs that were fed on them; similarly, when they paid on grain used to feed chickens."215

An important, if secondary, source of horizontal injustice was recruitment to the militia. Although everyone would prefer not to serve, just as everybody would prefer not to pay taxes, a fair system of selection could make the service more acceptable. As Tocqueville wrote, "What leads

213. McManners (1998), vol. 1, pp. 132–133; the number in square brackets is corrected from the original source. The implicit complaint in the last quoted sentence might seem illogical: if "their land" is better, a lower tithe may yield the same number of sheaves. Yet even though a regressive tithe could serve the goal of equalizing the income of the parish priests (if they were the tithe-holders), it would seem unfair to peasants with poor land that they should be doubly unfortunate: paying a higher percentage of the harvest from less productive land.

214. Nicolas (2008), p. 748.

215. McManners (1998), vol.1, p. 133.

to resistance [to military service] is unequal sharing of the burden and not the burden itself."[216] In the old regime the militia no less than the tax system was shot through with exemptions. While the members of the militia were initially chosen by majority vote in the parishes, a system that lent itself to revenge and favors, a reform in 1691 determined that they be chosen by lot. Nobles and higher officials were exempt, as were city dwellers, initially. The allotment of recruits to *généralités* and parishes did not respect proportionality, an objective injustice that was probably not perceived as such by the populations. The more visible exemptions within the parish did not necessarily generate resentment. Some were based on the nature of the village economy, such as the exemption for only sons of widows. Others were based on fairness, such as the immunity of brothers of a man who had already been selected. If the head of a family had raised foundlings, it was entitled to as many exemptions as it had taken in children, thus creating an incentive to volunteer for this task. Exemptions for servants of the privileged were not, however, perceived to have any such justification. Also, since many criteria were discretionary rather than mechanical, they invited abuses. Moreover, even in the supposedly mechanical selection among the non-exempt, officials often manipulated the lottery.

I now turn to *vertical forms of injustice*,[217] modes of surplus extraction that the peasants perceived as unjust. As noted, there were three institutional forms: the royal taxes (direct and indirect), seigneurial rents and monopolies, and the tithe.[218] Whereas taxes were (mostly) paid in money and the tithe (almost always) in kind, rents could be paid in either form. In addition, peasants were obliged to carry out forced labor (*corvée*) for the state and sometimes for the *seigneur*, mainly for road construction. Although variations in space and time were enormous and defy summary,

216. Tocqueville (2004a), p. 768. In the French militia in the old regime, where selection might lead to actual fighting, it would probably be more accurate to say that the unequal burden *increased* the resistance. As in the case of resistance to tax payment, it is impossible to quantify the relative importance of the burden and of its unequal distribution in generating resentment. Gebelin (1882), whom I generally follow here, affirms (p. 258) that the main cause of the unpopularity of the militia was the inequality and arbitrariness of the selection process. It seems, however, that the *burden itself was also a source of resistance*, as shown by the common practice in which all potential conscripts made a collection before the drawing of lots that would benefit the one who was eventually selected. "This consolation prize reduced the number of defaulters" (Poirier 1999, p. 91).

217. The distinction is not clear-cut, since many exemptions or rebates for individuals were due to their protection by a hierarchical superior.

218. Below, I also discuss non-institutional forms of surplus extraction, such as high prices of flour and bread that (allegedly) resulted from speculative hoarding.

a stylized reconstruction is all I need for my purposes. The central theme will be that the extractions were seen as legitimate if and only if they were part of a quid pro quo. "The problematic aspect in the cases of ecclesiastical payments and seigneurial rights is not the distribution of the burden at all, but rather *the assurance of getting what one pays for.*"[219] In addition to unfair extractions, I shall also discuss the prima facie unfair practice of seigneurial justice.

Let me first consider extractions by the state. The peasants probably had a more or less inchoate idea that taxes were needed to fund public goods, notably national defense and internal policing, that benefited the citizenry as a whole. By and large, the *taille* had a high degree of legitimacy, or at least higher than other taxes such as the hated salt tax.[220] The peasants wanted to be sure, however, that the tax was used for a good purpose, that is, that they got something back.

First, although they could understand that taxes had to be increased in wartime,[221] there was an expectation that they would be lowered once peace had been made.[222] There was often a ratchet effect, however. As John Donne wrote, "Princes do in time of action get / New taxes and remit them not in peace" (*Love's Growth*). If, as was usually the case, a war had been funded partly by loans, high taxes were needed to service them in peacetime. In the eighteenth century, the government tried to maintain wartime taxes on two occasions, failing in 1725 but succeeding, against

219. Shapiro and Markoff (1998), p. 403; my italics. As I discuss shortly, the observation is equally true for tax payments.

220. Ibid; Nicolas (2008), p. 198; Bercé (1974), p. 371. Boisguilbert (1707), pp. 31, 37–38, asserted that the French could afford to pay higher taxes if the arbitrary methods of collecting them were abolished; see also Esmonin (1913), p. 145, for the same comment by an *intendant* writing in 1669. Boisguilbert proposed to replace the existing taxes by various mechanical procedures that would eliminate the need for tax officials with discretionary powers.

221. Bercé (1974), p. 383. According to Maurepas, the principal minister of Louis XVI in the first years of his reign, taxes were seen as more legitimate when used to fund a defensive war than in funding an offensive one (Véri 1930, p. 67). Gomel (1892), vol. 1, p. 268, and Petitfils (2005a), p. 450, are perhaps wrong, therefore, when they affirm that the French would have accepted higher taxes to fund the offensive war against England during the American War of Independence. A tax increase to fund an offensive war may be as unacceptable as a tax increase in peacetime.

222. Bercé (1974), p. 617; Félix (1999), pp. 48, 438–439. Swann (2003), p. 158, writes that the "unwillingness of the Estates [of Burgundy] to pay [for billeting soldiers or for being exempt from billeting] at *a wartime rate after the Peace* of the Pyrenees in 1659 had been a significant cause of the conflict with Colbert in 1661–2." However, once the Estates complained about high taxes in peacetime, they were poorly positioned to complain about them in wartime (ibid., p. 160), just as trade-unions that insist on sharing windfall gains of the firm are poorly positioned to complain about sharing windfall losses (Elster 1989, chap. 6).

considerable resistance, in 1749.[223] In 1706, Vauban drew an interesting contrast between the behavior of the Spanish and French governments in the territories (Arras, Artois, Roussillon, and Luxemburg) that had recently come under French rule: "The Spanish avoided, as far as possible, overcharging the populations, and when they had to impose a new tax in wartime, they were very careful to abolish it in peace, far from prolonging and increasing them as we did and as we do every day. Let us not be surprised, therefore, if these populations are so badly disposed towards us, and if our government is hated and detested by all who dare speak up."[224] I do not know whether he was speaking truth to power or only writing a note to himself.

Second, taxpayers might not accept that a high proportion of the taxes went to pay tax officials. The many tax offices that were created to generate royal revenue "were a direct injury for the more ancient officials whose offices lost as much in value, but they also instilled ominous ideas in the minds of the taxpayers. When they saw in the tax documents the list of the duties levied by the tax officials, when they encountered in the streets the black-robed counselors, clerks or controllers from so many jurisdictions, the taxpayers concluded that all the monies levied on them did not go to the king's coffers. The king was being robbed; the tax was not due."[225] The cost of collecting the taxes could in some cases exceed 50 percent of the amount collected.[226] Although striking, this fact is somewhat irrelevant from a psychological perspective, since the peasants had no way of estimating the part of surplus extracted from them that went into the pockets of the tax officials. Even when the objective level of extraction by tax officials for their own profit was low, "the part of the costs of recovery probably seemed much more considerable to public opinion than it was in reality."[227]

Third, the peasants hated the compulsory work on the roads (*corvée*) because it was not part of a quid pro quo. (Another reason was that it could interfere with the harvest.) The roads were often designed to facilitate travel for nobles, notables, and merchants, not to benefit those who worked them. In 1769, the intermediate commission that handled affairs

223. Egret (1970), pp. 40–43. Argenson, vol. 6, p. 303, makes the Tocquevillian comment that the tax reductions in 1749 "were so puny that they shocked more than they pleased."

224. Vauban (1882), pp. 336–337.

225. Bercé (1974), p. 70; see also ibid., pp. 610–611; and Esmonin (1913), pp. 108–111.

226. Bercé (1974), pp. 69–70; for a more general discussion see ibid., pp. 112–118.

227. Ibid., p. 116.

in Burgundy between the meetings of the provincial Estates complained that the *corvée* was "a tax that falls not on the large landowners, who have the greatest interest in the construction of roads, but on the inhabitants of the countryside who have little interest and for the most part none."[228] In 1744, the inhabitants in one town refused to work for the passage of the king. Saint-Jacob, who cites this fact, sees it as a proof of the burden the *corvée* represented.[229] This may well be true, but the refusal could also be due to a perception that the work would be doing something for nothing.

Two anecdotal illustrations will also cast light on the old regime more generally. In 1766, the *Cours des Aides* (a tax court) of Montauban wrote an indictment of the *intendant* of the province, charging him with a number of abuses of the *corvée*. In a particularly striking case, he had ordered 4,000 people to work on a road for ten days so that his brother could visit him. The wine harvest was lost, as was the aftergrowth in the fields.[230] Arthur Young recounts "a curious anecdote of the bishop of Beziers cutting a road through the [farm of an abbot reputed for his husbandry], at the expence of the province, to lead to the house of his (the bishop's) mistress, which occasioned such a quarrel that [the abbot] could stay no longer in the country. This is a pretty feature of a government: that a man is to be forced to sell his estate, and driven out of a country, because bishops make love—I suppose to their neighbours' wives, as no other love is fashionable in France."[231]

Finally, the people might not accept taxes if they went to fund luxury at the Court. Edgar Faure writes that in the mid-eighteenth century, "the two subjects that most vividly interested public opinion were, on the one hand . . . , economies in the expenses of the Court and, on the other, the price of bread."[232] The first concern was a long-standing one, at least among the delegates to the Estates-General. These often claimed the right to monitor the use of the tax revenues, to ensure that they would serve the military purposes that the king cited in his convocation rather than maintaining the pomp at the Court. The Estates of 1321 affirmed that they

228. Saint-Jacob (1960), p. 368. In the preamble to the 1776 edict abolishing the *corvée*, Turgot (1844), vol.2, p. 291, makes the same point. Although the *corvée* was restored when he left office, the peasantry "did not forget the declarations of the preamble" (Gomel 1892, vol.1, p. 173). For any government, making a reform and then retracting it is worse than not making it.

229. Ibid., p. 295.

230. *Charges du procès Lescalopier*, pp. 93–94.

231. Young (1794), vol. 1, p. 46. As Arlette Jouanna points out to me, the "province" refers to the provincial Estates of Languedoc.

232. Faure (1961), p. 185.

would make a contribution to the Crusade only when it was under way.[233] For the same reason, the Estates sometimes offered to pay the subsidies in kind, for instance by equipping a certain number of soldiers.[234] When the Court resided in Paris, the urban population could see the splendor of the royals and nobles on a regular basis; even after they moved to Versailles their frequent presence in Paris for ceremonial or amusement purposes provided a reminder. In times of dearth, the contrast was striking. However, to my knowledge the expenses of the Court were not an important part of the grievances of the peasantry. They may have known them about them in an abstract way, yet out of sight, they were out of mind.[235]

As I suggested above, the *taille* was in principle accepted by the people. As a well-to-do peasant explained to his son, Rétif de la Bretonne, "All you need to know is that the king defends all the provinces of France with armies, which he supports with the money from the *taille*."[236] Indirect taxes, notably the salt tax (*gabelle*) and the wine tax, were deeply unpopular. Where the former was levied most heavily, around Paris, the tax amounted to 90 percent of the price. As salt was vital for preserving food, the tax could cut deeply into the consumption budget. The tax varied widely across regions, in a proportion of one to twenty, a situation that generated both smuggling and private armies raised by the tax farmers to prevent the smuggling. Smuggling of salt occupied tens of thousands of people on a permanent basis.[237] In "the borders between Brittany and Maine/Anjou the smuggling was extremely widespread, because of the enormous price difference between the two sides: a permanent civil war existed between the smugglers and the tax farmers and constituted for the whole population a school in depravity and crime."[238] The tax farmers deployed a panoply of repressive measures, including fines, whipping, branding, sentencing to the galleys, and execution.[239]

The deep unpopularity of the tax was due, in proportions that are impossible to determine, to its impact on the family budget, to its inequality across regions, and to the brutal methods used by the tax collectors and

233. Picot (1888), vol. 1, p. 29; Soule (1968), p. 69.

234. Picot (1888), vol. 3, pp. 53–54, but see also p. 83. In 1588, Henri III made a promise, which was non-credible yet apparently believed, that the coffer with the war funds would have two keys, one in his hands and the other in possession of the Estates (ibid., p. 413).

235. In their analysis of images of the king in the grievance books from 1789, Shapiro and Markoff (1998), chap. 19, do not cite any demands for economy at the Court.

236. Bretonne (1989), vol. 1, p. 146.

237. Ado (1996), p.71.

238. Marion (1927), p. 19.

239. Nicolas (2008), pp. 62–65.

the sergeants. Also, whereas indirect taxes have been praised (or at least more easily accepted) on the grounds that consumers are free to buy or not to buy the goods on which they are leveled,[240] in the *ancien régime* consumption of a stipulated quantity of salt was *obligatory*. In the grievance books for the parishes in 1789, the abolition of the *gabelle* was the most frequent demand, followed by demands for abolishing the tax on alcoholic beverages, the salt monopoly, the tax on legal acts, and compulsory labor service on the roads.[241]

To illustrate effects of indirect taxes, specifically on wine, I shall quote from the two major French autobiographies of the eighteenth century.

In his *Confessions*, Rousseau recounts how one day his walks took him to a peasant's hut, where he offered to pay for dinner. At first, he received only skimmed milk and some coarse bread, but when the peasant perceived that he was an "honest, good natured man," he opened a trap-door by the side of the kitchen and came back with ham and wine, and also prepared an omelet. "When I again offered to pay, his disquiet and fears returned; he not only would have no money, but refused it with the most evident emotion; and what made this scene more amusing, I could not imagine the motive of his fear. At length, he pronounced tremblingly those terrible words, "Commissioners," and "Cellar-rats," which he explained by giving me to understand that he concealed his wine because of the excise, and his bread on account of the tax imposed on it; adding, *he should be an undone man, if it was suspected he was not almost perishing with want.*[242]

In *Monsieur Nicolas*, Rétif de la Bretonne recounts how he and some friends were also walking in the countryside, getting hungry and thirsty. "Across from a house in a small village, we heard some laborers singing and enjoying themselves. We thought it must be a cabaret, although we had never seen one in such a remote place. [One of his companions] knocked on the door. Somebody opened, asking, "'Who is it?'—'Couldn't we have a *septier* [a quarter of a litre], and pay for it?'—'Yes, *messieurs*,

240. See, for instance, Slaughter (1988), p. 14. While generating less unrest, indirect taxes can also generate less income. If the demand for the taxed good is sufficiently elastic, as was the case for instance for tobacco in the *ancien régime*, raising the tax could reduce not only consumption but also the total income from the tax (Félix 1999, p. 56). "Taxes killed the taxes."

241. Shapiro and Markoff (1998), p. 380. In the grievance books for the urban notables and for the nobility, abolition of the *gabelle* ranked, respectively, as number nineteen and seventeen (ibid.).

242. Rousseau (1973), p. 217; my italics.

and even a *chopine* [half a litre], but not for payment, because the taxman [*gabeleur*] would take us to court."[243]

I now turn to the wide array of seigneurial extractions, some akin to the forms of economic exploitation found in agrarian hierarchies everywhere and others linked to the feudal past. The former included notably individual and collective forms of rent, paid in money or in kind. Among the many forms of individual rent the most widespread was the *cens*, usually paid in a fixed (nonadjustable) amount of money. Inflation ensured that its material value became insignificant, although it could retain a symbolic or "recognitory" value.[244] Because the rent could not be increased, "the old *censives* yielding a negligible income were the sore of the *seigneuries*."[245] Hence as time went on, "it was not rare for the *seigneur* to attack the old *censives* with their devalued rent, by profiting from the smallest nonobservance of the clauses in the lease."[246] This process must be seen in the context of the general "seigneurial reaction" of the late eighteenth century. Using the services of professional *feudistes*, who uncovered or reexamined old documents, the *seigneur* was constantly "searching for neglected rights" that he could activate.[247] In Burgundy, one *seigneur* picked a quarrel with his tenants on the basis of a charter from 1273.[248] The *feudiste* "became the most unpopular person in the life of the village, even more than the bailiff or the dragoon sent for the *taille*."[249]

By and large, however, the *cens*, like the *taille* and the tithe, was accepted as a fact of life. Like them, seigneurial rents "were not attacked for themselves, but for their illogical deformations"[250] Among 512 antiseigneurial incidents, Nicolas finds that only 88 took the form of a refusal to pay rent, whereas 158 involved the defense of collective rights and of

243. Bretonne (1989), vol. 1, p. 350. "*Gabelle*" usually referred to the salt tax, but was sometimes used about other consumption taxes as well, notably the wine tax. "*Gabeleur*" was often used as a generic term for all exploiters of the people. A "laborer" (*laboureur*) was a well-to-do peasant.

244. Pillorget (1975), p. 97.

245. Saint-Jacob (1960), p. 440.

246. Ibid., p. 245; see also p. 441.

247. Ibid., p. 425. Hayhoe (2008), p. 192, argues, however, that the seigneurial reaction in Burgundy "was characterized primarily by the rigorous policing of the land the lord owned, without much evidence of the invention or even reinvigoration of seigneurial dues."

248. Saint-Jacob (1960), p. 426.

249. Nicolas (2008), p. 280.

250. Saint-Jacob (1960), p. 519. According to Mill (2007), p. 147, it "is a political law of nature that those who are subjected to any power of very long standing never begin by complaining of the power itself, but only of the oppressive use of it."

communal lands.[251] This matches Saint-Jacob's claim that the most obnoxious seigneurial practice was the *champart*, the claim to a part of the product (often one ninth) of cultivated communal land.[252] As he explains, its unpopularity was due to the manifest lack of a quid pro quo: "By means of [the *champart*], the *seigneur* increased his income in a clever and most remunerative way. . . . Without any investment or risk, with no participation whatsoever in the cost of cultivation, free from the bother of finding the written charter, he levied a 'seigneurial tithe' *to which there corresponded no counterpart*. From these facts followed a violent hostility to these levies that was to trigger very acute conflicts until the end of the old regime. . . . The opinion is that the *seigneur* can take part of the communal land, but not [the product of] the work of others."[253] Elsewhere he writes that "resistance to the *champart* [was] always at the forefront of peasant rebellions."[254] In his study of the Sarthe, Paul Bois asserts that "the draining . . . of rural income [by absentee bourgeois owners] *without any counterpart*" generated the same resentment as the tithe paid to absent abbots.[255]

Other "illogical deformations" of the seigneurial regime were found in the innumerable small obligations that the *seigneur* could impose on his tenants, illustrated by some examples from Saint-Jacob. "What the peasant obviously found it hardest to support were the charges that *were not compensated by a right of use*. . . . In Argilly, the *seigneur* levies a toll on the land (*finage*), but maintains 'neither the bridge nor the boards.'"[256] Elsewhere, "the inhabitants refused to do repair work on a

---

251. Nicolas (2008), pp. 230–231. To explain this fact, he suggests that "while the use of collective rights reflects a common rule, valid for all, the payment of dues and charges for the fief involved a contact between the seigneur and each head of family taken separately" (ibid., p. 252). This proposal might seem to differ from the "fact of life" explanation I suggest in the text, but is in fact compatible with it. When collective action seems impossible because of the lack of a common grievance, acquiescence can be the natural outcome. One could speculate that the variety of contracts was used to "divide and rule," but I have not seen anything to substantiate this conjecture.

252. According to a royal edict of 1669, the seigneur could also claim the right of *triage*, that is, the right to exploit one third of the communal land. Although Saint-Jacob does not cite this right as an important source of peasant discontent (see the text cited below from pp. 119–120 of his book), Nicolas (2008), pp. 237–241, mentions several examples. Lefebvre (1924), p. 74, refers to strong peasant opposition to the *triage* in the marshlands of the North, and refers to plans by the government to defuse it by offering individual plots to the poorest peasants.

253. Saint-Jacob (1960), pp. 119–120; my italics.

254. Ibid., p. 215.

255. Bois (1960), pp. 357, 201.

256. Ibid., p. 137; my italics. Conversely, if the seigneur charged a toll for the passage of animals he was supposed to maintain the roads (Pillorget 1975, p. 98).

castle that 'was no more than a seigneurial house and not a fortress.'"[257] More generally, *"nothing was due without a counterpart,* no charge without the exercise of a right. The castle in Marcigny does not exist anymore, and yet one pays 12 *livres* for the refuge. The repairs of the moat and the castle in Avelange should be abolished 'since there is no longer any war or anything to fear for the life of the inhabitants from the enemies of the State.' The village oven in Bellenod-sous-Origny is fallen in ruins; the *seigneur* should return the wood for burning that he has received."[258]

Somewhat surprisingly, perhaps, the *banalités*—the seigneurial monopolies on milling, baking, and wine pressing—do not seem to have generated much resentment in the peasantry. In his study of 512 antiseigneurial actions, Nicolas finds only a single-digit number of incidents linked to these monopolies.[259] The reason may have been that these means of production, especially the mill and the wine press, were unaffordable for an individual household. Just as the peasant accepted to pay tax to the state in exchange for law and order, he was willing, as a quid pro quo, to pay the *seigneur* for milling his grain, baking his bread, or pressing his wine.[260] Some *seigneurs* no doubt abused their monopoly to charge unreasonable rates, but the paucity of recorded incidents suggests that such behavior was rare.[261]

Consider finally the tithe as a potential source of perceptions of injustice. The "tithe" (which actually averaged about one-thirteenth of the harvest, with large regional and even local variations) was levied in kind on the gross product of the land, always on grain and usually on wine, but sometimes on other products as well. In principle, it was supposed to provide an income for the parish priest, funds for repairing the church, and support for the poor members of the community. The ideal was a quid

257. Ibid., p. 416.

258. Ibid., p. 519; my italics.

259. Nicolas (2008), pp. 272–276; the estimate is inferred from his descriptions.

260. Shapiro and Markoff (1998), p. 403. Hayhoe (2008), p. 57, refers to the *banalités* as "partly a form of public service," contrasting them with "other seigneurial rights [that] were more overtly exploitative." As I discuss later, seigneurial justice, while it had some exploitative aspects, also provided a public service.

261. Marion (1923), entry "Banalité," claims, however, that the monopolies, notably on milling, were "among the heaviest and most detested seigneurial rights." Although he supports his claim by referring to the grievance books of 1789, the monopoly on milling was only "the 34th most common Subject in the Parishes, and tied for 87th place in the Third Estate documents" (Shapiro and Markoff 1998, p. 260).

pro quo.[262] In practice, the tithe was often farmed out, in the sense that it ended up in the hands of a *gros décimateur*, a tithe-holder who was external to the village and could be a bishop, an abbot, an abbey, or a layperson. The parish priest was then paid a fixed sum (*la portion congrue*) from the proceeds. To supplement his income, he often took a fee (*le casuel*) for baptisms, marriages, and funerals.[263]

The villagers accepted the tithe as such, but were hostile to its extension to products beyond grain and wine, and even more to the farming out. "The aggressiveness of the peasantry [towards the tithe] is expressed all the more forcefully when the beneficiary is outside the parish."[264] Saint-Jacob draws an analogy with taxes: "Just as the *forain* invaded and upset the old rural group, so did the outside *décimateur* almost everywhere introduce a focus on profit rather than on responsibilities. The tithe tended to lose its solidarity with agrarian and communitarian life, something that did not make it more bearable."[265] Every time the peasant had to pay a fee for a religious service, he would be reminded of the fact that the priest was supposed to live off the tithe. In Flanders, the peasants were hostile to the tithe not only because it was "diverted from its natural destination,"[266] the parish priest, but also because "it seemed unjust to the producers by targeting the gross product: seed grain and the part of the harvest destined for feeding animals and laborers were subject to the tithe like everything else; no account was taken of expenses to improve the land."[267] The fact that it would have been difficult in practice to calculate these deductions probably did little to make the inhabitants less hostile. The intuitive idea of a quid pro quo could be compelling even when one term of the equation could not be determined with precision.

This being said, the tithe was broadly accepted. In the grievance books from 1789, there are no demands for the outright abolition of the tithe. In the parishes, the demand that it be used for maintaining the parish

262. The quid that the priest provided might include the sacraments. Thus one priest "refused the sacraments to his parishioners because they refused him the tithe on their apples and pears to which he claimed a right" (Marion 1891, p. 332 note).

263. Unlike magistrates, who also charged a fee (*épice*) for their services (chap. 4), the parish priests had no opportunity to *create* occasions for performing them.

264. Nicolas (2008), p. 748. In some such cases, the parish priests encouraged their resistance (ibid., pp. 749, 751).

265. Saint-Jacob (1960), p. 132.

266. Lefebvre (1924), p. 113.

267. Ibid., p. 110; also McManners (1998), vol.1, pp. 133–134. Pillorget (1975), p. 80, notes that in Provence levying the tithe on the seed grain was seen as an abuse.

church is only the forty-ninth most common subject; in the Third Estate, the demand that it be used to pay the parish priest held the same rank.[268] Compared to the surplus extractions by the state and by the *seigneurie*, the tithe seems to have contributed little to the sentiment of injustice.

I return to the distinction between primary and secondary sentiments. The former were caused by perceptions of horizontal or vertical injustice, that is, by perceived violations either of the principle of *equality* or of the principle of a *quid pro quo*. The secondary sentiments could be caused by a subsistence crisis that induced its victims to seek for someone to blame. In most cases, peasants or urban consumers blamed the alleged hoarders or speculators for their selfish lack of concern for the welfare of the people. The basis for their anger could be the perceived violation of the principle of the *just price*. In a few cases, they claimed that the elites deliberately tried to starve the people, not as a collateral *by-product*[269] of profit maximization, but as the main *goal* of their actions. This charge was sometimes made, for instance, during the Flour War in 1775. More generally, secondary sentiments also include reactions to events that in themselves might have been seen as neutral or beneficial, but in a specific context could generate discontent.

The secondary sentiments arise from conjunctural causes, whereas the primary sentiments have more permanent and structural causes. At the same time, the perceptions of injustice due to structural causes heightened the sensitivity of the peasantry to conjunctural events and favored malign interpretations. Because of the pervasive horizontal and vertical injustice, peasants were always on hair-trigger alert. In 1789, the conjunctural factors were enormously important, but mainly because of the sounding board created by the structural factors. Unless I am mistaken, previous conjunctural episodes, such as the Flour War of 1775, were less important in shaping the mindset of the peasantry in 1789. This being said, some of these episodes may provide us with evidence about widely applicable mechanisms that operate in conjunctural events. I shall discuss two examples.

In note 170 above, I cited the statement by René and Suzanne Pillorget that when in the Paris uprising of August 1648 rumors that had triggered a panic turned out to be false, "the crowd was furious of having been afraid [and] unleashed its anger on the person or persons whom they deemed responsible for the panic." They add that in other cases, this reaction may lead to "the massacre or the flight of the person who is the

268. Shapiro and Markoff (1998), p. 381. In the grievance books of 1614, the third estate in Provence demanded the abolition of *le casuel* (Pillorget 1975, p. 109).

269. Hardy, vol. 4, pp. 198–199.

target of this anger," but that "on the evening of August 26, things came to an end for a much simpler reason: everyone went home for dinner." In 1789, however, we observe some of the "other cases." When peasants found out that rumors about impending attack by brigands were false, they sometimes responded by attacking the castle of a nearby *seigneur*. What is the underlying psychological mechanism behind this reaction? One can easily understand why a *disappointed hope* might give rise to anger against the person who disappointed one. It is less clear why the revelation of an *unjustified fear* would have the same effect—*relief* would seem a more plausible reaction than anger.

I can only speculate. (1) The Pillorgets suggest that a frustrated crowd might infer that the false rumor had been planted by a malignant agent, who would then feel the brunt of its anger. This explanation would fit with the general tendency for agents in the old regime to seek out an *agent* to blame for their misfortunes. (2) In *A Theory of Cognitive Dissonance*, Leon Festinger suggested an explanation for rumor formation following an earthquake in India that might apply, *mutatis mutandis*, to the present case: because the state of experiencing an emotion without a belief that would justify it is intrinsically unpleasant, agents can reduce their dissonance by inventing a belief.[270] Because of the salience of the *seigneurie* in their life, it would be a natural target. (3) Anger and fear share an action tendency—to fight. (Fear of course also has the action tendency of flight.) When the object of the fear turns out not to exist, the unfolding action tendency might be displaced towards the *seigneur* as a substitute object. Montaigne offers many examples in his essay on "How the soul discharges its emotions against false objects when lacking real ones."[271]

The second mechanism involves, I think, a deeper set of issues. The most famous single analysis in Tocqueville's book on the old regime is perhaps the following:

> It is not always going from bad to worse that leads to revolution. What happens most often is that a people that put up with the most oppressive laws without complaint, as if they did not feel them, reject those laws violently when the burden is alleviated. . . . The evil that one endures patiently because it seems inevitable becomes unbearable the moment its elimination becomes conceivable. Then, every abuse that is eliminated seems only to reveal the others that remain, and makes

270. Festinger (1957), p. vi and chap. 10. In Elster (2015a), p. 162, I explain why I am somewhat skeptical of this account.
271. Montaigne (1990), pp. 19–21.

their sting that much more painful. The ill has diminished, to be sure, but sensitivity to it has increased.[272]

We can illustrate the proposition by the abolition of the *corvée* by Turgot in 1776. Without citing him, Edgar Faure dismisses Tocqueville's idea: "The suppression of the *corvée* mattered only for a mass of ignorant peasantry, who lived from day to day far from the great centers and unused to express their gratitude, supposing they felt any. One misery suppressed, one misery forgotten: so many others remain. It is a constant fact of financial history that relief from a burden receives much less praise than its aggravation arouses fury."[273] If Tocqueville is right, however, the *relief would cause fury* and demands for more relief. Saint-Jacob cites a text affirming that after Turgot's decision "one cannot conceive the *spirit of vertigo* that has seized people in the countryside. One cannot understand by which motive they have persuaded themselves that they can evade with impunity the different duties they owe to their *seigneurs*."[274] A few days after the edict abolishing the *corvée*, the bookseller Hardy cites a popular song praising the decision and expressing a desire for its generalization to other burdens.[275] The demand for more relief might also, however, be due to a perception that the initial reform showed the weakness of the government. As I discuss below, if possible one should also distinguish between the reform triggering a *desire* for more reforms and triggering a *belief* that more reforms will follow. Whichever of these three mechanisms one prefers, they all provide a foundation for "the political doctrine inherited from Louis XIV, that the granting of any fragment of liberty would inevitably lead to anarchy."[276]

Seigneurial Justice

Tocqueville's analyses have inspired many claims of the present book. He got some things wrong, mainly because of his limited factual knowledge. In particular, one cannot defend his claim that *seigneurial justice* in the

272. Tocqueville (2011), p. 157. He refers to enhanced *motivations* for action. The same effect might result from enhanced *resources* due to less malnutrition (see note 154 above and Elster 2015a, p. 198).

273. Faure (1961), p. 458.

274. Saint-Jacob (1960), p. 465, my italics; see also Ado (1996), p. 67. For a related example, see Kaplan (2015), p. 93: after an *arrêt* in 1739 banishing internal tariffs, "customers . . . claimed—incorrectly—that the *arrêt* freed them from paying *all* fees, not just the transit tolls." See also the discussion below of Tourny's *intendance* in Guyenne.

275. Hardy, vol. 4, p. 507.

276. Félix (1999), p. 344.

old regime was a form of quid pro quo, and that its replacement by royal agents was one reason why the nobility lost popular support.[277] Nor can one defend the perhaps more common claim that seigneurial justice itself was invariably perceived as unjust and illegitimate. Although it is tempting to think that a system making the *seigneur* "judge in his own cause" must (1) *be* and (2) *be perceived as* intrinsically unfair, neither claim can be upheld.[278] The peasantry, in fact, seems to have had an ambivalent attitude towards that institution, as useful but in need of reform.

There were three degrees of seigneurial justice.[279] *High justice* covered most civil and criminal matters, including capital cases. Only those in possession of high justice could erect gallows on their land. Some decisions required approval by a royal court. *Middle justice* covered civil matters for small amounts. *Low justice* covered civil matters for very small amounts. I shall only consider civil matters, including horizontal relations among the villagers as well as vertical relations to the *seigneur*. According to one historian, one of the two most important questions is whether seigneurial justice "functioned only as the armed branch of seigneurial extraction or whether it also provided a public service."[280] One should add that the

---

277. Hayhoe (2008), pp. 29–30, 192, argues convincingly against Tocqueville's claim that seigneurial justice had lost its vitality and importance at the end of the *ancien régime*; see also Giffard (1903), pp. 214–224, for an argument that seigneurial justice actually encroached on royal justice rather than the other way around. Hayhoe does not cite textual evidence, however, for his claim (p. 29) that Tocqueville posited "that the royal government successfully orchestrated a transfer of jurisdiction, cases, and clients from seigneurial to *royal courts*" (my italics). In his most explicit statement on the topic, Tocqueville (2011), p. 35, says only that "*royal power* had gradually truncated, limited, and subordinated seigneurial justice" (my italics). It seems more likely that when referring to the royal power Tocqueville had in mind the *intendants* rather than the royal courts (*bailliages* and *sénéchaussées*), to which he never refers as courts, only as electoral jurisdictions. Among modern historians, Root (1987) is a prominent defender of the thesis that the *intendants* replaced seigneurial courts because the king wanted to limit feudal extractions to allow for higher taxes. In a book covering the same province (Burgundy), Hayhoe (2008), pp. 177–187, argues convincingly against his view.

278. For criticism of the first claim, see Vermeule (2012). The second claim is the object of the following discussion.

279. For details, see Follain (2002), pp. 22–23; and Crubaugh (2001), pp. 18–21.

280. Follain (2002), p. 36. The other question is whether seigneurial justice was equally active in all periods of the *ancien régime*. Six (vaguely functionalist) contributions to the volume to which this article serves as an Introduction also refer to seigneurial justice as a form of "social regulation" or "social control." More explicitly, Crubaugh (2001), p. 47, asserts that "the high cost of justice appeared to border on a form of social control, in which powerful and wealthy members sued their social inferiors and burdened them with court costs as a way of to keep them in line or to punish supposedly insolent behavior." In the case he describes to support this assertion, however, the imposition of high costs seems to have

apparatus of justice could also serve as a tool of extraction in its own right, by allowing its personnel to extract exorbitant fees in cases they could drag out for years.[281] Seigneurial justice involved no quid pro quo if the costs of litigation exceeded, as they sometimes did, the sums to be recovered. One cannot affirm unconditionally, therefore, that "in cases that did not directly involve the interest of the lord, judges worked as servants of the community"[282]—they could also work in their self-interest.

The vertical relations were limited to feudal matters: "a lord suing a villager to collect land rent would have to take the case to [a royal court], but he could take the same villager before the seigneurial court to collect seigneurial dues."[283] The seigneurial court and its agents also enforced feudal *rights*, notably those pertaining to the use of fields and forests. The main horizontal relations regulated by seigneurial justice were litigations among neighbors or family members. In a sample of Burgundian villages, each household was on average involved in 1.8 lawsuits over the decade from 1780 to 1789, with plaintiff and defendant mostly from the same village. Debts and inheritances were the most common types of case. Merchants and well-to-do peasants (*laboureurs*) were the most important categories of plaintiffs.[284]

Compared to the lower royal courts (*bailliages* and *sénéchaussées*), seigneurial justice was in some respects more efficient, because it was faster, cheaper, and above all closer. In Brittany in 1766, there were 2,300 seigneurial courts but only 23 *sénéchaussées*[285] (and one *parlement*), serving more than 2 million inhabitants. At the same time, seigneurial judges were often less competent, especially in small jurisdictions.[286] Their courts met at unpredictable intervals. Yet the alternative could be worse.

Judged in the abstract, seigneurial justice was *doubly unfair*: it was biased in favor of the *seigneur*, and it lent itself to chicanery by the personnel. As an example of the former, the *seigneur* could require that

been simply due to the greed of the legal personnel. I have not seen any evidence that the *seigneur* wanted to fill *their* pockets.

281. Many examples from Britanny, where seigneurial justice seems to have been unusually harsh, in Giffard (1903).

282. Hayhoe (2008), p. 16.

283. Ibid., p. 49.

284. Tables in ibid., pp. 103, 107, 109, 110–111.

285. Giffard (1903), pp. 37, 283.

286. To his question whether seigneurial judges in Burgundy were "legal professionals or greedy amateurs," Hayhoe (2008, pp. 33–36) opts for the first answer. For Britanny, the analysis by Giffard (1903), pp. 100–106, supports the second answer. For Normandy, Follain (2002), p. 29, seems to concur with Giffard.

declarations (*aveux*) of their holdings that the peasants were supposed to produce be written up by his notary.[287] As an example of the latter, consider the legal clerks who "ignored decrees mandating twelve syllables per line per page for writs and twelve lines per page; by using small sheets of paper and writing in large scripts, clerks could increase the costs [to the parties] of a document many times over. . . . In comparison, the clerks' handwriting for judicial registers, kept at the lord's cost, was minuscule. The formula was always the same: maximize revenue for officials, minimize costs for lords."[288] The *seigneur* had in fact a powerful tool in forcing the judges to promote his interest, since their offices were revocable at his will. To make them less dependent, many of the grievance books from Burgundy that discuss seigneurial justice demanded that the office of judges be made permanent.[289]

In Brittany, some peasants seem to have accepted the seigneurial courts as a "lesser evil."[290] Yet according to Giffard, "the grievance books that best express the true feelings of the peasants with regard to the judiciary system are those that demand both a reform of the royal justice and the abolition of seigneurial justice."[291] I conjecture that the demand for abolition was due not only to the actual and perceived abuse of seigneurial power, but also to the fact that the permanent *possibility of abuse* represented an affront to the dignity of the peasantry and not merely to their material well-being. Jean Nicolas argues that towards the end of the *ancien régime*, these symbolic insults became increasingly poignant.[292]

The Urban Populations

I now turn to the moral emotions of the *urban populations*, not counting nobles and royal officials. They included beggars, criminals, police informants, day laborers, servants, artisans (masters, journeymen, and apprentices), merchants, troops, gendarmerie, paralegals and sundry legal clerks (*la basoche*), lawyers, magistrates, clergy, and the world of finance. In addition, there were many retiree bondholders. The mere enumeration of these heterogeneous groups tells us that no generalizations can be made

287. Giffard (1903), p. 274.

288. Crubaugh (2001), pp. 16–17.

289. Hayhoe (2008) p. 204. Giffard (1903), p. 270, affirms that some grievance books in Brittany made the same demand.

290. Giffard (1903), p. 285.

291. Ibid.

292. Nicolas (2008), chap. 10.

about them. Our knowledge is much better for Paris than for provincial towns. For the capital, the journals that the lawyer Barbier kept from 1718 to 1762 and the bookseller Hardy from 1753 to 1789 provide us with a mass of information about what was happening in the streets and rumors about what was going on behind various closed doors. (Although many rumors did not correspond to the facts, they were themselves facts that could have causal efficacy.) To my knowledge, nothing comparable exists for provincial towns.

To identify some emotions of some these groups, I shall first consider four episodes recounted by Barbier.

In 1721, a coachman who had stolen a piece of iron worth thirty *sols* (about one day's wage) from his master, who rented out coaches, was sentenced to be branded and whipped. When the punishment was executed, in front of the master's door, his wife stood by and urged that he be whipped harder. A crowd that had gathered became so infuriated that it entered the house, broke the windows, and set fire to two coaches.[293]

In a second episode from the same year, a footman was condemned to the pillory and the galleys for having spoken freshly to the mistress of his master, the noble captain of the Swiss Guard. When he was led to the pillory accompanied by two hundred archers, they were met by a crowd of five or six thousand people who destroyed the pillory and broke the windows in the captain's house where he had retrenched himself. Several persons were killed. The next day, when the footman was taken back to the pillory under guard, nothing happened. Although a commoner, Barbier shared enough of the noble values to comment that "It was good that justice [*sic*] was done, for *footmen are already too insolent.*"[294]

A third episode occurred in 1726, when a cook sent anonymous threatening letters to his master to extract money from him. He was discovered and hanged. "The people [*le peuple*] and many others found this a rigorous judgment, to take the life of a man who had not killed or stolen and had never done a bad thing. The populace showed its resentment in breaking the windows of [the master]; but taking all things into consideration, and since the case is a new one, one did well in hanging the man as an example: *especially since he was a servant*, and one cannot purchase public tranquility too dearly."[295]

293. Barbier, vol. 1, p. 120.
294. Ibid., p. 171; my italics.
295. Ibid., p. 420; my italics.

In 1743, finally, the king for the first time called for recruitment to the militia in Paris. Rich merchants were indignant that their children were included along with their servants, whereas the people was indignant that artisans were included while the servants of the nobles were exempt.[296]

Each episode illustrates the difference between the anger (or indignation) of the urban elites, *born of a violation of the norms of hierarchy*, and the anger (or indignation) of the people, *born of the injustice of those norms*.[297]

One episode of the Flour War of 1775 took place on May 3 in Paris, when Hardy reports that "bandits and brigands" had entered Paris from outside to loot the bakeries. They forced his brother-in-law "to open his store, broke some of the windows, entered his apartment and took his personal provision of bread, the ringleaders recommending nevertheless not to touch his possessions but to take bread only."[298] On May 1, he had reported that in Saint-Germain-en-Laye people "ripped open the flour sacks and spread the flour in the streets, which certainly shows much more a desire to cause disorder and do harm than to procure relief to those who lacked bread."[299] On April 26, he had reported news from Dijon, where a suspected monopolist of grain had his house invaded and ravaged, and noted that "his silverware had not been looted but only damaged and thrown into a well."[300] A common factor in these narratives is the self-control of the rioters, who refrained from taking whatever they could lay their hands on. They were motivated by norms that transcended self-interest: it is permitted to destroy, but not to steal;[301] to take what you need, but not all you can get. As in the countryside, hunger and anger made a powerful combination that should be distinguished from mere greed.

Both Barbier and Hardy inform us about the role of the people of Paris in the conflict between the *parlement* and the Church—the royal government siding sometimes with the one, sometimes with the

296. Barbier, vol. 3, pp. 424–427.

297. In the contemporary United States, a similar difference exists between the ideology of white supremacists and the belief that "black lives matter."

298. Hardy, vol. 4, p. 181.

299. Ibid., p. 179.

300. Ibid., p. 173.

301. In some cases, the destruction of flour may have been due to a suspicion that it was adulterated rather than by a desire to exact revenge on hoarders and speculators (Faure 1961, p. 238). Yet this cannot have been the motive of all the destructive actions reported by Hardy. Another feature of many bread riots was that the rioters insisted on paying for what they took, at what they took to be the "just price" (the *taxation populaire*).

other—that was a recurrent feature of French politics in much of the eighteenth century. To simplify, the majority of magistrates in the *parlement* were Gallican, that is, opposed to the domination of the Roman curia, and a minority were also Jansenist, that is, opposed to the Jesuits. Although the people of Paris did not take much interest in religious dogma, their anger was triggered when the Church refused to offer the last rites to persons whose confessor had not signed on to the papal bull *Unigenitus* (1713), in which Clement XI declared 101 propositions in a book by a Jansenist theologian to be heretical. The legal clerks (*la basoche*) could drum up large numbers of people in the streets whenever one such episode occurred.[302] Popular flames were also fueled by Richerism, a low-church religious movement which emphasized the authority of the parish priests rather than of the bishops and shared the opposition of the Jansenists to the supremacy of the pope, notably in the *Unigenitus* affair. To control the steady stream of pamphlets and rumors, the government tried to supervise the printers closely, by forbidding their workshops to have back doors[303] and by forcing them to use noisy and heavy machinery that was easy to monitor and difficult to move,[304] but to little avail. A clandestine Jansenist weekly, the well informed *Nouvelles Ecclésiastiques,* appeared without interruption from 1728 to the Revolution (and beyond), reaching a circulation of 6,000 copies. In spite of their efforts, the authorities never managed to stop it.

Satirical and often scabrous sheets of verse directed against ministers, royal mistresses, at least one queen (Marie-Antoinette), and at least one king (Louis XV) offer a remarkable expression of urban emotions. The corpus of *Mazarinades* written during the Fronde amounts to about 5,000 verses.[305] During the tenure of Madame de Pompadour as royal mistress, the large body of verses disparaging her and other members of the elite was referred to as a *Poissonade* (her family name was Poisson, suggesting a pun on "poissarde," a vulgar fishwife).[306] Understood as gossip, the verses could provide amusement; understood as facts, they could trigger contempt, anger or indignation. Like underground political jokes in modern dictatorships, they may have offered *shared schemata* that, if conditions

---

302. Specifically, 550 lawyers, 800 procurators, 500 bailiffs, and a crowd of secretaries and clerks could be mobilized to support the magistrates (Chagniot 1988, p. 520).

303. Rocquain (1878), p. 50.

304. Chagniot (1988), p. 62.

305. Constant (2016), p. 226.

306. A collection can be found at "Poèmes satirique du XVIIIième siècle," https://satires18.univ-st-etienne.fr/.

were right, could facilitate the step from word to collective action. While possibly important, the issues are imponderable.

As I said, it is difficult to generalize about the psychology of urban life. What comes across most vividly from the writers I have cited is its volatile character: emotions were quick to arise, and quick to dissipate,[307] partly because many situations were ambiguous. The *intendant* Sauvigny noted that "the only reason why troubles arise and recur so frequently is that there is no law that is sufficiently precise to keep the workers to their duty, while also protecting them from the tyranny that the entrepreneurs might exercise on them."[308] When a disturbance arose, the authorities might not be able to tell whether the appearance of troops would calm or excite the crowds.[309] Although there were many conflicts around the workplace, there was no potential for organized *political* action. People could form crowds or gatherings spontaneously, after going to mass, when buying or selling in the marketplace or when queuing for bread, but only as (a not unwelcome) by-product of these activities.[310] Workers did, however, organize for *economic* purposes, sometimes showing considerable sophistication in exploiting a temporary weakness of their employers.[311] In 1753, a hatter in Falaise complains that when his workers learned that he had bought a large quantity of raw materials, they demanded a wage increase. In Beauvais the same year, a manufacturer of fabrics had to raise wages by 50 percent, as the vats were heating and the colors might turn. Workers in the ports could exploit the fact that boats did not wait.

The Clergy

The psychology of the Catholic *clergy* was as heterogeneous as its composition. It consisted of the *secular clergy* (parish priests and their auxiliaries, bishops, archbishops, and canons) and the *regular clergy* (monks,

---

307. Marais, vol. 1, p. 318.

308. Nicolas (2008), p. 506.

309. The authorities were sometimes afraid to let the troops appear in the streets (Barbier, vol. 1, p. 49) or ordered them to dress in *habits bourgeois* (Argenson, vol. 5, p. 317; see also Bercé 1974, p. 471). At other times, they may have overreacted to passing disturbances, because of their inability to anticipate the spontaneous decline of emotions: "In public commotions we cannot understand how the people can ever be appeased, nor in quiet times imagine as little what can disturb them" (La Bruyère 1881, IV.6). These two mechanisms are third-person analogues of the first-person hot-cold and cold-hot empathy gaps identified by Loewenstein (2000).

310. Lefebvre (1988), p. 24; also Kaplan (2015), p. 70.

311. The following examples are from Nicolas (2008), pp. 457–460.

Table 1. Types of Clergy in the Sénéchaussée of Nîmes

Type of cleric	Number	Number secular	Number regular
Bishops	3		
Cathedral chapters	73		
Collegiate chapters	87		
Curés	371	683	
Vicaires	123		
Professeurs	19		
Aumoniers	7		
Monks	263 (36 houses)		572
Nuns	309 (22 houses)		
Total	1,255		

Source: From Allen (1982), p. 62.

nuns, and their superiors). As an illustration, Table 1 shows their distribution in the diocese of Nîmes[312]:

There was no *archbishop* in Nîmes. Elsewhere, these prelates were at the summit of the ecclesiastical hierarchy. As Table 2 indicates, there was no clear correlation among the three dimensions of the hierarchy.[313]

These quantitative indicators can be put in a wider context. The clergy was the only of the three estates that was a corporate actor.[314] It met every year ending in a 0 in "small assemblies" and every year ending in a 5 in

312. From Allen (1982), p. 62.There were large variations in absolute and relative numbers of the various categories of clergy. From the data in Mousnier (2005), pp. 251–252, the numbers from Nîmes do not seem exceptional.

313. In addition to this general underestimation, there was also a geographical imbalance, dioceses south of the Loire paying more in proportion to their resources than dioceses north of the river. In 1701 the archbishop of Arles proposed to rectify the imbalance by a "cross-verification": a commission of prelates from north of the Loire would visit the south to check on procedures, and vice versa. The idea was rejected: "such an inquisitorial proposal was too unsporting [*sic*] to be accepted under the ancien régime" (McManners 1998, vol.1, p. 155).

314. In fact, the Church was the *only* nationwide corporate actor in the *ancien régime*. Although the provincial *parlements* tried from time to time to establish a united front against the monarchy (the *union des classes*), their efforts were undermined by rivalries, as noted above and further discussed in chapter 5. The nobility, too, tried to establish itself as a corporate actor, but except for a few general assemblies of nobles during the Fronde the kings repressed their attempts (Mousnier 2005, pp. 160–162). "Spontaneous assemblies of the nobility were illegal" (Swann 2017, p. 324). The power of the Church can be seen in the fact that it several times obtained important concessions by withholding its "voluntary

Table 2. Hierarchy of Archbishoprics in 1789

	Income	# of parish priests		# of bishops	
Cambrai	200,000 l.	Rouen	1,388	Tours	12
Paris	200,000	Besançon	812	Narbonne	12
Narbonne	160,000	Bourges	712	Auch	11
Auch	120,000	Sens	774	Bourdeaux	10
Albi	120,000	Lyon	706	Reims	9
Rouen	100,000	Cambrai	610	Toulouse	8
Toulouse	90,000	Reims	517	Lyon	8
Tours	82,000	Paris	479	Rouen	7
Sens	70,000	Vienne	430	Vienne	7
Bordeaux	55,000	Bordeaux	381	Embrun	7
Reims	50,000	Auch	359	Albi	6
Lyon	50,000	Tours	310	Aix	6
Bourges	50,000	Narbonne	242	Bourges	6
Arles	42,000	Albi	213	Arles	5
Aix	37,400	Toulouse	213	Cambrai	5
Besançon	36,000	Embrun	98	Paris	5
Vienne	35,000	Aix	96	Sens	5
Embrun	32,000	Arles	51	Besançon	4

Source: From Plongeron (1974), p. 20. He adds that the data for annual income are taken from official declarations and should probably be multiplied by a factor of two.

"large assemblies." In addition to internal regulatory matters, their main task was to vote the "free gift" to the king (a euphemism for negotiable taxes). Between the assemblies, the general agents of the clergy protected its interests efficiently. The common education of the upper clergy at the Saint-Sulpice seminary in Paris "was a powerful agent for unification of the kingdom"[315] and, we may add, for unification of the clergy. Although

---

gift" to the Crown (McManners 1998, pp. 162, 164; also chapter 5 below). The provincial Estates could try to play the same game, but in their case the government had a weapon it could not use against the Church, by suspending them (see chapter 5). Argenson, vol. 6, pp. 163–164, reports rumors that in 1750 the Church, inspired by a successful judicial strike in 1732, planned an "ecclesiastical strike" against Machault's attempt to tax it, by refusing to celebrate mass and give the sacraments. Whether a threat to strike was made or not, it would not have been credible. In 1751, Argenson, vol. 6, p. 404, also reports a more credible move: "there was *a great concert* among all members of the clergy that not one of them should yield on the refusal to pay [taxes]" (my italics).

315. Mousnier (2005), p. 254.

in this respect the clergy could act more effectively than the nobility and the third estate, one might think that the rule of celibacy would be an obstacle to intertemporal continuity, each generation having to start afresh, in contrast to the great noble families and banking dynasties who could consolidate their power over time.[316] However, among parish priests and especially in the upper clergy, links between uncles and nephews created a bridge across generations.[317] Richelieu must have known this perfectly well, although he argued for the admission of ecclesiastics to the royal council on the grounds that their celibacy guaranteed their personal independence.[318]

The secular clergy was divided into a first and a second order. Simplifying, the first order was made up of archbishops, bishops, their vicars general, canons, and abbots, while the second included parish priests and their vicars. Members of the first order were vastly more powerful. In the last Estates-General before the Revolution, in 1614, out of 135 deputies from the clergy only one "can be considered as an authentic member" of the lower clergy.[319] After 1680, parish priests were not elected to the quinquennial assemblies of the clergy.[320] They had neither active nor passive suffrage in the diocesan assemblies.[321] More important, they struggled to achieve representation in the assessment board (*bureau diocésain*) that allocated the ecclesiastical tax that members of the clergy paid to the Church, mainly to fund the "free gift." I shall return shortly to this issue.

The clergy reproduced within itself the division between the two other estates. The first order of the clergy was recruited almost exclusively from the second estate and the second order equally almost exclusively from the third estate. (In social terms, therefore, the distinction among the three orders

316. On banking dynasties, see Lüthy (1961), pp. 243–368.

317. The word "nepotism" is derived from the Italian word for "nephew." For uncle-nephew links in the lower clergy, see Julia (1956), p. 208; Plongeron (1974); p. 27; Tackett (1977), pp. 55, 73, 107, 138, 145, 234–235; and Mousnier (2005), p. 260, who refers to "veritable family dynasties." McManners (1998), vol.1, p. 632–633, describes how a benefice was often kept in the family by the parish priest resigning in favor of a relative. For the upper clergy, many examples in McManners (ibid.),who also cites succession from aunt to niece in the office of an abbess (p. 494). Plongeron (1964), p. 95 refers to "episcopal nepotism." It seems likely that the great strength of the Church—meaning the upper clergy—as a collective actor owed a great deal to these intergenerational links. The lower clergy also had an intertemporal continuity at a local level, but were not allowed to assemble.

318. Pillorget and Pillorget (1995), p. 135.

319. Pillorget and Pillorget (1995), p. 130. Hayden (1974), p. 94; and Major (1960), pp. 136–137, 163, give somewhat higher figures.

320. Olivier-Martin (2010), p. 430

321. Lavisse (1989), p. 360.

was somewhat artificial.) Among the 192 bishops appointed between 1774 and 1790, 173 were nobles, 2 commoners, and 17 of unknown origin. Among the parish priests, a small minority had noble background: 2.4 percent in the diocese of Reims, 2 percent in the diocese of Gap.[322] The bulk came from the well-to-do peasantry or urban bourgeoisie. A certain minimal income was needed for the family to guarantee the fee levied by the seminary during the studies: "an insurmountable obstacle for *le petit peuple*, whatever their faith or their desire for social promotion."[323] One study found that the percentage of families in the community paying less in *capitation* than the priest's family was concentrated in the 80s and 90s, but some as low as 40 or 50.[324] There were large regional variations, but in the words of one writer, perhaps referring to Stendhal's description of the seminary students in *Le rouge et le noir*, there is no doubt that the image of poor peasants in wooden clogs coming to the seminary to polish their manners was "appropriate for 1830, but not for the eighteenth century."[325]

Just as a magistrate derived income from his *office*, a member of the clergy could derive income from a *bénéfice*, a perpetual stream of income from the tithe and from products of Church property. Unlike an office, a benefice was not the personal property of the beneficiary; it could not be bought, sold, or bequeathed. Many parish priests held a *bénéfice*, entitling them to the income from the tithe (paid in kind). Others, however, were paid a fixed salary (*la portion congrue*) out of the income from a *bénéfice* held by someone from outside the parish. The income was the same in all parts of France and was adjusted periodically for inflation. In France as a whole one out of three parish priests were *congruistes*, with large regional variations.[326] In the diocese of Gap, which has been extensively studied by Timothy Tackett, they were two out of three.[327]

The psychology of the parish priests, whether tithe-holders or *congruistes*, was for a large part defined by opposition to their bishop. The psychology of the *congruistes* was also defined by opposition to the

---

322. Julia (1956), p. 207; Tackett (1977), p. 56. The noble priests might be younger sons of poor nobles of the sword (as suggested by McManners 1998, vol. 1, p. 324) or sons of newly ennobled.

323. Goubert (2008), p. 200.

324. Tackett (1977), pp. 61–62. McManners (1998), vol.1, pp. 329–330, summarizes studies of four other dioceses.

325. Plongeron (1964), p. 56. Stendhal's novel is subtitled "A Chronicle of 1830." See also McManners (1998), vol.1, p. 326. on the declining status and income of the parish priests in the nineteenth century.

326. Le Duc (1881), pp. 223–230.

327. Tackett (1977), p. 121.

tithe-holders, whether these were parish priests or external to the parish. (In fact, these two conflicts overlapped, since many bishops were also tithe-holders.) Concerning the first, a remarkable and influential book by Abbé Reymond, *Les droits des curés et des paroisses* (1776) argued on biblical and historical grounds that the priests had always been the near-equals of the bishops. Specifically, he claimed that the *curé* rather than the bishop should have the right to choose and to dismiss his vicar, as in any other form of procuration.[328] By the same logic, the parish priests should have the right to choose their own representative in the *bureau diocésain*. "[I]n most dioceses of France, the *curés'* single representative in this body was chosen by the board itself. Legally, this representative did not even need to be a *curé*."[329]

Reymond offered a powerful argument against this practice: "There are common law maxims from which one cannot derogate, because they *follow from the very nature of things.* . . . The present maxim is among these. It is in the nature of things that every Deputy to an economic assembly be chosen by those whom he represents. It is the essence of procuration that it be given *by* those who authorize the right to take their place. *In a word*, it is natural law to let an order of taxpayers choose *among* their fellow members . . . the one they believe most apt to uphold their common interest."[330] One common interest of the *congruistes* was to receive fair treatment from the tax board. Uniquely for the *ancien régime, their income was known*, with no possibility of evading taxes. "The congruistes were . . . indignant because they were convinced that the tithe owners undervalued their benefices in the tax declarations."[331] As noted above, the undervaluation might amount to 50 percent.

Officially, the preponderance of parish priests among the clergy at the Estates of 1789 was justified by their closeness to the peasantry, whose needs they knew better than any other group of delegates. Whether this was in fact the main reason for their presence, or whether Necker wanted to break the resistance to reform of the upper clergy, is another matter, to be discussed in Volume 3. Be this as it may, it seems likely that they were both well

---

328. Reymond (1976), p. 68. In an appeal to the *parlement* he had successfully opposed the appointment by the archbishop of his own vicar.

329. Tackett (1977), pp. 237–238.

330. Reymond (1776), pp. 288–289; my italics. Contrary to what Reymond implies, the principles that deputies should be chosen (1) by and (2) from those whom they represent are not equivalent. As I shall discuss extensively in Volume 3, neither principle was consistently followed in the elections to the Estates-General of 1789.

331. Tackett (1977), p. 237.

informed about their parishioners and sometimes allied with them against a common enemy. On the first point, we shall see (chapter 3) that Turgot used the parish priests as a channel of information from the periphery to the center and vice versa. On the second, we can cite Tackett's observation that "priests and parish in Dauphiné found themselves drawn closer together, mutually disadvantaged by the same ecclesiastical institution, united against the same common adversary, the absentee tithe owner."[332] At the same time, however, the tithe-holding curé was also brought closer to his parish by the fact that unlike the fixed salary of the *congruiste*, "his income was subject . . . to the same fluctuations as those of his parishioners [as he was paid in kind]. He understood their difficulties."[333]

For what it is worth, my hunch is that the opposition of the lower clergy to the upper was more potent than their solidarity with the villagers. Yet the curé might also support his parishioners in their struggles against the state or the *seigneur*. To illustrate solidarity against the government, we may cite the following episodes: "In 1713, in the Norman village Loucelles, the parish priest rang the church bells to prevent a salt brigade from searching the houses and the crowds gather straight away with sticks, torches, and flails."[334] In a strange case from 1753, "the Benedictines of Corbie encouraged their domestics to beat up the employees who were pursuing salt smugglers in their garden."[335] To preserve the cohesion of the community, some parish priests were reluctant to issue *monitoires*, instructions in their sermon to their flock to denounce, on pain of excommunication, villagers who had shown solidarity with the salt smugglers.[336] To illustrate solidarity against the *seigneur*, we may cite the following observation: "In 1754, when the villagers in the vast hunting ground of the Duc de Bouillon in the Mantes-Meulan area turned out in force to slay the game destroying their crops, the *curés* were in the van with their fowling pieces. . . . In the vexed question of the enclosure of common land, they spoke for the landless who could not afford to enclose a field for themselves, and for the village in general against the *seigneur*."[337] These are prima facie cases of *disinterested solidarity*, not induced by the presence of a common enemy.

332. Ibid., p. 221. As noted, this situation obtained only in about one third of the parishes.

333. Pillorget and Pillorget (1995), p. 373.

334. Nicolas 2008, pp. 168–169.

335. Ibid., p. 141.

336. Ibid., p. 632.

337. McManners 1998, vol. 2, p. 710.

CHAPTER THREE

The Psychology of the Main Social Groups

INFORMATION AND BELIEFS

I HAVE ALREADY, in various places, referred to the beliefs of individuals that occupied various positions in the structures of the old regime, such as the beliefs of the taxpayers about the imposition of others. In this chapter, I shall proceed more systematically. For the kind of *histoire des mentalités* I am trying to carry out here, determining popular beliefs, elite beliefs, and beliefs about beliefs is of course important. It is also difficult, for the reasons given in the Madisonian caveats cited in the Introduction.

The main agents in the economic and political system were the peasantry, the local authorities (*seigneurs*, *intendants*, and venal royal officials), the several urban groupings enumerated above, the *parlements*, provincial Estates, the royal administration, the royal Court, and finally the king himself. To understand the behavior of each group, we need to know not only their motivations, but also their beliefs about one another. Vertically, these include the top-down beliefs of the authorities about their subjects and the bottom-up beliefs of the subjects about the authorities. Horizontally, they include the beliefs of the members of any group in the social hierarchy about other members of the same group.

Top-Down Beliefs

To make decisions, the royal government needed both *factual information* about its subjects and *causal theories* about how they would respond to its measures. Among causal theories I shall also discuss views about military affairs.

Consider first the beliefs of the royal administration about the basic situation of the kingdom. According to Jean-Christian Petitfils, "the 'deciders' of the seventeenth century had only a vague, approximate, and fragmented knowledge of the basic geographical, economic, and demographic facts. Nobody knew if the French population amounted to 15, 20 or 30 million."[1] In Alsace, a census from 1715 reported 245,000 inhabitants, whereas one taken in 1731 asserted that the number was 335,650.[2] The number of parishes was known, but there were no proper registers of their inhabitants. The register of baptisms provided information about the flow, but not about the stock of the population. Hence taxation was top-down, based on the needs of the government, rather than bottom-up, based on the resources of the population. If the finance minister wanted to ensure the provision of grain to all parts of the kingdom, he had to act on the basis of information that was "characteristically incomplete, of uneven quality, and often tendentious."[3]

The successive ministries tried, over and over again, to gather more accurate information. As noted, the French people were adamantly opposed to the establishment of cadasters and, more generally, of public records of wealth.[4] The privileged, having more wealth, had more to fear; also, having greater connections, they were better able to resist. Among the reasons they adduced against publicity, two seem to stand out: the need to protect the secrets of families and the fear that reputations of solvency might be undermined by publicity. Both arguments are clearly stated by Saint-Simon:

---

1. Petitfils (2014a), p. 278.

2. Dupin (1745/1913), vol. 2, pp. 147–149.

3. Kaplan (2015), p. 16.

4. The French showed themselves to be wary of many other requests for information. "The very idea of counting the population (*dénombrement*) provoked . . . reactions in the population, which feared new taxes" (Petitfils 2014 a, p. 277); see also Bély (2015), pp. 266–267. In 1789, Necker's request to officials of the *bailliages* to send exact information about the number of households (*feux*) in each parish, to determine the number of deputies they could send to the Estates-General, "raised everywhere the strongest reprobation, as the populations had been accustomed for centuries to see in these investigations nothing but a basis or a pretext for new taxes" (Brette 1894, p. xix). In Paris, proprietors were opposed to numbering houses in the streets, since this operation was widely perceived as a prelude to a tax increase (Chagniot 1988, p. 269). Hardy, vol. 1, pp. 422–423, writes that when the king announced that holders of government bonds would not receive interest unless they could document that not only they *but also their servants* had paid their poll tax, the italicized clause was widely seen as a prelude to increasing the tax. A week later, the government backed down (ibid., p. 427).

To collect this tax [*le dixième*] it was necessary to draw from each person a clear and honest statement of his wealth, of his active and passive debts, and so on. It was necessary to demand sure proofs so as not to be deceived. Here was the difficulty. Nothing was thought of the desolation this extra tax must cause to a prodigious number of men, or of their despair upon finding themselves obliged to disclose their family secrets; of the turpitude of so many whose lack of wealth was offset by their credit and reputation, the suspension of which would throw them into an inevitable ruin, or of the breakup of families by these cruel revelations and the light cast on their most shameful parts. . . . Only the financiers would be saved, because of their unknown portfolios.[5]

I do not know *which* secrets were at stake. As Saint-Simon is clearly speaking on behalf of the nobility, one can speculate. Perhaps full daylight would reveal a noble engaging in retail trade (a fact that might cause him to lose noble status), or the possession of non-noble land for which he would be subject to taxation, or the details of a marriage contract. Be this as it may, the concern for a good financial *reputation* is well-documented. Nobles notoriously tended to delay paying their creditors, who accepted to wait as long as they believed the debtor to be solvent, even if perhaps illiquid. Full publicity and the revelation of insolvency would have caused the collapse of many houses of cards.[6] The system actually encouraged debt-funded spending, since the credit of individuals[7] as well as of the state (chapter 4) was based on conspicuous consumption, not on verifiable assets.

However, arguments from secrecy and reputation were probably vicarious or marginal. The main reason the privileged opposed publicity was that it would have made them pay higher taxes. As long as the tax assessments and collections were in the hands of individuals who possessed little hard knowledge but had discretionary powers and were susceptible to threats and bribes, the privileged could count on paying less, sometimes far less, than they would have done under a regime of full publicity. To be sure, the glass could also be seen as half full. In late eighteenth-century Normandy, the assessed revenue on which the poll tax and the *vingtième*

5. Saint-Simon, vol. 20, pp. 166, 178; see also Esmonin (1913), p. 319, for other contemporary texts that refer to the need to protect secrets and reputation.

6. When a taxpayer sued to have his tax reduced, the tax court (*cours des aides*) explicitly excluded the use of material evidence and relied only on reputation (Esmonin 1913, pp. 323–324). The court's argument was that a litigant might be ruined by having to document his assets.

7. Marion (1927), p. 17.

were based averaged about 65 percent of the real revenue, a proportion that was substantially higher than in the past because of the more effective procedures of verification introduced by Turgot and Necker.[8] The privileged still evaded paying taxes on 35 percent of their income, and did not pay the *taille*.

On occasion, the government and its officials bypassed the ordinary channels of information. In the 1680s, the finance minister Le Pelletier advised the *intendant* in Auvergne to "seek information from 'a few reliable and faithful persons' without giving them a public mission: he preferred secret agents of information to the regular agents of the government."[9] In 1789, Moreau de Beaumont also recommended the use of special commissioners for making the tax rolls, "given "the lack of enlightenment of almost all collectors and their interest in sparing their parishes."[10] As *intendant* in the Limousin, Turgot found it impossible to rely on village officials, "who usually could not read or write and on whose intelligence or probity one could not count." Instead he turned to the parish priests for gathering information about the villages as well as for conveying information to them.[11] As the parish priests were not part of the administration, their messages would be more credible than those of royal officials, at least in matters that did not affect the church. Yet these were second-best measures: they reveal but could not offset the flaws of the administration.

The most sustained information-gathering effort undertaken by the royal administration seems to have been the verification of titles of nobility in the 1660s. Since nobles were exempt from the *taille*, the unmasking of false nobles could potentially fill the royal coffers. The king also hoped to gain from the fines he imposed on the false nobles, and from the sums

8. Kwass (2000), pp. 92–93.

9. Esmonin (1913), p. 141, who adds that "the tax rolls made by such means could not be but mediocre."

10. Marion (1910), p. 47.

11. Follain (2008), p. 360; Faure (1961), pp. 276–277. The reformist curé Reymond (1776), p. 39, clearly refers to Turgot when he mentions the usefulness of the *curés* in the Flour War of 1775. Yet Kiener and Peyronnet (1979), pp. 83–84, affirm that after an initial burst of activity the main task of the *curé* became the reporting of the cattle lost to epizootics, a number needed to determine the compensation due to the peasants. (According to Faure 1961, p. 114–15, if one did not compensate them, they would not slaughter the cattle.) Also, "the government's attempts [to use the parish priests to disseminate knowledge] were often thwarted by the bishops, who feared, not without reason, that the bureaucracy might preempt the *curés'* loyalties to the detriment of the ecclesiastical hierarchy" (Tackett 1979, p. 163). Moreover, the fear that providing accurate information might lead to higher taxes could affect priests who were concerned for the welfare of their flock (ibid.).

they paid to transform their title into a true one, thus buying exemption. According to Esmonin, the second task was by far the most important undertaken by the officials charged with the verification.[12] Since the king always needed money urgently, he preferred a lump-sum payment to a steady income from the *taille*. The task was complicated, time-consuming, and subject to the corruption of those who performed it. Some authentic nobles thought the process dishonored them, and refused to cooperate. In Normandy, one registered 1285 families of authentic nobility and 172 usurpers, 39 of which maintained their noble status on appeal. This survey was feasible only because the numbers were relatively small.

To balance a budget, or to address the problems of an unbalanced budget, a government would obviously want know both sides of the ledger: income and debts. As discussed above, the government had only vague notions about taxable wealth and income. More surprisingly, perhaps, it did not know much it owed.[13] In addition to the *public debt* in the form of bonds (*la dette constituée*) there was the *royal debt* (*dette exigible et arriérée*), which basically consisted of unpaid pensions and wages to courtiers and officials, unpaid subsidies to allied countries, unpaid advances to financiers, and numerous other liabilities. Whereas the public debt was a matter of public record, registered by the *parlements*, the royal debt was the cumulative result of many promises to pay (*reconnaissances*) of which no tally was kept. One of the causes of the failure of L'Averdy's economic program was that it was based on largely erroneous assumptions about the royal debt.[14] Because of this double uncertainty, the finance minister was reduced to seeking precision in the second decimal while largely ignorant of the first. If "all the finance ministers who managed hundreds of millions were obsessed by the smallest economies,"[15] the reason may simply be that only the latter offered unambiguous opportunities for action.

From Louis XIII onwards, the kings resorted to another means for obtaining information, the *cabinet noir* that intercepted private letters, read them, and resealed them more or less perfectly.[16] Although some tried

12. Esmonin (1913), p. 203. The following relies on his analyses.

13. This paragraph draws on Félix (1999), pp. 160–167.

14. In addition, he had surprisingly naïve views about how to create a cadaster, ignoring both the costs and duration of the project as well as the lack of competent persons to carry it out (Félix 1999, chap. 7).

15. Félix (1999), p. 409.

16. Vaillé (1950), the only monograph on the topic, is useful, if sometimes more concerned with the technical aspect of mail interception (Vaillé was an employee of the post office) than with its political aspects. Boislisle (1890) has a good overview for the reign of Louis XIV; there are also many examples in Saint-Simon. D'Argenson, whose brother was

to circumvent the practice by writing in code, the Austrian ambassador to Versailles, Mercy-Argenteau, told the empress Maria Theresa that the French court had "such skilled decoders that there is no cipher to which they cannot rapidly find the key."[17] The practice originated in wartime, when it was mainly directed towards letters to and from the enemy, but soon began to target private letters within France. Its effects, apart from the anecdotal, are hard to assess. I shall discuss it at some length, more for the light it can shed on the mentality of the old regime, notably on the generation of universal distrust among members of the elite, than for any arguable effects on policy. There are, nevertheless, a few spectacular instances of the latter.

In some cases, opening letters could serve as a kind of opinion poll, or an attempt to obtain independent and reliable information. In 1659, Colbert asked the *intendant* of Alsace to "open the letters of the Jesuits in the province to learn their sentiments about the French administration there."[18] By 1719, the practice had become too well-known to work: "the Jesuits do not write to each other from one province to another, since their letters have been opened for a long time."[19] In 1752, when Louis XV learned that the crown prince was ill, "he broke the seal of several private letters to learn what one thought about the illness."[20] The king might also, by accident, be alerted to abuses or to news that nobody wanted to tell him. In his *Mémoires*, Olivier d'Ormesson writes that one day in 1665, "M. de Turenne told me a remarkable fact about an intercepted letter that was read in the king's presence and that indicated how the exile of Rocquesante was badly received and was seen as a violent and unjust action, and also mentioned the high favor of M. Colbert, who was the master and all-powerful; this kind of thing could make known to the king truths that nobody dared to tell him."[21] In his journal from 1775, the Abbé de Véri cites "puerile curiosity"

---

surintendant de la Poste during part of the reign of Louis XV, often refers to the interception of letters. Véri (1928, 1930) has many observations, several cited below, on the *cabinet noir* in the time of Louis XVI. Vaillé does not seem to have read him. It appears that even official correspondence was sometimes intercepted, so that one minister could learn what others were doing (Félix 1999, p. 319).

17. Mercy-Argenteau (1974), vol. 1, p. 469.

18. Vaillé (1950), p. 65.

19. Barbier, vol. 1, p. 29.

20. Luynes (1860–1865), vol. 12, p. 100. I conjecture that he opened the letters of the *doctors*, to see if what they said in private matched what they had told him. The kings' doctors were reluctant to be the bearers of bad news.

21. d'Ormesson (1860–1861), vol. 2, p. 322. Allegedly, Roquesante had been exiled because his impartial behavior in the trial of Nicolas Fouquet (see below) displeased Louis

as the motive of the king's "perfidious opening" of letters sent by the post, adding that "if this is how the king learns that one is not content with him, that would prove that a poison can sometimes have good effects."[22] After an attempt to assassinate Louis XV in January 1757, his mistress, Madame de Pompadour, asked the superintendent of police (the Comte d'Argenson, brother of the diarist) to shield the king from letters that might remind him of this event and reinforce his terrors, to which he responded that he would need direct instructions from the king himself.[23] The conflict may have contributed to his dismissal in February 1757.

Véri was extremely critical of this practice. In June 1774, shortly after the accession to power of Louis XVI, he deplores the king's tendency to judge people by their flaws rather than by their good qualities, adding that "among these obscure ways is one that was very common in the time of the late king, ascribed to curiosity rather than to a desire to do good: opening letters sent in the mail. One has made the king understand the odious and even dangerous character of this method. Once ill-intentioned people *know that it is used*, calumny and wickedness have a sure means of finding their way to the throne. The king felt the truth of this observation, and intends to limit this infamy."[24] On one occasion, in August 1775, he did in fact refuse to eat of the fruit of the poisoned tree, when he struck down a decision made on the basis of information in two intercepted letters.[25]

Later in the reign, however, Louis XVI made important decisions on this basis. In particular, it is possible that Turgot lost his post as finance minister because of manipulation of the mail (among other reasons: the dismissal seems to have been overdetermined). In an unpublished part of his Journal, Véri refers to a letter (possibly fabricated) to Turgot from a friend, who comments that "I did not think the king was as narrow-minded (*borné*) as you represent him to me." Edgar Faure, who cites this passage, comments: "One can imagine the effect of this reflection on the

---

XIV. We do not know how the king reacted to this criticism. In other cases, Louis XIV was vindictive when he read criticism of his policies (Saint-Simon, vol. 19, p. 428) and even more so when he intercepted letters that criticized or made fun of him personally. The critics were jailed or exiled.

22. Véri (1928), p. 274. On the high quality of Véri's observations, see the brief comments in the Appendix as well as Faure (1961), pp. 18, 34, 82.

23. Vaillé (1950), p. 162. Valfons (1860), p. 255, adds that Madame de Pompadour insinuated that d'Argenson had fabricated some of the letters that tormented the king, to enhance his own importance.

24. Ibid., p. 109; my italics.

25. Vaillé (1950), p. 184.

spirit of a sovereign suffering from an 'inferiority complex.'"[26] As we shall see shortly, Véri took it for granted that the king's officials would also prevent him from reading letters *praising* Turgot.

Among the means at the disposal of the man in charge of the *cabinet noir* was the practice of opening a letter and substituting a message that put the writer in a bad light.[27] Another was to show the king only the letters that officials wanted him to read. Véri cites a long letter written to him from Mme de Kaunitz (the wife of the principal Austrian minister), who characterized Turgot as "our hero." He comments that "M. d'Ogny, who is in charge of opening letters, will probably not have brought it to the knowledge of the king because of the praise it bestows on M. Turgot, whose operations he does not like."[28] Madame de Tencin, one of the great *intriguantes* of the eighteenth century, wrote to her brother, Cardinal Tencin, that if a certain letter "has not been communicated to the king by those in charge of breaking the seal, one must conclude that Dufort [the official in charge] is working with the ministers to show to the king only what suits him."[29] In theory, the selection bias could be avoided by having the letters opened by a subaltern official and forwarded directly to the king, without passing through the hands of ministers with a political agenda.[30] According to Dupont de Nemours, a close associate of Turgot's, such attempts invariably failed.[31]

Orchestration of letters in the expectation that they would be opened also occurred. A might fake or instigate a letter by B to C knowing it will be read by D (the king), the last being the real addressee.[32] Madame de Tencin fabricated a letter from Germany to someone whom she wanted to lose his post. On another occasion, she wrote to the Duc de Richelieu, one of the great rakes of the century, that he was about to receive an anonymous letter "written in order to be opened and brought to the king's attention."[33] Véri reports that Joseph II told him that Choiseul, longtime

26. Faure (1961), p. 530.

27. Argenson, vol. 6, p. 8.

28. Véri (1928), p. 352.

29. Vaillé (1950), p. 146.

30. Necker (1784–1785), vol. 2, pp. 500–501.

31. Vaillé (1950), p. 193.

32. In a comprehensive survey of eavesdropping in animals, Peake (2005), p. 30, finds that in some cases "it may be reasonable to assume that signals used here are, at least partly, 'intended' for eavesdroppers," i.e. that natural selection has favored these signals because their effect on third parties benefits the sender. In particular, these benefits might arise from third-party harm to a second-party recipient who is the rival of the first-party sender.

33. Vaillé (1950), p. 143.

the principal minister of Louis XV, manipulated his master by dictating to the Habsburg and Spanish ambassadors to France passages he wanted the king to read when their dispatches were intercepted.[34] In a somewhat obscure passage, Véri refers to a letter by a naval officer, Comte d'Estaing, to one of his correspondents, at a time when Necker's position in the government was vulnerable. Having intercepted the letter, the king found it "full of the praises for M. Necker that would sound in Europe. One must assume that M. d'Estaing knew that the king would see it, and that M. Necker was equally informed."[35]

Knowledge of the practice of interception might invite manipulation, but also caution. In his personal letters, Turgot never used the royal mail, only special courier. Madame de Sévigné used pseudonyms when referring to people at the Court;[36] others wrote in code. Even Madame de Maurepas, the wife of the principal minister of Louis XVI, "was too well informed about the opening of letters and the account that M. d'Ogny gives of them to the king every Sunday to explain herself clearly" in her letters to Véri.[37] Because Saint-Simon knew that his correspondence with his wife was intercepted, they limited themselves to "nothings" (*des riens*).[38] After making a critical comment in a letter on the foreign minister Torcy, Madame Palatine added that "I know that he will read this, but I don't care, and he will suffer the fate stated in the German proverb: Who listens at the doors will hear the tale of his own infamy."[39] Officials sometimes fabricated or intercepted letters to ruin a rival financially.[40] While one could not protect oneself against fabrication, one could neutralize

34. Véri (1930), pp. 46–47.

35. Ibid., p. 394.

36. An amusing, double-layered exception occurs in a letter to her daughter of December 23, 1671 (vol. 1, p. 398). She first reports a story of a courtier who offered to pimp for Louis XIV in procuring his niece for the king. The king dismissed him with a laugh, and later made the story public, shaming the would-be procurer. "And there is no cypher in all this; but I find that the king everywhere behaves so well that there is no need for mystery when talking about him." She presumably expected that her letter would be opened, and that the king would read it and appreciate her praise. Other letters also include extravagant, and seemingly pointless, praises for the king. In another letter from August 21, 1676 (vol. 2, p. 179), she first uses the private code-name Quanto for the king's mistress Madame de Montespan to communicate a rumor that she is about to be replaced, and then, in the next paragraph, uses her real name to inform her daughter about Madame de Montespan's travel plans.

37. Ibid., p. 419.

38. Saint-Simon, vol. 23, p. 134. He observes that such caution was very common (Saint-Simon 1996, p. 370).

39. Palatine (1985), p. 290.

40. Veillé (1950), pp. 126–127; Argenson, vol. 5, p. 437.

interception by not writing. If such caution led to undercommunication of business-related information, it could undermine efficiency.

Many writers observed that if it had been universally known that letters were opened, nobody would have confided anything important to the mail. The grievance book of the third estate in Nemours (written by Dupont de Nemours) states that "one could not learn anything from the letters when the authors know that they will be read," and asks "What purpose can it then serve? To harm someone in the eyes of the king."[41] Yet if the opening of letters had been *common* knowledge (everybody knowing that everybody knew, etc.), the king should have been able to infer that any letters containing incriminating information must have been fabricated. Since the kings sometimes did act on the basis of intercepted letters, they must have assumed that the practice was not generally known. If so, they were probably right. I conjecture that the practice of opening *many* letters (but not all) was *widely* (but not universally) *suspected* (but not known).

It is difficult to assess the effects of the *cabinet noir* on the formation and implementation of policy. Decisions based on fabricated or insufficient information could lead to the appointment of bad officials and the dismissal of good ones. Fear of interception of mail could act as sand in the financial machinery. A more important but also more diffuse consequence was the contribution to a general atmosphere of uncertainty, confusion, and distrust, making it "hard to see through the fog of rumour and disinformation with any confidence."[42] In the words of Robert Shiller, a recent recipient of the Alfred Nobel Memorial Prize in Economics, "There is substantial evidence that if an atmosphere filled with lies or presumed lies spreads throughout a society, the effect might reduce economic growth rates. Years of incremental damage would result in a substantially lower level of economic well-being than would otherwise have existed" (*New York Times*, November 10, 2019, p. B5).

By traveling amidst his subjects, a king could also glean a more general, if also more diffuse, impression of their beliefs. Hardy's journal includes the use of what he calls a "barometer" to measure the state of the opinion, namely the applause or silence of the people in the presence of the royal family or of magistrates.[43] "The silence of the people is the shame of the

---

41. AP 4, p. 153. The grievance book goes on to say, "This is how M. Turgot lost his place. The King, who will read this, will see that the fact is correct."

42. Swann (2017), p. 255.

43. Hardy, vol. 3, p. 685. Booing them was probably unthinkable and in any case dangerous.

kings,"[44] contrary to the maxim coined by pope Bonifatius VIII, "Qui tacet, consentire videtur," or that imputed to Alexander Dubcek after the Russian invasion of Prague in 1968, "Who is not against me is for me."

Hardy also reports that when Louis XVI departed on his annual trip to Compiègne, he took a detour "so that he would not witness the cooling of the people" caused by the high price of bread.[45] Furthermore, he reports that when Marie-Antoinette visited Paris the same year, she was "struck by the silence that reigned around her, compared to the noisy demonstrations one had already made for her so many times."[46] Hardy also used the applaudometer to measure the relative popularity of the two brothers of Louis XVI[47] and of the various princes and peers.[48] Using a different barometer, Hardy showed the lack of affection for the dying Louis XV by reporting that only three masses had been held for him during his illness, in contrast to the six hundred held after an assassination attempt in 1757 and six thousand during a serious illness in 1744.[49]

In 1725, the silence of the people caused the government to reverse a decision. In a *lit de justice* (a formal session of the *parlement* of Paris, under the presidency of the king), the king decided that magistrates with less than ten years' service would not in the future be allowed to vote on matters of state. The decision was part of the tug-of-war between the king and the courts that spanned the eighteenth century. The Court "knew it

44. Ibid., p. 544. See also Véri (1930), p. 178, commenting on an unsuccessful attempt by Louis XVI to buy popularity for himself and the queen by throwing money to the crowds: "the silence of the people is the lesson of the kings." The coincidence of expression suggests that this was a general idea at the time. It is worth while noting the ambiguous character of the practice of throwing money. According to one of the nieces of Mazarin, they amused themselves by throwing handfuls of gold coins from the palace windows, for the pleasure of seeing the guards fight over them (Lavisse 1989, p. 103). Hardy, vol. 2, p. 438, reports that when the equerries of the Maréchal de Brissac threw money to the crowds while traveling through Paris, "according to usual practice," three people were killed and several seriously wounded. In 1789, when a noble municipal official in Aix threw money at a crowd that demanded lower bread prices, it "took it as an insult" (Cubells 1987, p. 82).

45. Hardy, vol. 3, p. 545. Argenson, vol. 6, pp. 213–214, 234, reports that in 1750 Louis XV also avoided passing through Paris on his way to and from Compiègne, ostensibly to punish the people of Paris, but more likely to avoid being exposed to their silence. Barbier, vol. 8, p. 73, reports that on one occasion in 1762 nobody cried "Vive le roi!" when the king entered and left a *lit de justice*, although the expectation of applause was his reason for attending.

46. Ibid., p. 533. As observed in note 43 above, the "noisy" demonstrations could not have been unfavorable.

47. Hardy, vol. 3, p. 662

48. Ibid, p. 720.

49. Ibid., pp. 420, 423–424. I am not implying that the king was aware of these exact numbers, but perhaps he had a rough idea about the first two.

could count on most of the senior magistrates, who needed it to establish their families, and imposed silence on the younger ones, who like to talk and instruct themselves."[50] The session "lasted from 10 a.m. to 2 p.m. Afterwards, the king, who was impatient, got up and left. . . . In Paris, nobody shouted 'Long live the king!' On the contrary, the bourgeois prevented the people (*le petit peuple*) who wanted to shout."[51] The government inferred that it had gone too far, and reversed the decision.[52]

To be efficient, an administration needs not only factual knowledge, but also causal theories (or assumptions). In the economic domain, these mainly stemmed from mercantilist and, later, physiocratic doctrines.

Among the many dimensions of mercantilism that Eli Heckscher discusses in his classic work, most concern the levers that the royal administration could use to implement its policies. I discuss these in chapter 4. For my purposes here, the most relevant is Heckscher's account of the "Attitude to the factors of production," notably labor. He asserts that "[w]ith regard to the mercantilists' conception of industriousness and sloth, it must be said that there was hardly any point on which opinion was so unanimous as in its condemnation of idleness."[53] This moral condemnation went hand in hand with a causal theory, the doctrine of the "backward-sloping supply curve of labor," which assumed that workers were "satisficing" rather than maximizing their welfare.[54] To simplify,

---

50. Marais, vol. 3, p. 197. In an edict of December 13, 1756, the king tried to limit the access to the plenary sessions of all chambers to magistrates with ten years of service. Although never formally abolished, this "declaration of discipline" became a dead letter (Egret 1970, p. 86). Flammermont (1888–1898), vol. 1, p. lxxx, asserts that the government imposed the constraint because the high turnover among the magistrates, who saw their charges as a stepping-stone to other positions, created a majority that was "young, inexperienced, and turbulent." He also emphasizes that since the older magistrates opined first and could opine only once, they could not respond to and refute the proposals of the younger magistrates (ibid., p. lxxxvi). It may be impossible to determine whether the government mainly feared the incompetence or the radicalism of the young. Many details on this issue are found in Bluche (1986b), pp. 19–30.

51. Marais, vol. 3, p. 194; see also Barbier, vol. 1, p. 393. The episode confirms the belief of the people in the goodness of the king; the middle class knew better.

52. Rocquain (1878), p. 40.

53. Heckscher (1934), vol. 2, p. 154.

54. The hypothesis of "satisficing behavior" implies that peasants stop working when they have attained a satisfactory level of income or welfare. When the wages of day laborers or the income producers receive from selling grain or wine go up, they work shorter hours. While consistent with the large number of religious holidays in the *ancien régime*, it is harder to square with the many reports of deep misery in the French countryside. Grenier (2012–2013) discusses various explanations of an alleged shift around 1750 from a backward-slopping to a forward-sloping supply curve of labor.

producers had to be motivated by the stick of poverty rather than by the carrot of higher income. Heckscher also asserts that "Colbert exceeded all others in his condemnation of idleness."[55] As an example, we may consider his response to a letter from an *intendant* signaling much poverty in his district: "You must examine carefully the sources of this poverty to seek the means of diminishing it, either by relief from the *taille*, charging other districts that are better placed with what you subtract from the poorer, or by offering people the means to gain a living, or by examining whether this poverty results from a natural sloth (*fainéantise*), because in the last case they do not merit any relief."[56]

This attitude led naturally to what Heckscher called a *policy of low wages*. In the words of a French memorandum from 1786 that he cites, "In order to assure the prosperity of our manufactures *it is necessary that the worker should never enrich himself,* and he should have no more than he actually needs to feed and clothe himself properly. In a certain class of people, too much well-being lessens industriousness, and encourages idleness with all its attendant evils."[57] It seems that in France, unlike England, very few authors advocated a *policy of high wages*.[58] One argument for the latter was that "[c]oncern for *sales* made the worker's purchasing power, *ergo* high wages, appear desirable—the same principle, that is, as has become decisive in modern economic theory."[59] Another was the denial of "the fundamental mercantilist idea that a country might become rich through the poverty of its people."[60]

In the mid-eighteenth century, the government adopted, with hesitations and often inefficient implementation, the physiocratic doctrine of commerce and notably of free trade of grain. The immense practical importance of this issue was equaled only by the theoretical confusion

55. Ibid., p. 155.

56. Esmonin (1913), p. 527.

57. Heckscher (1934), vol. 2, p. 168; my italics.

58. Boisguilbert (1707) is one exception. For another, McManners (1998), vol. 2, p. 706, cites an interesting debate from the last decades of the *ancien régime* about two mechanisms by which consumption (by different classes) might increase employment: "Voltaire had justified self-indulgent spending [by the upper classes, including the upper clergy] by arguing it provided employment for the working poor. In 1786, the abbé François Pluquet, in his *Traité philosohique et politique sur le luxe*, demolished this comfortable contention: renounce your futile pleasures, he said, so you can reduce the leases on your property, enabling your farmers to pay their workers more; with this increased spending power, they will consume more, thus creating employment of a genuinely useful and permanent kind."

59. Heckscher (1934), vol. 2, p. 169. Written two years before Keynes's *General Theory,* Heckscher's book shares many of the assumptions of that work (Shackle 1967).

60. Heckscher (1934), vol. 2, p. 171.

surrounding it. Steven Kaplan cites how one high official could not accept another's "contention that the dearness (*cherté*) in the first years after the liberalization [in 1763–1764] was the product of a 'lack of liberty'; on the contrary, the [first official] frankly blamed the dearth and 'the uprisings of the people' on 'the liberty which has been accorded for the export of grain.'"[61] Faced with the misery of the population in 1767–1768, "the physiocrats insisted that the mischiefs [allegedly] caused by liberty were the result of insufficient liberty."[62] Whereas some officials claimed that "the free exportation of grain was the only measure capable of preventing starvation (*disette*) by encouraging agriculture and hence the production of grain," others asserted that in times of scarcity free exportation would lead to "excessive stockpiling and, as the grain would be hidden, a chimerical evil would create a real one."[63] The officials can hardly be blamed. They faced poor data, unreliable implementers, and causal issues that involved not only economics but politics and psychology as well. Sometimes, the government acted irrationally because it counted on the rationality of consumers. The upshot was that policy makers were fumbling in the dark.

Trade policy was not the only domain in which failures occurred because the government made wrong assumptions about the psychological effects of its actions. Specifically, the kings did not understand that *repression as well as concessions could backfire*. Also, they had no idea that invasion of a foreign country might stiffen its will rather than bending it, or that efforts to improve the economy could make it worse.

Concerning repression, Louis XIV thought the revocation in 1685 of the edict of Nantes, together with the brutal measures that preceded it, would extinguish Protestantism in the kingdom. Yet "Protestantism *did not only survive; it was regenerated* by the suffering of the persecuted, and shortly by the blood of the martyrs."[64] If the king had thought more deeply about the matter, he would have allowed the Protestants the *jus emigrandi* they had in Germany.[65] I return to other aspects of his policy in chapter 4. At the same time, *moderate* repression could also be counterproductive (chapter 4).

Concerning concessions, in 1764 the finance minister, L'Averdy, granted several rights to the *parlements*, "to reestablish an apparent peace in the

61. Kaplan (2015), p. 230.
62. Félix (1999), pp. 415.
63. Ibid., pp. 198, 199.
64. Pillorget and Pillorget (1995), p. 944; my italics. Droz (1860), vol. 1, p.70, makes a similar comment about how the Jansenists were saved by persecution.
65. Pillorget and Pillorget (1995), p. 939.

world of the judiciary. . . . *His views were too shortsighted*, and his trust of the magistrates too complete, for him to be able to anticipate that *their demands would increase in proportion to his concessions*."[66] These are the mistakes of autocratic rulers everywhere,[67] yet exacerbated here because of the short time horizon of the French kings. *Determining the long-term consequences of action takes time*, which the government rarely had.

One can offer, however, a more charitable interpretation of L'Averdy's mildness. In a letter from 1764 to the Duc d'Aiguillon, who advocated harsh measures in Brittany, L'Averdy wrote that "if we set about punishing at this moment, popular opinion will favor [the *parlements*] and those who are protesting on their behalf, a favor that will prevent us from pursuing what we have begun. It is better, therefore, to wait (*différer*). By virtue of their efforts and stupidity, [the *parlements*] will make the public come to its senses, it will not want to be governed by anarchy, it will return into the arms of authority."[68] While many of L'Averdy's economic views were naïve, this advocacy of crisis maximization is sophisticated, even if obviously risky. He assumed that harsh measures would generate more hatred than fear (see Introduction), and that it was more effective to give the *parlements* rope to hang themselves. "If he sometimes seemed to retreat, it was only to build up momentum and go forward."[69]

Concerning invasions, the foreign policies of Louis XIV and his minister of war Louvois were also dictated by flawed psychological assumptions. Like the instigators of the British repression of the American colonies and of the American war in Vietnam, they did not understand the emotional force of nationalism and assumed that their opponents were motivated only by material concerns and thus could be brought to heel by "compellence."[70] According to the most recent biographer of Louvois,

66. Marion (1927), p. 230; my italics. L'Averdy was a former magistrate. Antoine (1989), p. 834, refers to the "state of permanent revolt in which the magistracy had established itself, in spite of—*or because of*—all the concessions that had been made to it" (my italics). Commenting on events during the Fronde, Bluche (1986a), pp. 64–65, writes, "One must never make concessions from a position of weakness"; also (ibid., p. 505): "to endure, concessions must be given from a position of force."

67. "A king ought to wish to pardon while he has still grounds for being severe; if he acts otherwise, just as lopped trees sprout forth again with numberless boughs, and many kinds of crops are cut down in order that they may grow more thickly, so *a cruel king increases the number of his enemies by destroying them*; for the parents and children of those who are put to death, and their relatives and friends, step into the place of each victim" (Seneca, *Of Clemency*, 7; my italics).

68. Cited after Félix (1999), p. 345; my italics.

69. Ibid.

70. For the British in America, see Ramsay (1789), vol. 1, p. 58, vol. 2, p. 68; and Bourke

both the war against Holland in the 1670s and the devastation of the Palatinate in the 1680s were based on this assumption. With regard to the former, he writes that Louvois dismissed the idea that the Dutch might react to the king's humiliating demands by inundating their own country, as he thought it would be "too great a catastrophe for the Dutch."[71] They went ahead and did so. As for the latter, the king and his ministers "did not understand that states would undertake a war without the goal of obtaining concrete territorial or diplomatic gains."[72] Yet the passions of the Palatinate overrode their interest. The cumulative effect of these aggressive policies was not only the financial exhaustion of France, but the mobilization of most of Europe against it.

Concerning finally economic policy, well-intentioned efforts to improve an economic situation could also be counterproductive. In 1759, when the Seven Years' War was ruining the country, Louis XV "sent his gold and silver plates to the royal mint to be melted down and turned into specie. . . . This symbolic [gesture] had above all the effect of undermining the little trust that remained and of forcing a general suspension of payments."[73] As in the case of the grain subsidies in Champagne (discussed below), people may have thought that if things were revealed to be that bad, they were probably much worse.[74] In times of war or civil war, such measures could also send a signal to the enemy. During the Fronde, Paul de Gondi (the later Cardinal de Retz) reportedly made a proposal of this kind, which was turned down on the grounds that "such extraordinary measures would be seen as evident signs of an extreme necessity, from which the enemies would benefit."[75]

(2015), p. 294. For the Americans in Vietnam, see Lebow (1996), pp. 559–561. For the idea of compellence se note 144 to chapter 4.

71. Céant (2015), p. 137.

72. Ibid., p. 396.

73. Petitfils (2014b), p. 637; also Antoine (1989), p. 791. Among several striking examples, Kaplan (2015), p. 79, cites an occasion "in 1710 [when] the police decided not to publish an *arrêt* meant to dissuade people from pillaging convoys in order not 'to renew the sad ideas of dearth,' that is, in order not to incite them to pillage grain convoys!"

74. Rocquain (1878), p. 218: "The use of an expedient that was usually the last resort in calamities of the state scared the public." For an amusing experimental demonstration of this effect, see Spiegelhalter (2019), p. 107.

75. Chéruel (1879), vol. 3, p. 175. A century later, Argenson, vol. 3, p. 363, claimed that in 1709 the finance minister Desmarets pulled his punches by taxing the people less than an inept minister would have done, thus "scaring the enemies of France, who inferred (*qui y virent*) great resources" from his decision. Argenson also asserts, confusingly, that the decision was motivated by the severe economic crisis: 1709 was one of the worst years of the *ancien régime*. Presumably the enemies of France knew this fact and interpreted the decision to tax moderately as a sign of poverty rather than of abundance.

Conversely, ostentatious luxury could be used to send a signal of affluence to the enemy. As d'Argenson noted in 1739, however, this strategy could not justify luxury in peacetime: "One is still praising the cardinal [Fleury] for acting like the Romans who, besieged on the Capitol, threw bread from the windows to show that they still had some left; this had an effect, since it was a question of having the siege lifted, but *what good does a false reputation do us today*? Who is at our doors? Not our neighbors, but the real misery in our own country."[76]

Bottom-Up Beliefs

I shall now consider bottom-up beliefs, beginning with popular beliefs about the king.

It has often been argued that the people in the old regime blamed the advisors of the king both for causing their sufferings and for keeping the king ignorant about them. *"Si le roi savait!"* If only the king knew!

The people were wrong, since kings were not in fact ignorant. "[A]t the time he extracted extraordinary taxes from the kingdom, [Louis XIV] raised all of Europe against him and, at the same time, built Versailles, which could have waited. The means he used to overcome resistance were also abominable and his agents as well, as some of the highest among them admitted. Finally, many of the miseries and abuses that caused anger and insurrections could have been softened or abolished. Louis XIV was fully aware of the ills from which his people suffered and of their causes. The king 'knew.' The king did not care (*n'a pas voulu*)."[77] Saint-Simon cites an example of the king's knowledge of the abuses: when someone remarked on the great beauty of a terrace with a view on the Loire, "the king responded curtly, 'I can well believe it, it has been made at my expense, on the funds for bridges and roads of those districts, over many years.'"[78]

In his account of popular revolts in the seventeenth century Yves-Marie Bercé finds considerable evidence for the belief in the goodness of the king. In 1636, following the abolition of a detested tax, the *parlement* of Toulouse "spoke of 'the exceptional goodness of the king, who wanted only to relieve his subjects and not to establish any consumption tax (*gabelle*) or other taxes.' The very fact of the royal abolition showed that the enemies of the State had persuaded the subjects of 'the opposite of his good

---

76. Argenson, vol. 2, pp. 246–247; my italics.

77. Lavisse (1989), p. 324; also Argenson, vol. 6, p. 189.

78. Saint-Simon, vol. 27, pp. 130–131.

and saintly intentions.' The chimerical conclusion of these arguments was stated by the inhabitants of Aubeterre . . . , who understood that 'the king does not want any subsidy to be paid any more.'"[79] In 1639, seditious posters in Poitiers were signed *"in the name of the king and of the people,* a significant couple that was indissoluble in the minds of the rioters."[80] In 1648, following an edict on tax relief, the *parlement* of Bordeaux abolished the toll on certain products. It justified its decision by citing an "irresistible popular current: 'the people at that time, by a general and as it were contagious movement had formed the pretention to be discharged from all the subsidies that are weighing on them. The goodness of Their Majesties [the queen regent and the king] had excited these hopes.'"[81] Quite generally, "the discharge of taxes for one parish created an image in the whole *élection* of a king enlightened by the misery in the countryside, of the cessation of taxes, and of the departure without return of the armed tax collectors."[82]

In these cases, it seems that the abolition of one tax made people believe that it reflected the king's understanding that the whole system was flawed. When refusing to pay other taxes, they were simply anticipating and preempting the king's decisions. In other cases, as Tocqueville argued, the abolition made the taxes that had not been abolished seem more intolerable than previously. A third possibility, instantiated in the struggle between the Court and the *parlements* (see above), but not to my knowledge in popular riots before 1789, is that a concession might signal weakness and invite demands for more concessions. In 1789, however the reforms on August 4 may well have had this effect (Volume 3).

The political and administrative elites were under no illusion in this respect. They knew that the misery of the people was avoidable, caused by deliberate royal policies, and they knew that the kings knew. Some of them spoke truth to power, while others wrote eloquent denunciations that may never have reached the king. Six examples follow, taken from the reigns of Louis XIV and of Louis XVI. To my knowledge, nothing comparably explicit and harsh exists for the reign of Louis XV.[83]

79. Bercé (1974), p. 362.
80. Ibid., p. 590.
81. Ibid., p. 486.
82. Ibid., p. 611.
83. Malesherbe's short remonstrance from 1771 might count as an exception, but it is far less harsh and detailed than his great remonstrance from 1775 (both reproduced in Malesherbes 2008). The journal of d'Argenson (e.g., vol. 2, p. 149, see also Alem 2015, chap. 4) is explicit in its many descriptions of the horrors in the countryside, but was not written for publication.

In *Le détail de la France*, Boisguilbert wrote that "the main cause
of the reduction of the possessions (*biens*) in France is that in
both the ordinary and extraordinary means that are used to raise
money for the king, one considers the relation of the Prince to
France like that of an enemy country, or *a country that one is
never going to see again*, in which one does not find it unusual to
destroy a house worth 10,000 *écus* in order to sell 20 or 30 *pistoles*
worth of lead or to burn the wood."[84]

In *La dîme royale*, Vauban offers a similar example: "The *Taille* is one
of the causes of this ill [the reduction by one third of the yields of
the land over the previous 30 or 40 years], not that it is always and
at all times too high; but because it is levied unequally, not only
from parish to parish, but from one person to another; in other
words, it has become arbitrary, with no proportion between the
property of the taxpayer to his *taille*. Moreover, it is levied with
extreme rigor and at so great expense that it is certain that the
costs amount at least to a quarter of the tax. It is even common to
push the tax collection as far as unhinging the doors of the houses,
after having sold everything inside, and one has seen houses
demolished to take the beams, joists, and planks, sold for one fifth
or one sixth of their value."[85]

In 1693, the theologian Fénelon, who some twenty years later almost
became the guiding spirit of the prince who was expected to be
the next king of France (the prince died), wrote an anonymous
letter to Louis XIV in which he denounced the flaws of the reign
and of the king in extraordinarily strong and vigorous language:
"Your people, which you ought to love as your children and which
up to now have loved you with such passion, are dying of hunger.
Cultivation of the lands is almost abandoned. The towns and
the countryside are depopulating. All the trades languish and no

---

84. Boisguilbert (1707), p. 120. One pistole equaled 3 1/3 *écus*. In the phrase I have
italicized, Boisguilbert implies that the king behaved like a roving rather than a stationary
bandit (Olson 1991). Not only did the tax administration seize the possessions of the people,
but also caused there to be less to be seized (Félix 1999, p. 8). For other complaints that the
subjects of the king were treated like an enemy population, see Balzac (1665), p. 186 and
Esmonin (1913), pp. 47, 124.

85. Vauban (2007), pp. 766–767. The kings also wasted their own property in this manner. In 1693, "the gold and silver service of the king was melted down, a ruinous operation
[which] sacrificed the value of the handiwork" (Lüthy 1998, p. 97). In 1709, Louis XIV carried out the same operation (see below); his finance minister, also tried, unsuccessfully, to
use the royal jewelry as collateral for a loan (Lüthy 1998, pp. 223, 227).

longer nourish the workers. All commerce is destroyed. As a result, you have destroyed half of the real strength within your State, to make and defend vain conquests abroad. The whole of France is no more than a great poorhouse, desolate and without provision."[86] Although Fénelon blames the king's teachers and advisors for his bad policies, this language may have been tactical. He denounces the war against Holland in the 1670s, which he cites as "the source of all the ills of France," motivated only by the personal "glory and vengeance" of the king. The king probably never saw the letter, but his (secret) wife Madame de Maintenon, who had a strong influence on him, may have read it. It is the best indictment of the old regime, and notably of Louis XIV, that I have read.[87]

In 1712, Saint-Simon wrote a (much longer) anonymous letter to the king, perhaps inspired by Fénelon. Although, like him, he denounces the disastrous state of the kingdom, he overwhelmingly (a word here to be taken literally) concentrates on the causes of the misery, which he finds in the decision-making machinery of the royal government. He tells Louis XIV that he had become "the prisoner of [his] ministers" and that when he occasionally (one time out of twenty) refused to follow them, it was only to show or to pretend that he was the master.[88] Like Fénelon's, his letter probably never reached the king, but may have been read by one of his ministers or by Madame de Maintenon.

---

86. Fénelon (1983), p. 547.

87. It should be read together with his detailed reform program from 1711, the so-called "Tables de Chaulnes" (Fénelon 1997, pp. 1085–1106), which he wrote for his former pupil the Duke of Burgundy, then expected to be the next king of France (he died in 1712). His detailed proposals for change reveal much of what he thought defective in the regime. In his biography of Louis XIV, Bluche (1986a) systematically discredits the judgments of Fénelon (see notably pp. 670–675). For the non-specialist that I am, the biography seems biased by a desire to rehabilitate the king; for a specialist assessment along the same lines, see Dubief (1987). Another biographer claims that Fénelon, "presenting himself as the anti-Machiavelli, ignores that politics is tragic" and that "the nature of 'the political,' which is to preserve the fate of a human community in the face of the greed of its neighbors, escapes him completely" (Petitfils 2014 a, p. 564). This seems wrong, since Fénelon blames Louis XIV mainly for instigating the war against Holland, which was due to *his* greed (and desire for glory). Once that war had mobilized a European alliance against him, he did indeed have to defend himself, but that fact can hardly exculpate him. The assessment by Chaussinand-Nogaret (2002), p. 96, seems more accurate: "war exercised a pathological fascination on Louis XIV, since his ego took pleasure in the defeat and humiliation of enemies." Like many nobles, he suffered from *hubris* (see note 109 to chapter 1).

88. Saint-Simon (1994), pp. 371–372. The letter should be read together with his "Projet de government du Duc de Bourgogne" (in Saint-Simon 1996).

In May 1775, Malesherbes, as president of the tax court, wrote long
remonstrances that, rather than being, as was usually the case, a
response to a specific royal edict,[89] amounted to an indictment
of all aspects of the tax system of kingdom. According to Elisabeth
Badinter, "nobody had [previously] taken apart with so much
subtlety the mechanism of the administration and the system
of oppression that defined it."[90] In one of many poignant and
audacious remarks, Malesherbes writes: "Sire, one praises and at
the same time implores your benevolence; but, as defenders of the
People, we must appeal to your justice. We know that almost all
the sentiments to which the soul of a king is susceptible, the love
of glory, of pleasures, even of friendship, the natural desire of a
great Prince to provide for the happiness of those who approach
him, constitute perpetual obstacles to the rigorous justice he owes
to his people, because it is only at the expense of his People that a
king can be victorious over his enemies, magnificent in his Court,
and benevolent towards those who surround him."[91] He goes on
to spell out in great detail the tyrannical and arbitrary behavior
of the tax authorities, and recommends that the king order the
tax farmers to publish precise and detailed schedules for the taxes
they levy. Yet, he writes, "we must warn Your Majesty that the
Tax Farmers will perhaps only reluctantly lend themselves to this
publicity, and this reluctance itself will prove its necessity."[92]
On April 30, 1776, Turgot wrote a remarkable letter to Louis XVI
that, unlike those of Fénelon and Saint-Simon, was certainly
read by the addressee and may have contributed to Turgot's fall a
few weeks later. The principal minister Maurepas had proposed
to replace Malesherbes, who had resigned from his post in the
government, by Maurepas's notoriously incompetent nephew
Amelot. Turgot asks, "Sire, do you know to which point M. de

89. When, following the death of Louis XIV, the *parlements* regained their right to
write remonstrances, it was stipulated that they could protest only against the edicts that
had been submitted to them (Flammermont 1888–1898, vol. 1, p.xxxvii). I do not know
whether this restriction was lifted or simply fell into disuse.

90. Badinter (2008), p. 103.

91. Malesherbes (2008), pp. 180–181. Shortly after presenting this remonstrance to the
king, Malesherbes was appointed minister. Turgot managed to keep it secret, because he
thought it would undermine tax collection (Gomel 1892, vol. 1, p. 473), but it was leaked
in 1778.

92. Ibid., pp. 187–888. The "perhaps" was a manner of speaking; nothing was more
certain.

Maurepas has a weak character? To which point he is dominated by the ideas of those whom he sees often? . . . This weakness has created a singular variability in my relations to M. de Maurepas. My character, being more cutting than his, must naturally offend him, although at first my outward timidity may have offered some compensation. . . . *Never forget, Sire, that it was weakness that put the head of Charles I on the butcher's block* . . . and caused all the misfortunes of the [reign of Louis XV]."[93] Because of the weakness that eventually put *his* head under the guillotine, the king did not take Turgot's advice. As the Abbé de Véri wrote about a discussion he had with Maurepas, "it is useless to offer strong recommendations to those who do not have them in their soul."[94]

Even the vast majority of the educated elite who did not speak or whisper truth to power were probably under few illusions about the king. McManners affirms that the parish priests were not taken in: "The hoary pretence that it was evil councilors misleading the good king was a device to avoid the smack of treason in public complaints: in their registers, the *curés* revealed what they really thought."[95]

It seems likely that ordinary people viewed him as fundamentally good, although misled by his ministers.[96] For us, it may seem obvious that their blame implicitly extended to the king, at least for his bad choice of advisors.[97] We probably have to accept the fact—even if we (that is, I) cannot understand it—that during most of the old regime most of the French

93. Véri (1928), pp. 454–455; my italics.

94. Véri (1930), p. 119; see also Tocqueville (2011), p. 149, for a similar comment on Louis XV.

95. McManners (1998), vol. 2, p. 709.

96. Lavisse (1989), pp. 323–324. Fénelon asserts (1983), p. 547 on the contrary, that the people believed that "the king had no pity for their ills, that [he] only loved [his] own authority and glory," citing as evidence that the "popular insurrections, unknown for such a long time, are becoming frequent." As I note in the text, it would seem logical (to us) for the people to infer the responsibility of the king for choosing and maintaining in power the ministers or officials who enacted the policies that caused the insurrections, but there seems to be little direct evidence to support this inference.

97. "The first opinion which one forms of a prince, and of his understanding, is by observing the men he has around him; and when they are capable and faithful he may always be considered wise, because he has known how to recognize the capable and to keep them faithful" (Machiavelli, *The Prince*, chap. 22). Spanheim (1973), p. 53, makes a distinction between the king's ministers and his favorites, claiming that it's only by his choice of the latter that one can "recognize the nature of a prince, his *strength* and his *weakness*." He cites as examples the predilection of Louis XIV for the Comte de Lauzun, an adventurer, and for the Duc de la Rochefoucald, the mediocre son of the moralist. Petitfils (2008), p. 163, asserts that among the kings, only Henri IV did not have favorites.

believed unconditionally in the virtue and the wisdom of their kings, and even in their supernatural healing powers. Some of their glowing praise for "the best of kings" may have been cant[98] or *langue de bois*, but it would almost certainly be a mistake to impute to them hypocrisy on the scale found, for instance, in Communist regimes.

The kings tended naturally to encourage measures that would promote the unquestioning belief of their subjects in their goodness, and to suppress measures that would undermine it. Concerning encouragements, Madame Palatine wrote in a letter from 1701 that one day "I asked a person who should know, why all published writings praise the king. The answer was that printers have been told not to print any book that did not contain praise of the king, and that because of his subjects. The French usually read much, and as people in the provinces read everything that comes from Paris, the praise of the king inspires respect and consideration for him. That is why it is done, and not because of the king, who never sees [the books]."[99] Priests, too, were told to end their sermons with a couplet praising the king.[100]

Towards the end of the regime, however, the belief in the goodness and saintliness of the king came to be undermined. Marc Bloch reports a tell-tale change from the indicative to the subjunctive, when under Louis XV the traditional formula for the royal healing by touch, "The king touches you, God heals you," was replaced by "The king touches you, may God heal you." As he also notes, the government now published information about the number of successful royal healings, as if it felt the need to propagandize.[101] In 1766 Louis XV pronounced a dramatic "flagellation speech" in which he asserted, against the *parlement*, that "the rights and interests of the nation . . . are necessarily united with my own." As one of his biographers says, this dressing-down of the courts "spoke volumes about the crisis of power, which by this gloss seemed to strip itself of its mystery."[102] When absolute power has to be asserted rather than deployed, it is

98. Young (1794), vol. 1, p. 10, writes that "Travellers speak very much, even very late ones, of the remarkable interest the French take in all that personally concerns their King, shewing by the eagerness of their attention not only curiosity, but love. Where, how, and in whom those gentlemen discovered this I know not.—It is either misrepresentation, or the people are changed in a few years more than is credible." This observation from 1787 is relevant for the analysis of the Revolution, but not for the old regime as a whole.

99. Palatine (1985), p. 312.

100. Apostolidès (1981), p. 137.

101. Bloch (1983), pp. 397–405.

102. Petitfils (2014b), p. 681.

forfeited.[103] Although Louis XV may not have been the object of hatred, he "died under contempt,"[104] as evidenced (see above) by the small number of masses held for him when he was dying. In an entry from 1776, Véri writes, "[w]e are getting used to view the king as the manager (*homme d'affaires*) of the nation. . . . I have seen in my youth how the word *king* made the same impression on old officers as the word *God* did on the most religious minds. For them, this word justified everything and could lead to anything. It made them thrown themselves blindly into danger, with a kind of satisfaction. Today, the soldier wants to judge the king's intention, like that of any other man."[105] Like children who "believe" in Santa Claus yet ask their parents about the price of the Christmas gifts,[106] the subjects of the king were in an unstable state of half-belief, half-disbelief that is hard to capture in analytical terms. I shall pursue this issue in Volume 3.

Concerning repressive measures, a main concern of the kings was to prevent the *parlement* from criticizing them publicly.[107] Louis XIV successfully reduced the courts to passive instruments for registering the laws and verifying their consistency with earlier legislation. He did not tolerate protestations. For reasons I discuss later, the courts regained strength under the successor regimes (the regency and the two reigns), leading to a tug of war between the courts and the royal administration. Among the many dimensions of conflict, the question of publicity became increasingly important. As I noted, prior to 1753 the remonstrances were for the most

---

103. Gomel (1892), vol. 1, p. 26; Rocquain (1878), p. 257; see also ibid., pp. 217–218 on an earlier attempt by Louis XV to assert his "absolute power." In 1771 he ended the edict suppressing the *Grand Conseil* by saying "I shall *never* change" (Hardy, vol. 2, p. 227), as if thumping the table could make it so. This feature of the royal power was recognized by some officials at the time. In 1759, Chancellor Lamoignon wrote to the finance minister, Silhouette, that "to try to justify [the king's authority] is to cast doubt on it" (cited in Antoine 1970, p. 34).

104. Vovelle (1987), p. 84.

105. Véri (1930), pp. 8–9; see also ibid., p. 79, where he notes that "the popular love for the royal family has diminished prodigiously," citing as evidence the lack of popular expression of joy at the birth of a child of the king's brother. I have already referred to the "silence of the people."

106. Veyne (1976), p. 699.

107. In Burgundy, the provincial Estates and the royal government at various times tried to prevent publication of the "remarks" of the *alcades*, a body scrutinizing and sometimes criticizing the work of the administration (Thomas 1844, pp. 22–23; Swann 2003, p. 82). Their recommendations were not binding and were usually ignored, but it was "feared their publication might invite opposition" (Swann, ibid.). When the intermediate commission of the Estates (the *élus*) was "tempted to tolerate the expedient of raising loans without assigning revenue for their future reimbursement [and interest]" (ibid., p. 189), the *alcades* denounced the practice. "[The] mere presence of these criticisms of financial malpractice was a . . . source of reassurance for the investors" (ibid.).

part not published.[108] When that practice took hold, the courts spoke not only to the king, but also, sometimes mainly, to the general public. Louis XV disliked the publicity intensely, partly for reasons of state. According to Finance Minister Bertin, "The publicity of the *parlement's* resistance [to tax increases] was prompting Dutch, German, and Swiss financiers to lend money to England instead of France."[109] Other officials argued, however, that domestic concerns were more important. "The disparity between the negative image of the king that was being cultivated by the magistrates and the more benign image in the mind of the public rendered the remonstrances libelous."[110] In 1771, speaking in the king's name, the chancellor told the magistrates that they should be *"more zealous to do good than to appear to do good,* and not give [their] protestations a publicity that they should never have."[111] As noted earlier, the courts did indeed seek popularity by "appearing to do good," notably by refusing to register new taxes that would hurt the population at large as well as their own members. Thus "the powerful milieu of the high magistracy opposed the state technocracy, the latter pushing for innovation and the former fiercely defending the status quo under the mask of the general interest. . . . Without intending to, through the extravagant claims of the courts the great elites thus produced the 'revolutionary education' of their fellow citizens."[112]

The *parlement* did not like being scolded in public by Louis XV any more than he liked its public opposition. In the flagellation session of March 3, 1766, the minister Fleury read, in the king's presence, a declaration that denounced the recent remonstrances of the various *parlements* in the country and notably their pretention to form a single body that constituted the organ of the nation and the protector of its rights. In the king's view, this was "to forget that the courts owe their existence and authority only to [himself]." On March 8, a deputation of forty magistrates

108. In the mid-seventeenth century, the *debates* in the *parlement* were to some extent open to the public (Lavisse 1989, p. 35), generating a "formidable resonance board" (Bertière 1990, p. 198). This mode of publicity contributed to rousing urban crowds in the *Fronde*, but I have not seen any references to it for the later part of the old regime. Despite the general regime of censorship, lawyers had the privilege of publishing consultations written for their clients. In the struggle over the *Unigenitus*, this channel "operated a transfer of the internal problems of the Church into the politics of the kingdom" (Félix 1999, p. 85).

109. Kwass (2000), p. 173; see also ibid. pp., 179–180, 185; and Antoine (1989), p. 793.

110. Kwass (2000), p. 174.

111. Hardy, vol. 2, p. 230, my italics; see also ibid., pp. 154, 359. In its reply, the tax court said that "the reproach against the court that it had given too much publicity to its remonstrances shows the interest of those who surround our Lord-King in stifling the voice of the public and in preventing their behavior from being enlightened" (Grosclaude 1961, p. 240).

112. Nicolas (2008), p. 193.

complained of the *publicity* of the king's declaration and of the damage done to the *honor* of the *parlement* by the haste of the procedure. On March 10, the king responded curtly that "the expressions of my will are made to be known and public, whereas your deliberations ought to be kept secret."[113] On November 28, 1770, Louis XV issued an edict that amounted to a stronger version of the flagellation speech, and that eventually led to the collective demission of the magistrates. The public prosecutor, who was in an awkward intermediary position between the Court and the *parlement*, "humbly pleaded with [His] Majesty not to *publish a law that would become a monument of shame* for all the bodies that constitute the magistracy of your kingdom."[114] In both cases, the objections concerned the dishonor and shame that would follow from the publicity of the edicts, not their substance.

I shall cite some further examples that turn on the effects of secrecy and publicity, and on the choices undertaken to produce or to prevent them.

In 1775, Turgot took measures to alleviate the grain crisis in Champagne, by according a subsidy to importers. He wanted this measure to be kept secret from the exporting regions, where it might create a fear of penury, but be announced publicly in Champagne. However, the *intendant* in Champagne expressed his "fear that the announcement of these subsidies would trigger a fear of famine, in the very province they should help. This reaction seemed incomprehensible to Turgot, and rationally it is in fact absurd. But the *intendant* in Champagne had probably not invented anything: in a highly sensitized population, the very announcement of such exceptional measures could increase the panic."[115] As in the case of the king's donation of his gold and silver, the relief measures might appear as a signal that the situation was worse than one had thought.

Many believed that grain crises were due to hoarding by speculators, and suspected that Louis XV enriched himself personally in this manner, at the expense of his people. Véri, for instance, writes that "[t]he people says that the king and [the family of his mistress] have been profiting from the grains."[116] The belief was false,[117] but the king seems to have done his best to encourage it. Thus in 1774, the bookseller Hardy reports

---

113. Hardy, vol. 1, pp. 134–140; my italics. As a matter of fact, Louis XV sometimes abstained from giving full publicity to decisions he feared might be unpopular (ibid., pp. 216–217; also Hardy, vol. 2, p. 694; and, for an earlier part of his reign, Argenson, vol. 7, p. 124).

114. Hardy, vol. 1, p.786; my italics.

115. Faure (1961), p. 235.

116. Véri (1928), p. 75.

117. Antoine (1989), p. 609–610.

that one can "read on p. 553 in the Royal Almanac for the present year 1774, not without astonishment and not without being penetrated by pain, [the entry] *Treasurer of grains for the account of the King* [with his name and address]. This did not fail to arouse many mutterings in the public." A month later Hardy writes that "[o]ne learns that by the order of the government, *another page has been substituted* for p. 553 in the Royal Almanac, where one read for the first time the name and the address of Sieur Mirlavaud, treasurer of grains for the account of the king; one even affirms that Sieur Mirlavaud has lost his position, which has been given to a less well-known person. Unfortunately, this new arrangement, dictated by politics, did not destroy the first impression that the reading of this imprudent entry made on all the minds."[118] One might reasonably conjecture that this clumsy attempt to hide the facts was seen as a tacit admission of guilt, thus not merely not destroying but reinforcing an impression that might otherwise have faded. The substitution in the *Great Soviet Encyclopedia* of "the Bering Strait" for "Beria" after the latter's death comes to mind.

The royal government encountered a dilemma also found in other autocratic systems: public denunciation of critics of the regime may spread their views. Under Communism, if modernist painters were to be criticized, their works had to reproduced and hence made known.[119] Similarly, Barbier notes in his journal that the legal condemnation of the *Encyclopédie* allowed people to understand "the systems of deism, materialism, irreligion" by reading the thirty pages of the indictment rather than having to plow through the seven volumes of the work.[120] Elsewhere he comments on the publication of *Ne Repugnate*, an erudite work written under the guidance of the finance minister Machault that was directed against the tax-exemption of the clergy. In a condemnation of the book that was "put up on the street corners," Louis XV ordered its suppression as containing statements contrary to the honor of the clergy. In reality, the book was *published only to be condemned*, since the condemnation would

118. Hardy, vol. 3, pp. 305, 340; my italics.

119. Zinoviev (1981), p. 134. In Turkey in 1960, "many people first learned of various incidents when headlines announced a ban on publication of news about them" (Shibutani 1966, p. 59). More generally, "[p]eople sometimes confuse the denial with the charge. Those who had not heard the charge may hear the denial and may find the latter unconvincing." (ibid., p. 200–201).

120. Barbier, vol. 7, pp. 129–130. For another example, see Barbier, vol. 8, p. 41. Droz (1860), vol. 1, p. 65 writes that by confiscating books, the government, the *parlements*, and the Church "only excited the enthusiasm of the public for indestructible books, or channelled its curiosity to pamphlets whose existence it would have ignored."

create "a prejudice against the clergy in a public that does not read this kind of book."[121]

Secrecy can, in some circumstances, amount to publicity. For instance, a person who demands a secret vote can, by making that demand, enable others to infer how she will vote. More generally, the charge "The very fact that you want to keep something secret—as in 'taking the Fifth'—reveals that you have something to hide" is a powerful one, and often difficult to rebut. When a memorandum to the king from 1650 affirmed that the clergy evaded paying taxes on its vast properties, "[t]he clergy complained loudly about the rumors that circulated about its wealth, claiming that they were inspired by envy and impiety, and did not perceive that if anything substantiated the rumors, it was the extreme aversion it showed on all occasions to shed light on the extent of its possessions."[122] As noted earlier, this aversion permeated the old regime. The reason may not always have been that those who refused cadasters and verifications possessed *more* than they would admit. As we saw, Saint-Simon suggested that they might well possess *less*.

Until the publication in 1781 of Necker's *Compte rendu au roi*,[123] the finances of the old regime were shrouded in secrecy and, as noted earlier, in ignorance. Since these were in a permanent state of near-bankruptcy, the secrecy was justified both by the need to keep foreign enemies in the dark about the state of finances of the country and by the fear of discouraging lenders to the crown. Also, as the minister of justice said in 1734, "It is a rule of royal authority never to reveal what the king can do in France; soon it would become known what he cannot do."[124] When the *parlements* protested against new taxes or the maintenance of wartime taxes in peace, they had no way of knowing whether these measures were needed.[125] As one magistrate noted, they "discussed always on the basis of possibilities, appearances and [abstract] reasoning" rather than of objective facts.[126]

121. Barbier, vol. 4, p. 443. Marion (1891), p. 242, reads Barbier as affirming that the publication and condemnation of the book was intended to make more people *read* it. This seems unlikely. As in the condemnation of the *Encyclopédie*, the legal action simply made the public aware of the overall thrust of an erudite work; unlike that case, this effect was also the intended one.

122. Marion (1891), p. 205.

123. The accuracy of this work, which pretended to report revenues and expenses correctly, is still contested.

124. Argenson, vol. 1, p. 199.

125. Gomel (1892), vol. 1, p. 20; Swann (1995), p. 189.

126. Swann (1997), p. 336. Félix (1999), p. 15, writes that "the government found it more and more difficult to cover up the state of the finances. The establishment of new taxes, the sale of offices, and the emission of loans sufficed to allow observers to infer the difficulties." Observers and reformers could not infer, however, the actual numbers that would have

When the protestations were made public, the king did not (and, as noted above, often could not) provide facts and figures to contradict them.

Bottom-up beliefs could also target ministers, the Court nobility, and local authorities. For people in the French countryside, only the tax collector, the priest, and the *seigneur* (or his farmer and his judge) were the target of focused beliefs. As I discussed earlier, many of these could be stated in terms of the presence or absence of a quid pro quo. The *seigneur*, for instance, could be viewed either as a protector against the tax collector or as an additional predator. Beyond the level of the parish, the authorities— the governor of the province, the *intendant, élus* and other venal officials, deputies to the provincial Estates where these existed—were mostly too remote for ordinary people to have any clear idea of who they were and what they did. Here and there, an individual might be known and detested for his harshness, but not because of the category to which he belonged.[127] A fortiori, the same held for the king's ministers. Although the peasants often blamed them their misery, the charge was not supported by an articulated causal belief. Somebody had to be responsible; since it could not be the king, it had to be his ministers.

At a more abstract level, people might have more or less precise beliefs about the laws and the tax regulations to which they were subject. From Boisguilbert to Malesherbes, the lack of transparency was a major complaint against the system. For Boisguilbert, *uncertainty* about what one owed in taxes and the arbitrariness that followed from the uncertainty were the main flaws.[128] Almost any mechanical and non-manipulable procedure for assessing and collecting taxes was preferable, he argued, to a discretionary system that invited favoritism and led to waste by

---

allowed them to make constructive proposals. The constant demand for economies in the administration was an idling idea in the absence of any knowledge of the actual expenses. When after 1756 the *parlement* of Toulouse argued that the king's demand that taxpayers "declare their property and thus reveal the secret of their fortune obliged the royal government, by a principle of reciprocity, to also unveil the secret of its finances" (Jouanna 2014 d, p. 583), it was surely because the magistrates knew that the government would do no such thing. Similarly, if the *parlements* seemed to commit political suicide by demanding the Estates-General, it was because they were confident that the government would never dare to convoke them (Petitfils 2005 b, p. 584). When the princes of the blood demanded the Estates-General, it was only as a threat directed against the *parlements* (Pillorget and Pillorget 1995, p. 516). Such empty threats and demands were a regular feature of what substituted for politics in the *ancien régime*.

127. Venal tax officials were an exception (Bercé 1974, pp. 391–392): they were seen as purely parasitic.

128. Boisguilbert (1707), pp. 29–35.

generating disincentives to production, investment, and trade. Commenting on the tax farming, Malesherbes wrote that "the code of the [Tax Farm] is immense, and is not written anywhere. It is an occult science, which no one, except the financiers, have studied or been able to study, so that when a private person is the object of litigation, he can neither know for himself the Law to which he is subject, nor consult anyone: he must have recourse to the Clerk who is his adversary and his persecutor."[129] More generally, the old regime allowed for a "retained justice" (*justice retenue*), by which the king at any time could take a process out of the ordinary legal system and have it judged by *évocation* (chapter 4).[130] Apart from the inherent injustice of the practice, the uncertainty surrounding it generated inefficiency.

Horizontal Belief Formation

I now turn to instances of horizontal mechanisms of belief formation.

The beliefs that might trigger rebellions or riots include not only beliefs about the actions of hierarchical superiors, such as royal officials or *seigneurs*, but also, as explained in the Introduction, about the actions of horizontal peers in the same community or elsewhere. Before I consider the latter beliefs, I shall place them in a more general context.

The old regime saw a large number of isolated insurrections, riots, or smaller "emotions." There were also many spatial or temporal *clusters* of such events. Prior to 1789, the most important clusters occurred around 1630–1640 and in 1775 (the "Flour War"). According to Bercé, "the blaze of local insurrections [in 1635] that from the Loire to the Pyrénées stopped all tax payments . . . seems to form the most important insurrectional epidemic of the *ancien régime*."[131] Faure characterizes the Flour War as "a series of chain disorders that followed one another in a very rapid rhythm."[132] Both statements seem to presuppose a particular causal pattern, that of a *chain reaction* in which one "emotion" causes another, which would otherwise not have taken place. There are, however, two

---

129. Malesherbes (2008), p. 167.

130. Marion (1923), p. 226, defends *évocations* by the king against the *parlements* using the same argument that Malesherhes (1964, p. 72) as well as his great-grandson Tocqueville (2011, p. 108) used to defend the *parlements* against the king: they were an intrinsic evil that limited an even greater one. Given that *both* the government and the *parlements* often behaved in an arbitrary fashion, one might thus justify the encroachment of either on the domain of the other. The issue may be unresolvable.

131. Bercé (1974), p. 296.

132. Faure (1961), p. 249.

CHAIN REACTION

INSTIGATOR

INDEPENDENT, SIMULTANEOUS EVENTS (E.G. HARVESTS)

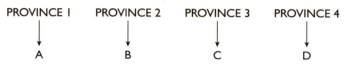

FIGURE 3.1. Patterns of events.

other possible patterns: an *orchestration* of the several local events by a deliberate instigator and the existence of *independent, simultaneous events* that, without any intentional coordination, might produce the same effect in many localities.[133] The three patterns are illustrated in Figure 3.1.

The most "common common" cause was probably the imminence of the harvest, which took place more or less at the same time in the various parts of a province or even in France as a whole. Just before the harvest, the dearth or the high price of grain might produce many local "emotions," which did not causally influence each other and were not traceable to one intentional agent. The tax collections could also serve as a common cause. Referring to the insurrections in Perigord in 1637, Bercé writes that "they were above all independent of each other. Each of them arose spontaneously, extended over a few days and a few miles, and ended also in isolation. Their simultaneity, their chronological coincidence at the end of April . . . corresponds only to the fiscal calendar and to the departure of tax commissions to the countryside."[134] Referring to tax revolts in 1675, Lavisse writes that "There was no coordination (*entente*) among these 'emotions' that occurred because of the same causes and at the same time. Brittany, Guyenne, Rennes, and Bordeaux act each by itself, they do not know each other. The scattered fires are not united into a general blaze."[135]

---

133. As we shall see in Volume 3, rebellions could also be triggered by *simultaneous but independent chain reactions*. This was notably the pattern of the Great Fear of 1789.

134. Bercé (1974), p. 442.

135. Lavisse (1989), p. 323.

In a footnote, Lavisse adds, however, that "in each province news from the neighboring provinces could encourage the rebels. . . . The military commander in the Angoumois, La Vieuville, wrote in May 1675 that 'the extreme poverty of the people, together with the impunity of its neighbors in Bordeaux and Bretagne, has persuaded them that they only had to oppose the execution of the recent [tax] edicts to be discharged from them.'" Commenting on events in the Angoumois and in Saintonge in the 1630s, Bercé similarly writes that "depending on local circumstances and on the vagaries of passion, each spring the center of the revolt shifts from province to province. Without any idea of following up, without organization, and without a conspiracy, popular uprisings flare up and spend themselves like flames in dry grass. The revolt came from Guyenne to Saintonge, and from there to Perigord and Gascony."[136] The "scattered fires" relayed each other rather than uniting into a "general blaze." According to Faure, "what one observed everywhere [in the Flour War of 1775] are the corroborating signs of popular manifestations that were at the same time *spontaneous* and *linked* (*en chaîne*), each justifying itself by the previous one and somehow transporting itself to the date and place of the next one."[137]

John Markoff spells out some mechanisms of contagion as follows: "one revolt stimulates another as the repressive forces appear weaker than previously known [Bayesian updating], as those forces are actually weakened by failure [a causal effect], and as organizational possibilities and tactics are debated and knowledge of successful organizational models and tactics becomes widely diffused" [imitation].[138] To these essentially rational mechanisms of belief formation, we must add the effect of *rumors*.[139] Given the pervasive secrecy of the *ancien régime* and the manifest lack of credibility of most public announcements, the natural *aversion to ignorance* of the human mind favored the formation of rumors.[140] Sometimes, it is hard to tell whether rumors were used as premises for behavior or whether they approximated more closely to gossip, valued as entertainment rather than as information. Also, it can be hard to locate the strength of the belief in a rumor on the scale from the possible through the plausible

136. Bercé (1974), p. 364.

137. Faure (1961), p. 311.

138. Markoff (1996), p. 369. A recent instance of Bayesian updating occurred in the Summer of 1989, when the non-intervention of Soviet forces in Poland encouraged the Hungarian opposition.

139. For a tentative analysis, see Elster (2015a), pp. 373–379. The phenomenon of rumor seems to be understudied and ill-understood.

140. Shibutani (1966), pp. 58–59.

to the probable or certain. For these and other reasons, the Madisonian caveats that I cited in chapter 1 apply in full to the comments that follow.

Earlier, I cited a verse from La Fontaine, "Each believes easily what he fears and what he hopes." As I noted, fear-driven beliefs were certainly rampant in the old regime. The "Great Fear of 1789" is a prominent example, but there are many others, such as rumors of a tax on children, of the dissection of living bodies, of an imminent scarcity of grain due to hoarding or speculation, and many others. Hardy's journal refers endlessly to positive as well as negative rumors in Paris, including *meta-rumors:* "One heard it said . . . that all the rumors (*bruits*) circulating about a new administration of the finances had reduced confidence and brought operations on the stock exchange to a halt."[141] Somewhat absurdly (to us), in a ruling of October 1774 the *parlement* pointed out to the king "that the rumors which have announced for a long time a project to destroy the *parlement* have reached such a level of notoriety that they keep the population in a state of fermentation that is harmful to the administration of justice and public tranquility," and asked for permission to meet with him. The king responded curtly that he was surprised that the court would render a ruling about rumors.[142] Argenson and Barbier, too, report numerous rumors, but unlike Hardy (and Véri) do not often question their plausibility.

Even when *émotions* had a common cause or were part of a chain reaction, the authorities often jumped to the conclusion that they were orchestrated.[143] Writing about the rural insurrections in the seventeenth century, Bercé observes that "the similarity of local situations [*common cause*] or the propagating function of travelers [*chain reaction*] may suffice to explain the dimension of the troubles, but this could not satisfy the contemporary official opinion, which tried to discover the existence of a conspiracy. . . . One wanted to find instigators among the local . . . officials or squires and, through them, recognize the troubles as the effect of high political intrigue [*orchestration*] rather than a popular antifiscal protest."[144] Just as the peasants imputed a dearth of grain to a malevolent agency rather than to a bad harvest, the "official opinion" imputed the decentralized revolts caused

141. Hardy, vol. 4 (2013), p. 391.

142. Hardy, vol. 4 (2012), pp. 632–633, 639.

143. The tendency to see a hidden hand behind uncoordinated actions was also observed in nineteenth-century France (Ploux 2003) or in eighteenth-century America (Anderson 2001, pp. 546, 561).

144. Bercé (1974), p. 357. Pernot (2012), pp. 91, 133, finds a similar tendency to interpret the urban insurrections in Paris of 1648 and 1649 as orchestrated. In 1649, the machinations of (the later) Cardinal de Retz did in fact stir up the people, but they came to nothing; see also D'Ormesson (1860–1861), vol. 1, pp. 695, 699.

by the bad harvests to organized plotters. Similar patterns recurred in the Flour War of 1775. The usually sober-minded Véri and Turgot both believed that it must have been due to a conspiracy.[145] Hardy writes that "one did not think that since the beginning of the French monarchy one had ever seen anything like the event one had the misfortune of witnessing; and one desired ardently that its principal instigators could be discovered. The plot seems to have been hatched with much art and secrecy."[146]

The imputations of dearth of grain to self-interested agents who were indifferent to the plight of the people were sometimes true.[147] The imputations of local riots to a hidden conspirator were *never* true. Why, then, did observers make them? Faure argues that "contemporaries were struck by the relatively reasonable and conscientious character of the [successive flour riots]. This nuance of *order in the disorder* appeared as a sign of premeditation and orchestration."[148] Bercé makes a similar comment on the riots in Bordeaux on May 14, 1635. There were signs of bourgeois complicity or at least passivity, and some "even talked about instigation, imagining a vast plot whose actors had stayed in the shadows behind the appearance of an unbridled mob. People noted the kind of *bloody order* respected in the insurrection, *the limited and virtuous execution of an unwritten decision* to kill the tax officials (*gabelleurs*). . . . Perhaps one should include this theme of a bourgeois conspiracy among the false rumors that accompany times of trouble, when information is scarce and danger is imminent."[149]

These observations suggest that observers assumed that a spontaneous popular uprising would be characterized by looting, rapes, and rampant destruction, with the implication that the absence of these features pointed to a hidden organized agent who decided on victims and dictated or limited actions. As I noted in my comments on Hardy's reports about the Flour War, this assumption can be false. If agents are motivated by a sense of injustice, some actions will be out of bounds.

145. Véri (1928), pp. 288–289. For Turgot's views, see the "Instruction sent by His Majesty to all the parish priests in the kingdom," in Turgot (1844), vol. 2, pp. 192–196.

146. Hardy, vol. 4, p. 193; see also ibid., pp. 198–199, for "various suspicions regarding the main instigators of the revolt," including financiers, Jesuits, and unnamed individuals who wanted to "starve the people to put the inhabitants of the capital in a state of revolt." See also Rudé (1964), pp. 26–27, as well as the rumor cited in note 172 to chapter 2.

147. Despite the rumors cited in the previous note, the imputation to a *malevolent* agent was never true. It could nevertheless be causally efficacious.

148. Faure (1961), p. 311; my italics. Bouton (1993), p. 99, also sees "the general recourse to the *taxation populaire* [sale at a fixed low price]" as a factor that "convinced many contemporaries, and especially Turgot, that the riots were directed by a conspiracy."

149. Bercé (1974), p. 307; my italics.

In his comments on the correspondence from the deputies of Anjou to the Estates-General of 1789 to their constituencies, Tocqueville noted the following statement from July 13: "In the midst of the tumult, those imprisoned for common crimes were going to escape; the people opposed the escape, saying that criminals were not worthy of mingling with the creators of liberty. . . . If, among the armed men, someone committed some baseness, he was immediately led to prison by his comrades." Such behavior, Tocqueville added, "is particularly French."[150] Commenting on the revolution of 1848, Tocqueville similarly states that he "never expected the rich to be looted. . . . [W]e have passed through such long years of insurrection that a particular kind of *morality of disorder* and a special code for days of riot have evolved. These exceptional laws tolerate murder and allow devastation, but theft is strictly forbidden."[151] The verbal similarity of the words I have italicized with the expressions used by Faure ("order in disorder") and Bercé ("bloody order") is striking. If my analysis is correct, this self-restraint is *not* particular to the French, but a normal component in actions motivated by a sense of injustice. In eighteenth- century Massachusetts, for instance, "when riots did happen, they were *regulated by custom in a curious way.* John Adams in 1774 drew a distinction between 'public mobs' which defended the law and the constitution, and 'private mobs' which took to the streets 'in resentment of private wrongs.'"[152]

Hoarding or suspicions of hoarding could produce strong reactions in third-party observers, even if they were not personally affected. In the following passage, the first episode refers to third-party *indignation* and the following to second-party *anger*:

> In Lyon on June 14, 1653, when a man named Varillon was heard in the marketplace offering a peasant 3 livres above the going price for his entire stock of wheat, a crowd attacked him, beat him until he took refuge in a nearby house and then proclaimed that the house should be burned down because he was a hoarder. This was not an isolated incident, for six days later a sergeant was attacked and beaten to death . . . after the wife of a metal founder screamed out in public "that he was hoarder of wheat who was causing the price of grain to rise."[153]

150. Tocqueville (2001 p. 125.

151. Tocqueville (1987), p. 72. One might add, conjecturally, that the norms of rebellion allowed killings, but not rapes.

152. Fischer 1989, p. 193; my italics.

153. Beik (1997), p. 40. For the distinction between anger and indignation, due to Descartes and further developed by Adam Smith, see Elster (forthcoming). My reading of the passage as implying that the wife of the metal founder was *personally* affected by the high

I conclude this discussion by turning to another set of horizontal beliefs, concerning the tax system. First, let me contrast two statements about the establishment of the tax rolls in the village. Goubert writes that "the tax schedules were *generally honest*: how could it have been otherwise? One took turns, more or less, to be the tax collector. The village opinion substituted for the most efficient verification; each peasant passed his life spying on this neighbor, whose resources he knew perfectly."[154] Saint-Jacob writes that "for the peasant the tax is heavy, above all because it is *shared unfairly*. He is constantly comparing the quotas. The whole village knows the tax roll; the collector brings it with him into each house; there is criticism, there is discussion. This publicity of the tax burden may have been one of the most original features of the old regime; it made peasant discontent more formidable and created an active revolutionary ferment."[155] He clearly implies that some villagers were lightly taxed, and that these cases were well known and generated resentment. My impression, for what it is worth, is that Saint-Jacob's deep immersion in the life of the peasantry enabled him to perceive patterns that did not strike Goubert, who mostly focused on the towns. It is also possible, of course, that the divergence reflects the fact that they wrote about different regions and, to some extent, different periods.

Esmonin does not discuss explicitly issues of justice among the taxpayers, with the exception of the relation between the bulk of the villagers and the tax collectors they have elected. If a tax collector imposed light taxes on himself or on his family, he risked being taxed heavily by his successor.[156] This homeostatic justice mechanism presupposes that the tax amounts were *known*. By another mechanism, which does not require this knowledge, a person who believed he had been taxed too heavily could, when he came to be tax collector himself, do the same to the person who had overcharged him.[157] As he would not benefit personally, his behavior would

---

price of grain is speculative, but consistent with the fact that the punishment meted out to the second hoarder was much worse than the one suffered by the first. As noted in the Introduction, there is a considerable body of evidence that indignation induces less severe punishment than anger does.

154. Goubert (2013), pp. 152–153; my italics. Argenson, vol. 6, p. 65, asserts that when he presided over the allocation of the *taille* in a village close to Paris where he rented a house, his "presidency made everyone declare [their property] and control others with great attention and freedom."

155. Saint-Jacob (1960), p. 512; my italics.

156. Esmonin (1913), p. 331.

157. Ibid.

fall under the heading of *altruistic punishment*.[158] A tax collector might, therefore, hesitate to impose unfair taxes if he knew his action might come back to haunt him.[159] From Esmonin's discussion, however, it seems that punitive taxation was more frequently a means of hurting the collector's personal enemies (including the villagers who had elected him)[160] than an attempt to restore justice.

In the observations on a project for tax reform that I cited earlier, Turgot comments on a proposed mechanism for allocating taxes across parishes. He believes the proposal is needlessly complicated, and that the allocation can safely be left to the *intendants*. "To suppose that the *intendant* will arbitrarily increase or reduce [the tax payment of] the parishes to favor or punish the inhabitants is to show a poor understanding of men. No man charged with the administration of a province would dishonor himself publicly without an interest in doing so. The allotment takes place in the presence of officers of the finance bureau, of the *élection*, and of the tax receivers, and an *intendant* who made a considerable change in the allotment, without a motive, would be disparaged in the whole province; and what interest could he have in exposing his reputation in this way?"[161] This argument repeats, at the level of the *élection*, Goubert's argument for the parish. Corruption can be kept in check by the disinfecting sunlight of publicity. When arguing for the power of the *intendant* to impose a *taxe d'office* in the parishes (see above), Turgot does not, however, point to any such reputational mechanism.

158. Fehr and Gächter (2002). For other examples of such behavior in pre-industrial societies, see Thompson (1971) and Lefebvre (1988), p. 40, both summarized in Elster (2015a), p. 84.

159. Esmonin (1913), p. 176.

160. "As the designation was not secret, everybody feared reprisals" (Esmonin 1913, p. 172).

161. Turgot (1844), vol. 1, p. 477. Marion (1910), p. 3, endorses this view, adding that the abuses in allocating individual tax rolls were far more serious than the minor issues that arose in the allocation of the total taxes to be paid by the parishes.

CHAPTER FOUR

The Royal Government
and the Courts

IN THE PREVIOUS chapters, devoted to the psychological structures of the old regime, I did not consider the psychology of the *kings*. This topic belongs, I believe, in a more general discussion of the royal government. The psychology of absolute power, in a sense to be defined shortly, is utterly different from the psychology of ordinary citizens or subjects.

My main focus will be on the obstacles to, and constraints on, the royal will. I first consider how their power was both constrained and enhanced by unwritten constitutional laws. Second, I argue that the psychology of the kings was in a sense self-defeating, in that their search for glory caused them to make choices that tended to diminish it. Third, I discuss how royal officials, venal as well as non-venal, were unreliable tools for the implementation of policy. I conclude by discussing the mechanisms by which the courts could thwart the king's will.

Unwritten Constraints

In countries that are governed by unwritten constitutional laws, notably Great Britain, there is usually a high degree of consensus about which laws these are. In the old regime in France, the notion of the unwritten *lois fondamentales du royaume* was ill-defined and mostly used for the self-serving purposes of various groups.[1] "Everyone claimed as funda-

---

1. Antoine (1970), pp. 15–29. refers to the "maxims of the kingdom," somewhat intermediate between the fundamental laws and ordinary legislation. He cites as an example the king's obligation to work with a council. The *parlement* of Paris made an explicit distinction between "the ancient maxims of the kingdom and the fundamental laws of the

mental laws whatever they had an interest in promoting to that dignity."[2] These rhetorical claims were probably taken seriously only (or at most) by exalted nobles, members of the provincial Estates, and magistrates who tried to reconstruct the history of France from the earliest times to prove their respective (and conflicting) immemorial rights.[3]

Scholars generally agree that the only fundamental laws that were universally accepted, and for that reason were capable of having causal efficacy, were the Salic law and the ban on alienating the royal domain.[4] I shall consider the former at some length. I shall preface the discussion, however, by mentioning some other putative fundamental or near-fundamental laws. Jean-Christian Petitfils writes that kings had to marry a foreign princess since "custom forbade the king from marrying one of his subjects."[5] This custom may have played a role in preventing the young Louis XIV from marrying Mazarin's niece, Marie Manzini, and, less consequentially, from making his morganatic marriage to Madame de Maintenon known to the public.

Another unwritten norm was that kings were not responsible for debts incurred by their predecessors. Lüthy refers to "the old monarchical tradition of inaugurating a new reign by the disavowal of debts of the old one."[6] This norm, in turn, was related to the norm that no king can bind his successor, just as no British parliament can bind a subsequent one. As the death of Louis XIV approached, Saint-Simon strongly advised Philippe d'Orléans, the future regent, to declare a bankruptcy, arguing that "Any

State" (Flammermont 1888–1898, vol. 1, p. 466). One important maxim it cited denied the right of the pope, seemingly affirmed in the bull *Unigenitus*, to excommunicate the king. The alleged maxims, as most of the alleged fundamental laws, were invoked in a purely opportunistic manner.

2. Marion 1923, p. 341, citing in particular the declaration of the Paris *parlement* on May 3, 1788.

3. Lüthy (1998), p. 276; see also the discussion in chapter 5 of conflicting historical narratives in Burgundy.

4. McManners (1998), p. 21, includes the age at which the king ceased to be a minor (thirteen years in the eighteenth century). Yet unlike the Salic law, the rule that the king became major at thirteen years was *created* by an opportunistic manipulation in 1574, when the Chancelier de l'Hôpital reinterpreted the expression "major at fourteen years" as "major at the beginning of the fourteenth year" (Jouanna 1998, p. 135). Montesquieu and Diderot both criticized this sleight of hand. Barbier, vol. 1, p. 210, reports that in 1722 the regent wanted to delay by four years the age at which Louis XV became major and adds that he thought only the Estates-General could change the age and, moreover, that it would have to favor the king by *lowering* the age. The fact that he perceived the situation in this way seems to undermine McManners's claim.

5. Petitfils (2014b), p. 130.

6. Lüthy (1998), p. 27; see also the passage from Meyer (1981), p. 206, cited below.

commitment made by the previous king died with him and has no power over his successor, and our kings pay for the height of power they exercise during their life with the total impotence that follow them into the grave."[7] This putative fundamental law was not as universally accepted, however, as it was in Spain, where people were reluctant to lend money to aging kings.[8] In France, it may have been tempered by considerations of moral hazard. There is also the intriguing suggestion that the only limitation on an absolute monarch is that he cannot abdicate any of his powers.[9] Nor does his omnipotence extend beyond his lifetime, as shown by the failed attempts by Louis XIII and Louis XV to regulate the regencies that would follow their deaths. Malesherbes, finally, included judges' tenure during good behavior among the fundamental laws, whereas venality and heredity of office had only the pragmatic justification of being "more advantageous than harmful in the present situation."[10]

Herbert Lüthy argues that the "absolute monarchy did have a constitution, but it was a constitution of rent, which strongly limited the power of the king to dispose of the resources of the kingdom."[11] More specifically,

Authority is no longer divided; the power of the king, the sovereign legislator and administrator who is not accountable to anyone, is limited only by property rights, which is the only claim that can be opposed to his arbitrary power. But this notion of property undergoes an extraordinary extension, mixing with private property all vested interests (*droits acquis*) and all particular appropriations of public dues and incomes: seigneurial rights, private forms of justice, administrative, judiciary, and military functions—all becomes part of the law of direct or "eminent" property, and in lack of other justification, possession equals title. The magistracy of the eighteenth century, the vigilant guardian of vested interests and also the foremost interested party in the matter, persevered in its effort to assimilate as completely as possible privilege and private property in one homogenous block of acquired possessions. . . . In sum, the monarchy could only liberate itself from all

7. Saint-Simon, vol. 27, p. 38.

8. Véri (1930), p. 396. Jouanna (1989), p. 332, refers to "a customary juridical rule that a law given by the king lasted only for his lifetime." She does not say specifically, however, that this rule covered the edicts that established loans.

9. Pillorget and Pillorget (1995), p. 263, citing Cardin le Bret. In the Danish Regal Law from 1665 (Art. XVII), this was the only limitation on the king' power. To my knowledge, this law is the only instance of *codified absolutism*.

10. Grosclaude (1961), pp. 239, 303.

11. Lüthy (2005), p. 19.

forms of political control by renouncing, in compensation, all power to "innovate."[12]

Lavisse affirms that in 1665 Colbert wanted to abolish all venal judicial offices *without compensation*, but that the king "was incapable of such an unjust violence."[13] The kings and their ministers were certainly capable of reducing the value of judicial and financial offices by all sorts of ingenious and dishonest stratagems, constrained only by "the obligation to find circumlocutions,"[14] but the fundamental law of respecting property prevented them from carrying out naked abolitions and confiscations. Similarly, Necker justified the low salt tax in some provinces by the fact that the king was bound to keep his promises that he made when they were annexed to the kingdom several centuries earlier.[15] When the absurdity of internal tolls finally forced a reform in 1779, they were not abolished outright, but made redeemable against compensation.

Some vignettes from the end of the old regime will show how the king and his family were constrained by the charges they had sold. "If [Marie-Antoinette] wanted a simple glass of water, it had to pass successively through the hands of three or four persons, each furiously attached to [his or her] charge. At this speed, the cool water arrived lukewarm in the queen's thirsty throat."[16] These courtiers served simultaneously. Others served successively, also creating a potential for absurdity. Thus "Louis XVI's valets served by quarters [of the year]. As one of them shaved him better than the others, he wanted to unite all the charges on his head. But as this desire met obstacles on the part of his colleagues, the king decided to shave himself."[17] Madame Palatine relates an accident in which her

12. Ibid., pp. 16–17. Tax exemptions linked to the office were also seen as personal property (Kwass 2000, p. 31). Pillorget and Pillorget (1995), p. 264, affirm that "respect for private property" was the only limit to the royal power, but do not follow Lüthy in extending the notion of property to venal offices. Argenson vol. 6, p. 159, reports that when he proposed to the finance minister Machault that the amount of the *taille* paid by individuals be fixed for nine years, "he yawned and said that one would then have to indemnify the *receveurs généraux* [venal tax officers at the level of the *élection*]. What, I said, because they would be the source of fewer costs and humiliations? That would be like indemnifying executioners because one had reduced crimes by good laws."

13. Lavisse (1989), p. 327.

14. Ibid., p. 164. It would be interesting, but perhaps impossible, to determine the quantitative importance of this "civilizing force of hypocrisy" (Elster 1999, pp. 341, 402).

15. Necker (1784–1785), vol. 2, p. 37.

16. Petitfils (2005a), p. 297. Mercy-Argenteau (1874, vol.1, pp. 69, 134–135) affirms that almost all of Marie-Antoinette's monthly allowance as crown princess was siphoned off by her staff before a trickle reached her.

17. Véri (1930), p. 180.

coach overturned because the two footmen, who had bought their charges, were old and decrepit.[18] I discuss less trivial examples later, related to obstructions by the *parlements*.

I now turn to the Salic law, requiring the crown to pass from male to male and only through the male line. Unlike, for instance, the Roman emperors, the French kings derived uncontested legitimacy from having an unwritten law of succession. In Rome, "[t]here was not, as there was in the Middle Ages and under the *ancien régime*, a dynastic superstition that made the throne into the property of a determinate family, always the same and an object of faith over the centuries; a superstition that from the Merovingians to the Bourbons prevented innumerable civil wars."[19] Pascal states the issue with unsurpassed clarity:

> The most unreasonable things in the world become the most reasonable because men are so unbalanced. What could be less reasonable than to choose as ruler of a state the oldest son of a queen? We do not choose as captain of a ship the most highly born of those aboard. Such a law would be ridiculous and unjust, but because men are, and always will be, as they are, it becomes reasonable and just, for who else could be chosen? The most virtuous and able man? That sets us straight away at daggers drawn, with everyone claiming to be most virtuous and able. Let us then attach this qualification to something incontrovertible. He is the king's eldest son: that is quite clear, there is no argument about it. Reason cannot do any better, because civil war is the greatest of evils.[20]

Because of their perceived legitimacy, the French kings did not have to fear a palace revolt or a military coup. The royal troops (*la maison militaire du roi*) were not a praetorian guard. Véri applauds the decision in 1775 by Saint-Germain, the minister of war, to "cut the totality or at least the greatest part of the military forces that are only for display (*faste*). The reform will fall almost wholly on the king's military establishment."[21] There is not a hint of a suggestion that the reform might reduce the king's

18. Palatine (1989), p. 199. She adds, ironically, that "This is the advantage of these charges that are bought and sold and of the *quartiers* [persons holding the office for a quarter of the year]. For if a *quartier* performs his task well, he leaves it after three months and is replaced by another who does not perform it well. But they have bought their office; they have to exercise it."

19. Veyne (2005), p. 19; see also Veyne (1976), p. 718.

20. Pascal, *Pensée* 786, trans. Krailsheimer.

21. Véri (1928), p. 173. Faure (1961), pp. 182, 308. thinks the decision a mistake, which "would prove disastrous for the monarchy." On July 14, 1789, he argues, troops loyal to the king might have crushed the popular insurrection. It is hard to assess this counterfactual.

power. By an abuse of language, one might say, therefore, that the power of a French king was "more absolute" than the power of a Roman emperor or an oriental despot, since he had less to fear.

At the same time, the Salic law and other unwritten laws limited the freedom of action of the kings. The Roman emperors often picked a successor, usually by adopting one. The French kings could not, and did not even try. The closest approximation occurred in 1714, when Louis XIV declared that his two legitimized sons with his earlier mistress Madame de Montespan could inherit the crown, in the absence of princes of the blood. This was a clear violation of the Salic law, which required the heir to issue from a "canonically valid marriage."[22] Since there were several princes ahead of the two sons in the line of succession, the violation had mainly a symbolic significance.[23] More important, in his will Louis XIV violated another unwritten rule (if not quite an unwritten "law") when he stipulated the composition and organization of the Council of Regency after his death. The king had wanted his two legitimized sons to be members of the council, his nephew Philippe d'Orléans to have a formal presidency only, and all decisions to be taken by a majority vote. In exchange for regaining its right to make remonstrances, the *parlement* struck down the will and made Philippe d'Orléans regent with full powers.[24] The older of the two sons received as a consolation prize the charge of educating the young king, a charge he lost in the *lit de justice* that Saint-Simon describes in the triumphant passage I cited earlier.

The deal that Philippe d'Orléans struck with the *parlement* was momentous. It ended the silence that Louis XIV had imposed on the magistrates in 1673 and restored some of their nuisance powers that I discuss later. "By these concessions, which were dangerous for the royal authority, the Duc d'Orléans bought the regency from the *parlement* of Paris."[25] If Louis XIV had not written the will, Philippe d'Orléans would have become regent without any need to the rely on the *parlement*. The absolute monarchy would have been stronger. It is impossible to tell what would have happened if the will had been respected.

22. Bluche (1986a), p. 863.

23. Mainly, but not only. Over the preceding years, the royal family had seen several presumptive heirs die of smallpox and other diseases. The health of the young Louis XV was viewed as fragile.

24. Petitfils (2013), pp. 294–295. According to Saint-Simon, vol. 25, p. 20, Louis XIV was aware that his will would have no effect, knowing that the attempt by Louis XIII to organize *his* regency had also failed.

25. Flammermont (1888–1898), vol. 1, p. v.

Overall, the Salic law was immensely stabilizing. The secure position of the kings made them immune to the psychological pathologies of the "bad emperors" in Rome who were obsessed with fears and suspicions and engaged in wholesale preemptive killings of potential rivals.[26] The kings were, however, subject to other structurally induced pathologies, in addition to more idiosyncratic character flaws.[27] The psychology of the four Bourbon kings with whom I am mainly concerned here—Louis XIII through Louis XVI—was shaped, in different ways, by their internalization of the idea of absolute power.

Louis XIII reigned in a time of extreme peril for the country. In addition to being ridden by internal disturbances that threatened to escalate into a civil war, France was engaged in the Thirty Years War (1618–1648) that was almost coextensive with his effective reign (1617–1643). If he succeeded in subduing both external and internal enemies, it was only because he could rely on his extraordinarily able and ruthless minister Richelieu, without whom France might have broken up in smaller kingdoms. Louis XIII knew he was dependent on Richelieu, but as an absolute king he hated being told what to do. Since "he was neither happy being with Richelieu nor being without him, he was never happy."[28] Other details about his life leave us in no doubt that he was an extremely neurotic person.[29] Of the four kings, he is the most enigmatic, with Louis XV as a second. Louis XIV was robustly non-enigmatic, yet he embodied a basic paradox

26. Veyne (1976), pp. 716–719.

27. I mention, without assessing it, the claim that the kings were constrained by their *fear of hell*, an attitude imputed to Louis XIII (Petitfils 2008, p. 744; Pillorget and Pillorget 1995, p. 431), to Louis XIV (Palatine 1985, pp. 193, 204 and Palatine 1857, pp. 367–368; Petitsfils 2014 a, p. 232), to Louis XV (d'Argenson, vol. 2, p. 395; Marion 1891, pp. 226–27; Petitfils 2014 b, p. 364) and to Louis XVI (Roland 1798–1799, vol. 2, p. 85). For Louis XIII, the fear of damnation was caused by the fact that he, a Catholic king, allied himself with Protestants in the war against Spain. For Louis XV, it was caused by his extramarital affairs. It seems that various elements in the Church deliberately nurtured these fears for their own purposes. The case of Louis XIII is particularly interesting: he feared that fear of hell (*attrition*) was insufficient for salvation, but he could not bring himself to feel the love of God (*contrition*) that some theologians required (see Spykman 1955). Richelieu managed to calm him. Louis XV also feared that he might be damned if he died too suddenly, before receiving absolution for his sins (Croÿ 1906–1907, vol. 3, p. 97). A violent satirical verse that circulated in 1749 states that "superstition opens for you the door to hell, the only thing you fear" (Argenson, vol. 5, p. 402). During the minority of Louis XIII, the papal nuncio "used and abused Marie de Médicis's fear of hell" (Petitfils 2008, p. 147).

28. Petitfils (2008), p. 614.

29. If we disregard its psychoanalytic framework, the study by Warvick (1974) of the journal that Louis XIII's private doctor kept for the first twenty-five years of the king's life provides sufficient details to support this claim.

"What do we do? We can't let the king die, but we also can't do anything that suggests he needs saving ..."

FIGURE 4.1. The King's predicament. © Zachary Kanin / The New Yorker Collection / The Cartoon Bank.

of absolute power. Because he tended not to like the successes of his own agents, he sometimes deliberately chose less competent underlings. The basic structural fact that I shall illustrate in the following is that when an average individual was imbued with an inordinate desire for glory, he could not succeed by the route of competence. Instead, he used his equally inordinate power to remove or resist competence in others. The paradoxical result was that the means he chose defeated their end. A cartoon in the *New Yorker* (August 6 and 13, 2018) illustrates the problem.

If we are to believe the character portrait that Saint-Simon sketched after his death, Louis XIV had what amounted to an inferiority complex. In his judgment, the king was "born with a spirit below the mediocre."[30]

30. Saint-Simon, vol. 28, p.4; confirmed by Spanheim (1973), pp. 35, 39. Petitfils (2014a), p. 179, disagrees with this assessment, but nevertheless asserts that because of his "slow spirit" Louis XIV hid himself behind a mask of impassibility. Bluche (1986a),

He "feared sense (*esprit*), talent, elevated sentiments even in his generals and in his ministers," and "was tired of the superior sense and merit of his former ministers [Colbert and Louvois] and generals [Turenne and Condé]."[31] Saint-Simon also reports a story about how a woman at the Court, Mlle de Chausserai, obtained all she wanted from Louis XIV "by pretending to be idiotic, ignorant, and indifferent about everything, and giving him the pleasant feeling of being entirely superior to her in spirit."[32]

Although Saint-Simon's judgment may have been biased by his visceral dislike of Louis XIV, it can be supplemented by other statements. Véri writes that "fate gave him first two competent ministers [Colbert and Louvois] whom he had not chosen and who were only moderately to his taste. When age gave him a pretext for deciding matters himself and choosing his cooperators in the ministry, in the army, and in high office, he made nothing but mistakes and the choices he made according to his preference (*par goût*) were all bad."[33] Although Véri does not explicitly say, as does Saint-Simon, that the king chose incompetent agents *because of* their incompetence, Louis XIV himself made it clear that this was the case. Lavisse writes that he "had an almost childish fear not only of being, but of 'appearing to be,' governed. He was suspicious of anyone who was someone in his own right and who was conscious of himself (*se sentait*). He avows it frankly: 'I thought it was not in my interest to choose men with a more eminent dignity, because, needing to establish my own reputation in all domains, it was important that the public knew, by the rank of those who served me, that I did not intend to share my authority with them, and that they themselves, knowing who they were, should not conceive greater

---

pp. 726–727, argues for his superior intelligence. As I noted, his book is too close to a hagiography to carry conviction. Louis XV was probably the most gifted of the four kings, but paralyzed by indecisiveness and "modesty carried to the length of a vice" (Petitfils 2014 b, p. 448). The native talents of Louis XVI may have been non-negligible (he translated Hume and Gibbon), but he was stunted in his development by a dictatorial grandfather (Louis XV) and by a wife who held him in open contempt.

31. Saint-Simon, vol. 28, pp. 88, 91. In the case of the two generals, another factor may also have mattered: during the Fronde; both had betrayed his father.

32. Saint-Simon, vol. 30, p. 161.

33. Véri (1930), p. 225. On the king's inferiority complex towards Louvois, see also Tellier (1987), p. 427. To my knowledge, Véri had not read Saint-Simon, but he might have. Parts of the manuscript of the *Mémoires* circulated in the second half of the eighteenth century. The first (partial) publication dates from 1781, two years after the date of Véri's entry. Since the first (partial) publication of Spanheim's report also dates from 1781, it could not have been the basis for Véri's comments.

hopes than the ones I chose to give them.'"[34] According to Saint-Simon, who should always be read with a grain of salt on the topic of Louis XIV, the king also preferred to appoint very young people to important positions, to "show that he governed by himself."[35] The German ambassador Spanheim, finally, refers to the king's "immoderate and limitless desire for glory," which made him "capable of sacrificing his true interests."[36] Although Spanheim does not explicitly say so, the king's choice of inferior executants of his will would illustrate this effect. Louis XIV wanted, impossibly, both to achieve great results *and* receive sole credit for them.

Montaigne wrote that "just as we honor kings and festive days by putting on our best clothes, there are regions where they emphasize the disparity between themselves and their king and mark their total submission to him by appearing in their shabbiest clothing; as they go into the palace they put a tattered robe over the good one, so that all pomp and glory should belong to the king alone."[37] Louis XIV certainly wanted to monopolize pomp and glory, as shown in 1661 when he dismissed and tried the superintendant of finance, Nicolas Fouquet, for (among other things) having organized a feast at Vaux-le-Vicomte that surpassed in splendor anything the king had offered.[38] Intolerably, he made the king look like a poor cousin, or a "January sun." The trial of Fouquet that followed was a travesty of justice.[39]

Louis XV and Louis XVI were perhaps less obsessed with glory, but equally obsessed with having, and being perceived as having, ultimate decision-making power. Writing about Louis XV, d'Argenson says that he had "the mutinous spirit of a child, whose *amour-propre* makes him ridiculously watchful against the rumor of being governed."[40] Referring to Louis XV by the anonymous "on," the general and military writer Guibert wrote that "one prefers to entrust the troops to mediocre men, who are

34. Lavisse (1989), p. 136; also Saint-Simon, vol. 20, p. 264. The expression "se sentait" is probably taken from the comparison of Henri IV, Louis XIII and Louis XIV in Saint-Simon (1996), p. 1262. For an example, see Lavisse (1989), p. 644. After the success of the king's brother in the conduction of the war against Holland, Louis XIV made sure that he never held command again (Saint-Simon, vol. 28, p. 15; Petitfils 2014 a, p. 415). Saint-Simon (vol. 13, p. 392) affirms, more generally, that the king was "not inclined to give his blood relatives the command of his armies, lest they aggrandize themselves."

35. Saint-Simon, vol. 16, p. 487; also vol. 14, p. 247; and vol. 20, pp. 264, 278.

36. Spanheim (1973), pp. 40, 255.

37. Montaigne (1990), p. 648.

38. Bluche (1986a), pp. 155–156; Petitfils (2005b), p. 358; Bertière (2013), pp. 244–246. This interpretation of Fouquet's fall is contested by other historians.

39. Dessert (1984), chap. 13.

40. Argenson, vol. 4, p. 60.

incapable of training them, but are passive, docile towards all wills and all systems, rather than to a superior man *who might acquire too much credit* and resist the opinions that one has adopted."[41]

Nobody likes to be contradicted. Yet, as Arthur Young noted, without the risk of offending there is no instruction. In the old regime, people took offense very easily, and no one more so than the kings. Their *amour-propre* reached monstrous proportions, matched only by their power to punish offenders. As a result, their officials and generals were often reluctant to express disagreement with the kings and even to make suggestions to them.[42] In fact, one expression of *amour-propre* is what psychologists call *reactance*, the tendency of an agent to reject suggestions or recommendations to perform some action, even when it would be in her interest.[43] According to d'Argenson, Louis XV was tainted by this tendency: "If it was discovered that he was going to fight his enemies on the Rhine, that was enough to make him turn his steps towards Normandy; the announcement of anything always made him do the opposite: the announcement of the disgrace of [the officer and diplomat] Bellisle made him a duke, and the announcement of his great favor on the return from [a much admired defense of] Prague caused him and those close to him to appear as being in disgrace."[44]

Concerning Louis XVI, Edgar Faure cites a distinction he takes from de Gaulle: he "did not have the *passion for power*, but he did have the *jealousy of decision*."[45] Véri reports Louis XVI as saying, "*M. Turgot wants to be me, and I do not want him to be me.*"[46] Any suggestions had to be made indirectly, to make the king believe that the idea came from him. Moreover, to prevent the appointment of someone to an important position one could praise the candidate so excessively that the king felt crowded.[47] Such praise might in fact trigger both the king's aversion to excellence *and* his reactance.

41. Guibert (1772), p. 40; my italics.

42. Thireau (1973), p. 115, cites one of the *Mémoires* that Louis XIV (actually his officials) wrote for his heir, in which he affirms his fear of lacking people willing to contradict him. This was one of the many commonplace ideas with which these *Mémoires* abound (Perez 2004, p. 35). To my knowledge, there is no evidence that the king ever practiced it; it was attractive *en gros*, but not *en détail*. As we saw, in 1665 nobody dared tell the king that the exile of Roquesante was seen as unjust and Colbert as too powerful.

43. For a brief discussion of reactance, see Elster (2015a), pp. 175–177.

44. Argenson vol.4, p. 60; see also ibid., p. 113.

45. Faure (1961), p. 28; he also refers (p. 428) to the king's "sulking egocentrism."

46. Véri (1928), p. 448.

47. Saint-Simon, vol. 13, p. 244, claims that when there was a question of appointing him ambassador to Rome, he was the victim of "poisoned praise."

I have discussed some obstacles to will *formation*. Among the many obstacles to the *execution* of the king's will, the most important was perhaps an internal one: his omnipotence. (I discuss external obstacles later.) An absolute ruler is unable to make credible promises, because he can undo them at any time.[48] If he does not have the ability to make credible promises, the subjects will not trust him. *Credit*, in particular, will be undermined. Hence France never managed to establish the English institutions of the *floating debt* and the *sinking fund*. The reason, Lüthy asserts, was the generic incompatibility of absolutism and a system of public credit.[49]

A floating debt makes it possible for lenders to the Crown to withdraw their capital at short notice, thus making them more willing to lend. (The certificates of loan deposits can then serve as paper money, at least if the assurance of withdrawal at will is credible.) Colbert established the *Caisse des Emprunts* in 1674 for this purpose, but "this institution was too contrary to the habits of the Treasury: it presupposed the maintenance of a certain amount of liquid cash, but from 1680 the *Caisse* was empty."[50] When he died a few years later, his successor "immediately suppressed the *Caisse*, whose deposits were not reimbursed, but converted into bonds; this was the avowal of the incapacity of the State to contract effectively reimbursable loans."[51]

A sinking fund (*caisse d'amortissement*) is based on earmarked revenues from various sources that are to be used *exclusively* for the purpose of reducing the public debt.[52] The system originated in England in 1716, but never worked as intended. "Experience . . . demonstrated that it was next to impossible to devise laws fool-proof enough to prevent diversion of the fund for purposes other than debt reduction."[53] Several French finance ministers struggled unsuccessfully with this problem, which became increasingly urgent as the proportion of government revenue used to pay interest on the public debt approached 40 percent. In 1725, the Pâris brothers, de facto controllers of the finances of the kingdom, created a 2 percent tax on all wealth and income in the kingdom, to be perceived in

---

48. Holmes (1988), pp. 225–228; Olson (1991).

49. Lüthy (1998), p. 423; see also ibid., pp. 95, 210–211, 289–296, 414.

50. Ibid., p. 106.

51. Ibid.

52. Félix (1999), pp. 167–170, asserts, however, that the real purpose of the reimbursements was to create confidence in creditors and induce them to subscribe to new loans carrying lower interest.

53. Swanson and Trout (1992), p. 109.

kind (following a proposal by Maréchal Vauban) and to be used exclusively to reimburse the public debt. The tax was quickly abolished, not because the fund was raided for other purposes, but because the privileged were opposed to its in-kind nature. "The in-kind tax . . . took little where there was little and much where there was much, thus realizing the equal apportionment that one had never succeeded in achieving."[54]

In 1749, the finance minister Machault established two funds, in principle completely separated from the daily expenses of the treasury, which were to serve to reimburse capital and pay interest on the bonds.[55] Marion asserts that "this *barrier* that the sovereign claimed to establish *against his own inclinations* . . . was not absolutely illusory," and that the promise to respect the autonomy of the fund was sufficiently credible to "raise serious worries among our English enemies" (my italics). Marion concludes, nevertheless, that the English worries proved unwarranted.[56] His successor, Bertin, adopted the principle of a sinking fund, without specifying the modalities of its application. Unlike the fund itself, these modalities did not have to be registered by the *parlements*, leaving the finance minister free to divert the funds from their intended purpose.[57] Bertin's successor, L'Averdy, a former magistrate himself, responded to the refusal of the *parlements* to register edicts over which they had no control by the "Edict of the liberation of the debts" (1764) whose "main goal was precisely to create a mechanism that would be independent of the vicissitudes of power [and] of the unpredictable needs of the ministers."[58] These royal mechanisms for self-binding disappeared when the edict was repealed after L'Averdy's departure from the ministry in 1768. The very existence of the fund created an irresistible temptation to raid it, just as

54. Marion (1927), p. 131; see also Félix (1999), p. 152.

55. Félix (1999), pp. 42–43.

56. Marion (1891), pp. 365, 366. Slater (2018), p. 48, confirms that eighteenth-century British governments were "haunted by two nightmares," one of which was "that the French might actually get their public finances in order and be able to rearm quicker than the British could."

57. Félix (1999), p. 153.

58. Ibid. In a critical comment on L'Averdy's edict, an anonymous English observer proposed that "the fund be administered by commissioners chosen by the *parlement* among its members" (ibid., p. 171). L'Averdy himself may have been sympathetic to this idea (ibid., p. 176), which nevertheless would hardly have been acceptable to the king. From a different perspective, in a book from 1749 the Marquis de Mirabeau "asserted that the operations of a sinking fund had greater chances of succeeding in the provinces than in Paris, where the incessant demands of the courtiers made it impossible for the ministers to cut expenses" (ibid., p. 254). As noted earlier, Malesherbes made a similar comment, but blamed the king rather than his ministers.

taxes supposed to replace the *corvée* were easily diverted to other uses while the corvée was maintained.[59]

The most important *rente perpétuelle* was the interest (technically paid by the City Hall, *hôtel de ville*, in Paris) on government bonds. By and large, the interest was paid in full, although, as I mentioned, actually laying one's hands on the money could be a struggle. When Saint-Simon proposed a general bankruptcy after the death of Louis XIV, he suggested that the *rentes sur l'hôtel de ville* be exempted.[60] The edict of 1749 that established the financing of the sinking fund by a new tax, the *vingtième* (twentieth), explicitly exempted Paris bondholders from the tax.[61] Even in the virtual bankruptcy organized by the finance minister Terray in 1770, the *rentes sur l'hôtel de ville* were initially spared. One reason was that many of the magistrates in the *parlement* of Paris, which would have to register the bankruptcy edicts, had much of their fortune in these papers.[62] In 1771, however, Terray first suppressed the tax court and then, "being assured of not meeting any unwelcome protestations," reduced the *rentes sur l'hôtel de ville*.[63] Magistrates in the provincial *parlements*, who had most of their fortune in real estate, were less inclined to defend the bondholders.[64]

The Paris bourgeoisie included a large number of *rentiers*. According to Jean-Christian Petitfils, around 1650 they amounted to 100,000 in a population of 430,000.[65] In an estimate for 1780 cited by David Garrioch, the Parisian bourgeoisie, defined as those who "lived from investment or rent rather than by trade or manual work," amounted to about 14 percent of the population.[66] Whatever the exact numbers, there is no doubt that there was a substantial number of *rentiers* in Paris. As noted, the government may have spared them because it feared the remonstrances of the *parlements*. Marion writes that the *rentiers* were "the

59. Faure (1961), p. 422; Véri (1928), pp. 258–259.

60. Saint-Simon, vol. 27, p. 75.

61. The edict is cited in Marion (1910), pp. 287–292.

62. Bluche (1986 b), pp. 111–112, lists the names of magistrates whose wealth was mainly in *rentes* and those who held it mainly in land, and asserts that the latter were "slightly less numerous" than the former. From Terray's point of view the *size* of the fortunes must also have been important: if the bondholders were wealthier than the landowners, they could be expected to resist more strongly. Although Bluche (ibid., pp. 108–109) also gives data for the size, he does not disaggregate them into bonds and land.

63. Gomel (1892), vol. 1, p. 40.

64. Egret (1970), pp. 13–14.

65. Petitfils (2014a), p. 73. It is likely that this number includes some persons who held government bonds while also exercising a profession (Roche 1981, pp. 131–134).

66. Garrioch (2002), p. 104.

least badly paid, because the government knew what problems it would incur if it ceased to 'keep the pot of Paris on the boil,'"[67] suggesting fear of social unrest as the motivation. The government also knew that if it did not pay interest promptly and fully, it would have difficulties finding subscribers to new loans.[68] These two reasons combined to make the government somewhat committed to keeping its promises to the bondholders, even without the institutional constraints that emerged in England after 1688.[69] If the *rentiers* were mistreated, it was mostly through the action (or inaction) of the *payeurs de rentes*, venal paymasters who dragged their feet while they made the funds fructify for their own profit.[70]

After 1726 and until the Revolution, the kings were also able to resist the temptation to manipulate the value of the coins they issued. Prior to this date, Gresham's law operated. France was "a country of hidden treasures, where precious metals seemed to be absorbed by the subsoil."[71] Louis XIV had solemnly announced that specie would remain immutable, but in wartime he yielded to pressure. Lüthy discusses several factors that may explain why the declaration of May 1726 "stuck," as earlier ones had not. The most important were a long period of peace and the fact of inflation, which "replaced favorably the debasement of the *livre tournois* in the only virtue one had always attributed to it, that of progressively alleviating monetary debts and dues."[72] By the mid-century, "monetary stability had become a routine that was so well engrained that no finance minister, even in the middle of new wars and financial crises, would dream of touching it."[73] Only

67. Marion (1927), p. 41. In 1741, Argenson, vol. 3 p. 380, predicted the order in which various groups would have to make sacrifices to avoid a bankruptcy: "first the troops, especially those who are in the field, then the expenses of the king and the court, and finally the *rentes sur la ville* whose non-payment would ruin many poor families and *make Paris rise up*" (my italics).

68. Taxing the interest on bonds, when lenders had relied on an explicit promise that they would not be taxed, could have the same chilling effect (Marion 1927, p. 238). In reimbursing loans, the finance minister L'Averdy distinguished between bonds that were part of a familial patrimony and were fully reimbursed, and those that had been bought by speculators at lower prices or with paper money, which were not (Félix 1999, p. 148). In other words, the promise was attached to the original bondholder, not to the bond.

69. Given the short time-horizon of the government, the first reason was probably the most important.

70. Claeys (2011), p. 451.

71. Lüthy (1998), p. 95.

72. Lüthy (2005), p. 29.

73. Ibid., p. 30. This statement, however, seems to provide a description of the explanandum rather than an explanation. According to Claeys (2011), p. 614, lenders never believed that this stabilization was definitive. North and Weingast (1989), p. 804, write

Voltaire complained that oppressed debtors were hurt by the stable value of money.[74]

The Tools of Government

To better understand the *external* obstacles to the king's will, we must consider the instruments he had at his disposal. They include the members of the various royal councils, notably his ministers; governors and *intendants* of the provinces, both revocable; the *Grand Conseil* (a royal court that rivaled with the *parlements*); the first presidents of the *parlements*, who were appointed by the king and whose office was not venal; and finally the many tools he could use in the trench warfare against the courts.[75]

Some of the ministers were highly competent, while others, as noted, may have been chosen for their incompetence. Some were chosen on the whims of a royal mistress[76] or (in the case of Louis XVI) the queen. Regardless of competence or lack of it, they were often hindered in their work by intrigues at the Court. Thus, when Machault, as finance minister, wanted to increase the royal revenues by awarding tax farms and subfarms to the highest bidders, Madame de Pompadour and others at the Court made him choose their protégés instead.[77] As noted, Saint-Simon asserted that Louis XIV had a policy of randomly rejecting 1/20 of the demands of his ministers, to remind them that they could not make any promises without his approval. The powerful finance ministers seldom stayed in office for long, a fact that must have prevented them from learning their complex

---

that of the two ways of establishing a credible commitment, that of setting a "precedent of responsible behavior" is "seldom observed." The other way, which is the topic of their article, is that of "being constrained to obey a set of rules that do not permit leeway for violating commitments."

74. Picard (1912), p. 364.

75. I shall say nothing about the provincial governors, who spent most of their time in Paris. According to Petitfils (2014a), pp. 281–282, the king kept the governors close to keep them away from their local clients. When one of them asked the king's permission to leave for his province, Louis XIV replied that "When you can govern your own affairs, I will let you take care of mine" (Sévigné, vol. 2, p. 67). They were largely supplanted by the intendants after 1661 (Harding 1978). The governors of Burgundy, who belonged to the powerful Condé family (Swann 2003), were an important exception.

76. "The most harmful influence that Mme de Pompadour exercised over [Louis XV] was probably to rashly remove his scruples regarding the choice of [ministers]" (Antoine 1970, p. 622).

77. Argenson, vol. 6, p. 48; see also ibid., p. 82 (but also ibid., p. 63 for a seemingly contradictory statement).

and arcane business. A contemporary observer estimated their probationary period to two or three years.[78] Between 1754 and 1763, spanning the crucial Seven Years War, five persons held the office. During the equally crucial pre-revolutionary years from 1768 to 1783, eight persons occupied it. During the last two years of the regime, two persons held it. The mean length was about four years, largely due to the long tenures of Colbert (eighteen years) and Orry (fifteen years). Finally, they were hindered by the strict separation of their domains. Finance ministers were supposed only to take care of revenue, not of expenses. D'Argenson cites a person close to Louis XV as saying that the king would, as a matter of principle, never inform the finance minister about foreign policy nor the foreign minister about financial affairs.[79] The lack of trust among the ministers is shown by the fact, cited earlier, that they were not above intercepting letters to their colleagues. Defending the need to censor criticisms of the administration, the principal minister, Choiseul, wrote to Louis XV that "among your ministers, M. de Praslin, M. de Laverdy and I are the only ones who are attacked; the others, in truth, by their knowledge (*lumières*) merit neither regard nor consideration; it is not possible to be more deprived of talent than your other ministers." Joël Félix, who cites this letter, adds that "Nothing could better have revealed the deep divisions that were eroding the government of Louis XV."[80]

The king could not appoint, instruct, promote, transfer, and if need be dismiss, venal officials. He could abolish their office, but only against compensation. He could, however, try to influence them by exile and occasionally by bribes.[81] The vast majority of these officials held royal or municipal offices that were private property, handed down from father to son or sold on an open market, sometimes to speculators who bought up large batches to resell them.[82] Their number varied from around 45,000 in the middle of the seventeenth century to about 70,000 at the time of the Revolution, around 1 percent of the adult male population.[83] The complex and often baroque character of the venal offices, many of them serving only the purpose of filling the coffers of the treasury, defies summary. The more important ones, which did have a genuine function, were offices of finance and

78. Félix (1999), p. 370.

79. Argenson, vol. 3, p. 424.

80. Félix (1999), p. 343.

81. For examples of bribery, see Swann (1995), pp. 76, 288–289; Egret (1962), p. 185.

82. On the speculators, see Doyle (1996), pp. 76, 141, 202 n. 3; also Lüthy (1998), p. 108, on the farming-out of venal offices.

83. Doyle (1996), pp. 58–60. The overlapping group of adult male nobles numbered approximately as many individuals; estimates vary widely.

of law.[84] With regard to the former, the venality had a purpose, since the purchase sum could serve as collateral in cases of embezzlement, squandering, or bankruptcy.[85] The venality of legal offices had no justification, Montesquieu notwithstanding.[86]

Finance officials collected taxes and provided loans to the king; legal officials carried out the tasks of civil and criminal justice and, crucially, that of registering royal edicts and ordinances. Officials were paid a salary (*gages*), which technically represented the interest on what they had paid for the office. From time to time the government would increase the salary, to justify a request for a new down payment. This practice, which amounted to a forced loan, was but one of the many arrows in the government's quiver of chicanery.

Finance officials could also profit in various ways from the money that passed through their hands, by retaining some of it for themselves and lending it out. They constituted a huge deadweight loss for the economy. As noted, the costs of recovering the *taille* could be high when it was collected by the *élus*. Even when the task was transferred to the *intendant*, the *élus* retained their offices because abolishing them and paying compensation would be too expensive. The tax farmers who collected indirect taxes did not have their charge by virtue of a venal office,[87] but by their ability to provide a steady and predictable lump-sum payment each year. There were no legal obstacles to transferring their task to the royal administration itself, but, as always, the short time horizon blocked reform. "A unified system would certainly have yielded the state a much greater revenue, but the old method of snatching whatever lay to hand was followed. A radical change would have meant a longer period of waiting before the new results materialized and nobody could afford to wait."[88]

Law officials mostly did what magistrates are supposed to do, administer criminal and civil justice. (I shall return to their task of registering royal edicts.) In their case, abolishing their offices and transferring their tasks to the royal administration was not an option, not only because it would have been too costly, but also because the old regime for the most

84. Higher military offices were also venal, but did not carry full property rights. The venality served mainly as guaranty against indebtedness (Cénat 2015, p.p. 114–118).

85. Claeys (2011), pp. 100, 213, 258; Dessert (1984), pp. 53–54.

86. Montesquieu (1748), V. 19.

87. De facto, however, they were often hereditary (Claeys 2011, p. 106).

88. Heckscher (1934), vol. 1, p. 124; see also Hayden (1974), p. 117: "There never was a breathing space to allow for reorganization." Reform would have required the government to take one step backward to take two steps forward, *reculer pour mieux sauter*.

part respected the separation of the executive and the judicial powers.[89] The occasional practice of *justice retenue*—taking individual cases out of the ordinary judicial system to have them decided by the executive or by special courts—obviously undermined the independence of the judiciary to some extent. Yet such interventions were relatively uncommon, the role of the *intendants* in handling tax disputes being perhaps the most frequent case.[90] To an unknowable extent, the patrimonial rather than meritocratic character of the legal system must have generated miscarriages of justice, false convictions as well as false acquittals. There are plenty of anecdotes[91], but no data.

Intermittently, and from 1653 definitively, the *intendants* were the main instruments for implementing the royal policies. Over time, they accumulated vast powers. In 1721, the financier John Law told d'Argenson that France was ruled by thirty *intendants*.[92] Unlike the magistrates, they were in theory both revocable and transferable.[93]

Concerning revocations, outright dismissals of *intendants* seem to have been very rare. While it is arguable that the mere possibility of losing one's office would keep the *intendants* in line, some actual dismissals from time to time would have been needed to give bite to this risk. As far as I can judge, dismissals were too rare to sustain a mechanism of "anticipated reactions."

Concerning transfers, the king and his ministers faced a dilemma that often arises in posting officials to supervise policy implementation in provinces located far from the center.[94] In order to become familiar with the local conditions, the agents of the central administration should stay for

89. On this complex issue, notably concerning the influence of Montesquieu, see Olivier-Martin (1997), pp. 500–511.

90. Tocqueville (2011), p. 56; Egret (1970), p. 120; Kwass (2000), p. 53. To some extent, therefore, the royal administration practiced *seigneurial justice writ large*, judging in its own case.

91. See for instance Swann (1995), p. 11.

92. Argenson, vol. 1, p. 43.

93. In its insatiable demand for fresh money, in 1704 the government made the office of their subdelegates a venal one, an anomaly that was abolished in 1715 (Saint-Jacob 1960, p. 209).

94. For the Roman empire, see Olivier-Martin (2010), pp. 64, 106. For the Chinese empire, see Skinner (1975), p. 341. In China, rotation was supplemented by the "law of avoidance" that kept officials from serving in their native provinces (ibid.). Tocqueville (2011), p. 41, affirms that this principle was followed for the *intendants* in the old regime. I have not seen this statement confirmed elsewhere, but the principle was certainly applied in the appointment of bishops (McManners 1998, vol. 1, pp. 210, 237). For them, exceptions were made for Béarn and sometimes for Brittany, where knowledge of the local dialect was important (ibid., p. 218–219).

some time in the province for which they are responsible. Moreover, as Necker observed, if the *intendant* "sees his nomination as a mere step in his career (*un lieu de passage*) . . . , he has no incentive (*n'est point excité*) to prepare reforms whose success is not attributed to him."[95] Yet to avoid being captured by local interests, they should rotate often. Roland Mousnier writes that in the first years of the reign of Louis XIV, the government intended to "move [the *intendants*] from *généralité* to *généralité* so that in a few years they would have done the tour of the kingdom, *to acquire a better knowledge of the whole*."[96] He does not cite any sources for the motive he imputes to the administration, and it seems intrinsically implausible. François Olivier-Martin affirms, more plausibly, that "in the beginning of the institution the king changed the posting of the *intendants* very often, every three years for example, *to avoid local attachments*."[97]

I have no firm evidence regarding the two motives I have italicized. What is clear is that over time, the *intendants* became increasingly immobile. "There were 68 *intendants* under Louis XVI. 29 stayed in the same posting 10 years or more; 24, more than 20 years; 13, more than 25 years; 7, more than 30 years; 2, more than 40 years. . . . In addition, for many *intendances* a kind of inheritance had been established. 15 *intendants* were sons of *intendants*."[98] The effect of immobility was capture by local interests. In the mid-seventeenth century, when the *intendants* rotated frequently, many of them were rigorous in the pursuit of the king's interest. As Bercé writes, some were "truly terrorist representatives of the *raison d'Etat*."[99] Later, their loyalty shifted, because of the attachment to their province. Marion writes that "the *intendants* were much less afraid of displeasing their minister than those whom they administered." Also, whereas the enlightened *intendant* Tourny "was accused in Bordeaux of rigor and tyranny in levying taxes for the king, in Paris he was accused of weakness and timidity. The second reproach was certainly the most justified."[100] Follain writes that in Provence, the *intendant* was "more a negotiator charged by the province to defend its interests—meaning the

95. Necker (1778), p. 2. The phrase is revealing: Necker himself had no such incentive.

96. Mousnier (2005), p. 1073, my italics.

97. Olivier-Martin (2010), p. 626. Mousnier (2005), p. 1077, affirms that three years was the average before 1661. A proposal that *governors* rotate every three years did not go anywhere (ibid., p. 1031).

98. Mousnier (2005), pp. 1107–1108; see also ibid., pp. 505, 507, for some data on the latter part of the reign of Louis XVI, showing a steady increase in the length of posting. For a fuller discussion, see Ardascheff (1909), pp. 129–133.

99. Bercé (1974), pp. 666–667.

100. Marion (1891), p. 58.

interests of the privileged—than an agent of the government charged to make Provence submit to the interests of the central power."[101] These examples all refer to the mid or late eighteenth century, when the power of the *intendants* was steadily increasing. In an important monograph on the subject, a Russian scholar, Ardascheff, cites the archbishop of Aix as saying in 1787 that "The king's man becomes the man of the province."[102] Yet the *intendant* had to obey direct orders, while, for instance, the *élus* of the Estates in Burgundy "had no such constraints and they could, and did, put what they believed were the interests of the province first."[103]

Which local interests did the *intendant* defend? Follain explicitly refers to the interest of the local elites. When Marion refers to "the tendency of many *intendants* to seek the favors (*les bonnes grâces*) of their *administrés*, at the expense of the king's interests," he probably also refers to the privileged. Why, in fact, would the mighty *intendant* care about what ordinary people, who probably did not know who he was, thought about him?[104] Esmonin, too, writes that "the protestations of the *intendants* were not always disinterested. It was normal that an administrator sought relief for his district to be well regarded by his *administrés*."[105] This statement refers to Normandy, where three *intendants* were charged with administering 4,000 parishes, with more than a million and half inhabitants.[106] If they sought approval, it must have been that of a small elite.

Earlier, however, I observed that some *intendants* defended the interests of the peasantry, not in the search of popularity but out of an impartial concern for their welfare. At the level of intentions, Turgot's passage as *intendant* in the Limousin remains the exemplary model, although his achievements were constrained by the contradictory decisions of the central administration, the hostility of the *parlements*, and the lack of qualified personnel at the local level. The *intendant* in Guyenne, Tourny, deliberately "substituted the public interest (*le service public*) for the king's interest (*le service du roi*), the public good for the *raison d'Etat*."[107] He preferred, for instance, to improve the roads rather than spend huge sums on the passage

---

101. Marion (1891), p. 58.

102. Ardascheff (1909), p. 116, with many examples in ibid., pp. 120–128. Kaplan (2015), p. 99, cites a text from 1748 in which a tax-farmer complains about "the unfraternal and 'cowardly' attitude of *intendants* who sealed off their province as if 'surrounded by enemies.'"

103. Swann (2003), p. 226.

104. Marion (1891), p. 44.

105. Esmonin (1913), p. 31.

106. Follain (2008), p. 27.

107. Poirier (1999), p. 90.

of a princess; the king had the opposite preference.[108] In 1748, a year of famine in his province, he asked and obtained the permission of the finance minister to relieve the harshness of taxation. Yet because—for reasons I discussed in chapter 3—the "taxpayers thought too easily that they would enjoy a general suspension of taxes," he eventually had to limit the tax cuts.[109] Obstacles to improving the welfare of the peasants might come from their excessive expectations, not only from the administration.

Although one probably cannot make any generalization about *what* the *intendants* substituted for the king's interest, the relevant point is that such substitutions did occur, on an important scale. There is other evidence that the king could not simply push a button or press a lever and count on the intended effect being produced. Pierre Goubert asks, rhetorically, whether Colbert's vast reform program "did not boil down to a collection of intentions."[110] His answer is revealing: Colbert and the king succeeded at least in *destroying* any independent source of power, rebellious nobles or obstructionist *parlements*. Measures aiming at improvements were more difficult. Commenting on Colbert's attempt in 1664 to reform or abolish internal tolls, Heckscher cites a comment from 1701: "these tolls have remained in existence since; they are so contentious and intricate that no merchant has ever completely grasped them, but have always freely paid them in order to avoid lawsuits."[111]

A further sign of the ineffectiveness of the royal edicts is that they often had to be issued several times, revealing their inefficacy. The long series of edicts banning the seizure of farm animals and tools to pay tax arrears suggests that the practice was difficult to uproot. In 1753, bans from 1666, 1667, and 1713 were renewed.[112] Commenting on an edict from 1666 banning the establishment of new religious establishments without special permission, Lavisse writes that "the edict was only a reminder of earlier edicts. It was followed by others, proof that the will of the king here, once again, remained inefficacious."[113] Even draconian measures failed to achieve their end. "It is estimated that the economic measures taken [to prevent the import and production of printed cotton fabrics] cost the lives of some 16,000 people, partly through executions and partly through

---

108. Lhéritier (1920), p. 189.

109. Ibid., p. 264.

110. Ibid., p. 191.

111. Heckscher (1934), vol. 1, p. 106.

112. Saint-Jacob (1960), p. 331; see also Pillorget and Pillorget (1995), p. 69; Bercé (1974), pp. 99, 384; Nicolas (2008), p. 203; Lavisse (1989), p. 312.

113. Lavisse (1989), p. 355.

armed affrays, without reckoning the number of people who were sent to the galleys or punished in other ways. On one occasion in Valence, 77 were sentenced to be hanged, 58 were to be broken on the wheel, 631 were sent to the galleys, one was set free and none were pardoned. But even this vigorous action did not help to attain the desired end."[114]

Discretionary Tools

I conclude with some comments on various extra-legal or discretionary tools the government had at its disposal to punish recalcitrant individuals, render them harmless, or force them to comply with royal policies. In addition to the opening of private letters that I discussed in chapter 3, the government had several other arrows of harassment in its quiver: lodging soldiers in private homes, sending individuals who displeased the king in one way or another into exile, or censoring their writings.

The coercive quartering of soldiers or former soldiers (*garnissaires*) in private homes was often used to extract taxes, and sometimes to punish the parents of a young man who had tried to evade military service.[115] These might be active soldiers, who had to be fed and lodged somewhere in the middle of a campaign, but sometimes they were raised only for this purpose.[116] The costs went beyond just feeding and lodging them, since they often engaged in licentious and destructive behavior. In the terminology explained later, this tool was a form of *compellence*: making life so hard for the taxpayers that they finally decided that compliance was the lesser evil. Nevertheless, Marion claims that the system was less costly than the alternative legal process. For instance, in 1781 "the substitution of *garnissaires* for process servers in the *élection* of Bourges made the cost of collecting taxes fall by more than a half."[117]

114. Heckscher (1934), vol. 1, p. 173.

115. The practice could also be motivated by private revenge. To humiliate the magistrates, a governor could send soldiers to quarter in their country houses (Bercé 1974, p. 57). "The Duc d'Epernon used the forced residence of his guards as a regular instrument of revenge" (ibid., p. 58). The tactic may also have been used for the purpose of behavior modification.

116. Bercé (1974), p. 98, distinguishes among five repressive strategies used by the tax receivers (officials at the level of the *élection*). By "increasing order of severity," they were confiscation, debtor's prison, the solidarity constraint, quartering of soldiers in wartime, and quartering of troops raised merely to harass.

117. Marion (1923), p. 256. Not surprisingly, the magistrates opposed the procedure (Nicolas 2008, p. 209). Seigneurial justice (see above) provides another case in which arbitrary decision making could be preferable to the slower and more costly court procedures.

However, the variant of this system called *dragonnades* had no such justification. Even before the revocation in 1685 of the Edict of Nantes (1598), which had offered guarantees for freedom of worship to the Protestant community, zealous officials sent elite troops (*dragons*) to lodge in the houses of Protestants, with the tacit or explicit encouragement to loot and bully until they converted, which they often did in large numbers. After they converted, some bishops continued to use the *dragons* to force them to go to mass and take communion.[118] The reasoning behind this strategy has been described as follows:

> The mechanistic philosophy, together with Cartesianism, was the dominant philosophy. . . . In this perspective, human beings are made up of two parts: the automaton and the mind. The anti-Protestant policy of Louis XIV follows this scheme. First, it regulates the automaton. It manufactures N. C.s [Newly Converted] who go to mass only because one has forced them to. Next, the task is to persuade them. . . . The "Conversion fund" [used to pay Protestants to convert] or the *dragons* come first, for the automaton. Next, come the preachers, for the mind.[119]

This policy rests on a perverted version of Pascal's wager argument. Pascal wrote that "we are as much automaton as mind" and that "we must . . . make both parts of us believe: the mind by reason which needs to be seen only once in a lifetime, and the automaton by habit."[120] However, it is *the agent herself* who must make this effort, and take the first outward steps of going to mass etc., in the hope that the mind will follow. Pascal's argument is addressed to the unbeliever, not to the government. In fact, as I discuss later, the attempts to force conversion had, predictably (in retrospect), the opposite effect of the intended one.

I shall now comment on an extraordinary tool of government that the French kings used frequently as part of their *justice retenue*, that of sending recalcitrant individuals or persons who displeased them for some reason into *exile*, not outside France but to some place more or less distant from their principal residence, be it Paris, Versailles, or a provincial town.[121] The

---

118. Pillorget and Pillorget (1995), p. 938.

119. Ibid., p. 940–41.

120. *Pensées*, 661.

121. Arthur Young noted a positive effect of exile: when nobles were banished to their estate, they improved it. "As soon as the sentence [of exile] was reversed, the Duke [d'Aiguillon] went to Paris, and has not been here since, and consequently all now stands still" (Young 1794, vol. 1, p., 59; see also ibid., p. 67). Swann (2017), p. 269, refers to the practice of the exiled to modernize their castles as "tried-and-trusted."

recent work by Julian Swann was the first to submit the use of exile to a systematic analysis.[122] The government could also take other measures to neutralize its opponents, such as house arrest and imprisonment,[123] but exile seems to have been the more common tool. More subtly, but with much of the same effect, the king might *expel* a disgraced person *from* the Court, or refuse to grant an expected favor.[124] More bizarrely, he might exile a courtier for *withdrawing* from the Court.[125] One encounters hundreds of references to threats and executions of exile in the journals of Barbier, Marais, d'Argenson, and Hardy. According to the empress Maria Theresa, the "bizarre" practice of sending ministers into exile existed only in France and Turkey.[126] In France, as we shall see, it covered not only ministers, but was also extended to many other groups and individuals.[127]

122. Daubresse, Morgat-Bonnet, and Storez-Brancourt (2007) is a partial exception, but they focus only on the exile of magistrates and for the most part on the period prior to 1650. A chapter in that book by Storez-Brancourt (2007), the Journal by one of the clerks during the exile of 1720 that she has edited (Brancourt 2013), and the study by Durieux (2010) of the exile in 1753–1754 give a vivid image of the procedures and consequences of exile in the eighteenth century.

123. As an alternative to the exile of magistrates, the king could summon a *parlement* to Versailles for an audience, and then leave it in limbo by refusing to arrange a time for the reception of the deputation. This tactic was "frequently employed when dealing with provincial magistrates, who found themselves burdened with the cost of seeking accommodation close to court, while they awaited the king's orders" (Swann 2017, p. 189). Another tactic was to "exile" magistrates to their home town, as when the government confined the magistrates of the *parlement* of Dijon within the city walls for a year, presumably believing "that this would inconvenience the judges, who could not visit or attend to their country estates, without causing the stir of sending them into exile elsewhere" (Swann 2017, p. 188; also Swann 2003, pp. 269–270).

124. Swann (2017), pp. 50, 54, 64.

125. Ibid., p. 63. Others "found it less painful to withdraw from court rather than face daily reminders of disgrace" (ibid., p. 68). They might then have to ask permission to do so (Barbier, vol. 1, p. 195).

126. Faure (1961), p. 27. Although Swann (2017), p. 283, may be correct in asserting that "Bourbon kings saw themselves as absolute monarchs, not tyrants or despots, and property or offices were rarely confiscated in the manner of Russian tsars or Ottoman sultans," the arbitrary use of exile nevertheless had some of the flavor of "Oriental despotism."

127. For the nobility, presence or absence at the Court could present a collective action problem, in one of two forms. "In one view the [English] barons regarded this attendance as their principal privilege; in another, as a grievous burden. That no momentous affairs could be transacted without their consent and advice, was in general esteemed the great security of their possessions and dignities: but as they reaped no immediate profit from their attendance at court, and were exposed to great inconvenience and charge by an absence from their own estates, *every one was glad to exempt himself from each particular exertion of this power*; and was pleased both that the call for that duty should seldom return upon him, and *that others should undergo the burden in his stead*" (Hume 1983, vol. 1, p. 462; my italics). Tocqueville made the opposite argument with regard to France: the

From Louis XIV onwards, the French kings used the tool of exile against members of the royal family, ministers, magistrates, lawyers, writers, ecclesiastics, and sundry other persons who for some reason displeased them. Saint-Simon cites, as an instance of the last category, an episode from 1664 when the governess of the *demoiselles d'honneur* of the mother of Louis XIV closed an opening that the king had had made into their bedchamber so that he could visit them at night.[128] In his anger, he exiled her and her husband to Guyenne. In 1740, Louis XV exiled the husband of his mistress for having received freemasons in his home; "even the august quality of being cuckolded by the king could not exempt him from banishment."[129] Another episode with ironic consequences occurred in 1749, when the Comte de Maurepas was exiled from the Court for allegedly having written a song making fun of the king's mistress. When Louis XVI came to power, one reason for calling Maurepas to the office of principal minister was apparently the virtue the king inferred from this exile.[130] There were probably many domestic episodes of this kind, which the memorialists and diarists either did not know about or viewed as too trivial to mention.

When used for such personal reasons, or deployed against magistrates or clerics, the exiles probably did not have strong tangible effects one way or another. Sometimes they worked as intended, by quelling incipient flames of rebellion; at other times, they had the opposite effect, nourishing the unrest. In the larger scheme of things, they probably did not affect military or financial matters. When magistrates responded to the exile of their colleagues by going on a judicial strike, they could throw some sand in the machinery of administration, but like other forms of passive resistance this strategy had mainly a nuisance value. More consequential were the exiles of competent administrators or military officers. According to Julian Swann, the dismissal and exile in 1757 of the finance minister Machault and the secretary of state for war d'Argenson "had damaging military

---

nobility as a class would have benefited if the nobles had stayed on their estates, but the individual noble preferred the lures of the court. "The limbs gained at the expense of the body" (Tocqueville 2011, p. 84). The implications are that if the English nobles had developed class consciousness they would have stayed at the Court, whereas class-conscious French nobles would have stayed on their estates. As the English nobles preferred to stay on their estates, the use or threat of exile was not available to the kings.

128. Saint-Simon, vol.7, p. 34. The fact is attested by many accounts.

129. Argenson, vol. 3, pp. 58–59.

130. Gomel (1892), p. 52: Louis XVI "praised himself for choosing the victim of a favorite as his adviser."

repercussions as it was surely not a coincidence that French military fortunes, on both land and sea, took a decisive turn for the worst [*sic*]."[131]
Generals, too, could be dismissed and exiled for political rather than military reasons.[132]

Exiles were initiated when the king's musketeers delivered, often in
the early hours of the morning, a *lettre de cachet*. Although most famous,
or infamous, for their arbitrary use in detaining persons who were seen
as a menace to the public order or to the "peace of families," these letters
could also serve to give notice to persons whom the king for political or
personal reasons wanted to remove from Paris, Versailles or a provincial
town.[133] The removal could serve three purposes: incapacitation, retribu-
tion, and behavior modification. It is likely that in many cases two or all
three motives were involved.

Incapacitation

When a minister was dismissed from office, he was usually also exiled
dans ses terres (to one of his landed properties), where he could
not serve as a focus of intrigue and opposition. When necessary,
he could also be sent to some other place more distant from the
Court.[134]

Often, the measures were taken against many people simultaneously,
to prevent them from conspiring with each other. Thus in 1727,
the king's principal minister Fleury exiled to their dioceses twelve
bishops who had signed a letter defending the views of a bishop
accused of Jansenism, "to prevent them concerting with one
another."[135] When the Pâris brothers, important financiers under
Louis XV, were exiled in 1726, they were sent to four different
towns.[136]

In 1750, when the finance minister Machault wanted to make the
clergy pay the *vingtième*, "the king ordered all the bishops who
were in Paris and who were not members of the future assembly of
the clergy to return within three days to their diocese; the marked
intention was to intimidate the clergy and *prevent them from*

---

131. Swann (2017), p. 138.
132. El Hage (2016).
133. Quétel (2011) offers a myth-puncturing account of the *lettres de cachet*.
134. Swann (2017), pp. 95, 247.
135. Vaillot (1974), p. 204.
136. Claeys (2011), p. 619.

exciting one another against the demand for the *vingtième*."137
The king also used such divide-and-conquer tactics against
individual magistrates and against the *parlements*.

Concerning the magistrates, Swann reports a divide-and-conquer
tactic: "During an exile it was common to see individuals receive
signs of favour, such as the right to visit Paris for pressing affairs,
in the hope that it would cause resentment."138

As the *parlements* were divided into several chambers, the king
could exile them to different places. Thus in 1753, Louis XV sent
members of the lower chambers into individual exiles to nine different places, whereas the higher *Grand'Chambre* was allowed to
remain in Paris where the king hoped it would register his edict in
a matter of refusal of sacraments to alleged Jansenists.

When the *Grand'Chambre* did not do as he hoped, he sent the
magistrates in collective exile to Pontoise, near Paris, hoping that
the cramped living conditions there (see below) would make them
reconsider. Yet some of the individual exiles communicated with
the *Grand'Chambre* and persuaded the magistrates in Pontoise to
resist the effort to divide the *parlement*.139

A person could also be exiled for revealing facts the king did not want
to become known, such as the true construction costs of his castle
at Meudon.140

Retribution

In one notorious instance, a pure punishment motive seems to have
been dominant. In 1770–1771, the Comte de Maupeou, the last
minister of Louis XV, abolished the *parlements*, replaced them
by non-venal institutions that would render justice free of charge,
exiled 60 magistrates *dans leurs terres*, and dispersed 107 all
over France. Among the latter, he exiled his personal enemies

---

137. Argenson, vol. 6, p. 195; my italics; see also Rocquain (1878), pp. 258–259, for
a similar occasion in 1767. More subtly, in 1754–1755 the king took preemptive action by
exiling bishops who had countenanced the refusal of sacraments to alleged Jansenists, to
prevent the *parlements* from condemning them and causing a scandal he wanted to avoid
(Egret 1970, pp. 68–69.)

138. Swann (2017), p. 186; my italics; see other examples in ibid., pp. 289, 401.

139. Durieux (2010).

140. Argenson, vol. 6, p. 251. The motive may also have been to punish him for the
indiscretion.

to "deserted and unhealthy places; he showed his pleasure from knowing that they suffered."[141]

Also, when Maurepas was exiled to Bourges in 1749 and not allowed to live on his own estates,[142] punishment may have been the motive.

Behavior Modification

In some cases, the king used a threat of exile as a tool of *deterrence*, to prevent the *parlements* and other bodies from disobeying the king.[143]

In other cases, he hoped to achieve his ends by *compellence*: making life in exile so unpleasant for the magistrates that they ultimately complied.[144] The greater the distance from the seat of the *parlement* and the harsher the living conditions, the stronger the exile was felt.[145]

If an exiled person refused to comply, he could be sent to a more distant place.[146]

Conversely, when the *parlement* of Paris was exiled to Pontoise rather than to the much more distant Blois in 1720, Saint-Simon commented that "in this way the punishment became

---

141. Véri (1928), p. 73; see also Egret (1970), p. 179; and Gomel (1892), p. 32. Specifically, "Michau de Montblin and president Jean-Hyacinthe-Emmanuel Hocquart, two of the leading figures in the Parlement, were exiled to the Île d'Yeu and the Île de Noirmoutier respectively. These were considered to be particularly grim destinations on account of the rudeness of the local climate and the fact that both men were reputed to suffer from respiratory ailments, and it was subsequently claimed that they died prematurely as a result" (Swann 2017, pp. 185–186).

142. Antoine (1989), p. 613.

143. Examples in Rocquain (1878), pp. 25, 55, 69; Argenson, vol. 6, p. 309; Barbier, vol. 8, p. 127.

144. According to Schelling (1966, p. 70) deterrence and compellence are two types of coercive threats, the difference being that "the threat that compels rather than deters often requires that the punishment be administered *until* the other acts, rather than *if* he acts." See also Brattan (2005). For some doubts about the efficacy of compellence that relies only on worsening the material situation of the target, see Lebow (1996) as well as the comments above on the policies of Louis XIV in Holland and the Palatinate.

145. Also, hot-heated leaders were sometimes exiled to a more distant place than those who were seen simply as fellow-travelers (Marion 1898, pp. 356–357). The motive could be incapacitation as well as behavior modification.

146. When the Archbishop of Paris opposed the king in a matter of sacraments, he was first exiled to Conflans, then to the more distant Lagny, and finally to the very distant Perigord (Roquain 1878, pp. 185–187, 206). Again, the motive may have been both incapacitation and behavior modification.

ridiculous."[147] Nevertheless, the royal government "counted on there being enough annoyance and harassment [in Pontoise] in the very fact of moving to subdue this rebellious body."[148] To make magistrates feel "the rigors of exile," they were not allowed to lodge in the suburbs of the town.[149]

In 1763 magistrates were exiled "in two poor villages where honest men can find neither a place to stay nor anything to eat."[150]

Censorship of publications was a constant feature of the *ancien régime*.[151] All books needed the *prior* approval of the royal librarian, either explicitly or by tacit permission. The *parlements* and the Church could exercise *posterior* censorship, by condemning books or ordering them to be burned.[152] In banning a book, the government could refer to royal declarations that stated its reasons in general and sometimes excessive terms. Thus in its panic after the attempts to assassinate Louis XV in 1757, the government issued a declaration asserting that "All those convicted of having written, caused to be written, or having printed writings tending to attack religion, to upset (*émouvoir*) the minds, to subvert our authority and to disturb the order and peace of our States, shall be punished by death." In a writing from 1759 on the institution (*la librairie*) that implemented the censorship, and of which he was the director, Malesherbes wrote that "There have been, at all times, severe laws against the authors, printers, and distributors of scandalous, seditious, and slanderous pamphlets, and they have never been executed. . . . The *death penalty* for a crime described a vaguely as that of having written works tending to *upset the minds* displeased everyone and deterred no one, since one understood that such a harsh law would never be executed."[153] Also, the short half-life of emotions probably caused the persecution of subversive writers to fade away once the panic subsided.

---

147. Saint-Simon, vol. 37, p. 361. The distance between Paris and Pontoise is about 35 km., that between Paris and Blois about 185.

148. Storez-Brancourt (2007), p. 675. An indication of the rigors of exile is that nine out of eleven legal clerks died when the *Grand'Chambre* was in exile in Pontoise in 1753–1754 (Egret 1970, p. 60).

149. Storez-Brancourt (2007), p. 656.

150. Egret (1970), p. 151.

151. The following draws heavily on Félix (1999), pp. 19–31.

152. Not surprisingly, these two institutions fought for the upper hand. In 1532, the king "laid down that [theologians] were not allowed to search bookshops without the presence of two members of parliament" (Jones 2001, p. 847).

153. Malesherbes (1809), pp. 108–109.

Other declarations were more specific, such as that of March 28, 1764, "forbidding all others than our courts [the *parlements*] from printing, selling or peddling any writings, works, or projects concerning the reform or the administration of the finances, for just as much as the wise dissertation of our courts may be useful for this great purpose, the dissertations and projects written by dissolute persons (*des gens sans caractère*) who publish their writings, instead of submitting them to persons who by virtue of their situation are capable of judging them, may be contrary and harmful."[154]

The finance ministers, in particular, did not see the value of independent reflections. L'Averdy banned the writings of Turgot's close collaborator Dupont de Nemours, and "Calonne, like Necker, banned the publication of almost all manuscripts that touched on financial matters. . . . The only financial writings that received Calonne's approval were those that criticized Necker."[155]

In this domain as, in many others, the government was *fortiter in modo, suaviter in re*, speaking strongly but carrying a small stick. As noted, some of the strong language was self-defeating. When he was director of the *librairie*, Malesherbes, protected writers rather than persecuting them, going so far as to conspire with them to assure the continued publication of the banned *Encyclopédie*. Many writers circumvented the bans by having their books published abroad. As noted in chapter 3, some books were published only for the purpose of being banned, since a summary indictment could provide a more accessible version of an erudite volume. Some writers took pride in having their books banned, and complained when they were not. Tocqueville wrote, "The half-measures that were imposed on the enemies of the Church at that time did not diminish their power but rather increased it. . . . Authors were persecuted just enough to elicit complaint but not enough to provoke fear. They were subjected to enough restraint to provoke resistance but not to the heavy yoke that might quell it."[156] Counting on the laziness of the censor, authors could also use anodyne titles or subtitles to escape his attention.[157]

154. The declaration did not specify the punishment these dissolute writers might incur. The unusual royal deference to the courts must be seen in the context of L'Averdy's accession to the post of finance minister in December 1763 (Félix 1999).

155. Félix (1999), pp. 29–30.

156. Tocqueville (2011), p. 139.

157. Henry (2001), p. 1620, notes that Montaigne often used such "'facade titles' (titles that conceal more than they reveal about the subject matter of an essay." For a similar practice by Marx, see Elster (1985), p. 438 note 1.

Revenues and Spending

I have referred repeatedly to various aspects of the royal finances. I now propose a more systematic discussion of the revenues and expenses of the administration. I shall first present an overview, and then a more detailed discussion of some of the events and choices that would ultimately lead to the bankruptcy of the country and the calling of the Estates-General.

Under Louis XIII and Louis XIV, direct taxes accounted for most of the royal revenue. Under Louis XV and Louis XVI, indirect taxes were the most important. Among the direct taxes, there was an important distinction between the *impôts de répartition* and the *impôts de quotité*. The former, notably the *taille*, started from a determination of the total amount to be collected and then fixed the allocation of subtotals to *généralités*, *élections*, and parishes, as explained earlier. For the government, it had the advantage that the amount of taxes collected was unaffected by fraud, since evaded taxes were shifted onto others. The latter, which fixed the amount to be paid by individuals according to their income or status, was vulnerable to tax evasions.[158] Some of these taxes were assessed as a proportion of estimated income—2 percent, 5 percent, 10 percent, or 15 percent depending on the needs of the treasury. In 1695, the government introduced the *capitation*, a graduated head tax, which was assessed on a schedule of twenty-two groups ranked by social status, roughly but imperfectly correlated with income or wealth.

Unlike the *taille*, these income-based and status-based taxes were in principle supposed to be paid by everyone. In practice, the privileged were usually able to use their influence and connections to obtain exemptions or rebates. Cities and provinces often negotiated fixed lump-sum payments (*abonnements*), which offered the government the advantage of certainty and individuals the advantage of paying lower taxes than accurate individual assessments would have required. Among indirect taxes, the salt tax was the most important and the most hated. Indirect taxes were mostly collected by tax farmers, in symbiotic collaboration with bankers and financiers. This mode of collection, which also had the advantage of certainty, generated waste by the numerous middlemen and speculators. Throughout the old regime there were many proposals and attempts to

---

158. Félix (1999), p. 281, paraphrasing Turgot, writes that "the *vingtième* [a 5 percent *impôt de quotité*] placed the king alone facing his subjects, whereas the *ancien régime* relied fundamentally on a corporatist conception," in which members of the parish were collectively responsible for taxes and could hold each other individually responsible for tax evasions.

put these taxes in *régie*, as a regular part of the royal administration, with mixed results.

The main "ordinary" (peacetime) expenses included the cost of maintenance and improvement of infrastructure, the budget of the army and the navy, the salaries of venal office-holders and of non-venal officials, the expenses of the royal household, pensions to courtiers, and the interest on government bonds and annuities. In wartime, there were also "extraordinary" expenses. The terms "ordinary" and "extraordinary" are somewhat misleading, however. From 1632 to the beginning of the "personal reign" of Louis XIV in 1661 France was more or less continuously at war against Spain and the Austrian-Hungarian Empire. After 1661, wars spanned the periods 1672–1679 (the War against Holland), 1688–1697 (the War against the League of Augsburg), 1701–1714 (the War of the Spanish succession), 1733–1735 (the War of the Polish succession), 1740–1748 (the War of the Austrian succession), 1756–1763 (the Seven Years War) and 1776–1781 (the War of American independence). As these add up to more than half of the whole period 1632–1789, war was in fact a more "ordinary" state than peace. Moreover, even in peacetime the government devoted important resources to preparations for war.

In peacetime, "ordinary expenses" might be covered, at least approximately, by "ordinary revenues" from existing taxes. According to Marion, the "short period that separated the War of the Polish succession from the War of the Austrian succession was the best in the financial history of the *ancien régime*," when revenues and expenses came close to being in equilibrium.[159] The 1660s and the early 1770s were also periods of approximate balance. To address the deficit that existed for most of the old regime, successive finance ministers tried to reduce the expenses and/ or increase the revenue. Many effected cuts in pensions and in the royal household, to some, but not very large, effect. As Malesherbes observed in a text I cited earlier, "the love of glory, of pleasures, even of friendship, the natural desire of a great Prince to provide for the happiness of those who approach him" constituted perpetual obstacles to such cuts. Some ministers also wanted to eliminate venal offices, but were deterred by the costs of reimbursing them. Less honestly, they often cut expenses by reducing the interest paid on government bonds and annuities, by reducing the salaries of venal officers, or (as explained earlier) by increasing them in exchange for a one-off payment. These and other short-term expedients, which amounted to concealed bankruptcies, undermined themselves in

159. Marion (1927), pp. 160–161.

the long run. More generally, in practice the finance ministers had little control over expenses, except for those allocated to roads and bridges.[160] Their main task was to gather the funds the king requested.

In practice, the government had to focus on increasing its revenues. As noted earlier, a more equal allotment of the *taille* could have increased the total that was collected. By exposing "false nobles" claiming exemption from the *taille* one might also increase the mass of taxpayers. The establishment of cadasters or the verification of self-reported estimates could also have increased the taxes that were collected. None of these proposals, when implemented, succeeded on a large scale.

Among many other measures, four seem to stand out: confiscation of the profits of bankers and financiers, the creation of new venal offices, tax increases, and loans. The first was implemented by the establishment of a *chambre de justice*, a special court created after a change of reign or in the aftermath of war to demand that financiers regurgitate some of their profits, either because these were (rhetorically) deemed excessive or because of the classical "adage that the living king is not in any way responsible for the actions of the dead king."[161] It does not seem that these prosecutions brought in substantial sums, and in any case they were one-off operations.[162] The second measure was a stop-gap expedient, which recreated penury when the officers had to be paid. I shall discuss the last two measures, which were the most important, at greater length.

To a large extent, the old regime survived day by day, month by month, year by year, by using the tricks of the trade of bankers and financiers, juggling with currencies, repackaging loans, issuing paper money of various kinds, including certificates that were backed by future taxes, and so on. Many of these devices involved a chain of middlemen, who siphoned off a part of the taxes, or lent them out at high rates of interest, before they finally reached the royal treasury. Two outstanding finance ministers of the old regime, Machault (1749–1754) and Turgot (1774–1776), eschewed such short-term stop-gap measures (*expédients*).[163] Marion writes about

160. Claeys (2011), pp. 147–148.

161. Meyer (1981), p. 206. As noted earlier, the status of this adage as a "fundamental law" is uncertain. In an attenuated form of this principle, a new administration could also refuse to honor the promises of its predecessor (Velde and Weir 1992, p. 9).

162. Dessert (1984). The motive behind the *chambres de justice* of 1661 is revealed by the fact that "the fines were set proportionally to the wealth of the accused and not as a function of the gravity of the embezzlements" (Claeys 2011, p. 548).

163. Slater (2018, pp. 7–8) writes that "[i]n the short run, management of the National Debt is highly technical, even arcane. It is difficult even for the most intelligent outsider to grasp what is going on. This complexity and lack of transparency can be a great help to

Machault that "he had no special knowledge of finance; far behind professional bankers . . . in the art of finding resources and in imagining *expédients*; he had the thankless task of making sure that in the future one would be able to do without *expédients*."[164] Instead he tried to improve the efficiency of tax collection. Turgot's principle was to rely neither on tax increases, nor on loans, nor on (full or partial, open or concealed) bankruptcies, but to improve tax collection and reduce expenses.[165] Both failed. By contrast, Turgot's successor Necker (1776–1781) relied on loans, a policy that seemed to succeed miraculously well, but, in the opinion of some historians, proved disastrous.

Necker Cause of the Revolution?

The proximate financial causes of the calling of the Estates-General will concern me in Volume 3. Here, I want to take few steps back in the causal chain, to discuss the decision to join the Americans in the War of Independence. At the time, the French "burned with the desire to make England atone for its success in the Seven Years War."[166] The American Revolution was "the occasion that had been awaited for a long time, and, as far as possible, even provoked, to take revenge on British imperialism—a pointless revenge, with no other gain or aim than the humiliation of the traditional adversary."[167] In fact, the revenge was not only pointless, but arguably needless. As early as 1750, Turgot (aged twenty-three) had observed that "colonies are like fruits that remain attached to the tree only until they are ripe: once they are self-sufficient they do what Carthage did [when gaining its independence from the Phoenicians in 650 B.C.] and *what America will do one day*."[168] Great Britain would have lost its colonies without any French intervention, and hence at no cost to France. Yet, as Lüthy remarks, "it would probably have been superhuman to resist the temptation" to

---

politicians and technocrats in constructing their short-term fixes, which usually depend on some sleight-of-hand to obscure where the real burdens have been transferred." I suspect that this statement is even more true for the *ancien régime* than it is today.

164. Marion (1891), p. 11.

165. Marion (1927), p. 290.

166. Gomel (1892), vol. 1, p. 230.

167. Lüthy (2005), p. 592–3.

168. Turgot (1844), vol. 2, p. 602; my italics. In a memorandum he wrote to Louis XVI in 1776, immediately before he was discharged as finance minister, Turgot (ibid., pp. 552–553) repeated this prediction, in more nuanced form. In 1765, Louis XV's principal minister Choiseul (1904, p. 393) also made the same prediction to the king, urging him to refrain from increasing the French debt and to do his best to make the British increase theirs.

humiliate Britain.[169] It seems appropriate here to invoke a famous maxim by La Bruyère: "Nothing is easier for passion than to overcome reason; its greatest triumph is to conquer interest."[170] Although the government might have been deterred by the prospect of raising taxes for the war, Marion affirms that the success of subscriptions to the loan of December 1777 overcame any hesitations it might have had.[171]

The "financial causes of the French Revolution" is a much-debated topic, on which experts differ. According to a traditional view, defended by Marcel Marion, René Stourm, Charles Gomel, and more recently by Herbert Lüthy, the root cause was not so much the expenses that France incurred in supporting the American War of Independence as the decision by Necker, as de facto finance minister, to fund them by loans rather than by taxes. That decision, in turn, has usually been ascribed to his extraordinary vanity and his desire to be acclaimed for achieving a "painless war."[172] Much of the literature is psychologizing and, occasionally, moralizing. This body of mostly older studies may be held up against recent Anglo-American literature, which tends to argue that "the repeated crises of the Old Regime owed more to institutional, even constitutional, flaws than to errors by individuals."[173] Whereas Gomel argues that "the crisis that led to the convocation of the Estates-Genera and the fall of the royalty can be imputed to the shortsightedness of Necker's management during his first period as minister,"[174] Robert Harris affirms that the abuse of Necker by historians is "incomprehensible."[175]

It is hard to assess the validity of these competing claims. It seems worthwhile, nevertheless, to comment on how Necker's psychology may

169. Lüthy (2005), p. 593. In his *Mémoires*, Louis XVI's minister of war, the Comte de Ségur (1859, vol. 1, p. 102) writes that Louis XVI opposed the war, not because it would be costly and risky, but because "his conscience made him view the violation of treaties and of peace, without any other motive than humiliating a rival power, as a perfidy." Yet, as he goes on to write, influenced by popular pressure the government took the first steps towards what became a large and costly war effort.

170. La Bruyère (1881), 4.77. Adam Smith (1976, p. 465) notes, however, that in some cases "national animosity" and national interest converge in their aims.

171. Marion (1927), p. 299.

172. See also Thomas Jefferson's character assassination of Necker cited in the Appendix.

173. Velde and Weir (1992), p. 3. They also affirm that the life annuities that were a major source of revenue towards the end of the old regime were "based on realistic expectations about the differential default risks of the different assets" and "can be explained without recourse to assumptions of noncompetitive behavior, conspiracy, or irrationality on the part of the government or any other party" (ibid., p. 4).

174. Gomel (1892), vol. 1, p. 255.

175. Harris (1970), p. 255.

have shaped his decisions. Contemporaries as well as historians agree on his excessive need for approval and popularity. Even his daughter Madame de Staël, who adored him, wrote that "the goal of his actions, the wind that carried him, was the love of approval (*amour de la considération*)."[176] Véri refers to his "somewhat childish desire for glory and popular favor."[177] The *constituant* Malouet said that "he had a timid pride, which rested on the means at his disposal and on his fame, and which constantly made him fear to go against public opinion,"[178] and the economist Montyon that "the core of his character was a degree of self-love that exceeds the common measure of human vanity."[179] Senac de Meilhan writes that his *Compte-Rendu* was motivated "by the unique and imperious need for success and praise."[180] Modern writers use stronger language. Marion writes that his love of glory was carried to "an almost pathological (*maladif*) level" and that he was "devoured by the need for applause that was the dominant passion of his whole life."[181] Commenting on the *Compte-rendu* (1781), Petitfils writes that "it reveals on each page, in bombastic language, the self-importance and self-satisfaction of its author."[182] Commenting on his *Eloge de Colbert* (1773), Lüthy observes that it was "in reality a praise of Necker by himself."[183] As a final and revealing testimony, one may cite Necker's self-adulation in 1776 when he wrote to the principal minister of Louis XVI, Maurepas, to assuage the latter's doubt about how the king would react to an unknown face: "Even a person made of bronze will not be able to resist reason and wisdom, joined to the sensibility and frankness of manner which announce the purity of the soul and necessarily create attachments. This has been the experience of my whole life."[184]

The cumulative effect of these characterizations, which could be multiplied, leaves little room for doubt about Necker's extreme vanity and desire for popularity. The crucial question is whether they affected his choices.[185] Contemporaries and some historians have certainly thought

176. De Stäel (2000), vol. 1, viii.

177. Véri (1930), p. 173.

178. Malouet (1874), vol.1, p. 217.

179. Montyon (1812), p. 192.

180. Meilhan (1795), p. 180.

181. Marion (1927), pp. 202, 324, 332. Petifils (2014a), p. 341, also refers to Necker's "vanité maladive."

182. Petitfils (2005a), p. 343.

183. Lüthy (2005), p. 407.

184. Cited in Egret (1975), pp. 46–47.

185. Implicitly arguing against the policies of Robert Walpole, Hume (1985), p. 352, explains the preference for loans over taxes by a less idiosyncratic trait of politicians: "It is very tempting to a minister to employ such an expedient, as enables him to make a great

so. Véri thought his preference for loans over taxes was due to his desire for popularity, claiming that "he could not make up his mind to demand [new] taxes, fearing he might lose his fame and popular favor in the provinces."[186] More generally, he wrote, "in each operation of M. Necker . . . I find rather the desire to merit praise than a judicious understanding of the public utility."[187] Senac de Meilhan explains his resort to loans by his desire to "seduce the multitude, which was enchanted by the sight of a war conducted without tax increases."[188] Among historians, Gomel also cites Necker's desire for "personal success" to explain the extremely favorable conditions he offered for life annuities.[189] Others have explained his preference for loans over taxes by his background as a banker,[190] in which case his popularity might be an *effect* of his policies rather than an intended *aim* that would explain them. Also, the fear that the *parlements* might have refused to register new taxes may have induced the same preference.[191] Finally, Necker explained to Louis XVI that by multiplying the number of bondholders one would create a social group that was attached to the stability of the regime.[192]

Be this as it may, there is evidence that Necker counted on the subscribers to his loans being *less rational than himself.* In the *Eloge de Colbert*, written before he became finance minister, he noted as an argument "in favor of loans, compared to taxes, [the fact that] the annual increase in Europe of precious metals alleviates the weight of the taxes one pays to the Sovereign and *reduces the value of the interests that he pays to the bondholders*, for a million is worth much less today than it was twenty years ago."[193] We know from Véri's report of a conversation he had with Necker in 1780 that the latter also expressed this view during his first tenure as finance minister. "He talked to me about raising a loan in the province [of Berry]. 'That would also be my opinion, I told him, but one must also

---

figure during his administration, without overburthening the people with taxes, or exciting any *immediate* clamours against himself. The practice, therefore, of contracting debt will almost infallibly be abused, in every government" (my italics).

186. Véri (1930), p. 376. He also cites, as one possible explanation of Necker's reluctance to tax, his "susceptibility to the praise by some people of his financial skill in supporting the costs of war without taxes" (ibid., p. 268).

187. Ibid., p. 305.

188. Meilhan (1795), p. 181.

189. Gomel (1892), p. 276.

190. Augeard (1781), p. 16; Marion (1927), p. 295.

191. Egret (1975), p. 93.

192. Petitfils (2005a), p. 322.

193. Necker (1773), pp. 122–123.

establish a tax, either to pay the interests or to create a reimbursement fund.' Why worry so much about reimbursement, he said. All this does not affect the general course (*marche*) of nations. In any case, the capital always diminishes with time."[194] Elsewhere, Véri notes that his "uncertainty [concerning the reimbursement of the loans] leaves doubts about [Necker's] principles of justice and humanity."[195] Unlike finance ministers before 1726, Necker did not advocate or—when in office—practice debasement of the coinage, a form of endogenous inflation, but counted on exogenous inflation having the same effect.

If bondholders had rational expectations and anticipated the inflationary outcome stated in the phrase I italicized above, they would of course have demanded higher nominal yields to offset the inflation, thus undercutting Necker's argument. Implicitly, therefore, he assumed that they were irrational. With respect to small bondholders, at least, he may have been right. To my knowledge, this issue is not discussed in the literature. Instead, scholars have focused on the demand for higher nominal yields to offset the risk of default, differentiating among more and less risky assets.[196] Prospective lenders had plenty of evidence to back their estimates of default risks, and the government knew it had to offer better rates on the more risky assets. By contrast, I have not come across any discussions of how anticipations of inflation driven by an influx of precious metals affected market rates.[197] Nor is it clear that Necker had a firm basis for his prediction. His statement may simply have been a weak rationalization for a preference for loans over taxes that he had adopted on other grounds.[198]

As we have seen, there are many possible causes for the government's preference for loans over taxes towards the end of the old regime. I believe that the most important factor was its desire to defer financial sacrifices, under the pressure of diffuse public opinion as well as the sabotage potential of the *parlements*. Be this as it may, the *effect* of that preference was the build-up of the debt to an unsustainable level (see Volume 3).

194. Véri (1930), p. 269.

195. Ibid., p. 360.

196. Velde and Weir (1992).

197. Velde and Weir (ibid.), p. 18, discuss inflation caused by endogenous (government-initiated) currency devaluation, and note correctly that it is "more logically subsumed under default risk." They do not, however, discuss the exogenous cause of inflation that Necker cites. When White (2001), p. 60, writes that "without a commitment to price stability, it would be difficult for [the French] government to use debt finance," he also refers to endogenous sources of inflation.

198. For obvious reasons, he did not publicly repeat this argument while in office.

The Legal System

Above, I discussed the use of exile in the perennial struggle between the courts and the king, interrupted only between 1673 and 1715 and between 1770 and 1775. This struggle was only one aspect of their relation. I shall now propose a fuller account.

Up to now, I have used the terms "court" and *parlement* more or less as synonyms. It is time for a more fine-grained description.[199] The *parlements* were at the core of the legal system. Because they were the highest courts of appeal, they called themselves "sovereign courts." The king referred to them as "superior courts," since he could override their decisions by several forms of *justice retenue*. There was a varying number of *parlements*, thirteen at the eve of the Revolution. The *parlement* of Paris had a vast jurisdiction, ranging over time from one third to one half of the kingdom, and was generally in the forefront in the conflict that opposed the *parlements* to the king. In the eighteenth century, an influential mythomaniac, Lepaige, went back to the times of Clovis (fifth century) and even to the German tribes of the first century, to justify his claim that the *parlements* had originally formed a single court, which had been artificially dismembered and now had to be reconstituted in a *union des classes* capable of confronting the king as unitary agent.

The highest court in a *parlement* was the *Grand'Chambre*, whose *Premier Président* was the only legal officer who was appointed directly by the king and whose office was revocable. On some occasions, the *parlements* "had to defend their rights against [among other things] the energetic or insinuating action of the presidents, who were in reality the king's men."[200] Lower courts, *chambres des enquêtes* and *chambres des requêtes*,

---

199. Bluche (1986b), pp. 10–17, offers a concise yet comprehensive survey.

200. Egret (1970), p. 179; see also Flammermont (1888–1898), vol. 1, pp. lxxxix–xci, for some of the tactics the *Premier Président* used to manipulate the opinions of his body. Marion (1898), pp. 57–64, 178, 258–259, 396, shows how the *Premier Président* of the *parlement* in Britanny variously defended the king against the body he presided and the body against the king. In 1764, Miromesnil, the *Premier Président* of the *parlement* of Rouen, had to tell the chancellor that he could no longer restrict his rebellious magistrates (Félix 1999, p. 119). Barbier, vol. 2, p. 109, cites an example from Paris in which the *Premier Président* was subject both to the contempt of his magistrates and to the displeasure of the Court. Storez-Brancourt (2007), p. 715, cites a text from the exile of the *parlement* in 1753, reporting that "the hot spirits are furious that the *Premier Président* went hunting with the Prince [of Conti], saying that the *Premier Président* did not go to kill partridges, but rather themselves." In 1720, the *Premier Président* of the normally government-friendly *Grand Conseil* was outvoted by his body when he asked it to comply with the wishes of the regent (Brancourt 2013, pp. 207–209; see also Durieux 2010, p.77). In 1750, the *parlement*

carried out the bulk of ordinary legal business. There were several of these courts, each with its own president, opening for the *préséance* conflicts and divide-and-conquer tactics by the Court that Saint-Simon described. Among several other courts, the most important was the *cour des aides*, a tax court. I have often cited the remonstrances that Malesherbes wrote for this court. Another court, the *chambre des comptes*, had some nuisance power if it refused to verify the royal accounts, but by the eighteenth century it had lost most of its powers. A third court, the *cour des monnaies*, had the task of overseeing coinage and judging counterfeiters.

In addition to the first presidents, the kings could also shape the law by bringing edicts before the *Grand Conseil*, a special court that was under their direct influence. Its jurisdiction was ill-defined, and always contested by the *parlements*. In 1755–1756, a trivial conflict of jurisdiction escalated, when the king first tried to impose the authority of the Grand Conseil and then, after strong remonstrances by the *parlement*, had to retreat.[201] When the *parlements* were reestablished in 1774, after the abolition by Maupeou in 1771, the *Grand Conseil* acquired a new function, to which I shall return, as a latent threat to the courts.

Conflicts between the courts and the king could arise in adjudication, if the king chose to exercise his *justice retenue*, and in legislation. The former interference, to which I have referred earlier, was a constant bone of contention, but less significant than the latter, to which I shall turn shortly.[202] First, however, let me briefly survey the motives that animated the magistrates. As I noted earlier, one cannot exclude that they sometimes viewed themselves as guardians of the interests of the French,

---

of Paris withdrew from its *Premier President* the right to formulate its remonstrances and to "modify them if the style of the head of the company seemed to soften or misrepresent the discussions in the assemblies" (Félix 1999, p. 235). Exceptionally (Cubells 1987, p.74; Swann 2017, p. 199) the *Premier Président* could also serve as *intendant*, thus cumulating two positions as "the king's man." Conjecturally, the cumulation of roles may have weakened his efficacy in both.

201. Egret (1970), pp. 72–74.

202. The best-known form of *justice retenue* was known as "evocation," the transfer of a case from the jurisdiction under which it would normally fall to another instance, often the *intendant* or the royal council. Marion (1923), p. 226, writes that "the progress or decline in royal power could be measured almost precisely by the number and the ease of evocations." Barbiche (2012, p. 299), writes that the procedure was used only exceptionally in the eighteenth century, the time when the *parlements* repeatedly and successfully encroached on the royal power. (Tocqueville 2011, p. 56 overestimated the frequency of evocations.) A separate issue, which I mentioned earlier, is that an *évocation* might actually provide superior justice to that of the *parlements*. It might also be much cheaper for the litigants, as noted by d'Argenson, vol. 2, p. 18.

as distinct from the interest of the king. The remonstrances penned by Malesherbes are outstanding instances, and there may be others. Yet when they presented themselves in this light, both contemporaries and historians affirm that they were often moved by the desire for popularity. As I have noted, Parisians magistrates had a strong interest in the integrity of the *rentes sur l'Hôtel de Ville*. The *parlements* also had an institutional interest in litigation. In addition to the salary that went with office, the litigating parties paid them fees (*épices*).[203] Hence they opposed any reforms that threatened to reduce the number or duration of lawsuits. Thus when Turgot abolished the guilds in 1776, the *parlement* resisted the reform because it "would lose the great benefits that they generated."[204] For the same reason, it resisted any form of *justice retenue* that would take their business away.[205]

The magistrates were far from a homogeneous body. They might be unanimous in defending their privileges and income, but not necessarily in other matters. In plenary sessions, many votes were close.[206] There were several sources of heterogeneity. As noted, older magistrates tended to be more compliant with the royal demands than were the younger ones.[207] Also, recently ennobled magistrates "were among the most vocal in defending their hard-won rights and privileges."[208] Although most magistrates were Jansenists or Gallicans, some defended the papal bull *Unigenitus*. Powerful ministers such as the Duc de Choiseul, principal minister from 1760 to 1771, used their powers of patronage to "build a party within the *parlement*."[209] Finally, matters of *préséance* within and across the *par-*

203. Malesherbes proposed to pool the *épices* and share them among the judges (Grosclaude 1961, p. 283), a reform that would have limited their greed (and their income). Unsurprisingly, it was not accepted.

204. Letter from the Swedish ambassador to Paris to his king, cited in Marie-Thérèse and Mercy-d'Argenteau (1874), vol. 1, p. lii. Not only did law suits generate profits; Argenson, vol. 2, p. 18, asserts, among many others, that the courts generated law suits.

205. Argenson, vol. 2, p. 18.

206. For examples of close votes see Swann (1995), pp. 108, 118, 171, 179, 280, 345; and Hardy, vol. 1, pp. 176, 190, 192, 214, 325, 592, vol. 2, pp. 243, 253, 332, 490, and vol. 3, pp. 348, 363.

207. Hardy, vol. 2, p. 244, notes that "everybody was surprised to see that the oldest and richest [among the prosecutors] who were most able to resist the events were precisely among those whose lack of firmness made them fall into the trap that had been made for them; whereas the younger, who had the most to lose, gave an example to their elders in showing that they cared more about conserving their honor and were less attached to their interest." Note their concern with honor, not with the public interest.

208. Swann (1995), p. 301.

209. Swann (1995), p. 298. In this respect, at least, the *parlement* had a more than verbal similarity to the homonymous British institution.

lements constituted a permanent source of divisions and oppositions. As I
noted, the kings and their ministers could exploit these differences. However, the government itself was no more unitary than the opposition in the
parlements, as ministers were constantly intriguing against each other,
seeking to promote their clients and demote their opponents. The conflict
between the government and the *parlements* cannot be viewed as a game
between two unitary actors, or not even as the exploitation by one unitary
actor of the divisions of the other.

To introduce the role of the *parlements* in legislation, let me mention
two non-legislative bodies that assess legislation, or proposed legislation,
in contemporary France: the *Conseil d'Etat* and the *Conseil Constitutionnel*. The former has mainly a technical role, that of ensuring that a law is
consistent with existing legislation and satisfies usual criteria of legal construction ("control of legality"). The role of the latter, as its name implies,
is that of ensuring that a law is consistent with the constitution ("control
of constitutionality"). The history of the *parlements* might be stated, in
simplified form, as their struggle to go beyond a role similar to that of the
Conseil d'Etat and appropriate for themselves a role similar to that of the
Conseil Constitutionnel, in the absence both of a written constitution and,
a fortiori, of a constitutional basis for that appropriation. At times, they
also compared themselves to the British parliament, but with a right to
veto rather than to initiate legislation.

In the absence of a written constitution, the *parlements* justified their
protestations by appealing to the unwritten or customary "fundamental
laws of the kingdom." As I discuss later, they were not the only institutions of the *ancien régime* that tried to limit the power of the kings by
these putative or alleged laws. The Estates-General that met with irregular intervals from 1302 to 1614 as well as the provincial Estates of the
pays d'états, notably Brittany, Burgundy, and Languedoc, used similar
arguments and similar rhetoric.[210] Not surprisingly, a king could benefit
from conflicts between the institutions that contested his power (*tertius
gaudens*) and sometimes actively turn them against one another (*divide et
impera*).[211] I discuss some examples in chapter 5.

210. Magistrates and deputies argued, for instance, that "the establishment of new
taxes required the respect for certain formalities that called for the intervention of several
organs, such as: the king and the sovereign courts [the *parlements*]; the king, the provincial estates, and the sovereign courts; the king, the Estates-General, and the sovereign
courts; or the king and the Estates-General" (Vergne 2006, p. 207).

211. For this distinction, see Simmel (1908), pp. 82–94.

In 1935 Stalin dismissed the importance of the pope, asking how many divisions he had. He might have been surprised if he had observed the role of Pope John Paul II in bringing down Communism in Eastern Europe. When the young diarist d'Argenson argued the case of the *parlement* to his father, the redoubtable *lieutenant de police*, the Marquis d'Argenson, echoed Stalin in his answer: "My son, does the *parlement* have any troops? On our side, we have 150,000 men; that's what it comes down to."[212] He cannot have ignored the real—if short-lived—power of the Paris *parlement* during the Fronde, based largely on the effect of its decisions on the people of Paris. According to one historian, "the political propaganda of the *parlement*, which accused the rulers of the country, notably Mazarin, of being tyrannical and corrupt, finally made the Parisians find unacceptable a relatively moderate fiscal policy. . . . Although the magistrates did not directly provoke the uprising, there is an evident link between the rebellion and the policies they had pursued since 1643."[213]

D'Argenson *père* may have been right in dismissing a similar influence in 1718. Although the *parlement* had regained its power to remonstrate as part of a deal struck with the Regent in 1715,[214] the monarchy was stronger than it had been in 1648.[215] He ignored, however a source of parliamentary power that was to prove important later in the century, the control over the judicial system. Just as the kings could use *exile* as a tool of deterrence or compellence, the courts could use *judicial strike* and *collective resignations* for the same purposes. Although, to my knowledge, the courts never threatened explicitly to use these tools, there was a standing implicit threat. Egret refers to "the two dangers that obsessed the power: the coalition of the sovereign courts and the judicial strike."[216] The edicts from 1725 and

212. Argenson, vol. 1, p. 20. Voltaire observed that "you cannot pay armies with remonstrances" (Swann 1995, p. 216).

213. Pernot (2012), p. 90.

214. Swann (2017), p. 174, asserts that in 1715 the Regent reestablished remonstrances as "a much needed safety valve that helped personal monarchy to avoid appearing capricious." I have not seen evidence that this was the *intention* of the Regent. It may or may not have been the *effect* of the remonstrances.

215. In 1720, there were rumors that the *parlement* was about to stage a coup d'Etat and depose the regent (Marais, vol. 1, pp. 333–334; Barbier vol. 1, p. 53; Buvat 1865, vol. 2, p. 114–15). According to these writers, this conspiracy was the cause of the exile of the magistrates. Saint-Simon (vol. 37, pp. 355–363) explains the exile by the refusal of the court to register a financial edict. As he was much closer to the Regent than the diarists were, I tend to dismiss the rumors they report. Egret (1970), p. 37, characterizes the imputation of an intention to depose the regent as "dubious."

216. Egret (1970), p. 48. Swann (1995), p. 227, refers to the scenario of a concerted judicial strike of the *parlements* as the crown's "nightmare."

1756 that I cited earlier, and which would have required magistrates to have at least ten years of service before being allowed to vote in certain matters, were intended to neutralize this threat. (As I noted, the imposed silence of the people forced the government to withdraw the edict of 1725, while that of 1756 was never implemented.) The implicit threat was credible because the magistrates did in fact suspend their work on a number of occasions in the eighteenth century, in the hope that the costs their strikes or resignations imposed on the government would cause it to retract the offending edicts. Referring readers to Egret's comprehensive account and to a briefer, more conceptual overview by Olivier-Martin,[217] I shall limit myself to some aspects of these episodes. For reasons of space, I focus on the *parlement* of Paris, although much of what I shall say also applies to the provincial courts.

The edicts that triggered strikes or resignations varied. In 1648, the magistrates went on strike when the government created twenty-four additional offices, thus devaluing the existing ones.[218] Similarly, in the first half of the eighteenth century magistrates resorted to these measures only when their individual or collective privileges were threatened. In the second half, this motivation could still operate, as it did in 1756, but financial and notably religious matters were more important. The long shutdown from May 1753 to September 1754 was caused by the long-simmering controversy over the papal bull *Unigenitus*, condemning Jansenism. Although the magistrates were not for the most part Jansenists, they were Gallican, meaning that they resisted interference from Rome in French affairs. The courts were embedded in a larger judicial system, which also included lawyers, prosecutors, clerks, ushers, and jailers, whose inaction could paralyze any alternative court the government might establish. Thus when the government established a *Chambre Royale* in Paris in 1753, "it was almost totally inactive and soon fell into total disgrace among the pleaders. [Four] prosecutors who had been in this chamber were told by their colleagues that when the *parlement* was reestablished, they would no longer be received in the community and that none of them would plead against these four. There are immense charitable works among them and among the poor lawyers to support them in the interest of the common cause of the *parlement*."[219] The work

217. Egret (1970); Olivier-Martin (1997), pp. 399–418.

218. Pernot (2012), p. 68. The government backed down, by reducing the number of new offices to twelve.

219. Argenson, vol. 8, p. 200. On jailers who refused to release prisoners, see Marion (1898), p. 353.

of the *Grand'Chambre* exiled in Pontoise in 1720 was also undermined by the concerted absence of the lawyers.[220]

I conclude this discussion of the struggle between the courts and the royal government by a summary of the tools that each side had at its disposal.

As for the courts, they could

Write remonstrances and, if the king insisted by a *lettre de jussion*, repeat them (*remontrances itératives*).

If the king then imposed his will by a *lit de justice*, the courts could refuse to implement the law. This refusal was called an *arrêt de défense*, "a ruling that would prohibit royal officials from executing [an edict] under the penalty of being prosecuted."[221] This extreme measure had a striking "scandal effect but relatively little impact, since the royal council was quick to strike it down."[222]

Less drastically, magistrates could drag their feet in applying a law they didn't like.[223]

Magistrates could resign their office, individually or collectively. This measure was risky, since the resignations might be accepted.[224]

Magistrates and other officers of the courts could suspend their functions, without formally resigning.[225]

The courts could count on or encourage go-slow actions or abstentions by other actors in the legal system, as well as on their ostracism of cooperators with the government.[226]

---

220. Brancourt (2013), pp. 12, 25; see also Saint-Simon, vol. 37, p. 367. The sabotage by the lawyers mattered only for civil cases; criminal cases could be pursued as usual (Storez-Brancourt 2007, p. 665–666). In 1753–1754, by contrast, one observed "an obstinate silence of the judges, even in criminal matters for which the old regime did not tolerate any delays" (ibid., p. 704). Bargaining theory tells us that this fact must have strengthened the hand of the courts. Regarding the "affaire des avocats" in 1730–1731, Bell (1990), p. 570, asserts that because the lawyers did not form an official body, the government could deploy against them only "the threat of going hungry" (*la menace de la faim*). As he nevertheless observes, lawyers no less than judges were sometimes exiled.

221. Kwass (2000), p. 186.

222. Egret (1970), p. 179.

223. Jouanna (1998), p. 130.

224. Ibid.

225. Moderate judges could also abstain from attending plenary sessions of the *parlements* (Swann (1995, pp. 78, 118, 356). Whether intentionally or not, their abstention strengthened the radicals and worked against the crown.

226. For examples, see Bluche (1986b), p. 97.

They could also take steps to ensure the reluctance of magistrates to
replace those that had gone on strike or resigned, to instill fear of
future retaliation when the regular courts were restored.[227]

Because of the great publicity of these measures, and the public-
interest language in which they were phrased, the court could also
count on the people of Paris to support them.

In the *pays d'états*, courts might in some cases count on the support
of the provincial Estates,[228] although conflicts between the two
bodies were more frequent (chapter 5).

Among these measures, the fourth and the fifth were the most efficacious but also the most costly, in terms of lost *gages* or *épices*. As in
many other cases of bargaining, the question was always whether the
magistrates and their allies could stand their losses for longer than the
king could tolerate the paralysis of the judicial system, notably of criminal justice (see note 220 above). An entry in the journal of Barbier from
January 1754, during the long exile of the *parlement*, is revealing: " [In
the radical opposition] one had hoped that the suspension of activities of
the *parlement* would have stirred up trouble; that is what the [radical]
party demanded. Instead, everything is calm and the partisans [*gens de
parti*] are ruining themselves to support the indigent."[229] In other words,
the magistrates had hoped that the paralysis of the judicial system would
cause unrest in Paris and force the king to yield; instead, it drained the
finances of those who had to support the loss of income of lawyers and
others during the suspension.

As for the king and his ministers, they could

Use the tools of exile and, more rarely, of house arrest and
imprisonment. These instruments could be deployed in a divide-
and-conquer fashion, as when "on the night of January 19–20, 1771
[each] magistrate was awakened by two musketeers and asked
to give a straightforward answer of 'yes' and 'no' to the question
of whether he would resume his duties suspended since the
assembly of January 13. The aim was to drive a wedge between the
moderates and the implacable opponents of the crown."[230]

227. Ibid., p. 62. The fears were real, as shown by the treatment of the substitute magistrates when the *parlements* were restored in 1774 (Véri 1928, p. 226).

228. Lavisse (1995), p. 150; Pillorget and Pillorget (1989), pp. 530–531.

229. Barbier, vol. 6, p. 7.

230. Swann (1995), pp. 348–349. Some judges in the opposition answered "yes," but
recanted when the *parlement* assembled at 3 p.m. Barbier, vol. 1, pp. 17, 71, offers acute

The government could also try to bribe the magistrates, by offering them tax exemptions, pensions, or plain cash. When Mazarin imposed a "tax on the well-off" (*taxe des aisés*) in 1644, the *parlement* registered the law without objections since the magistrates were explicitly exempt.[231]

As noted, the government could try to manipulate the *parlements* by having the *Premier Président*—the king's man in the court—bring pressure on his colleagues or influence their remonstrances. As also noted, this tactic could backfire.

The government could also try to divide the courts by offering selective benefits to some of them, as in an episode from 1648 when Mazarin offered more advantageous financial conditions to magistrates in the *parlement* than to those in the *Cour des Aides*, la *Chambre des Comptes*, and le *Grand Conseil*. Although the magistrates in the *parlement* were initially tempted to accept the more favorable treatment, they finally joined the other courts in a "revolt of the judges."[232]

As explained in chapter 2, the king could try to paralyze the *parlement* by playing on conflicts of *préséance* among its chambers.

The government could also use its dominant position vis-à-vis the provincial Estates to undermine the *parlements*. Egret writes that the courts "were obliged to defend themselves . . . against their sustained and manipulated rivalry with the provincial Estates, which were too docile to the seductions of power and deliberately thwarted the actions of the parliamentarians."[233] It is likely that the government also benefited from conflicts between the *parlements* and the provincial estates even when it had not instigated them (*tertius gaudens*). I return to this question in chapter 5.

The king could also try to undermine the *parlement* by strengthening its rival, the royal *Grand Conseil*. The intention behind the edict of 1768 reestablishing the *Grand Conseil* was arguably "to weaken the position of the *parlement*."[234] After Louis XVI in 1774

---

insights into the collective action problem that the magistrates would face when told to either go into exile or accept the king's demands, while not knowing what their fellow judges would do.

231. Pernot (2012), p. 52.

232. Moote (1972), p. 127 and *passim*. In the next century, this solidarity was often undermined by questions of *préséance* (Egret 1970, pp. 154–156).

233. Egret (1970), p. 179.

234. Swann (1995), p. 291.

restored the *parlement* that Louis XV had abolished in 1771, he gave a new role to the *Grand Conseil,* which would *automatically* replace it if the magistrates suspended their functions or resigned collectively. This device—invented or inspired by Malesherbes— seems to have had the intended effect of taming the *parlements,* at least until the years immediately before the Revolution.[235]

Following a long-standing practice, in 1763 the finance minister Bertin "ordered . . . the financial decisions to be registered on a *lit de justice* the very day of the judicial vacations. In this way, he hoped that tempers would cool over the summer."

The government could try to *negotiate* (using bribes, threats, or promises) its edicts with the *parlement* before formally presenting them for registration. Thus when the finance minister L'Averdy worried whether the *parlement* of Britanny would register the declaration of November 1763, the Duc d'Aiguillon told him not "to hesitate in sending it, because if it is registered, as I hope, without other modifications than those made by the *parlement* of Paris (*agreed upon and accepted beforehand*), it will be all the much easier for us to make the Estates agree to the taxes that it contains."[236]

Each side—the government and the courts—was fully aware of the tools that the other side had at its disposal, and refined its own tools to deflect attacks and counterattacks. Although the ingredients of the successive crises were more or less the same, their deployment and combination varied too much for any generalizations to be possible.

235. Ibid., p. 226. For the role of Malesherbes, see Grosclaude (1961), pp. 277, 300, 307; Véri (1928), p. 177.

236. Félix (1999), p. 328; my italics. D'Aiguillon's hope was disappointed when the *parlement* refused, by thirteen votes to twelve, to register the declaration (ibid., p. 331). Jealousy of the pretentions of the *parlement* of Paris to speak for all the courts may have been more important than substantive disagreements (ibid., pp. 351–352).

CHAPTER FIVE

Deliberating Bodies

ALTHOUGH THE *PARLEMENTS* OFTEN ASSERTED that they represented the people against the crown, this claim had no substance.[1] There were, however, some genuinely representative bodies in the old regime: the Estates-General, the provincial Estates in the *pays d'états*, the quinquennial assemblies of the clergy, the occasional assemblies of notables, and the provincial assemblies that were created in the last decade before the Revolution.[2] Village assemblies, too, claimed to be and sometimes were (somewhat) representative. Like many representative bodies in earlier times, these were far from satisfying democratic criteria of suffrage, eligibility, and apportionment, but they did offer platforms for discussions, recommendations, and sometimes decisions that involved a substantial minority or even a majority of the community in question.

The Estates-General (1302–1614)

The Estates-General were perhaps the most important of these institutions. During the three centuries of their effective existence, they served a valuable function in preparing legislative reforms, although never vested with formal powers of legislation. The kings were more concerned, however, with their opposition to new or increased taxes. For reasons that are hard to nail down, they got away with not calling the Estates-General for almost two centuries. One might argue, or speculate, that in doing so they

1. See the comments by Malesherbes cited in Augeard (1866), pp. 40–41.
2. I shall write "Estates" with a capital *E* when referring to the assemblies and use "estates" with a lower-case *e* to refer to the three orders (clergy, nobility, and commoners) that met in the Estates. I shall not here discuss the assemblies of notables or the provincial assemblies, which I shall consider in Volume 3.

prepared the ground for their own demise. For one thing, the Estates-General might have served as a safety-valve for popular discontent. It is hard to assess the value of this claim. For another, one might argue with Tocqueville that

> if the French had still participated in government through the Estates General, as they had in the past, if they had even still participated in the daily administration of the country through their provincial assemblies, it is safe to say that they would not have been inflamed by the ideas of these [men of letters], as they were now. They would still have possessed a certain familiarity with government, and this *would have alerted them to the dangers of pure theory*.[3]

In retrospect, this argument is more plausible than the first, but nobody made it at the time. For the kings, meetings of the Estates-General and other deliberating bodies had few redeeming virtues, and none at all within their short time horizon.

The Estates-General were meetings of the three estates: clergy, nobility, and commoners.[4] The last category included originally only voters and deputies from the towns, but gradually came to include voters in the countryside as well.[5] On one count they met twenty-one times, but not all were equally important. I shall limit myself to the Estates of 1302, 1307, 1355, 1484, 1560–1561, 1576, and 1614. It is important to keep in mind that the estates were split along two dimensions: the two privileged orders against the commoners, and the two secular orders against the clergy. As in countries split on both an economic and a racial or ethnic dimension, this duality could be an obstacle to concerted action.

The first Estates met in 1302, as the reaction of Philippe le Bel to a papal bull that "contained the germ of the right [of the pope] to depose the kings" and to the pope's subsequent convocation to a Council in Rome that would work for "the reformation of the kingdom, the correction of the king and a good government of France."[6] The king "reacted to this

---

3. Tocqueville (2011), p. 129; my italics.

4. Picot (1888), vols. 1–5 is the standard history. Soule (1968) is a useful short account. Hayden (1974) is perhaps the best monograph on one meeting of the Estates-General (in 1614). Exceptionally interesting contemporary accounts are those of Masselin (1835) for the Estates of 1484, Bodin (1788) for those of 1576, and Rapine (1651) for those of 1614. Griffiths (1968) has a useful overview and a rich collection of documents for the Estates-General of the sixteenth century.

5. Soule (1968), p. 60. To my knowledge, no villager was ever elected as deputy; see for instance Hayden (1974), p. 75.

6. Picot (1888), vol. 1, p. 21.

threat of a common deliberation by the French bishops by instantaneously assembling the barons and the prelates of the country; but to avoid a division of the two orders on an issue of this importance, he convoked deputies from the independent towns (*les bonnes villes*) to take place in this assembly: for the first time the bourgeoisie as a body would participate in the affairs of state."[7] Being in a minority, the clergy did not dare to oppose the king's wishes. These events repeated themselves in the Estates of 1307, when the king "needed the [two] secular orders to smother the opposition of the clergy" to the abolition of the Templars and the confiscation of their wealth.[8] De facto, the two secular orders imposed their will (and that of the king) on the clergy.

De jure, there was never a majority vote among the three orders, an issue that first became important in 1355, when the Estates attempted to prevent any two-against-one alliances in the future. In the first edition of his history of the Estates-General, Georges Picot imputed that attempt to the third estate, whose influence was then at its highest at any time before 1789: "The third estate . . . did not dream of maintaining forever the preponderance that it had so recently acquired, but it was keen to retain from that momentary triumph at least a perpetual independence: four times in the great ordinance [of 1355] the deputies made the king promise that the decisions in future assemblies should be made by the unanimity of the orders, and that no two among them should be able to bind the third."[9]

Picot goes on to say, first, that "the third" (*le tiers*) did not yet have the meaning of "the third estate" (the commoners) that it acquired in the next century, but, second, that in reality only the third estate had reason to fear being outvoted by the other two. The generality of phrasing might thus have been purely opportunistic and chosen for the purpose of providing an impartial guise for the interest of the third estate. Once the principle had been stated in that form, other estates could appeal to it if they felt threatened. In 1576, both the clergy and the third estate invoked the dictum.

According to Picot's later ideas, however, the 1355 dictum was *not* simply opportunistic. In a letter he wrote to the politician-historian Guizot that was reproduced in the second edition of his treatise, he read the 1355 text as expressing a unanimous agreement by the three orders that all future decisions would have to be taken unanimously: "At first glance it

---

7. Ibid. Olivier-Martin (2010), p. 263, traces this development back to 1263.

8. Ibid., p. 24.

9. Picot (1888), vol. 1, p. 99.

seemed possible to suppose [as he had done in the first edition] that the deputies from the towns wanted to be protected from a joint action by the clergy and the nobility, but a closer reading of the texts made me reach a more solidly based opinion: it is certain that the three orders had reached an agreement to *protect themselves mutually* against an alliance of two against the third."[10]

Although he does not cite the texts on which he based this interpretation, Picot goes on to mention the fact that in 1576 the clergy used the maxim "no two estates can bind the third" to protect itself. Instead of referring to this subsequent fact, whose relevance seems to presuppose backward causation, he might have cited the events of 1302 and 1307. In 1355, the clergy could not predict the wars of religion, but they could remember how Philippe le Bel had summoned the third estate to impose his will on them. The weak point of Picot's argument lies in the absence of any plausible reason why the *nobility* should have an interest in an agreement. It might possibly gain by forming an alliance with the other privileged order or with the other secular order, and had, at that time at least, no reason to fear an alliance of these two orders against itself.[11]

Arlette Jouanna[12] has classified the main demands made to the king by Estates-General in the following categories.

10. Ibid., pp. 397–398; my italics. The agreement must have been somewhat fragile. In the Estates of 1561, the clergy was not represented, as its delegates were engaged in the *colloque de Poissy* which tried in vain to reach a compromise between Catholics and Calvinists (Elster 2013, pp. 58–59). The two other orders profited from their absence by adopting measures to repay the royal debt that fell mainly on the clergy (Picot 1888, vol. 2, pp. 204–209, 385–391). This fact suggests that the agreement amounted to each order having a veto, which the clergy obviously could not exercise if it was absent. Also, in 1614 the clergy and the nobility tried to impose financial sacrifices on the third estate, which responded in kind by proposing a reduction in the pensions of the nobles, while also accepting, "to show its disinterestedness," to assume its part of the burden (Picot 1888, vol. 4, p. 187). By this time, the "agreement" was clearly in abeyance.

11. The only reference to a possible alliance of the clergy and the third estate against the nobility I have come across is in Lefebvre (1988), p. 59, where he describes the attitude of the nobles in the spring of 1789: "In their mind, the Estates-General ought to remain divided into three orders, each having one vote, so that the clergy and the nobility would have an assured majority. Some nobles, fearing a coalition of the clergy and the third estate against the nobility, even pretended that each order had a veto." I shall return to this puzzling statement in Volume 3.

12. Jouanna (1989), p. 301. These demands refer to Estates-General held in the sixteenth and seventeenth centuries. In earlier centuries, they also demanded a stable money and the right to delay subsidies to the Crusades until they were underway (Picot 1888, vol. 1, pp. 29, 37).

Meetings of the Estates-General at regular intervals, without
  convocation, every two, five, or ten years.
Consent to taxation
The right to enact laws that neither the king nor the *parlements* could
  modify
The right to ask the administration for financial accounts.
The right to consent to war and peace.
The right to call for a national (religious) council.
When the king is minor, the right to choose the regent and nominate
  members of the Royal Council.
The right to reject some members of the Royal Council
The right to choose some members of the Royal Council

The deputies also came with grievance books (*cahiers de doléance*) with
demands for specific legislation and for abolition of abuses.[13]

The most important concession the Estates demanded of the king in
exchange for consent to taxation was the achievement of constitutional
status, with the right for the Estates-General to meet periodically and to
impose their will on the king when they were in unanimous agreement.
(They never proposed constitutional rules that would govern their own
proceedings.) As noted in the Introduction, the fact that taxes had to be
raised immediately while the Estates lacked any machinery to enforce the
royal promises of regular convocations implied that the king was at liberty
to break them.[14] The financial accounts the kings presented as part of the
bargains with the Estates were utterly unreliable, except for those presented in 1561 by the chancellor L'Hôpital.

In the early modern period, many other European countries were
Ständestaaten with written or unwritten constitutions that regulated
joint decision making by the king and the Estates.[15] With its obsession
with *préséance*, France is more accurately characterized as a

---

13. For an overview, see Griffiths (1968), p. 123.

14. Referring to the Estates of 1484, Picot (1888), vol. 1, p. 390, asserts that they "lost all
authority" when they voted the taxes before they had obtained the concessions of reform.
The temporal sequence was not the main problem, however. Even if the concessions had
been *granted* before the vote on taxes, the Estates would be dissolved when the time came
to *implement* them.

15. Around 1600, a French writer observed (with some exaggeration) that "When the
Parliament of England, the Estates of Sweden, of Poland, and those of all the neighboring
countries meet, the kings are obliged to respect their decisions without changing anything,"
and asked, "Why should not the French have the same privilege?" (Cayet 1836, vol. 1, p. 79).

Ständegesellschaft. The estates were so viscerally jealous of each other that the degree of cooperation required for a concerted opposition to the monarchy proved impossible. I have cited the furious reaction of the nobles in the Estates of 1614 to the claim of the third estate deputies to be their "younger brothers." According to Picot, "at no other time did the Estates-General show such a fierce antagonism between the orders. Quarrels of *préséance*, petty susceptibilities aroused by vanity and sustained by *amour-propre*, this in a nutshell was the history of these sterile fights."[16] Elsewhere, he refers to the "contemptuous haughtiness [of the nobles] which seemed to increase from assembly to assembly until the Estates-General of 1614, when their quarrels with the third estate brought out the full insolence of their haughty disdainfulness (*morgue*)."[17] He cites many specific episodes. Picot notes that these quarrels were avoided in 1484, because cross-voting induced "the fusion of interest and the absence of these deplorable rivalries."[18]

One cannot prove conclusively that the struggle for *préséance* explains why France never became a *Ständestaat*. The European countries with that form of government were also concerned with rank, but mostly not in the same virulent form. Spain provides a counterexample, however, being both a *Ständestaat* and rank-obsessed. Be this as it may, in France an important reason why the Estates-General remained an episodic and not a periodic institution[19] was the careful avoidance behavior of the kings. "The modes of convocation, election and holding of the Estates-General had never been clearly determined."[20] The successive kings had a strong interest in cultivating this procedural indeterminacy. "The king was careful not to enact rules of order that might be used as argument for regular meetings of the Estates. . . . The royal prudence avoided any enactment of general statutes."[21] Guy Coquille, a deputy to the Estates-General of 1560, 1576, and 1588, stated the matter clearly: "The government of this kingdom is a true monarchy, which has no relation to democracy or aristocracy, as some have claimed because of the existence of the Estates and of the *parlements*. This opinion is far from the truth; for if the Estates were a form of democracy, there would be regular times and places for their meetings,

16. Picot (1888), vol. 5, pp. 113–114.
17. Ibid., p. 224.
18. Ibid., vol. 1, p. 351.
19. For this distinction, see Vermeule (2011).
20. Marion (1923), p. 217.
21. Tanchoux (2004), pp. 24, 25.

which is not the case."[22] The mode of electing the delegates was up for grabs, as was the mode of voting by the delegates, within each estate and by the Estates once elected and assembled. Although the Estates-General had some tangible effects, notably in proposing legislative reforms, their indeterminate character was an obstacle to durable success. None of their demands received lasting satisfaction.

Before 1789 the number of delegates each electoral district could send to the Estates-General was indeterminate.[23] The convocations specified sometimes that in each district one should elect *one* deputy, sometimes *at most one* deputy, and sometimes *at least one* deputy from each state.[24] Actual numbers varied a great deal. In the third estate, "some *bailliages* sent two deputies, others six or eight."[25] In 1614, several *bailliages* elected deputies only for one or two of the estates. The voters were usually members of the order the deputy would represent. On several occasions, however, the choice was made by *cross-voting*, so that within a given electoral district members of all orders cast a vote on the choice of the deputies from a given order.[26] This regime was the rule in 1484, and occasionally adopted in 1789. In 1576 and in 1614, the elections in Brittany of delegates to the Estates-General took the extreme form of having delegates by each order *elected only by members of the other two orders*.[27] In 1484, in 1576, and in 1614, the intention behind cross-voting seems to have been to promote the spirit of the province at the expense of the spirit of the orders.[28] The delegates came, as it were, as ambassadors from their province.

In some cases, the government might try to influence the selection of deputies. In 1614, "Marie de Médicis and her advisers acted as Louis XVI and his advisers did not desire to do in 1789," by working to ensure

---

22. Coquille (1789), p. 294–295.

23. The king deliberately also left the agenda for the Estates to which they were convoked under a veil of indeterminacy, reckoning that it was "easier to circumvent an assembly than the mass of voters" (Soule 1968, p. 69).

24. Necker (1797), pp. 85–86.

25. Picot (1888), vol. 5, p. 262.

26. For other instances of cross-voting, see Elster (2013), chap.5.

27. Picot (1888), vol. 5, pp. 271–272.

28. Picot (1888, vol. 5, p. 251) asserts both that in the 1484 Estates "the provincial spirit prevailed over the spirit of caste" and that "the spirit of the province *and that of France* were stronger than that of the rival interests" (my italics). Yet the spirit of the province could easily undermine that of the nation: collective action problems were as likely to occur among the provinces as among the orders. "The provincial spirit and the class spirit, both combated by the king, rivaled involuntarily between themselves" (Konopczynski 1930, pp. 68–69).

"that the choice of deputies to the Estates-General fell on persons who depended absolutely on the king and the queen."[29] Her task was facilitated by the fact that the nobles, considering themselves as natural leaders, did not bother to do the necessary electoral work.[30]

In 1356 the numerous Estates-General (800 deputies in total) elected 80 delegates (presumably by and from the estates) to deliberate and vote in common. This seems to have been the only example of one-tier decision making prior to 1789. Other Estates-General voted by aggregate units and often aggregate subunits. In 1484, when the deputies had been elected by cross-voting, voting by estate presumably seemed inappropriate. Instead, the aggregate units were six provinces: Paris and Île de France, Burgundy, Normandy, Guyenne, Languedoc with the Dauphiné and Provence, together with half a dozen regions in the center of France. From 1560 onwards, the aggregate units were the three orders. They deliberated separately, and communicated through envoys.

Within each estate, voting was always by majority of subunits. There was no agreement, however, as to what these subunits were. Referring to the Estates-General of 1614, Roland Mousnier writes that

Each order met by government and by subdivision of government. There were twelve governments in each order, each with its own president. But *the problem of voting was never solved*: should one vote by government, each having one vote; by *bailliage*, each having one vote; or by head? Depending on the mode of voting, the results could be very different: the government of Île-de-France included 16 *bailliages*; that of Burgundy 12; that of Normandy 7; that of Picardy 5; that of Guyenne 16; that of Orléans 19. Opposite results might occur if the deputies voted by *bailliage* and *sénéchaussée* instead of voting by government.[31]

This dilemma (or trilemma, if we also include voting by head)[32] may be illustrated by the Estates of 1484, 1576, and 1614. In his Journal from the

29. Pillorget and Pillorget (1995), pp. 129–130.

30. Jouanna (1989), p. 345. Nor, as we have seen, did they bother to achieve administrative competence.

31. Mousnier (2005), p. 791.

32. According to Konopczynski (1930), p.72, voting by head was rarely used and only for "minor agenda-setting issues." As we know, however, agenda issues can be far from minor. Rapine (1651), pp. 9 ff. indicates that in 1614 voting by head (*pluralité [*=majority*] des voix*) was also used in electing the President and other officers of the third estate. Moreover, it seems that the decision to vote by governments rather than by *bailliages* on all other issues was itself taken by majority voting by head (ibid., p. 11). The phrase "pluralité des voix" is ambiguous, but in this context it seems reasonable to read it as voting by

Estates of 1484, Jean Masselin cites the President of the Estates as asserting that

> Our division in six sections does not seem to be an equal one, for the first, that of Paris and the adjoined deputies, surpasses indubitably two or three other sections, by the extent of its province, by the number of its *bailliages* and by the number of its deputies. The section of the Langue d'Oïl is in the same case. It seems fair, therefore, that votes on this subject be taken by *bailliages* or by deputies, and not according to the procedures used up to this point.[33]

The "subject" in question was the composition of the Council that would guide the king, who was not yet major. The President, who was strongly influenced by the princes in Paris, wanted to ensure their predominance in the Council. Although his effort was rebutted, the President and the princes managed to split the near-unanimous opinions by playing on the rivalry among the provinces.

For the Estates-General of 1576 we can draw on the Journal of Jean Bodin, who complained about the practice of voting by governments within the third estate. In a crucial vote on his proposal that the union of religion should be brought about "without war," Île-de-France, Normandy, Champagne, Languedoc, Orléans, Picardy, and Provence voted against that additional clause, with Burgundy, Brittany, Guyenne, the Lyonnais and the Dauphiné voting for. Bodin noted that "the government of Guyenne had seventeen deputies, and that of Provence only two,"[34] adding that there were "great altercations and complaints" in the five minority governments. Although it is not clear whether Bodin thought the vote should have been taken by head or by *bailliages*, he certainly thought it arbitrary or unfair to assign equal voting rights to units of unequal size. In the end, however, he got his way, when the Estates refused to vote the war subsidies.

The Journal of Florimond Rapine shows how the same issue arose in the Estates of 1614 and effectively caused their collapse. From the beginning, there was considerable confusion within the third estate as to whether votes should be taken by governments or by *bailliages*. Early on, the question arose how to elect the deputies that would make the closing

---

head, since other votes usually indicate the votes of the various governments. Finally, voting by *bailliages* when these had sent several deputies would seem to require voting by head among the latter to determine the vote of the *bailliage*.

33. Masselin (1835), pp. 99–101.

34. Bodin (1788), p. 228. For the context, see Ulph (1947).

speeches. "One debated whether the election should be made by provinces or by *bailliages*. The provinces of Paris, Guyenne, and Orléans were of the opinion that one should vote by *bailliages* so that they could have more votes, since in these three provinces there were many *bailliages*. But it was decided by majority vote (*à la pluralité*) that one would vote by province."[35] We may note the self-serving motivation that Rapine attributes to the three provinces favoring *bailliages*.

Next, a revealing debate occurred over a proposal to allow for a vote among all the governments on an article that had been proposed by one *bailliage* but rejected by the government to which it belonged.[36] If a *bailliage* were to go over the head of its government and appeal to the estate as a whole, the article would presumably need to be adopted by majority voting (by head or by *bailliage*) in a majority of governments. A majority of the governments rejected the proposal, apparently because of its impracticality. As the example shows, the idea of nested majority voting is ambiguous. Although a final decision would always require a majority vote in a majority of the governments, the rejected proposal would have allowed an article proposed by any *bailliage* to be put on the agenda, not only the articles approved by the government to which it belonged.

On December 15, 1614, the third estate voted, ten governments to two, an article condemning regicide (a fanatic Catholic had assassinated Henri IV four years earlier) as well as interventions by the pope in French politics. A month later, after the king under pressure from the clergy asked the estate to withdraw the article, the question came up again. As it seemed that a majority of the governments would now vote against the article, some deputies asked for a vote by *bailliages*. "It was nevertheless decided to vote by province."[37] While the vote by provinces was being taken, one by one, a deputy for Picardy spoke before his turn to make a general claim:

> As this matter is of extreme importance, and as what is at stake is the dignity of the kingdom and life of our kings, it is reasonable to vote by *bailliages* and not by provinces, because the latter are not equal in their number of deputies, and that if one voted by provinces those which have only three or four deputies would have as many votes as those which have thirty or forty *bailliages;* and at the beginning one had voted by *bailliages*; and even though it had since been decided to

35. Rapine (1651), p. 90. As noted above, I believe the estate voted by head on this issue.
36. Ibid., pp. 100–101.
37. Rapine (1651), p. 362. We do not know *how* that second-order decision was taken.

vote by provinces, that ought only to be understood to apply to ordinary matters; but as nothing had come up as important and serious as the matter they were discussing, he asked the assembly to decide to vote by *bailliages*.[38]

Although "a great many deputies rose to their feet to express their agreement," the president of the estate decided to continue the vote by provinces. The delegations from Languedoc and Lyon having left, the article was rejected by six to four governments. Somewhere between 100 and 120 deputies (out of 192 in the whole third estate) then signed a formal complaint against this "decision by the smallest number." This unresolvable trilemma—voting by governments, by *bailliages*, or by head—effectively caused the Estates of 1614 to collapse.

From voting by subunits *within* each estate, I now turn to voting *by* the estates within the Estates-General. There is not much to say on the topic, because strictly speaking no voting ever took place. Decisions were never taken by a binding up-and-down vote on a proposal made by the king or by one of the estates. Yet, as noted, the question of unanimity versus majority of the orders was often highly salient. Sometimes, as in 1560, the king yielded when the estates did achieve unanimity. At other times, as in 1484, the deputies lost out when they voted the taxes before they obtained the concessions they demanded.[39] Most of the time, the kings and (during the regencies) the princes or the queen-mother either sabotaged unanimous decisions or used divide-and-conquer tactics to prevent them. Given the inability of the Estates to reach and impose binding decisions, it is surprising that so much energy and argument were invested in voting within each estate, another form of second-decimal precision.

We may ask what tools the kings, the estates, and the Estates-General had at their disposal in their struggle, as I did with respect to the struggle between the king and the courts. The two cases differ radically, since the Estates-General and the estates could not effectively prevent the collection of taxes or the raising of soldiers the way the courts could suspend the operations of justice. They were episodic rather than ongoing institutions, and had no leverage for making credible threats. Had they been *periodic*, they might have developed the necessary instruments. (As we shall see, the provincial Estates seem to have been in a more favorable position to extract concessions, by dragging their feet when bargaining

38. Ibid., p. 364.
39. Picot (1888), vol. 1, p. 380.

with the Crown.) Although the Estates-General never demanded to collect taxes, they sometimes demanded control over how they were spent. As noted, in 1321 the third estate asserted that its contribution to the funding of the Crusades would become effective only when the expedition was under way.[40] In 1576, the clergy declared that it would pay its taxes in kind, by providing the king with a certain number of soldiers and paying them directly.[41] Although the clergy, unlike the nobility and the third estate, constituted an corporate body that could have carried out this plan, they were forced to yield.

Elections to, and voting in, the assemblies of the clergy took different forms over the centuries. At all times, especially under Louis XIII, the kings tried to influence the election of the deputies as well as their proceedings. In 1700, chancellor Pontchartrain asked an archbishop who presided over the provincial elections to the general assembly to ensure that a certain bishop was not chosen, adding that if it could not be done in secret he should just inform the electoral assembly that this was the king's will.[42] In 1635, when the king did not succeed in preventing the assembly from meeting, he "did at least try to reduce the number of deputies, since, in addition to the fact that large assemblies usually lead to more heated debates, they are less likely to yield to pressure."[43] Once the general assembly met, the government could put pressure on the delegates to adopt a mode of voting that would favor the decision it desired. These were the kind of harassment measures that were routinely deployed to force the compliance of other deliberating bodies such as the provincial Estates or the *parlements*. However, the clergy had greater powers of resistance. As noted in the Introduction, by virtue of their regular and frequent assemblies they could constrain the kings to keep their promises. Also, as shown by one of the most salient defeats of the royal government, there were limits to what it could do to punish the Church. In 1750, when the finance minister Machault tried to make the provincial Estates and the clergy pay the tax of the *vingtième*, he had only a limited success:

> In Brittany, Artois, Languedoc and Provence, the [provincial Estates]
> voted against the new tax, and the bishops were not less zealous in

40. Picot (1888), vol. 1. p. 29. The Estates had no effective control, however, over the funds (Soule 1968, p. 69).

41. Ibid., vol. 3 pp. 53–54. Under pressure, the clergy agreed to pay the tax in money (ibid., p. 83).

42. Mousnier (2005), p. 285.

43. Maury (1879), p. 793.

fighting it. In Languedoc the opposition of the latter took a particularly violent form. To make it desist, the government exiled the bishops and several deputies of the nobility. But it *could not deploy the same means towards the assembly that represented the French clergy as a whole* and thus force it to yield. All its efforts to make it accept the tax of the *vingtième* failed.[44]

The Main Provincial Estates

The *pays d'états* had provincial Estates (*Etats*), whence their name.[45] Their main tasks were to levy taxes for the king, usually in the form of a lump-sum *abonnement*, and to carry out public works in the province. Their importance varied a great deal, both over time and across space. The Estates of Languedoc, Burgundy, and Brittany, on which I focus below, were always powerful. Those of the Dauphiné were revived in 1788 after a long dormancy, and had a strong influence on the electoral procedures for the Estates-General (see Volume 3). In Provence, the traditional Estates, which Richelieu had abolished in 1630 and replaced by a functionally similar Assembly of Communities, were reestablished in 1787. Small frontier provinces in the South and in the North also had Estates, the most important being those of Artois. In the following, I shall make no attempt to generalize. My aim is only to point to some recurrent mechanisms that bring out, if more evidence were needed, the multiple and conflicting sources of power and authority in the *ancien régime*.[46] It is difficult to generalize about the overall role of the estates in the political system. Were they mainly agents of, and collaborators with, the royal government or sources of income, patronage, and power for local elites? Or were the latter functions a condition for the efficient exercise of the former?

Unlike the Estates-General, the proceedings of the provincial Estates had a well-defined structure. They met at regular intervals, annually in Languedoc, biennially in Britanny, triennially in Burgundy. The rules for designating members of the Estates, and the voting procedures once they met, were also well-defined. Also unlike the Estates-General, the provincial Estates had a *commission intermédiaire* (called *élus* in

44. Maury (1880), p. 647; my italics.

45. I shall not discuss the provincial assemblies that were established in the last years before the Revolution. While perhaps important as a training ground for deputies to the Estates-General of 1789, they were no part of the *system* of the *ancien régime*.

46. The most important books on which I rely in identifying the mechanisms are Rébillon (1932), Legay (2001), Swann (2003), and Durand, Jouanna, and Pélaquier, eds. (2014).

Burgundy[47]) representing them between the sessions, had permanent quasi-ambassadors in Paris, and sent envoys on missions there from time to time.

In Languedoc, there were twenty-three deputies for the clergy, twenty-three for the nobility, and forty-six for the Third Estate, foreshadowing the *Règlement* of the Estates-General of 1789. The deputies voted by head, foreshadowing the decision by Louis XVI on June 27, 1789.[48] According to Marion, these formal resemblances between representation and voting in the Estates of Languedoc and in the Estates-General made Tocqueville overestimate the progressive and liberal nature of the former.[49] In reality, the Estates of Languedoc were dominated by a clerical aristocracy. In Brittany, all nobles who satisfied the changing genealogical requirements could meet as of right, a right they often exercised for the sake of free meals and drink as well as payment for attendance. Their exact number did not matter, since the Estates "voted by order." This expression hides an important ambiguity: would decisions require unanimity, or would a majority of "two against one" suffice? In theory, the Estates of Brittany followed the latter procedure, but when the rambunctious nobles were in a minority they usually succeeded in generating a chaos that prevented the other orders from outvoting them. In the Estates of Artois, majority vote by the orders was the rule and also the practice, the third estate being unable to block the two privileged orders from outvoting it.[50] In the Estates of Burgundy, too, two orders could bind a third.[51]

The *pays d'Etats* collected taxes in the province on behalf of the king and also for internal purposes. They usually obtained an *abonnement* (an

47. Not to be confused with the *élus* in the *pays d'élection*.

48. Because the crucial vote on the "free gift" could not be reduced to a binary choice, the assembly used a procedure (described in Jouanna 2014 a, p. 79) guaranteed to produce a Condorcet winner on the assumption (plausible in this case) that preferences were single-peaked ("qui donne le plus donne le moins"). The Languedoc Estates also practiced a rule (Pélaquier 2014 a, p. 31) that in 1789 would be demanded by the third estate and opposed by the clergy and nobility, that of *cross-verification* of credentials by the three orders. As noted above, the Estates in Brittany sometimes practiced *cross-voting* when electing deputies to the Estates-General.

49. Marion (1891), p. 89; see also the Appendix on Languedoc in Tocqueville (2011).

50. Legay (2001), p. 24.

51. Swann (2003), p. 88. In 1788, the nobility demanded a change from majority vote to unanimity for decisions to be valid (ibid., p. 378). This is the only instance I have come across of these two ways of voting by order being explicitly compared. In the Estates-General of 1789, when voting by head versus voting by order was a key issue, nobody to my knowledge asked whether voting by order, if accepted, would proceed by majority vote or by unanimity (Elster 2014, p. 86).

annual lump-sum payment), sometimes referred to as a "free gift," for direct or indirect taxes. This arrangement was in the *perceived* interest of both parties: the province paid less than it would have done if taxes had been levied under the auspices of the *intendant*, and the government benefited from punctual and certain payments.[52] In another sense, of course, the government lost. As noted several times in earlier chapters, the urgent need of the government for "money yesterday" truncated its time horizon and induced a preference for smaller earlier payments over larger delayed payments. Given its situation, the government cannot be characterized as irrational. Getting more money later has no value if one expects to be invaded and defeated in the meantime. The government was not subject to "pure time preference," but simply constrained by the need to survive.[53] This being said, the kings might have used the few periods where the country was not under acute foreign threat, such as the 1670s, to create a breathing space (one step backward) that would have allowed the transition to a less wasteful administration (two steps forward).[54] That Louis XIV chose not to do so, but instead waged an offensive war against Holland, was not irrational either, in the technical sense of that term, but immoral. It reflected his preference for the glory of France, and above all that of his person, over the welfare of the French.

The kings had another reason for outsourcing tax collection to the provinces: unlike the royal government, the Estates could make credible promises of interest payment and reimbursement. In Burgundy, "the crown obliged the Estates to borrow on its behalf. Crucially, by alienating the revenues from the *crues* [salt tax], *octrois* [internal tolls], and, after 1710, direct taxation, it provided the means to underwrite those loans. The Estates were happy to accept the bargain, as provincial elites were the principal beneficiaries of a sound investment opportunity."[55] In other

---

52. The lump-sum *don gratuit* paid by the Church offered the same advantage, but in that case it is more difficult to compare it to what direct taxation would have yielded.

53. See Elster (2015a), p. 103, for the several reasons an agent might have to prefer earlier over later reward.

54. Marion (1927), p. 381, makes a similar observation about the financial reforms of Calonne in the last years of the regime: "The State had *the time to perish ten* times before the new taxes he imagined could take effect."

55. Swann (2003), p. 192. As he notes (ibid., p. 300), the "Estates were seeking to provide a system that guaranteed a good return [5 percent] for them, regardless of the fact that they could almost certainly find the necessary funds at a lower interest rate. The losers in this arrangement were the *taillables* [taxpayers], who supported an unnecessarily heavy burden."

words, the Estates were able to earmark income from direct and indirect taxes to interest on, and reimbursements of, their loans, whereas the royal government was always tempted to divert taxes intended for that purpose to other and more urgent needs. Later, the crown invented "a new strategy for obtaining money by forcing the Estates to borrow two million *livres* directly for the king, allowing them to retain part of the proceeds of direct taxation to cover interest and repayment charges."[56] With many variations, similar schemes were used to extract money from the other *pays d'Etat*.[57]

As in my discussion of the relations between the king and the *parlements* and between the king and the Estates-General, we can try to determine the strategies deployed in the relations between the royal government and the provincial Estates.

Consider first the tools at the disposal of the government.

The "nuclear option" of dissolving the Estates was used only once, but may have served as an implicit threat once Machault had resorted to it in Languedoc.

In 1658, the Estates of Burgundy were *exiled* from Dijon to Noyers, "where the effects of disgrace persuaded them to promise [the sum] requested by the king."[58]

The government could, within limits, exercise prior or posterior control over the selection of deputies.[59]

Since it usually sent commissaries to attend the meeting of the Estates, these could bribe or threaten the deputies to vote the way the king wanted.[60]

As I discuss below, the government could also play on the opposition between the Estates and the *parlements*.

---

56. Ibid., p. 322.

57. Legay (2001), pp. 220–224; Rébillon (1932), pp. 730–735; Pélaquier (2014c).

58. Swann (2003), p. 156. Elsewhere, Swann (2010) refers to the "much more inhospitable" environment in Noyers, suggesting that *inconvenience may have added to disgrace* in order to bring about the desired behavior modification.

59. Pélaquier (2014a), p. 49; also Legay (2001), p. 92. In Brittany, the royal government tried, without success, to regulate the representation of the nobility (Rébillon 1932, pp. 42–79). In Burgundy, one member of the intermediary commission (the *élu du roi*) was supposed to represent the king, but "as so often under the *ancien régime*, a position initially intended for a devoted royal servant had been transformed into a venal office" (Swann 2003, p. 102).

60. Jouanna (2014a), p. 89.

The government could also, more ambiguously, reward the Estates by offering a rebate on the "free gift" if they accepted the king's demands without objections.[61]

Moreover, the government could try to play the various provincial Estates against one another, "either to inspire fear by referring to the sanctions that had struck the most recalcitrant or, on the contrary, to cause emulation by praising the more docile."[62]

It is hard to assess the causal efficacy, if any, of the last two strategies. The provincial Estates, had fewer arrows in their quiver.

They might try to present a united front to the king. As noted earlier, in the eighteenth century the *parlements* sometimes attempted or at least hoped to form a national *union des classes*, which would replace the Estates-General as representatives of the popular will. The idea never took hold. Rather, "it was a sheer fiction (*fantôme*)" that, if anything, "provided a powerful pretext to break the back of the magistracy."[63] The prospect of concerted action among the Estates was even dimmer. "The provincial Estates could not claim to have a common constitution and an esprit de corps that might have nourished a solidarity similar that of the *parlements*."[64] The fact that they met at different intervals could also be an obstacle to cooperation, although their permanent delegates in Paris could exchange information and, on at least one occasion, cooperated to block an almost-made royal decision that would have been to their common detriment.[65]

Although one contemporary text refers to the need for "mutual help,"[66] the main interaction among the Estates was the exchange of information, notably about how other Estates reacted to proposed tax increases. The government was aware of these exchanges, partly fearing them and partly exploiting them for its own advantage. In a letter from the 1750, the *intendant* in Languedoc, Le Nain, warned the finance minister that "too brutal

61. Swann (2003), p. 163.

62. Jouanna (2014c), p. 346, adding, with several examples, that these strategies could be counterproductive.

63. Egret (1970), p. 180.

64. Legay (2001), p. 72. Cooperation among the estates would probably not, how-ever, have been undermined by the questions of (inter-body) *préséance* that plagued the *parlements*.

65. Jouanna (2014c), p. 351.

66. Legay (2001), p. 189.

measures could provoke 'contagious [excesses] in the other *pays d'Etat*, especially in Provence, which regards with great attention what is happening here.'" In 1752, Le Nain's successor Saint-Priest wrote that "it was absolutely necessary to prevent Languedoc from 'producing the second volume of what happened in Brittany.'"[67] At the same time, the "brutal measures" were sometimes undertaken deliberately to signal to other Estates that they could not expect clemency. At the opening of the sessions of the Estates in Languedoc in 1662, "the kings' commissioners worked at . . . disquieting the minds 'by the examples of the punishment of Burgundy, Provence, and more recently Béarn.' "[68] This ambiguity was characteristic of the *ancien régime*: punishment was as likely to induce fear-based compliance as resentment-based resistance. The government could never know which was the more likely reaction.

Although the details are fuzzy, the main bargaining tool of the Estates seems to have been the exploitation of the government's urgent need for money, by dragging out the negotiations. In sequential bargaining, a party who can credibly cite the need to consult its constituency unless the other party makes a better proposal will always have an edge. Marie-Laure Legay mentions the slowness of the Estates of Artois as a "force of obstruction," and contrasts it with the "impatience" of the royal negotiators.[69] She does not, however, explicitly mention its effect on the bargaining outcome, seeming to treat the slowness as a given fact, caused by the cumbersome apparatus of the Estates, not as a strategic tool.[70] In her discussion of the determinants of the size of the "free gift," she mentions only the financial state of the central government and that of the province.[71] In his discussion of

---

67. Jouanna (2014c), p. 348.

68. Ibid., p. 346.

69. Ibid., p. 24.

70. The crucial question, to which I have not found an answer in the literature, is whether a provincial Estate could credibly *threaten* to consult its constituents (or perhaps the *parlement*) unless its offer or counteroffer is accepted, or *warn* that its constituents (or perhaps the *parlement*) might demand to be heard unless the offer or counteroffer is accepted. The abstract, unctuous, and evasive language used by all deliberating bodies in the *ancien régime* allowed them to elide the crucial distinction between threats and warnings (Elster 2015 a, pp. 423–425), an elision all the more necessary as overt threats might be construed as treason.

71. Ibid., p. 58.

Burgundy, Julian Swann writes that "[c]onsent to taxation was grudging at best, and the *élus* revealed themselves to be masters of the art of procrastination."[72] In her discussion of "the bargaining (*marchandage*) over the fiscal demands" in Languedoc, Arlette Jouanna writes that the "capacity of negotiation and even resistance of the Estates should not be underestimated."[73] Neither of the two latter authors provides a mechanism that would explain why sometimes the king and sometimes the Estates got the upper hand. In one case cited by Jouanna, they essentially split the difference, the finance minister demanding 600,000 livres, the Estates offering 315,000, with a compromise agreement of 450,000. In another case, the corresponding amounts were 130,000, 40,000. and 50,000. [74] Clearly, the Estates got the better in the second deal, but why?

The Provincial Estates and the Parlements

Finally, I shall consider the relations—of both cooperation and conflict— between two provincial bodies, Estates and *parlements*. Although I have not come across any relevant prosopographical studies, the fact that the two bodies recruited their members from the same local elite families must have encouraged a modicum of cooperation. A possible example from Languedoc is the practice of the *parlement* and other courts in protecting the Estates by suspending litigation against deputies during the session.[75] More important, perhaps, is the commonality of interests. In Burgundy, "[the members of the Estates] and *other provincial elites* were the principal beneficiaries of [the] sound investment opportunity" of subscribing to provincial loans.[76] Presumably these other elites included the magistrates in the *parlements*, who would thus share an interest in taxation with members of the Estates that would facilitate joint action. In Artois and Brittany, where many buyers of provincial bonds lived outside the province,[77] this (conjectural) solidarity between the two bodies may have been less pronounced.

72. Swann (2003), p. 157.
73. Jouanna (2014a), 83.
74. Ibid., p. 82.
75. Pélaquier (2014b), p. 322.
76. Swann (2003), p. 192; my italics; see also ibid., p. 299.
77. Legay (2001), p. 223; Rébillon (1932), pp. 734–735.

At the structural level, there were built-in tensions between these two bodies that made for endemic conflict.[78] The courts took pride in protesting the king's demands for new taxes or an increase of old taxes, while the Estates had a vital role in collecting the taxes.[79] As I noted, they sometimes dragged their feet or held out for a reduction, but much of the time they were docile in complying with the demands of the government. Apart from the period from 1673 to 1715, "docility" is not a word that one would apply to the *parlements*. Related to this fact were the conflicts over the registration of edicts and decrees. While "the *parlement* in Rennes, although created later than the Estates [of Brittany], never admitted the superiority of the powers of the latter,"[80] it might on occasion yield to them. As an example we may cite Rébillon's rhetorical question about Brittany: if "the *parlement* accepted the appeal by the Estates against the execution of a law, even if it had been registered [by the *parlement*], threatening for instance to prosecute all those who had participated in levying a tax not approved (*consenti*) [by the Estates], what power did it not lend the other assembly?"[81]

Yet, the two Breton bodies were not equally powerful. Citing Rébillon again,

Of the two assemblies, [the *parlement*] was best placed to lead the other. In fact, to the king it always appeared as the most redoubtable. As a *homogeneous and permanent body*, it was much more capable than the Estates of pursuing a consistent policy. . . . The judicial powers of the *parlement* allowed it to hamper the government much more seriously than the political powers of the Estates have ever done; the latter *had no weapons* that could compare with the cessation of services or even the *arrêts* of its magistrates, and its remonstrances stirred the opinion much more efficiently than theirs.[82]

---

78. Somewhat exceptionally, the judiciary in Normandy "called for provincial Estates even though it would lose some of its authority, because "their desire for the fiscal-administrative independence that Estates would bring to the province outweighed the narrower interests of corporate jurisdiction" (Kwass 2000, p. 176).

79. Swann (2003), pp. 281–282, 292–294; Pélaquier (2014b), p. 326.

80. Legay (2010), p. 69.

81. Rébillon (1932), p. 210. Jouanna (2014a), p. 69, cites a letter from 1672 referring to an old divide-and-conquer custom in Languedoc according to which the Estates were not allowed to meet in the same town as the *parlement*, to avoid "collusion."

82. Rébillon (1932), p. 211; my italics.

Also, the two bodies in Brittany had different priorities. It was not mainly, as it seems to have been in Languedoc, a conflict over which had the best claim to represent itself as the bastion of resistance to new taxes,[83] but a choice between two evils: "the basic loyalty of the towns and of the large majority of the Breton nobles made them tend to support the royal authority, in which they saw a salutary safeguard against *return to civil war* [La Fronde, in which the *parlements* had been a main instigator] rather than to defend the claims of the *parlement* against the *growing absolutism*."[84] While the Estates feared anarchy, the *parlement* feared, or claimed to fear, tyranny. Perhaps, as I suggested earlier, it mainly sought popularity.

The triangular relations king-Estates-*parlement* in Brittany are particularly well brought out in a letter from 1759 to the finance minister Silhouette by the governor of the province, the Duc d'Aiguillon, that is worth citing at some length:

> There has been at all times between the *parlement* and the Estates an invincible jealousy, which increases each time the administration entrusted to the commissioners of the Estates receives a new extension. The magistrates, who were in the habit of being solicited and as a consequence feared and respected by the nobles, the lower judges, and the mayors, find themselves painfully obliged to stoop before [the commissioners] to obtain tax rebates, and the latter *return hundredfold, on this occasion, the rebuffs they suffer when they have a lawsuit. This discord between the two bodies has often been useful for the king's service.* . . . However, after the system [of the union des classes] has come into favor, and one has tolerated that [the *parlements*] have attributed to themselves the right of mutual defense and to represent the Estates-General of the kingdom, the Estates, which are currently governed by five or six muddlers [*brouillons*] whose insolence and tyranny increase by the day, believe they have found a *support* in the *parlement* that is all the more firm for its links to all the other [*parlements*] in the kingdom, and have become extremely close to it. . . . Moreover, as the muddlers and the factional are always united in their conspiracies, and for some time have governed the multitude which is too weak and desultory to resist their violence, *the Estates and the parlement act in concert in all circumstances and*

---

83. Jouanna (2014b), p. 303.
84. Rébillon (1932), p. 263; my italics.

nothing is done without the unanimous agreement in the one and the other body.[85]

Under Louis XIV, the Estates of Languedoc cooperated with the *parlement* after it lost much of its power after 1673. Prior to that date, however, there were frequent conflicts. "Among 76 conflictual events between the two institutions in the period from 1648 to 1789, more than half took place in the years 1649, 1650, and 1651."[86] In struggles over which institution should have the right to consent to taxes, the *parlement* might condemn members of the Estates to the galleys or even to death, while the king granted the members of the Estates the right to have their law suits adjudicated in other jurisdictions.[87] When the Estates met in Montpellier, the deputies were influenced by the magistrates in the *Cour des Comptes* in the same town, who "held every day in their hands the means to ruin them."[88] By virtue of their judicial powers the magistrates could affect the economic situation of the deputies to the Estates, a strategy to which the latter could respond only by having their cases tried elsewhere.

After 1759, conflicts in Languedoc revived, when the Estates allied themselves with the king against the *parlement*. The government wanted to rule by dividing. An internal memorandum written to the finance minister states that "it is easy to see how important it is for the king's service to support the Estates . . . because this is a sure way of causing the failure of all the efforts of the *parlement*."[89] An additional reason for

85. Cited from Marion (1898), pp. 123–124; my italics. In 1764, the finance minister L'Averdy wrote to d'Aiguillon in similar terms: "If we provoke the *parlement* [of Britanny], it will act on the sly to make the proposal fail in the Estates; if your efforts make the Estates agree to it, it will not register it" (Félix 1999, p. 327).

86. Pélaquier (2014b), p. 326.

87. Ibid., p. 327. In 1651, "at the request of the Estates [of Brittany], the royal council referred to the *parlement* of Paris all lawsuits affecting their members, to protect them from the hostility of the Breton magistrates" (Rébillon 1932, p. 215). Similarly, Bercé (1974), pp. 163–164, writes that "agents of the state obtained an automatic *évocation* of all their court proceedings to a tribunal outside their province, because, as stated in the decision in the [king's] private council that granted this favor, 'someone and his children cannot expect justice by said court given the animosity of all the inhabitants of said town and neighboring towns towards them'" (see also ibid., p. 502). This second-best practice is characteristic of the *ancien régime*. As Tocqueville (2011, p. 108) wrote in a different context, "a great evil [here: trial outside the normal jurisdiction] limited a still greater one" [here: magistrates acting as persecutors rather than as judges]."

88. Cited after Jouanna (2014a), p. 90.

89. Cited after Jouanna (2014d), p. 585. This letter dates from the same year (1759) as the letter from the Duc d'Aiguillon arguing that in Brittany divide-and-conquer was no

supporting the Estates was the need to maintain their ability to obtain loans, urgently needed in the middle of the Seven Years War, on favorable terms.[90] On their part, the Estates were willing to consent to new taxes, paying the price of unpopularity, in exchange for an official statement by the king that in the future all new taxes would need their consent, thus implicitly undermining the claims of the *parlement*, which responded by decreeing that the Estates could not consent to a tax that it had not validated.[91]

In Burgundy, conflicts between the two bodies took an acute turn in "the Varenne affair," in the mid-eighteenth century.[92] Jacques Varenne was an official gifted with legal and literary skills, whom the *élus* employed to refute the remonstrances of the *parlements* (as noted earlier, these began to be published around 1750). The debate had the form of competing historical narratives offered to justify the pre-eminence of the one or the other body. "On the disputed question of consent to taxation, [Varenne] argued that the dukes of Burgundy [prior to the annexation by France in 1477] had regularly assembled the three orders of the province in order to demand a *don gratuit*, which once voted was collected by the *élus*. Rather cuttingly he added that the *parlement* had nothing to do with this procedure: it did not exist. . . . [A]s a *coup de grâce* Varenne pointed out that the Estates had petitioned Louis XI to establish the *parlement* of Dijon in 1476," thus adding the pre-eminence of begetting to that of antiquity. The magistrates "offered an alternative historical scenario. . . . In their published remonstrances of March 16, 1762, they argued that the *parlement* had been in existence for thirteen centuries, and that long before the reign of the dukes Burgundy had been part of the kingdom of France. . . . As in other provincial crises . . . , the magistrates ostracized their opponents. All social contact with the members of the chamber of *élus* was forbidden, and 'the proscription was extended to their wives, children, and even their servants.'"

These conflicts were largely futile and sterile. If magistrates and deputies disagreed over who should decide what, it was mostly due to their

---

longer a viable strategy for the government, indicating the local character of these power struggles.

90. Ibid., p. 586.

91. Ibid., p. 588.

92. The discussion of this affair relies heavily on Swann (2003), pp. 270–282. I do not give page references to the passages cited from his exposition.

egoism and egocentricity[93] rather than to different conceptions of the public good. As for egoism, the following example is probably typical: in 1759 "the *parlement* of Languedoc refused to validate several decisions that aimed at preventing lawsuits that were ruining [the local communities], but that evidently served its interest" by the fees they generated.[94] As for egocentricity, I refer to the earlier discussion of *préséance*. Yet to an indeterminate and indeterminable extent, the deliberations and votes in these bodies must have contributed to a political culture in which questions increasingly required answers, and arguments from authority became increasingly hollow and shallow. The Enlightenment may have been a contributing, if elusive, causal factor.

Because of the limited documentation, it is difficult to say anything with confidence and generality when we move to the lowest level of deliberating bodies, the *village assemblies*. There were about as many of these as there were parishes, that is, around 40,000. There is no reason to believe that those whose deliberations left written traces are representative.[95] A classic study by Albert Badeau relies on records from Champagne and Burgundy, whereas the most recent study by Antoine Follain mainly focuses on Normandy, with occasional excursions to other provinces. Hence I limit myself to comments on some practices that, while not necessarily representative, nevertheless illuminate the *ancien régime* by the sheer fact that they were *possible*.[96]

The village assembly was often convoked by the *seigneur*, or needed his authorization to meet, sometimes against payment of a fee. In some cases, custom or charter allowed the village to convoke an assembly as of right. The frequency varied, ranging in Normandy from once a year to ten times a year. The *seigneur* might or might not be allowed to attend the deliberations. In some matters, the decisions of the assembly were final and enforceable, whereas in other cases they needed the approval of a court

93. For this distinction, see the Conclusion to Elster (2009b). The egocentric, unlike the egoist, is willing to sacrifice some material welfare in exchange for the applause of an outer audience or the "warm glow" provided by an inner audience.

94. Pélaquier (2014b), p. 329. For the same phenomenon in Burgundy, see Saint-Jacob (1960), pp. 336–337, and Swann (2003), pp. 199–200.

95. Follain (2008), p. 217, asks, "Will one reproach me for having based my study on the history of some dozens of localities while having nothing to say about the others?" He answers that "This has always been the case for studies of *The Village in the Ancien Régime*."

96. To avoid overburdening the text with footnotes, I shall not give references to the examples I cite. They are all taken from Badeau (1878), chap. 2, and from Follain (2008), chs. 7 and 8.

or of the *intendant*. Usually, all adult males could attend, except, in some cases, for new arrivals to the village, unmarried men, municipal employees, and villagers who did not pay taxes or own property. Voting seems to have been mostly public, such as by raising hands, but sometimes by secret ballot. School teachers were usually the last to vote, so as not to influence the deliberations. The assembly could be quite turbulent and tumultuous, sometimes to the point where no decisions could be reached. As a remedy, the village might elect a smaller council to manage its affairs. In large villages, plenary assemblies were called only when there was a question of initiating or sustaining a lawsuit.

The tasks of the assemblies included sales, purchases, and exchanges of communal property, as well repairs of churches, vicarages, roads, and bridges. They also appointed municipal officials, shepherds, constables, tax assessors, and tax collectors. In some cases, they set the date for the wine harvest and determined wages or prices. Their most consequential decisions concerned litigation (sometimes against the *seigneur*), selling communal property, taking up loans, negotiating the tariffs for the *seigneur's* monopolies, or imposing a new tax. In such cases, there might be a quorum of one-half or two-thirds of the heads of households in the village. When the assembly met, decisions often required unanimity: since each would be affected by the decision, each should not only be heard, but have a veto. In decisions that did not require unanimity, votes were sometimes weighted by income. As noted in note 199 to chapter 2, non-attendance was sometimes subject to a fine. In one ingenious arrangement, the punishment of a non-attendee was combined with a reward for attendees, since the former had to give a quarter liter of wine to each of the latter.

Although we perceive these assemblies through a glass darkly, I believe Tocqueville went too far in denigrating them.[97] In one of his scathing comments, he wrote: "When we recognize that these empty semblances of liberty went hand in hand with the absence of any real power, we can already see on a small scale how the most absolute rule can be combined with some forms of the most extreme democracy, compounding oppression with the ridicule engendered by failing to notice it." When he asserts that "the resemblance between the [New England township and the French village] was as close as that between a living individual and a corpse can be," he probably underestimated the vitality and autonomy of many village assemblies. He got many facts wrong, as when he writes that

97. The following passages are quoted from Tocqueville (2011), pp. 52–54.

in the village assembly "there was no deliberation . . . , nor was a vote taken" or that "it was not free to meet until the express permission of the *intendant* had been sought and granted." Just as he generalized recklessly about the grievance books on the basis of a tiny sample,[98] his comments on the village assembly were based on a small, and certainly not random sample of the 40,000 parishes.[99]

98. For every demand, one can find an assembly that made it, but no assembly made every demand: "Within a certain range of possibility one can always find in these materials what he wants to find, and by quoting them selectively make them say what he wants them to say. Tocqueville, whose errors have been repeated by many others, tells us 'I carefully read the grievance books . . . I saw that here one demanded the change of a law, there of a custom, and I took notes. I continued that immense labor to the end, and, when I set about putting these separate wishes together, I discovered with a kind of horror that what was demanded was the simultaneous and systematic repeal of all laws and customs prevailing in the country; I saw at once that this was going to involve one of the vastest and most dangerous revolutions ever to appear in the world.' [Tocqueville 2011, p. 131, using a different translation.] The method of Tocqueville, of course, is illustration rather than proof. In effect, he asked each cahier, 'What can you contribute to my composite forecast of the Revolution?' Sagnac and others have done the same. In this way, by pointing out that nearly everything done by the first revolutionary assembly was prefigured in the mind of some Frenchman who contributed something to a cahier, they exaggerate the foresight and intent with which the electors approached the Revolution. They ignore the thousands of parishes, bourgs, and urban corps that asked for none of the constitutional changes fundamental to the Revolution, and they fail to observe that no electoral assembly demanded anything approaching the full agenda that the National Assembly was to undertake" (Taylor 1972, p. 482).

99. Root (1987), pp. 12–13, writes that "Tocqueville consulted the administrative archives of Tours, where village records had all but disappeared."

CHAPTER SIX

Conclusion

I SHALL NOT SUMMARIZE the claims and arguments—already quite summary—made in the course of this book, but draw attention, in no particular order, to some general themes.

The Limits of Our Knowledge

The documentation from the *ancien régime* is massive, but tantalizingly incomplete, often unreliable, and hard to aggregate.

Incompleteness arises at all levels. As a non-specialist, I am awed by the efforts of historians to mine the archives and triangulate the sources, while also noting—as they do—that they are trying to reconstruct a puzzle from which many pieces are missing. As noted at the end of chapter 5, the surviving archives from the 40,000 villages do not give a representative sample, especially since the mere fact of their survival might be due to a selection effect.[1]

The same argument applies, in varying degrees, to the records of towns and provinces. To my knowledge, deliberating assemblies such as the *parlements*, assemblies of the clergy, provincial Estates, and the Estates-General never kept records that would enable us to identify those who argued and voted for or against proposals. If, as seems likely, many votes

---

1. Montaigne (1991), p. 44, cites a bias of this kind when he referred to Diagoras as being "shown many vows and votive portraits from those who have survived shipwrecks and . . . then asked, 'You, there, who think that the gods are indifferent to human affairs, what have you to say about so many men saved by their grace?'—'It is like this,' he replied, 'there are no portraits here of those who stayed and drowned—and they are more numerous!'" Similarly, villages that left records to posterity may have escaped the most brutal forms of destruction that at one time or another affected many of them.

were cast by the ephemeral methods of standing and sitting or of raising one's hands, even the numbers of votes pro and con might not be recorded, except when they were so close that they had to be counted by roll-call votes. In this case, too, the fact that many votes were recorded as close (chapter 5) might be due to a selection effect rather than to permanent deep divisions.

The incompleteness of our knowledge of key economic variables is in part due to the reluctance of individuals, from all social classes, to comply with requests for information, as these were invariably seen as a first step towards a tax increase. Even when individuals did comply, we may question the *reliability* of their answers. As I have noted several times, individuals as well as institutions had an incentive to misreport— exaggerate or understate—their income and property. At a different level, statements by royal officials, venal magistrates, and elected deputies can rarely be taken at face value. For each Vauban, Turgot, or Malesherbes, there were innumerable perpetrators of deception or victims of self-deception. The tendency of speakers or writers to disguise self-interest or group interest as the public interest is, of course, universal. In democracies, it is to some extent kept in check by the disinfecting sunshine of *publicity*, as Bentham—long before Judge Brandeis—argued.[2] In the *ancien régime*, especially towards the end, *public opinion* substituted to some extent for publicity. It was a poor substitute, often based on rumors rather than on facts in the public domain, but it was perhaps better than nothing. It kept the government in a constant state of nervous tension, even when it tried to do good, and may have limited the emission of blatant lies.

Finally, the problems of *aggregating* findings across time and space are almost insurmountable. Some books whose titles hold out the promise of applying to the old regime as a whole turn out to be devoted to one province and one reign. To synthesize their findings would be close to impossible. One scholar studying patterns of insurrection in a given time-space window might decide to limit insurrections to events involving at least ten persons. Another, focusing on a different window, might choose a higher or lower threshold. If the first proposes generalizations based on the patterns she observes, they might contradict the extrapolations of the second. To create a national index of average grain prices on the assumption that grain is qualitatively equal everywhere, as did Ernest Labrousse, is invalid

2. Bentham (1999), p. 149.

if, as is arguable, high prices of grain in one province could reflect better-quality grain rather than conjunctural factors.[3]

For these reasons, I doubt we will ever see the emergence of a canonical interpretation of the old regime. As more pieces of the puzzle are revealed, some interpretations will be discarded, but the accumulation of pieces will not converge to a unique picture.

Exemptions and Exceptions

These problems would have mattered less if local practices had been imposed and enforced in a uniform manner by the central government. France, after all, was not a federal country, in which the several states have a large degree of autonomy, resulting in widely diverging practices. Nevertheless, although a rigorous comparison is not feasible, the old regime seems to have been more heterogeneous than any federal system known to me. It was shot through with exemptions and exceptions at the level of individuals, institutions, social orders, towns, and provinces.

The genesis of this patchwork system is complex. Provinces that joined the kingdom in the Middle Ages and in the early modern period often did so with explicit stipulations that they would be treated more favorably in one respect or another, notably taxation and the right to self-government by provincial Estates. Although many privileges became diluted with time, others remained in force. Towns could buy tax exemptions in exchange for a lump-sum payment. In one respect, this transaction was an "integrative bargain" in which both parties gained (given their preferences): the towns paid less, and the king benefited from the certainty and punctuality of the payment. The clergy, as well as individuals, could strike similar deals. The nobility's exemption from the *taille* can be traced to the decision by Charles VII in 1439 to create a royal army funded by this new tax, which he was not strong enough to impose on the nobles even as they became exempt from the duty to provide him with soldiers.

The nobles benefited from numerous other formal or informal exemptions, which can be illustrated by the length of study required for a law degree. An ordinance from 1499 allowed nobles to obtain their law degree after three years, rather than the usual five.[4] In the eighteenth century, such formal exceptions had been replaced by informal ones. Thus among

---

3. Heers (2010), p. 19. His anti-Marxist bias may have shaped his criticism of Labrousse's Marxist views.

4. Jouanna (1977), p. 68.

eighty-four *intendants* whose career is known, seventy-four "becam[e] certified *avocats* or enter[ed] judicial office before attaining the minimum age or completing the full period of training."[5] Magistrates were able to find an office for their sons at an early age, an abuse reflected in (and attenuated by) the rule that when two blood-related magistrates cast a vote for the same proposal, their votes counted for one. For another example, one can cite the letter where Madame de Sévigné expresses her happiness when Monsieur and Madame (the king's brother and his wife) granted her an exemption from quartering soldiers.[6] These exemptions all conferred substantial material advantages. Others were mainly symbolic, and even disadvantageous from a material point of view. One reason why many commoners sought ennoblement was to obtain the fiscal advantages that went with noble status. Yet in the seventeenth and the eighteenth centuries, "the ennobled had to pay for the confirmation of his nobility: at the end of the day he paid more than the value of his fiscal privileges."[7]

The heterogeneity has also psychological roots in the desire for status and *préséance*. The tax exemption for the *seigneur* did not necessarily matter in economic terms, since the taxes paid by his tenants often lowered the rent he could extract by a comparable amount. However, the honorific nature of the exemption made it worth struggling for. In court society and beyond, the desire to distinguish oneself was a fertile ground for the creation of innumerable artificial privileges, which the king could grant and withdraw at his pleasure. This "narcissism of small differences" (Freud) was a regular obstacle to concerted action in all social groups. Hence it is tempting to argue that the kings actively encouraged the cult of *préséance*, as a tool of divide and conquer. More likely, they simply benefited from the cult, except when struggles for *préséance* occurred within the military where it led to the inefficient practice of generals taking turns to command. The kings themselves were intensely preoccupied with their *préséance* over other heads of state.

Scarcity, Urgency, and Uncertainty

At both extremes of the social hierarchy—the peasantry and the royal government—life was characterized by extreme scarcity, which truncated the time horizon of the agents. Investments and reforms that take time

5. Gruder (1968), p. 26.

6. Letter to her daughter of January 12, 1676 (vol. 2, p. 23).

7. Meyer (1981) p. 203, noting that some would-be nobles were deterred by this fact. Others were not (Nicolas 2008, p. 315).

to bear fruit were not undertaken because one could not afford to wait. (Among the peasantry, even those who could afford to invest in cattle or put new land under the plough often refrained from doing so, lest the increased revenue be offset by higher taxes.) For the peasant, the scarcity was mostly imposed by hard natural constraints.[8] To some extent, the scarcity the government faced was of its own making. Some of the wars that were a semi-permanent feature of the old regime and that created a constant need for money had an offensive character and were thus avoidable. But for the kings—especially Louis XIV—offensive wars were the logical consequence of an obsessional craving for glory.

Scarcity leads to *urgency*, that is, to a desire to act immediately. As explained in the Introduction, although urgency can be a rational response to scarcity, it can also be an effect of a strong emotion even when there is no objective need to act sooner rather than later. The urgency of revenge is the most striking example. In such cases, "inaction-aversion" captures better the psychological reality of urgency. From descriptions of riots and insurrections (*émotions*) in the old regime, it seems clear that the steps from suspicion to accusation and from accusation to action often skipped the requirement of gathering information before forming the beliefs on which the actions were based. Although I cannot provide any examples, I assume that the kings, too, sometimes acted on impulses, in spite of efforts by their ministers to delay their decisions, either for the emotion to abate or for more information to be gathered. Decisions did not have to be filtered through political or legal processes that would have permitted careful examination of possible long-term effects of the various options. In fact, as I noted in the Introduction, because the identification of delayed effects is itself a time-consuming process, it could be truncated by emotion-based urgency.

Uncertainty is a pervasive, although sometimes neglected, feature of decision making at any level. It is characterized by the *lack of reliable estimates* of the value of key variables and by the *lack of confirmed causal theories* of the relations among them. In its presence, even a rational agent is at a loss about what to do, and must rely on intuitions or heuristics or flip a coin. Reliance on the maximin heuristic—assume the worst and act accordingly—was probably prevalent. The peasantry were subject to the

---

8. Mullainathan and Shafir (2014), chap. 6, define a "scarcity trap" as "a situation where the person's behavior contributes to her scarcity." While there is no quarreling with definitions, and some peasants of the *ancien régime* may well have been caught in a scarcity trap in this sense, my strong impression from the literature is that the main reason peasants didn't save or invest was that they couldn't afford to. "It is expensive to be poor."

vagaries of the weather and of disease, as well as to governmental demands that may have seemed no less unpredictable. As noted, urgency contributed directly to the government's uncertainty about factual matters, by preventing the collection of data that might have resolved it. Also, impenetrable social relations, then as now, can prevent officials from predicting how the citizens at large will react to an edict or a measure. As I noted in the Introduction, harsh measures may deter some persons while inciting others to rebellion, the net effect being indeterminate.[9]

Injustice and Norm Violations

Injustice could generate strong emotions and many *émotions* (riots). In chapter 2, I distinguished between horizontal and vertical forms.

Horizontal injustice took the form of *arbitrary differences* in taxes, tithe, and recruitment to the militia, within each of the 40,000 parishes, among the parishes in each of the roughly two hundred *élections*, among the *élections* in each of the roughly 30 *généralités*, and among the latter. With few exceptions, only the within-parish differences were subjectively experienced as unjust, as most people knew little about conditions in other villages in their *élection* and a fortiori in other *élections* or *généralités*. An important question is whether the improved means of transportation towards the end of the old regime extended people's horizon and made them aware of injustice on a larger scale, and possibly capable of broadly based collective action.

Vertical injustice took the form of *asymmetric relations of exchange*, in which the lord, the church, or the state failed to provide a sufficient counterpart for the surplus, whether monetary or in kind, that they extracted from the peasantry. These three extractors did to some extent moderate each other, as each protected the peasantry from the others to make sure that enough was left for itself. Yet the total burden was at all times overwhelming, at an order of magnitude of perhaps 75 percent of the product of the soil. It was accepted only as long as the peasantry thought the provision of public goods by the lord and the state and of church services by the parish priest constituted a reasonable quid pro quo.

Some cases of perceived injustice do not fit neatly into the vertical/horizontal framework, as when peasants or town dwellers reacted against

9. The indeterminacy is illustrated in a cartoon from the London *Observer* on January 4, 2009. It shows a young boy on a heap of rubble in Gaza, watching Israeli bombers in the sky and asking himself, "Is this going to make me more or less likely to fire rockets at Israel when I grow up?"

what they perceived as the callous disregard of their welfare by speculating hoarders of grain or bread. Even when scarcity of grain or bread was due to natural causes, a pervasive "agency-bias" led consumers to impute it to human action.[10] In these cases, *hunger was transmuted into anger.*[11] Hence the determinants of the subjective welfare of the peasantry, as well as of their potential for insurrection, included (1) the absolute level of their burden, (2) horizontal inequities, (3) vertical asymmetries, and (4) allocation of blame for scarcity. Heavy burdens might be accepted if they were seen as fairly shared, fairly reciprocated, and due to nature rather than to human agency. Conversely, the alleviation of a burden might increase subjective misery if it went together with greater horizontal or vertical injustice. Tocqueville also argued that the *abolition* of a burden might increase subjective misery if other burdens remained in place. Equally plausible, perhaps, the abolition of a burden might create the expectation that other burdens would also be abolished, with disappointment and increased subjective misery following when they were not. The relative weights of absolute levels of burdens and the fairness of their distribution and reciprocation were no doubt conjunctural, and will often remain conjectural, but Tocqueville was certainly right in arguing that fairness mattered.

Adding to the comments in the Introduction, I shall consider some factors that shaped the translation of subjective *perceptions* of injustice into collective *action*. (In addition to perceptions, we might also invoke

10. In some societies, natural causes as the proximate cause of misery have been explained by *divine* (or supernatural) action as the ultimate cause: disasters revealed the anger of the gods. In a brilliant summary of the hermeneutics of suspicion, Gibbon (1996), p. 586, writes that "Ambiguous actions are imputed to the worst motives: error is confounded with guilt, accident with design, and laws with injustice; the partial injustice of a moment is dexterously applied as the general maxim of a reign of thirty-two years: the emperor alone is made responsible for the faults of his officers, the disorder of the times, and the corruption of his subjects; and *even the calamities of nature, plagues, earthquakes, and inundations, are imputed to the prince of the demons, who had mischievously assumed the form of Justinian* (my italics)." In my readings about and from the *ancien régime* I have not come across divine wrath as an explanation for the people's misery, but I may have missed something. In other societies, "dearth might become a weapon at the disposal of demagogues. . . . 'how easy would it be,' [Edmund] Burke speculated [in the mid-1750s], 'to give the people's fluctuating Minds some dangerous turn, to *confound natural with political Evils* to animate them with the hopes of Gain and Plunder.' Scarcity provided conditions for opportunistic attacks on property" (Bourke 2015, p. 200; my italics). Again, I have not come across this particular causal constellation in the *ancien régime*, although it was observed after 1789. Prior to that date, people attacked property *en détail*, not yet *en gros*.

11. A study of feeling "hangry" (MacCormack and Lindquist 2019) does not discuss the cases I consider here, in which hunger triggered anger towards an agent (usually an alleged hoarder or speculator) based on the belief that he was also *the cause* of the hunger.

rumors of injustice.) In some cases, the *anger* of the victim of an injustice must have fused with the *indignation* of those who observed it. Large numbers could then offset the fact that the latter emotional reaction is weaker. When the injustice targeted many individuals, their responses would depend on their expectations about what others would do. Coordination was facilitated by having a common complaint, and hindered when, for instance, a lord submitted his various tenants to different systems of exploitation. Again, it is tempting but probably invalid to interpret the latter case as "divide and conquer" or "social control." Collective action might merely involve passive resistance (see below), but could also take the form of attacks on property, property records, or persons. As a rule, insurrections did not involve indiscriminate looting.

Reactions to injustice must be sharply distinguished from reactions to violations of status-related *norms*. Although the reactions—anger and indignation—could be the same in both cases,[12] status norms differ from conceptions of justice in that they seek to enforce the asymmetries, exceptions, and exemptions that the latter condemn. Recruitment to the militia is a case in point. The urban elites would be angry if their servants were not exempt, and the bulk of the urban population would be angry if they were. The obligatory work on the roads (*la corvée*) provides another example—nobles were angry if roads were not diverted to their *château*, and the peasantry were angry if they were.

Conspiracy Theories and Agency-Bias

The human mind seems to prefer agency-based explanations over those that appeal to "blind," non-intentional mechanisms. One may cite, for instance, Hume's comment on an episode in the English Civil War: "whatever hardships [the troops] underwent, though perhaps derived from inevitable necessity, were ascribed to a settled design of oppressing them."[13] Many other examples could be cited.[14] Although alleged conspiracies almost by definition have two features, that of involving several persons and that of being kept secret to a larger public, I discuss some

12. According to the editors of a handbook on anger, "there is quite a broad agreement that typical triggers of anger include frustration; threats to autonomy, authority, or reputation; disrespect and insult; *norm or rule violation; and a sense of injustice*" (Potegal, Stemmler, and Spielberger 2010, p. 3; my italics). As shown by the comments by the lawyer Barbier cited in chapter 2, that "footmen are becoming too insolent," rule violations could also trigger indignation in third-party observers.

13. Hume (1983), vol. 5, p. 484.

14. Elster (2015a), pp. 168–169.

cases that have the second feature only. I limit myself to theories that had consequences for behavior, that is, were used as premises for action.

Unlike most other alleged conspiracies, those in the *ancien régime* were often two-layered.[15] At the bottom level, we find spontaneous charges by peasants or urban dwellers that scarcity of grain or of bread was due to hoarders and speculators who acted with reckless disregard for the welfare of producers and consumers, caring only about their own profit.[16] In an entry of his journal from 1721, Marais observes that the edicts from 1539, declaring that monopolies harmful to the public were illegal, did not specify a punishment.[17] In some cases, the rumors involved *cartels* of hoarders or speculators, as in an entry of his journal from 1725: "In neighboring places, it has been forbidden to bring grain to Paris, *in order to* maintain the scarcity and the horribly high prices, and nobody doubts that in two or three market days it has produced nine millions in profit. In this secret game, one is playing with the fate of Paris and perhaps of France."[18] While these accusations were sometimes based on observations, they were often based on rumors and speculations derived from long-standing mental schemata,[19] themselves fueled by the agency-bias. "The people would never admit that nature was the sole responsible for its misery."[20]

The rebellions and riots triggered by "hunger transmuted into anger" often took place simultaneously in different provinces, or followed upon each other in close succession. From the chronology, the authorities often inferred that there must have been a hidden conspiracy guiding the uprisings, ignoring the more obvious explanation that harvests or tax collections took place at the same time. These higher-level conspiracy theories show that *the government as well as the peasantry was subject to agency-bias.* Even the usually sober Turgot fell into this trap.

In 1766, the *parlement* of Paris invoked the common-cause argument in its response to the king's implicit charge that the courts of the kingdom

---

15. Similar two-layered conspiracy theories persisted in nineteenth-century France (Ploux 2003, pp. 103, 109).

16. Occasionally, the people also blamed the administration for its inefficient responses to penury (Faure 1961, p. 313). In such cases, the emotions, caused by the perception of incompetence rather than of profit-seeking, were likely to be less virulent. Actions, notably in the countryside, would not have a well-defined target.

17. Marais, vol. 2, p. 73, referring to the prosecution of the Duc de La Force for hoarding (Lecestre 1925).

18. Marais, vol. 3, p. 215; my italics.

19. For the importance of memories of the remote past in peasant movements, see Nicolas (2008), p. 655; and Lefebvre (1988), pp. 85–86. Shibutani (1966), pp. 76–86, has a useful discussion of "rumors as plausible extrapolations."

20. Lefebvre (1988), p 47.

were engaged in a subversive conspiracy. It asserted "That the magistrates of the different courts of the kingdom are constrained to follow the same laws [and] that from these common obligations there must result, *not an association or confederation of resistance*, which does not exist and never will, but an unintentional agreement (*concorde indélibérée*)."[21] This disclaimer was disingenuous, as the king certainly had reasons to fear coordinated actions by the courts (the *union des classes*). However, even if the *parlements* had operated independently of each other, simply reacting in the same way to the same abuses, the king's spontaneous agency-bias might still have led him to view the similarity of their remonstrances as the expression of a "confederation of resistance."

Among the possible explanations of agency-bias, two seem to stand out. First, the mind gravitates towards intentional rather than "blind" causal interpretations, because the former provides intrinsically satisfying *meanings*. In this perspective, the agency-bias is closely related to a teleological bias, as shown in the frequent refusal to believe that any benefits of action can be accidental: "cui bono" followed by "post hoc, ergo propter hoc." Second, one can find consolation in the idea that what is *caused* by human agency can also be *changed*, to the better, by human agency. These two mechanisms can, of course, work together and reinforce each other.

Passive Resistance

Resistance to the three powers that be—the *seigneur*, the state, and the church—could be *overt or covert* and take the form of acts of *commission or of omission*.

The most visible form was acts of *overt commission*, active resistance in the form of attacks on property or persons, as in most of the 8,528 episodes catalogued by Jean Nicolas.

In the religious domain, subjects sometimes reacted to oppression by *covert commission*. Their resistance sometimes aimed at being invisible and non-violent, as when Protestants assembled in "the desert" after the revocation of the edict of Nantes in 1685. "In the eyes of the law, these assemblies were rebellious by the very fact of being held."[22]

In theory, people might also engage in *covert omissions*. Yet this category raises a question: covert from whom (if any)?[23] If a peasant did

---

21. Cited from Hardy, vol. 1, p. 144; see also ibid., pp. 773, 775.

22. Nicolas (2008), p. 795.

23. For a general discussion of this issue, see the Introduction to Elster (2015b), pp. 4–5.

not show up for the *corvée* or for the sermon of an unpopular priest, his follow peasants might be aware of his abstention, but not necessarily the *seigneur*, his manager, the *subdélégué* of the *intendant*, or the priest. One might think that the peasant would want his peers to know what he did, to incite them to join him, but not his superiors, lest they punish him. Yet he might also fear that his peers might inform on him, or that if too many join him repression might be forthcoming. As I have not come across clear instances or explicit discussions of this category, I shall not pursue it.

By contrast, there is much testimony to the pervasive if sometimes diffuse forms of *overt commission* (passive resistance), which I discuss in the remainder of this section and which could take the forms of disobedience, sabotage, and tacit abstention from cooperation.[24] They mainly targeted the royal administration, but could also be directed against landowners. The resisters could be nobles, priests, abbots, magistrates, seigneurs, and other village notables, as well as the mass of the peasantry. To my knowledge, there are no systematic studies of passive resistance, but I suspect that it slowed down the machinery of government to a considerable degree.[25] When directed against landowners, it served as a brake on competition.

Jean Nicolas titled one of the chapters in his book, "United against the tax farmers" (*Unis contre la ferme*), referring to the hated collectors of the salt tax. "The collective acts of overt or covert resistance would not have been conceivable without the spirit of community which to a smaller or larger extent animated the elites of all the three orders."[26] In his data base, he finds that nobles and notables siding with popular tax rebellions included the partly overlapping groups of 71 municipal officers, 78 ecclesiastics, 100 seigneurs and nobles, 39 "men of the law," 41 magistrates, and 164 well-off commoners. Moreover, nobles as well as ecclesiastics blatantly violated the ban on cultivating tobacco, sometimes beating up the tax officials if they ventured onto their lands. "A beating from a nobleman's lackey was a professional hazard for all officers of the law."[27]

When tax farmers and their private armies met with active violence, they could "solicit the Church to issue a *monitoire*, a statement

24. Passive resistance must be distinguished from the *virtual* (anticipated) resistance that could act as a brake on surplus extraction by state or lord.

25. I shall not consider the case of soldiers refusing orders to shoot on the people. Although important in 1789 (see Volume 3), this form of resistance does not seem to have been common in the prerevolutionary *ancien régime*.

26. Nicolas (2008), p. 138.

27. Carroll (2006), p. 201.

obliging the faithful to reveal what they knew about the facts, on pain of excommunication."[28] This practice was deeply resented by the villagers, who could retaliate by the means of sabotage they had at their disposal. In Savoie in 1716, "following a well-known tactic the faithful darkened the church . . . by holding their hats against the windows to prevent the reading of a *monitoire*. . . . Afterwards, they rang the three church bells to cover the voice of the priest."[29] If they could not prevent him from reading out loud, they could at least ensure that he wasn't heard.

Passive resistance could also take the form of refusing to bid for or take care of properties that had been confiscated for non-payment of taxes. As noted in chapter 2, if the tax collector seized cattle in lieu of tax payments, neighbors might refuse to take care of them. In Guyenne in 1635, "if bailiffs succeeded in seizing animals in the fields or fruits on the trees from those liable for taxes, they would not find a neighbor to take them in or any bidder willing to sell them."[30] In Brittany in 1750, "one attempted to sell the assets of a *gentilhomme* . . . for non-payment of the *dixième*. All the buyers withdrew, and one made a point of honor in assisting him."[31] In Languedoc in the same year, the attempt to collect the *vingtième* failed for the same reason: "Because of a unanimous agreement not to pay and to prevent the use of force, nobody would acquire properties that might be seized."[32]

In *Les paysans du Nord*, Georges Lefebvre documented a particular form of passive resistance due to ill-will (*mauvais gré*). As in the cases discussed in the previous paragraph, the underlying cause is community solidarity, but opposed to the landowner rather than to the tax collector. Social norms prevented the owner of the land from evicting his manager (*fermier*) and replacing him by another who was willing to pay a higher rent. If he tried to, and ignored the symbolic warnings signs, the community would punish his replacement: "his harvests were destroyed, his trees cut, his animals mutilated, his ploughs broken, his house and tools burned; he himself could be beaten up or killed by gunshot."[33] These were, of course, forms of *active* resistance. Yet even after these were attenuated

28. Nicolas (2008), p. 169; see also p. 630 for a fuller description.
29. Ibid., p. 749. As Nicolas explains (ibid., p. 632), the practice was seen as unjust (punishing all for the silence of some) and as relying on denunciations that undermined village solidarity. The priests could also drag their feet or refuse to cooperate with the secular authorities (ibid., p. 631).
30. Bercé (1974), p. 353.
31. Argenson, vol. 6, p. 164.
32. Marion (1891), p. 156.
33. Lefebvre (1924), p. 95.

by severe legal punishments, "no power in the world could eliminate the second [passive] kind of peasant vindictiveness, which was ostracism. The intruder found nothing to buy; he could not sell anything in the province; no worker or artisans would work for him; nobody would have any relations with him, and the excommunication would also reach his children, who would not be marriageable. Hence more than one piece of land remained uncultivated, because a stubborn owner could not find a manager."[34]

Yves-Marie Bercé writes that a "[tax] rebellion by definition presupposes violence and physical resistance against an official. Yet the notion can be *extended to passive resistance*, such as the refusal to prepare the tax rolls or to elect solvable tax collectors."[35] Specifically, the "nomination by a community of beggars or idiots of the village as tax collectors, or the refusal to name one, were considered as serious cases that justified legal action against the community. This was a low-grade form of rebellion (*guerre larvée*). In the areas of traditional refusal to pay taxes, huge groups of parishes persisted in this practice for years, avoiding repression by resorting to a jungle (*maquis*) of procedures."[36] In doing so, however, they might ruin themselves, since litigation was costly and artificially prolonged by the courts. As in other litigation-prone societies, the remedy was sometimes worse than the ill.

As I discussed in chapter 4, the courts and the legal community more generally also engaged in various form of passive resistance, most radically by going on strike and by ostracizing non-strikers. In addition to the cases cited there, I can mention reactions to the creation of new courts in the Southwest around 1630, which included lack of buyers (passive resistance) as well as threats towards buyers.[37] A religious community expressed its opposition to a nomination by passive resistance, as when the archbishop of Paris refused in 1766 to give his approbation (*visa*) to a Vatican-appointed canon in Notre-Dame, suspecting simony (purchase of the benefice). The candidate appealed to the *parlement*, which authorized him to get a *visa* from the archbishop of Lyon, the primate of the French church. On the first occasion he presented himself in the church as officially appointed canon, "there was not a single canon who was willing to

34. Ibid., p. 96. The fear of this kind of civic death is also known from other communities; see, for instance, Busquet (1920), pp. 357–358; and Mason (1970), pp. 116–117.

35. Bercé (1974), p. 563; my italics.

36. Ibid., p. 103.

37. Bercé (1974), p. 154. As always, it is hard to tell whether the passive resistance was due to solidarity or to fear (chap. 1).

accompany him to the different members of the chapter in the visits that precede the inauguration, as required by custom . . . , which put him in the situation of having to use the office of two notaries for the inauguration; the chapter also refused to receive the three hundred *livres* that each recipient customarily pays to cover the expenses of his funeral."[38] Given the intense theological controversies of the period, together with the clergy's obsession with *préséance*, I would be surprised if there were not many such cases of ostracism in the Church.

Finally, we can extend the notion of active resistance to include overt expressions of disapproval, and that of passive resistance to include the absence of overt expressions of approval (chapter 3). Towards the end of the *ancien régime*, these two forms of resistance fused, when tacit condemnation received active approval. Thus in 1788, the audience in a theatre cheered when the maxim "The silence of the people is the lesson of the kings" was invoked from the stage.[39]

Second Best?

Tocqueville as well as his great-grand-father Malesherbes argued that institutions that may seem inappropriate to us, such as the venal and highly politicized courts, could be defended on second-best grounds, as *an evil that limited a still greater one.* This idea is an early version of the "principle of the second-best"—that "it is not true that a situation in which more, but not all, of the optimum conditions are fulfilled is necessarily, or is even likely to be, superior to a situation in which fewer are fulfilled."[40]

The evils of the legal system were numerous. Since offices of judges were private and inheritable property, there was no guarantee that they possessed the requisite competence. Since judges (not only lawyers) were partly paid by the parties to a suit, they tended to encourage litigation and oppose measures that would limit it. (However, their self-interest could also benefit the people, as when they opposed the substitution of brutal military force for legal means of enforcing tax collections.) As in many other times and places, judges often *argued from conclusions to premises.*

---

38. Hardy, vol. 1, pp. 177–178.

39. Swann (2017), p. 329. More generally, people could express emotions in the theater that they could not manifest in the streets. In 1762, after Maréchal de Broglie was exiled for insubordination, the public was so opposed to this decision that when a character in a play by Voltaire uttered the line, "It is the fate of heroes to be persecuted," the audience applauded wildly. The play was then banned (Barbier, vol. 8, p. 14).

40. Lipsey and Lancaster (1956), pp. 11–12.

As Montaigne said, "Just as no event and no form completely resembles another, neither does any completely differ. . . . All things are connected by some similarity; yet every example limps and any correspondence which we draw from experience is always feeble and imperfect; we can nevertheless find some corner or other by which to link our comparisons. And that is how laws serve us: they can be adapted to each one of our concerns by means of some twisted, forced or oblique interpretation."[41] The conclusions the judges wanted to reach were not necessarily motivated by self-interest, but the flexibility of judicial language certainly enlarged the scope for self-serving arguments. Because judges could not be removed, and their judgments could not be appealed, there was no control on arbitrary or interest-driven decisions.

The preceding comments apply to the ordinary functions of the courts in civil and criminal cases. In addition, the *parlements* took upon themselves a task somewhat similar to modern judicial review of legislation, by issuing remonstrances against royal edicts. The similarity breaks down, however, in that there was no authoritative, written constitution that the courts could cite in objecting to legislation. In several countries with constitutions that did not at the outset explicitly authorize judicial review— the United States, Norway, France, many Latin American countries, and Israel—supreme courts or constitutional courts have taken it upon themselves to exercise it. As Hamilton argued in *The Federalist* No. 78, given that there *was* a constitution, it would be anomalous if it could not be enforced. In the *ancien régime*, by contrast, the *parlements* took upon themselves not only the enforcement of "the constitution" but even the invention of the constitution—"the fundamental laws of the kingdom"— they claimed to enforce. These laws were invented in an opportunistic manner as the need for justification arose.

I have argued that the remonstrances of the *parlements*, by and large, did not aim at promoting the long-term public interest, but mostly the interests of the magistrates and their popularity. This assessment is controversial, but even if correct would not prove that Malesherbes and Tocqueville were wrong. Especially after 1750, the government's constant fear of urban unrest, nourished by the close links between the *parlement* of Paris and the bourgeois and artisans of the city, made it wary and cautious. If the government had had a free hand, unencumbered by remonstrances,

---

41. Montaigne (1991), p. 1213. Two hundred years later, Malesherbes, as noted earlier, referred to the "subtlety and falsity" of the magistrates.

as was briefly the case between 1770 and 1774, it might have implemented harsher policies. I leave this counterfactual unresolved.

Second-best issues could also arise in other contexts. Optimally, justice should be inexpensive, speedy, and impartial. Assuming for the sake of argument that the *parlements* and the lower-level courts, *bailliages* and *sénéchaussées*, were impartial, their proceedings were expensive and slow. Adding the layer of seigneurial justice, which was partial, speedy, and inexpensive, may have provided better outcomes overall. Also, because local courts could be vindictive when magistrates used their power to pursue private feuds, the practice of transferring litigation to other jurisdictions could be defended on second-best grounds.

Wars, Taxes, and Loans

In the *ancien régime*, as in many other times and places, wars were a major drain on public finance. They could be financed in four ways: by taxes only, by loans only, by loans that were later followed by taxes to pay the interest on the loans, and by loans followed by full or partial bankruptcy.

The first option might appeal to moral purists. As James Madison wrote in 1792, "each generation should be made to bear the burden of its own wars, instead of carrying them on, at the expence of other generations."[42] This might make sense for offensive wars, assuming that they do indeed occur at the initiative of a "generation" or have wide popular support, but not for defensive wars. However, the French offensive wars, notably in the 1670s and 1680s, occurred at the initiative of Louis XIV, for whom the glory of France, and even more his own glory, counted for more than the welfare of the French. Defensive wars present a different category: since they presumably benefit future generations, it is not unreasonable to let them bear some of the burdens by paying interest on the loans. It is possible, but hard to document, that the incidence of tax revolts was shaped, at least partly, by the perceived legitimacy of the wars.

The second option might seem unfeasible, at least in the long run, since the common practice of taking out new loans to pay interest on the old ones eventually had to come to a halt. Nevertheless, as I argued in chapter 4, there is some evidence that Necker assumed that inflation caused by the influx of gold and silver from America would erode the value of the loans and hence the real cost of paying interest. If he did make

---

42. Madison (1983), p. 208. David Hume (1985) also argued strongly for funding wars fully by taxes.

that assumption, he must have tacitly also assumed that lenders would *not* make it, since they would otherwise require a higher interest rate to compensate for inflation. The issue is complex, not least because there are competing explanations of Necker's preference for loans over taxes, including his desire to acquire popularity by managing an apparently cost-less war.

The third option was the dominant one. During a war, both taxes and loans funded current military operations as well as interest on loans incurred in earlier stages. Once the war ended, there was a general expectation that wartime taxes would be reduced. The expectation was reasonable to the extent that taxes had funded military operations, but the expectation that taxes would fall all the way to their prewar level was not, since loans did not end with the operations they had funded. It is more than doubtful that the French people at large made this distinction, since their knowledge about higher finance was nil. They remembered what they paid in taxes before the war, and inferred that at the end of the war, taxes would return to that level. These comments, to be sure, are speculative, and based on general psychological principles rather than on documentary evidence.

The last option, bankruptcy, hovered in permanence over the *ancien régime*. There were no outright cancellations of sovereign debts, for instance on the grounds that they had been incurred by previous kings, but many small and medium-sized measures that cumulatively had much of the same effect.[43] The tools of the government included debasement of the currency (a practice that for ill-understood reasons ceased after 1726), suspension of reimbursements, cuts in interest rates, issuance of increasingly devalued paper currencies, "flights forward" that used future tax revenues to pay for current expenses, and other tricks of the trade. The upshot was a lack of confidence in the promises of the government, forcing it to offer a high risk-premium on its bonds that inevitably increased the share of interest-payments in the national revenue, leaving less for ordinary expenses, some of which were incompressible. As has often been remarked, the escalation of debts was due in large part to the fact that the kings were *unable to make themselves unable* to break their promises. If

---

43. The most drastic measures were those taken by finance minister Terray in 1770. According to Marion (1927), p. 247, because of Terray "the *ancien régime* survived for another twenty years." In his opinion, Terray's main claim to fame was his attempt to force the privileged class to have *skin in the game*: "the day it seriously felt the burden of taxes, it would have understood the need to moderate pretentions that would have affected its own purse" (ibid., p. 271).

the "central paradox of American [colonial] history" was the "inconsistency of slaveholders devoting themselves to freedom,"[44] the *impotence of omnipotence* may be the central paradox of the *ancien régime*.

Tocqueville

In the present book I have repeatedly cited Tocqueville's *Ancien régime*, usually as an inspiration and occasionally as a target of criticism.[45] Compared to his previous study of America, it is less exuberant and more coherent, less speculative and more firmly anchored in the facts. The fascination the book will always exercise on readers owes a great deal to the seamless way in which historical analysis is overlaid with a sense of tragedy as well as of irony. In addition to being a literary masterpiece, it is a pioneering study in political psychology. Compared to the Marxist tradition that mostly emphasizes objective (material) misery as the cause of rebellion,[46] Tocqueville stresses the subjective perception of misery and oppression, and even suggests that alleviation of objective misery may go together with, and in fact cause, an increase in subjective misery.[47]

Tocqueville's emphasis on lived experience goes together with his attention to *emotion* as the spring of action. In the tripartite relations among the peasantry, the urban third estate, and the nobility, he focuses (albeit in somewhat inconsistent terminology)[48] on the *hatred* the first class harbored towards the third, the *envy* the second felt towards the third, and the *contempt* of the third for the second. His many references

44. Morgan (1975), p. 4. In the revolutionary era, the same paradox would reappear in France (see Volume 3).

45. In Volume 3 I shall also cite and discuss his notes for the unpublished second volume of that book, in which he comments on the Revolution and the *Constituante* as they unfolded. In the present summary, I do not dwell on Tocqueville's factual mistakes, cited at various places above, concerning the grievance books, seigneurial justice, and the village assemblies.

46. Marx himself was aware, however, of the importance of subjective factors, when he emphasizes that the worker's subjective satisfaction depends on a comparison between his actual and expected consumption and on a comparison between his own consumption and that of the capitalist (Marx 1849).

47. As we saw, in his book on the 1789 Revolution he emphasized neither of the two mechanisms cited in the previous note, but rather the tendency for the alleviation of one form of oppression to cause others to be more acutely felt. In his retrospective analysis of the 1848 Revolution, however, he asked, "Had no one noticed that for a long time the people had continually been gaining ground and improving their condition, and that their importance, education, *desires*, and power were all constantly growing? Their prosperity had also increased, *but not so fast* (Tocqueville 1987, p. 75; my italics).

48. Elster (2009a), pp. 3, 67.

to the *fear* that could on occasion animate all social classes are sometimes ambiguous, lending themselves to understanding in terms of prudential as well as visceral fear,[49] although the context will usually allow us to determine the meaning Tocqueville had in mind.

Let me make a speculative remark about contempt, in what I hope is in Tocqueville's spirit. The emotion of contempt in an observer is usually thought to go together with the emotion of *shame* in the person being observed. In many standard cases, shame is indeed the effect of the expression of contempt. Often, however, for that effect to be produced the expression has to be spontaneous and involuntary, such as a turning away of the head or not responding to an invitation. If the observed agent believes, rightly or not, that the expression was *intended* to shame her, she will often react with anger rather than with shame. Anger is, in fact, the standard reaction to the deliberate imposition of pain, and few things are as painful as shame. I suggest that the French Revolution became inevitable when the reaction in members of the third estate to the contempt of the nobles changed *from shame to anger*. I leave this remark as an unverifiable speculation.

One might ask why the reaction of those who lacked the privileges did not take the form of hatred of the king (who granted them) rather than envy of those who possessed them (see the ice cream example from the Introduction). In a letter Tocqueville simply notes that "what most prevented the French from being worthy and capable of freedom was that they always detested the neighbor more than the master."[50] However, this descriptive statement does not provide an explanation, which may be found in the well-known mechanism of *neighborhood-envy*.[51] "Potter envies potter" (Hesiod, cited by Aristotle in *Rhetoric* 1381 b).The king might be the object of contempt, as was the case for Louis XV at the end of his life, but was too distant to trigger envy.

While many of Tocqueville's counterintuitive insights have inspired me, it may be worth while noting that some of them probably did not originate with him. As he never cites other historians of the *ancien régime* and even asserts that he made it his policy not to read them,[52] any claims about influence must rely on textual comparisons. I believe he had read and was influenced by Joseph Droz as well as by Madame de Staël, although one

49. To get the sense of this distinction, we can imagine Franklin Roosevelt saying, "The only thing of which we have to be prudentially afraid is our visceral fear."

50. Tocqueville (2003), p. 1098; also p. 1107.

51. Elster (1999), pp. 170, 182.

52. Tocqueville (2003), p. 1200.

cannot exclude the possibility that the textual similarities stemmed from a common source or simply expressed ideas that were "in the air." Be this as it may, let me simply cite some strikingly similar texts, leaving the possible causal links to the interpretation of the readers.[53]

The broken contract. A central idea in Book II of the *Ancien régime* is that the French nobility had broken the two implicit contracts that justified its privileges in the public eye: to do military service in exchange for tax exemptions (pp.77–78) and to provide public goods to the peasantry in exchange for feudal dues (p. 37). Madame de Staël was fully aware of the first breach of contract (p.145) as well as of the second (ibid.).

The failure of half-measures. A central idea in Book III (and in the notes for the second volume) is that under Louis XV and Louis XVI, the administration constantly failed to see that half-measures would work contrary to their intended purpose, an idea that Tocqueville applied to concessive (p. 133) as well as to repressive (p. 139) policies. Mme de Staël (p. 148) refers to the ineffectiveness of the repressive half-measures taken on the day of the oath of the Jeu de Paume. Droz refers both to concessions (volume 1, p. 315) and to repressive measures (volume 1, p. 369) that were counterproductive because they did not go far enough in their respective directions.

Contempt mixed with sympathy. Another important idea in Book III is the inconsistent attitude of the privileged classes towards the people, an amalgam of sympathy and contempt (p. 163). Droz (volume 1, p. 71) makes the same point and, like Tocqueville (but referring to a different behavior), spells out how the attitude also led to inconsistent practice.

The difficulty of fighting a two-front war. In his notes for the second volume, Tocqueville claims that one cannot at one and the same time be courageous against despotism and against anarchy (p.162). Having successfully resisted the king, the *Constituante* could not also stand up against the people of Paris. Again, we find Droz (volume 2, p. 271) making the same observation.

---

53. With one exception, page numbers refer to Tocqueville (2011), Droz (1860), and Stäel (2000). The exception occurs in the last reference to Tocqueville, which is to his notes for the unfinished second volume (Tocqueville 2001).

Bibliographical Overview

HERE I SHALL state the main sources on which I have relied, beginning with the historians. In addition to the great work by Tocqueville, the writings I have found most valuable fall in two categories. First, there are the great French doctoral *Thèses d'Etat*, sometimes running to a thousand pages and written over twenty years. This species of scholarship now seems to be extinct, perhaps because historians no longer accept the toll it takes on their personal life. Second, over the last half century there has been an amazing blossoming of Anglo-American scholarship on the *ancien régime*. Needless to say, much recent French work is also extremely useful.

No scholar, working from primary sources, could possibly cover the full spectrum of institutions and behavioral patterns of 15–25 million people over several centuries.

Many historians focus on one part of the spectrum in one period and in one province. Examples include Yves-Marie Bercé, *Histoire des Croquants: Etude des soulèvements populaires au XVIIᵉ siècle dans le Sud-Ouest de la France* (covering some 450–500 episodes), and Pierre de Saint-Jacob *Les paysans de la Bourgogne du nord au dernier siècle de l'ancien régime*. Another title is less explicitly selective, Michael Kwass's *Privilege and the Politics of Taxation in Eighteenth-Century France*. Despite the title, it is largely a book about Normandy.

Other historians focus on one part of the spectrum and one period, but covering France as a whole, examples being Arlette Jouanna, *Le devoir de révolte: La noblesse française et la gestation de l'Etat moderne, 1559–1661*; Guy Chaussinand-Nogaret, *The French Nobility in the Eighteenth Century*; and the two volumes of

a playful, anecdote-studded, and fact-studded book by John
McManners, *Church and Society in Eighteenth-Century France.*
Here I also place Herbert Lüthy's *La banque protestante en France,*
which combines formidable technical and detailed financial history
with acute observations on the nature of the old regime.

More rarely, perhaps, a study may cover the whole spectrum in
one province and one period, an example being Pierre Goubert,
Beauvais et le Beauvaisis de 1600 à 1730.

Unlike the many books that deliver less than the titles promise, a
book by Joël Félix, *Finances et politique au siècle des Lumières: Le
ministère L'Averdy 1763–68*, delivers more.

Some historians finally, cover one part of the spectrum for the whole
period and for the country as a whole, examples being the five
volumes of Georges Picot, *Histoire des Etats Généraux*; Jean
Nicolas's study of 8,528 episodes of popular violence, *La rébellion
française 1661–1789*; and Julian Swann's *Exile, Imprisonment,
and Death.*

Some historians who write about *one individual* also manage to illuminate many parts of the spectrum. The classical biographies of Machault
and the Duc d'Aiguillon by Marcel Marion fall in this category, as do the
biographies of the Cardinal de Retz by Simone Bertière, of Malesherbes by
Pierre Grosclaude, and of Mirabeau by Guy Chaussinand-Nogaret. (Biographies of the kings tend to be somewhat hagiographical.) One may even
find useful studies of *one day*, such as Edgar Faure's *La disgrâce de Turgot,*
published in a series of books, *Thirty Days That Made France.*

I have also drawn on works of synthesis that provide basic information
about the main institutions and events of the old regime. These include
the comprehensive survey *France baroque, France classique 1589–1715* by
René and Suzanne Pillorget; François-Olivier Martin, *Histoire du droit
français*; and the two volumes by Roland Mousnier on *Les institutions
de la France sous la monarchie absolue.* The numerous writings by Jean
Egret on eighteenth-century politics are invaluable. Two books by Marcel
Marion, Volume 1 of his *Histoire financière de la France depuis 1715* and
his *Dictionnaire des institutions de la France aux XVIIe et XVIIIe siècles*
are partly dated, but still useful. The same two adjectives apply to a classic
work by Ernest Lavisse, *Louis XIV: Histoire d'un grand règne*, crammed
with telling examples provided to him by his assistant Edmond Esmonin,
who is also the author of an unsurpassed study of the macro- and micro-
finances of the old regime, *La taille en Normandie au temps de Colbert,*

often cited above. If asked to recommend one book that shows the *ancien régime as it really was,* this is perhaps the one I would choose.

My hope is that these and similar surveys, which spell out what more specialized studies usually take for granted, have kept me honest. Yet because of my emphasis on the *psychology*—motivations and beliefs—of the agents, I have taken my main inspiration from micro-historical studies based on primary sources. Marc Bloch wrote that "the good historian resembles the giant of the fairy tale. He knows that wherever he catches the scent of human flesh, there lies his quarry (*son gibier*)."[1] The good historian can also convey this sense of excitement to his or her readers. Let me cite from three authors on whom I have drawn extensively:

> The systematic exploration of the archives can bring out a multitude of hitherto buried incidents, of which one element may bring to our attention, luck helping, a novel interpretation. Only the total immersion (*bain de foule*) in the mass of material can deliver this intimate knowledge, this kind of empathy that is inseparable from the study of the past.[2]

> In dealing with the history of mentalities, the seemingly futile detail can have its value. A quasi ethnographic approach to the facts must therefore be added to the demands of erudition.[3]

> I have tried to stay as close as possible to the village, at the heart of daily life, in my search for the color of an agrarian civilization that is no longer ours. I am persuaded, moreover, that general life is perhaps strongest at the level of the cell, and that it is possible to find there the large currents that traversed all of France at the time. An ambition to reach general history through local history: certainly. And believing also in the virtue of the significant detail, I have not been afraid to seek it out when it could reveal an important fact.[4]

I do not attach equal importance to all statements in these passages. I do not believe in empathy as a scientific method, nor do I think that the study of village life in Burgundy will allow us to understand village life

---

1. Bloch (1964), p.26. LeRoy Ladurie (1966, pp. 15–50) adds that the history of the *climate* is also worth studying.

2. Nicolas (2008), p. 19. Quoting Ernest Labrousse, he adds that "everything that is important is repeated": a detail is not telling until it has been confirmed.

3. Bercé (1974), p. 2.

4. Saint-Jacob (1960), p. xxxviii; see also p. 425.

elsewhere,[5] the way a single cell contains information about the organism as a whole. Rather, I cite these writers because their work illustrates the "infinite capacity for taking pains" that is sometimes cited as a definition of genius.

Although the monumental monographs on the French peasantry by George Lefebvre, Pierre Goubert, René Pillorget, and Emmanuel Le Roy Ladurie also exhibit this virtue, they do not, to the same extent, focus on the peasant *psychology*. The writings by Pierre de Saint-Jacob, Yves-Marie Bercé, and Jean Nicolas confirm Tocqueville's insight that the French peasantry felt oppressed not mainly because of the objective weight of its burdens, but because of a burning feeling of their *injustice*. The perception of injustice can be partly explained by the behavior of the local nobles, who continued to cling to their privileges long after they had ceased to perform the functions that, in the eyes of the peasantry, had once justified them. This, too, was one of Tocqueville's main insights. The psychology of the Court nobles, for whom residence in their *seigneurie* was (often literally) a punishment rather than a source of pride, evolved over time. I draw on Arlette Jouanna, *Le devoir de révolte*, and on Guy Chaussinand-Nogaret, *La noblesse au XVIIIe siècle*, for the earlier and the later periods. To my knowledge, there is no comparable study of the psychology of the pre-revolutionary urban populations. Nicolas, *La rébellion française*, has valuable chapters on artisans, merchants, and day laborers. Magistrates, bankers, financiers, ship-owners, and industrialists existed in an increasingly symbiotic relationship with the upper nobility, an affinity that did not prevent the latter from showing their *morgue* when they were provoked or wanted to provoke.

Consider next works by contemporary *observers* and *actors*. The most useful are by authors who are well-informed, not moved by partisan or personal interest, and not subject to retrospective fallacies (or to failing memory) The first criterion is obvious, but open to various interpretations. Although many personal journals report rumors rather than facts, the existence of rumors can itself be an important fact. The second induces a preference for observers over actors.[6] The last criterion induces a preference for journals over memoirs. With a few exceptions, the authors I cite

---

5. See Follain (2008). As an example, the *taille personnelle* in Burgundy had effects that differed radically from the *taille réelle* that obtained, for instance, in the Dauphiné.

6. This preference is not obvious, since even when they have an axe to grind, actors may be better informed than observers (Walpole 2000, p. 5). Yet since actors with few exceptions write memoirs after leaving the stage rather than journals while occupying it, their (motivated) bias may be compounded by (unmotivated) errors of recollection.

are mostly silent on the life of people in the countryside. They lived at the Court, or had a professional practice in Paris.

Let me first mention some foreign observers, including some who commented on the revolutionary years.

In 1609, Sir George Carew wrote up a "Relation on the State of France" that, among other observations, contains a prescient reply to Sully, the minister of Henri IV. "In way of vaunt, [Sully] once told me, that his master levied more out of his only province of Normandy, than mine did out of all the countries under him. To which I answered, I took that to be the way to make his Majesty's subjects desirous to change their master, and those of my master to continue their old."[7]

John Locke spent more than three years in France in the 1670s, writing a journal that deals mostly with agricultural and other practical matters, with occasional comments on social affairs. He has several comments on the tax system, some of them cited above.[8]

The reports by ambassadors are often the most reliable sources: they were usually well informed and had no other motive than that of informing their national government. The Prussian ambassador Spanheim, *Relation de la Cour de France* from 1690, is exceptionally insightful and for the most part confirmed by recent scholarship.[9] Throughout the whole *ancien régime*, the reports by the Venetian ambassadors to France are invaluable because of their disinterestedness.[10] For the period 1770–1780, the reports to Maria Theresa from Mercy-Argenteau (the Austrian envoy to the French Court) that provided information about petty court intrigues, while less scintillating than Saint-Simon's set-pieces, are also more reliable.[11]

7. Carew (1749), p. 464.

8. For a survey of his observations on the French tax system and its inequities, see the editorial introduction to Locke (1953), pp. xlv–xlix.

9. Spanheim (1973). Meyer (1981), p. 20, characterizes this book-length report as "singularly accurate."

10. See Fontana, Furlan, and Saro (1997) for a full compilation of these reports for the period 1786–1795.

11. It is worthwhile citing, though, a prescient comment on a more important matter: "given the character and the comportment of *M. le dauphin* [the future Louis XVI], it is virtually certain that *Mme la Dauphine* will one day be called upon to govern France" (Mercy-Argenteau 1874, vol. 1, p. 349). This prediction appeared in a letter to her mother, but as it was also conveyed to Marie-Antoinette herself (Bertière 2002, p. 114), it may have

In his letters, Horace Walpole, a gadfly who was an arbiter of taste in
France as well in England, offers many succinct characterizations
as well as telling details. Among the former, one may cite his
descriptions of life at Versailles as "a mixture of parade and
poverty" or, in a different vein, "a mixture of piety, pomp, and
carnality."[12] Among the latter, we find a striking anticipation of
Tocqueville's assertion that in its blindness the French nobility
neglected a basic rule, *pas devant les domestiques*: "I dined to-day
with a dozen *savants*, and though all the servants were waiting,
the conversation was much more unrestrained, even on the Old
Testament, than I would suffer at my own table in England, if a
single footman were present."[13]

In the years before and during the French Revolution, the British
agronomist Arthur Young crisscrossed France and observed the
state of agriculture as well as the roads, fields, buildings, and
the mindsets of those—cultivators as well as nobles—whom he
met. After July 14, 1789, he was in the thick of events both in the
countryside and in Paris. Being accustomed to English practices,
he was particularly struck by the *lack of windows* in the houses in
the French countryside: "can a country be likely to thrive where
the great object is to spare manufactures?"[14]

Gouverneur Morris, one of the main actors at the Federal Convention
in 1787, spent the time from February 1789 to 1798 in Europe,

---

become (to some extent) a self-fulfilling prophecy. Maria Theresa did not want it to become
true: "If the state of this monarchy were to deteriorate even more, I would rather they
blamed some minister than my daughter" (Mercy-Argenteau 1874, vol. 2, p. 35).

12. Walpole (2017), pp. 485, 505.

13. Ibid., p. 483. For a similar observation, see Argenson, vol. 6, p. 91: "One is too free
to criticize the government, and with great arrogance at high table, with lackeys present."
Tocqueville (2011), p. 162 wrote that "As for the people, it was taken for granted that though
they listened, they would not understand." Towards the end of the *ancien régime*, a chronicler
complained that apprentice hair-dressers who overheard what their clients said were led to
a "secret revolt" against their masters (Mercier 1789, p. 198). In 1788, "it is not impossible
that criminally irresponsible exchanges between the privileged were captured in passing by
servants, spread and deformed by word of mouth, and inflamed the hatreds" (Lefebvre 1988,
pp. 52–53). For two American examples of the dangers of talking in the presence of slaves,
see Phillips (1999), p. 147, and Wood (2009), p. 536. In Elster (2015a), p. 303, I refer to this
behavior as an instance of the "younger sibling syndrome," which consists in assuming that
other people are less rational and capable of strategic behavior than oneself. As noted by Chwe
(2009), p.11, "If you can't think of [other] people as strategic, you completely misrecognize
strategic situations involving them, and they can use this misrecognition to their advantage."

14. Young (1794), p. 19; see also pp. 29, 97, 190, 194, 273.

much of the time in France. Like Arthur Young, he met many high-ranking nobles and, like him, observed closely the proceedings of the Constituent Assembly. Among his many prescient observations, I shall cite one from July 1, 1789: "The Court are about to form a camp in the neighborhood of Paris of 25,000 men, under the command of the Maréchal de Broglie. . . . All my information goes to the point that he will never be able to bring his army to act against the people."[15] In the event, the Maréchal was, crucially, unable to make the soldiers shoot on the crowds.

Thomas Jefferson, as ambassador to France from 1784 to September 1789, wrote many letters about pre-revolutionary and constitutional events that testify to his exceptional acuity. Here I shall only quote from his character assassination of Jacques Necker, the king's first minister at the end of the period I consider: "Eloquence in a high degree, knowledge on matters of account, and order, are distinguishing traits in his character. Ambition is his first passion, Virtue his second. He has not discovered that sublime truth that a bold, unequivocal virtue is the best handmaid, even to Ambition, and would carry him further in the end than the temporizing wavering policy he pursues. His judgment is not of the first order, scarcely even of the second, his resolution frail, and upon the whole it is rare to meet an instance of a person so much below the reputation he has obtained."[16]

One might add, as a semi-foreign observer, Princess Elisabeth-Charlotte of Bavaria ("Madame Palatine") who married the brother of Louis XIV and spent fifty years in France writing some sixty thousand letters, mostly to her German relatives; 10 percent of them have survived. Her robust common sense enabled her to perceive, and her directness of language to express, without caring if her letters were opened, the many absurd and malign features of the royal court. Anyone who believes that Norbert Elias provides a credible interpretation of the Court of the Sun-King should read her.

For the reign of Louis XIII and that of Louis XIV under the regency, the *Historiettes* of Tallemande des Reaux provide what the title promises—chatty, anecdotal portraits of prominent and less prominent members of French society. His editor assures us that they are mostly

15. Morris (1939), p. 130; see also a letter from July 4 on p. 137.
16. Jefferson (1958), p. 190.

reliable,[17] but they show only intermittent psychological insight and tend towards the picturesque and the scatological. He is sometimes referred to as the poor man's Saint-Simon. Vastly more insightful, while entirely abstract (no proper names or dates), are the *Maxims* of La Rochefoucauld. When decoded, they reveal many of the psychological mechanisms that governed life at the Court. For instance, Maxim 225, "What makes false reckoning, as regards gratitude, is that the pride of the giver and that of the receiver cannot agree as to the value of the benefit," may reflect his disappointment at the way he felt that the Queen (Anne d'Autriche) had failed to reward his loyalty.[18] While his *Mémoires* are disappointing, those of his exact contemporary Cardinal de Retz are riveting, if unreliable.

For the personal reign of Louis XIV (1661–1715) and the subsequent regency, the *Mémoires* of Saint-Simon, running to some 7000 pages and 43 volumes in the best annotated edition, are an outstanding source. They are complemented by other of his writings, notably an anonymous letter to Louis XIV from 1712 about the state of the kingdom. Once the reader learns to ignore his near-pathological obsession with rank (*préséance*) and genealogies, the *Mémoires,* written in language of inimitable direct-ness and spark, offer invaluable analyses of the psychology of the king and the sociology of the court. Relying on hundreds and perhaps thousands of episodes, he shows how the courtiers, like planets, moved around the Sun-King in elliptical movements, sometimes close and sometimes fur-ther away. (To stretch the metaphor, the king's mistress or wife could be the other focus of the ellipse.) Saint-Simon knew some of the facts and events he reports from first-hand observations, others from his wife, who was lady in waiting to the king's niece, still others from his close friend-ships with members of the king's inner circle, and many from a small army of mostly female informants. In some of the episodes he recounts, notably from the Regency, he was also a central actor. He emphasized the need for the telling detail: "it is by the detailed narrative of these particulars at the court that one can understand it, and above all the king, so closed in

17. Antoine Adam, in Réaux (1960), vol. 1, p. xxii.

18. Swann (2017), p. 112 captures the ambiguity of the situation: "Service whether mili-tary or at court, or in the royal administration was *not only a duty, but also a gift* that the monarch was expected to recognize and repay" (my italics). See Bertière (1990), pp. 211–212 and Jouanna (1989), p. 102, on the numerous sources of misunderstanding and discontent in relations of clientelism at the Court. Bertière (1990), p. 340, cites another maxim by La Rochefoucauld that may reflect affairs at the Court.

upon himself and so difficult to penetrate . . . . All these things must be felt palpably, by narratives rather than by any other words."[19]

Two other great observers of the Court of Louis XIV were Madame de Sévigné, who left about a thousand letters, mostly to her daughter, and La Bruyère (both died in 1696). While her letters combine a smothering mother's love with penetrating, witty, and sometimes racy comments on current events, he wrote as a moralist. The maxims of his *Characters* are for the most part not at the same abstract level as those of La Roche-foucauld, but take the form of stylized portraits, in which courtiers could easily recognize some among themselves, and of pithy comments on their psychology. Two examples: "The Court does not satisfy a man, but it prevents him from being satisfied with anything else."[20] "No courtier cares to take the initiative in anything, but he will offer to second him who does, because, judging of others by himself, he thinks that no one will make a beginning, and that therefore he shall not be obliged to second any one."[21]

Maréchal de Vauban was the foremost military engineer of the reign of Louis XIV. In the course of his many fortifications and sieges, he travelled to all parts of France and had the opportunity to observe the life of ordinary people.[22] He may have known the state of the country better than anyone at his time, and had no axe to grind. His grasp of detail is documented in his fine-grained "Description géographique de l'élection de Vézelay" and in his *Projet de dîme royale* (1707), which also provides much information about other parts of France. In *Le détail de la France* (1707), his contemporary Pierre de Boisguilbert, discussed both "the cause of the reduction of goods" and "the facility of remedies." They cite many of the same causes of the misery of the people, notably the disincentives to production and trade created by the arbitrary and unpredictable tax system.

For the Regency, the personal reign of Louis XV, and the reign of Louis XVI, we can rely on several journals. That of the lawyer Marais, who was close to the proto-Enlightenment philosopher Pierre Bayle, covers the period from 1715 to 1727. Another lawyer, Barbier, covers the period from 1718 to 1762. He was knowledgeable about the world of the judiciary, but also offers observations on foreign policy and on Parisian *faits divers* that

19. Saint-Simon, vol. 11, p. 369; see also vol. 28, p. 280. However, some of his character portraits consist of a cascade of adjectives and are hard to get into focus.

20. La Bruyère (1881), 8.7. McManners (1998), p. 44, suggests that Saint-Simon embodied this maxim. In the same spirit, Madame Palatine (1989), p. 233, wrote that "it would be sad if [the visits by the king and the court] did not take place, because that would show contempt, but they do not give much joy when they do take place."

21. La Bruyère (1881), 8.29.

22. Blanchard (1996), pp. 454–455, 519–523.

came to his attention. That of the bookseller Hardy covers the period from 1753 to 1789. The parts I have read[23] also discuss *faits divers* at great length, as well as the constant triangular struggles among the government, the Church, and the *parlements*.

Marais, Barbier, and Hardy were observers, but many actors also kept journals. The best-known is that of the Marquis d'Argenson, who was for two years minister of foreign affairs under Louis XV and held several other positions. He was extremely well-informed about the inner political circle (his brother was also a minister), but his interpretations were often shaped by prejudices and wishful thinking.[24] Although I have often cited him, his judgments cannot always be trusted. A more analytical and reliable document is the journal of the Abbé de Véri, which covers the years from 1756 to 1781. Although he never held political office, he was an *éminence grise* in the ministry of Maurepas (1774–1781), and was able to persuade him to persuade Louis XVI to bring Véri's close friend Turgot into the ministry. Together with Turgot and their common friend Malesherbes, also briefly a minister after having been a courageous magistrate, Véri stood for a disinterested concern for the common good and social justice equaled, among the writers I cite, only by Vauban, Boisguilbert, and Fénelon. The three friends differed radically from their contemporaries in politics by their lack of concern for their reputation, at a time when reputation mattered more than achievements. They were positively unwilling to draw attention to themselves.[25]

23. Although the manuscript in Hardy's handwriting can be consulted at the Bibliothèque Nationale, I have not done so. I cite from the six published volumes, covering the years from 1753 through 1781, of an edition that will ultimately include the whole manuscript.

24. Swann (2017), p. 210, observes that Argenson was "[n]ever one to miss an opportunity for gloomy foreboding." At the same time, his incessant reports about the imminent recall of the exiled minister Chauvelin and the imminent fall of the principal minister Fleury, of the finance minister Orry, and of Madame de Pompadour show his vulnerability to wishful thinking. See also Ogle (1893) for a character portrait of Argenson.

25. On Turgot, see Meilhan (1795), pp. 147–148; and Véri (1928), pp. 321, 373, as well as a line, "the most sublime virtue has no vanity," in a poem to his praise cited in Hardy, vol. 4, p. 610. He quit his promising theological studies because he did not want to "devote all [his] life to wearing a mask on [his] face" (Nemours 1844, p. xiv). On Malesherbes, see Grosclaude (1961), p. 11. On Véri, see Mornet (2010), pp. 401–404, and the editorial Introduction to Véri (1928), p. 37. For a contrast, see Argenson, vol.1, p. 130, who affirms that his "voluntary disinterestedness can lead [him] farther than if it had been artificial and contrived." See also similar comments on the benefits of appearing to be disinterested in Bernis (1980), p.496. The debunking comments by Bourdieu (1994), p. 161, on disinterested behavior may seem appropriate in these two cases, but not for Malesherbes, Turgot, and Véri; see also Elster (2009b), pp. 43–46.

REFERENCES

(Starred works are freely available online.)

Ado, A. (1996), *Paysans en révolution*, Paris: Société des études robespierristes.

Alem, A. (2015), *Le Marquis d'Argenson*, Paris: Institiut Coppet.

Allen, E. (1982), *The Genesis of Revolution in the Gard*, Unpublished Ph. Dissertation, Tuale University.*

Anderson, J. (2001), *Crucible of War*, New York: Random House.

Antoine, M. (1970), *Le conseil du Roi sous le règne de Louis XV*, Paris: Droz.

Antoine, M. (1989), *Louis XV*, Paris: Hachette.

AP = Archives Parlementaires, Serie I: 1787–1799, Paris 1875–1888.*

Apostolidès, J.-M. (1981), *Le roi-machine*, Paris: Editions de Minuit.

Ardascheff, P. (1909), *Les intendants de province sous Louis XVI*, Paris: Felix Alcan.*

Argenson, Marquis de (1859–1867), *Journal et Mémoires*, Paris: Renouard.*

Arrow, K. (1982), Review of A. Sen, *Poverty and Famines*, *The New York Review of Books*, 29, pp. 24–26.

Aubertin, C. (1880), "L'éloquence politique dans le parlement de Paris: Les orateurs de la Fronde," *Revue des Deux Mondes* 39, 194–216.*

Augeard, J.-M. (1781), *Suite des observations du citoyen*, Utrecht.*

Augeard, J.-M. (1866), *Mémoires secrets*, Paris: Plon.*

Babelon, J.-P. (1982), *Henri IV*, Paris: Fayard.

Badeau, A. (1878), *Le village sous l'ancien régime*, Paris: Didier.*

Badinter, E. (2008), "Introduction" to Malesherbes (2008).

Balzac, G. de (1665), *Aristippe*, in *Œuvres*, volume 2, Paris.*

Barbiche, B. (2012), *Les institutions de la monarchie française à l'époque moderne*, Paris: Presses Universitaires de France.

Barbier, E.-J.-F. (1858), *Journal de la Régence et du règne de Louis XV*, Paris: Charpentier.*

Bastid, P. (1970), *Sieyès et sa pensée*, Paris: Hachette.

Beik, W. (1997), *Urban Protest in Seventeenth-Century France*, Cambridge University Press.

Bell, D. (1990), "Des stratégies d'opposition à Louis XV: L'affaire des avocats," *Histoire, économie et société* 19, 567–90.

Bély, L. (2015), *Les secrets de Louis XIV*, Paris: Tallandier.

Bentham, J. (1999), *Political Tactics*, Oxford University Press.

Bercé, Y.-M. (1974), *Histoire des Croquants*, Paris: Droz.

Bernis, Cardinal de (1980), *Mémoires*, Paris: Mercure de France.

Bertière, S. (1990), *La vie du Cardinal de Retz*, Paris: Editions Fallois.

Bertière, S. (2002), *Marie-Antoinette l'insoumise*, Paris: Editions Fallois.

Bertière, S. (2013), *Le procès Fouquet*, Paris: Editions Fallois.

Blanchard, A. (1996), *Vauban*, Paris: Fayard.

Blaufarb, R. (2010), *Une lutte de deux siècles et demi contre l'exemption fiscale, 1530–1789*, Aix: Presses Universitaires d'Aix-Marseille

Bloch, M. (1930), "La lutte pour l'individualisme agraire dans la France du XVIIIe siècle. Deuxième Partie," *Annales d'Histoire Economique et Sociale* 2, 511–556.*

Bloch, M. (1983), *Les rois thaumaturges*, Paris: Gallimard.

Bloch, M. (1964), *The Historian's Craft*, New York: Vintage Books.

Bloch, M. (1999), *Les caractères originaux de l'histoire rurale française*, Paris: Armand Colin.

Bluche, F. (1986a), *Louis XIV*, Paris: Hachette.

Bluche, F. (1986b), *Les magistrats du Parlement de Paris au XVIII siècle*, Paris: Economica.

Bodin, J. (1788), "Journal de Bodin," in C. J. Mayer (ed.), *Des états generaux et autres assembles nationales*, vol. 13, Paris.*

Boigne, Comtesse de (1999), *Mémoires*, Paris: Mercure de France.*

Bois, P. (1960), *Paysans de l'Ouest*, Paris: Editions de l'Ecole des Hautes Etudes en Sciences Sociales.

Boisguilbert, P. de (1707), *Le détail de la France*, Paris.*

Boislisle, A. de (1890), "Le secret de la poste sous le règne de Louis XIV," *Annuaire-Bulletin de l'Histoire de France* 27, pp. 229–245.*

Bossuet, J.-B. (1836), *Œuvres Complètes*, vol. 4, Paris.

Bourdieu, P. (1994), "Un acte désintéressé est-il possible?," in *Raisons pratiques*, Paris: Seuil, pp. 149–167.

Boureau, A. (1995), *Le droit de cuissage*, Paris: Albin Michel.

Bourke, R. (2015), *Empire and Revolution: The Political Life of Edmund Burke*, Princeton: Princeton University Press.

Bouton, C. (1993), *The Flour War*, University Park: University of Pennsylvania Press.

Brancourt, I., ed. (2013), *Le Régent, la Robe et le commis-greffier. Introduction à l'édition intégrale du Journal du parlement de Pontoise, en 1720*, Saint-Agnan-sur-Sarthe: AAGA.

Brattan, P. (2005), "When Is Coercion Successful?" *Naval War College Review* 58, 99–120.

Bretonne, R. de la (1989), *Monsieur Nicolas*, Paris: Gallimard (Bibliothèque de la Pléiade).

Brette, A. (1894), *Recueil de documents relatifs à la convocation des Etats Généraux de 1789*, vol. 1, Paris: Imprimerie Nationale.

Brioist, P., Drévillon, H., and Serna, P. (2008), *Croiser le fer*, Paris: Champ Vallon.

Busquet, J. (1920), *Le droit de vendetta et le paci corse*, Paris: Pedone.

Buvat, J. (1865), *Journal de la Régence*, Paris: Plon.*

Carew, G. (1749), "A Relation of the State of France under King Henry IV," in T. Birch (ed.), *An Historical View of the Negotiations between the Courts of England, France, and Brussels*, London, pp. 414–528.*

Carroll, S. (2006), *Blood and Violence in Early Modern France*, Oxford University Press.

Cayet, P. (1836), *Chronologie novenaire*, Paris: A. Desrez. *

Cénat, J. P. (2015), *Louvois*, Paris: Tallandier

Chagniot, J. (1988), *Paris au XVIIIe siècle*, Paris: Hachette.

Charges du procès Lescalopier (1765).*

Chaussinand-Nogaret, G. (1985), *The French Nobility in the Eighteenth Century*, Cambridge University Press.

Chaussinand-Nogaret, G. (2002), *Le Cardinal de Fleury*, Paris: Payot.

Chéruel, A. (1879), *Histoire de France pendant la minorité de Louis XIV*, Paris: Hachette.*

Choiseul, Duc de (1904), *Mémoires*, Paris: Plon.*

Chwe, M. (2009), "Rational Choice and the Humanities: Excerpts and Folktales," *Occasions: Interdisciplinary Studies in the Humanities* 1.*

Claeys, T. (2011), *Les institutions financières de l'ancien régime*, vol. 1, Paris: Editions SPM.

Colbert, J.-B. (1673), "Mémoire sur les affaires de France," in D. Dessert, *Colbert ou le serpent venimeux*, Paris: Editions Complexe 2000, pp. 99–164.

Constant, J.-M. (2016), *C'était la Fronde*, Paris: Flammarion.

Coquille, G. (1789), "Comment on doit considérer les Etats, et quelle est la nature de leur pouvoir," in C. Mayer (ed.), *Des états generaux et autres assembles nationales*, vol.. 7, Paris.*

Cosandey, F. (2016), *Le rang: Préséances et hiérarchies dans la France d'Ancien Régime*, Paris: Gallimard.

Croÿ, Duc de (1906–7), *Journal inédit*, Paris: Flammarion.*

Crubaugh, A. (2001), *Balancing the Scales of Justice*, University Park: Pennsylvania State University Press.

Cubells, M. (1987), *Les horizons de la liberté*, Aix-en Provence: Edisud.

Dainville, F. (1952), "Un dénombrement inédit au XVIIe siècle," *Population* 7, 49–68.

Daubresse, S., Morgat-Bonnet, M., and Storez-Brancourt, I. (2007), *Le parlement en exil*, Paris: Honoré Champion.

Davies, J. (1962), "Towards a theory of revolution," *American Sociological Review* 27, 5–19.

Deffand, Madame du (1866), *Correspondance compléte*, vol. 1, Paris: Levy.*

Dessert, D. (1984), *Argent, pouvoir et société au grand siècle*, Paris: Fayard.

Devyer, A. (1970), *Le sang épuré*, Brussels: Editions de L'Université de Bruxelles.

Doyle, W. (1974), *The Parlement of Bordeaux and the End of the Old Regime 1771–1790*, London: Benn.

Doyle, W. (1996), *Venality*, Oxford University Press.

Dravasa, E. (1965), *"Vivre noblemen": Recherches sur la dérogeance de la noblesse du XIVe au XVIe siècles*, Bordeaux: Chez l'Auteur.

Droz, J. (1860) *Histoire du règne de Louis XIV pendant les années où l'on pouvait prévenir ou diriger la Révolution française*, Paris: Renouard.

Dubief, H. (1987), Review of Bluche (1986a), *Bulletin de la Société de l'Histoire du Protestantisme Français* 133, 315–320.

Dupin, C. (1745/1913), *Oeconomiques*, Paris: Marcel Rivière.*

Dupont-Ferrier, G. (1930), *Essai sur la géographie administrative des élections financières*, Paris: Daupeley-Gouverneur.

Duchêne, J. (1985), *Françoise de Grignan*, Paris: Fayard.

Durand, S., Jouanna, A., and Pélaquier, E. (eds.) (2014), *Des Etats dans l'Etat*, Geneva: Droz.

Durieux, A. (2010), *La dispersion du Parlement de Paris 1753–1754* (unpublished, accessible at www.scribd.com/doc/ 31247434/Alain-Durieux).

Egret, J. (1962), *La pré-révolution française*, Paris: Presses Universitaires de France.

Egret, J. (1970), *Louis XV et l'opposition parlementaire*, Paris: Armand Colin.

Egret, J. (1975), *Necker, Ministre de Louis XVI*, Paris: Champion.

El Hage, F. (2016), "'Cela peut se dire au coin du feu, mais ne s'écrit pas': The Criticism of Generals in Eighteenth-Century France," *French History* 30, 31–50.

Elster, J. (1985), *Making Sense of Marx*, Cambridge University Press.

Elster, J. (1989), *The Cement of Society*, Cambridge University Press.

Elster, J. (1999), *Alchemies of the Mind*, Cambridge University Press

Elster, J. (2004), "Mimicking Impartiality" in K. Dowding, R. Goodin, and C. Pateman (eds.), *Justice and Democracy*, Cambridge University Press, pp. 112–126.

Elster, J. (2006), "Tocqueville on Revolution," in C. Welch (ed.), *The Cambridge Companion to Tocqueville*, Cambridge University Press, pp. 49–80.

Elster, J. (2007), "The Night of August 4 1789: A Study in Social Interaction," *Revue Européenne des Sciences Sociales* 45, 71–94.

Elster, J. (2009a), *Alexis de Tocqueville: The First Social Scientist*, Cambridge University Press.

Elster, J. (2009b), *Le désintéressement*, Paris: Seuil.

Elster, J. (2011), "The Indeterminacy of Emotional Mechanisms," in P. Demeulenaere (ed.), *Analytical Sociology and Social Mechanisms*, Cambridge University Press, pp. 50–63.

Elster, J. (2013), *Securities Against Misrule*, Cambridge: Cambridge University Press.

Elster, J. (2014), "Nested Majorities," in S. Novak and J. Elster (eds.), *Majority Decisions*, Cambridge University Press, pp. 34–55.

Elster, J. (2015a), *Explaining Social Behavior*, rev. ed., Cambridge University Press.

Elster, J. (2015b), "Introduction" to J. Elster (ed.) *Secrecy and Publicity in Votes and Debates*, Cambridge University Press, pp. 1–14.

Elster, J. (2016), "Tool-Box or Toy-Box? Hard Obscurantism in Economic Modeling," *Synthese* 193, 2159–2184.

Elster, J. (2017), "On Seeing and Being Seen," *Social Choice and Welfare*, 49, 721–734.

Elster, J. (2018), "Collective Action in America before 1789," in T. Christiano, I. Creppel, and J. Knight (eds.), *Morality. Governance, and Social Institutions*, New York: Springer, pp. 157–195.

Elster, J. (forthcoming), "Enthusiasm and Anger in History," *Inquiry*.

Esmonin, E. (1913), *La taille en Normandie au temps de Colbert (1661–1683)*, Paris: Hachette.*

Faure, E. (1961), *La disgrâce de Turgot*, Paris: Gallimard.

Fehr, E., and Gächter, S. (2002), "Altruistic Punishment in Humans," *Nature* 415, 137–140.

Fehr, E., and Fischbacher, U. (2004), "Third-Party Punishment and Social Norms," *Evolution and Human Behavior* 25, 63–87.

Félix, J. (1999), *Finances et politique au siècle des Lumières: Le ministère L'Averdy 1763–68*, Paris: Comité pour l'histoire économique et financière de la France.

Fénelon, F. (1983), *Oeuvres*, vol. 1, Paris: Gallimard (Editions de la Pléiade).

Fénelon, F. (1997), *Oeuvres*, vol. 2, Paris: Gallimard (Editions de la Pléiade).

Festinger, L. (1957), *A Theory of Cognitive Dissonance*, Palo Alto, CA: Stanford University Press.

Fischer, D. H. (1989), *Albion's Seed*, Oxford University Press.

Fisher, R. N. E. (1992), *Hybris*, Warminster, UK: Aris and Phillips.

Flammermont, J. (1888–1898), *Remontrances du Parlement de Paris au XVIIIe siècle*, Paris: Hachette.*

Follain, A. (2002), "Justice seigneuriale, justice royale et régulation sociale du XVe au XVIIIe siècles," in F. Brizay, A. Follain, and V. Sarrazin (eds.), *Les justices de village*, Rennes: Presses Universitaires de Rennes, pp. 9–58.

Follain, A. (2008), *Le village sous l'Ancien Régime*, Paris: Fayard.

Fontana, A., Furlan, F., and Saro, G. (1997). *Venise et la révolution française*, Paris: Robert Laffont.

Garrioch, D. (2002), *The Making of Revolutionary Paris*, Berkeley: University of California Press.

Gebelin, J. (1882), *Histoire des milices provinciales, 1688–1791: Le tirage au sort sous l'ancien régime*, Paris: Hachette.*

Gibbon, E. (1996), *History and Fall of the Roman Empire*, vol. 2, London: Penguin.

Giffard, A. (1903), *Les justices seigneuriales en Bretagne aux XVIIe et XVIIIe siècles*, Paris: Arthur Rousseau.*

Gomel, C. (1892), *Les causes financières de la Révolution Française*, Paris: Guillaumin.*

Goubert, P. (2010), *Louis XIV et vingt millions de Français*, Paris: Fayard.

Goubert, P. (2013). *Beauvais et le Beauvaisis de 1600 à 1730*, Paris: Publications de la Sorbonne.

Granovetter, M. (1978), "Threshold Models of Collective Behavior," *American Journal of Sociology* 83, 1420–1443.

Grenier, J. -Y. (2012–2013), "Temps de travail et fêtes religieuses au XVIIIe siècle," *Revue Historique* No. 663, 609–641.

Griffiths, G. (1968), *Representative Government in Western Europe in the Sixteenth Century*, Oxford University Press.

Grosclaude, P. (1961), *Malesherbes témoin et interprète de son temps*, Paris: Librairie Fischbacher.

Gruder, V. (1968), *The Royal Provincial Intendants*, Ithaca NY: Cornell University Press.

Guibert, Comte de (1772), *Essai général de tactique*, London.*

Harding, R. (1978), *The Anatomy of a Power Elite: The Provincial Governors of Early Modern France*, New Haven CT: Yale University Press.

Hardy, S-P. (2009), *Mes loisirs, ou journal d'événements tels qu'ils parviennent à ma connaissance*. Vol. 2, Québec: Presses de l'Université Laval.

Hardy, S-P. (2012), *Mes loisirs, ou journal d'événements tels qu'ils parviennent à ma connaissance*. Vol. 1, Paris: Hermann.

Hardy, S-P. (2012), *Mes loisirs, ou journal d'événements tels qu'ils parviennent à ma connaissance*. Vol. 3, Paris: Hermann.

Hardy, S-P. (2013), *Mes loisirs, ou journal d'événements tels qu'ils parviennent à ma connaissance*. Vol. 4, Paris: Hermann.

Hardy, S-P. (2014), *Mes loisirs, ou journal d'événements tels qu'ils parviennent à ma connaissance*. Vol. 5, Paris: Hermann.

Harris, R. (1970), "French Finances and the American War, 1777–1783," *Journal of Modern History* 48, 233–258.

Hayden, J. (1974), *France and the Estates General of* 1614, Cambridge University Press.

Hayhoe, J. (2008), *Enlightened Feudalism: Seigneurial Justice and Village Society in Eighteenth-Century Northern Burgundy*, Rochester, NY: University of Rochester Press.

Heckscher, E. (1934), *Mercantilism*, London: Allen and Unwin.

Heers, J. (2010), "Le trafic des épices et autres légendes historiques," *La Nouvelle Revue d'Histoire* 46, 18–19.

Henry, P. (2001), "Montaigne," in E. Jones (ed.), *Censorship: A World Enyclopedia*, London: Fitzroy Dearborn, vol. 3, pp. 1620–1621.

Holmes, S. (1988), "Precommitment and the Paradox of Democracy," In J. Elster and R. Slagstad (eds.), *Constitutionalism and Democracy*, Cambridge University Press, pp. 195–240.

Hume. D. (1978), *A Treatise of Human Nature*, ed. Selby-Bigge, Oxford University Press.

Hume, D. (1983), *The History of England*, Indianapolis IN: Liberty Fund Press.*

Hume, D. (1985), "On Public Credit," in *Essays Moral, Political, and Literary*, Indianapolis IN: Liberty Fund Press.*

Jardin, A. (1988), *Tocqueville: A Biography*, New York: Farrar, Strauss, and Giroux.

Jaurès, J. (1968), *Histoire socialiste de la Révolution Française*, vol. 1, Paris: Editions Sociales.

Jefferson T. (1958), *Papers*. Vol. 15. Princeton: Princeton University Press.

Jones, E. (2001), "Ancien Régime: 1500–1789," in E. Jones (ed.), *Censorship: A World Encyclopedia*, London: Fitzroy Dearborn, vol. 2, pp. 846–848.

Jouanna, A. (1977), *Ordre social: Mythes et hiérarchies dans la France du XVI siècle*, Paris: Hachette.

Jouanna, A. (1989), *Le devoir de révolte: La noblesse française et la gestation de l'Etat moderne*, Paris: Fayard.

Jouanna, A. (1998), "Le temps des guerres de religion en France," in A. Jouanna et al. (eds.), *Histoire et Dictionnaire des Guerres de Religion*, Paris: Laffont, pp. 3–445.

Jouanna, A. (2014a), "Le déroulement de session," in S. Durand, A. Jouanna, and E. Pélaquier (eds.), *Des Etats dans l'Etat*, Geneva: Droz, pp. 67–93.

Jouanna, A. (2014b), "Les relations directes avec la Cour," in S. Durand, A. Jouanna, and E. Pélaquier (eds.), *Des Etats dans l'Etat*, Geneva: Droz, pp. 293–316.

Jouanna, A. (2014c), "Les contacts et les liens idéologiques avec les autres Etats provinciaux," in S. Durand, A. Jouanna, and E. Pélaquier (eds.), *Des Etats dans l'Etat*, Geneva: Droz, pp. 345–363.

Jouanna, A. (2014d), "Les dernières décennies de l'ancien régime: La périlleuse alliance avec la monarchie contre le parlement 1759–1789," in S. Durand, A. Jouanna, and E. Pélaquier (eds.), *Des Etats dans l'Etat*, pp. 581–604.

Julia, D. (1956), "Le clergé paroissial dans le diocèse de Reims à la fin du XVIIIᵉ siècle," *Revue d'Histoire Moderne et Contemporaine* 13, 195–216.

Kaplan, S. (1982), "The Famine Plot Persuasion in Eighteenth-Century France." *Transactions of the American Philosophical Society* New Series 72, 1–79.

Kaplan. S. (2015), *Bread, Politics, and Political Economy in the Reign of Louis XV*, London: Anthem Press.

Kemp, S. (2007), "Psychology and the opposition to free trade," *World Trade Review* 6, 25–44.

Kiener, M., and Peyronnet, J.-C. (1979), *Quand Turgot régnait en Limousin*, Paris: Fayard.

Knapp, R. (1944), "A Psychology of Rumor," *Public Opinion Quarterly* 8, 22–37.

Komlos, J. (2003), "An Anthropometric History of Early Modern France," *European Review of Economic History* 7, 159–189.

Konopczynski, L. (1930), *Le liberum veto, étude sur le développement du principe majoritaire*, Paris: Champion.

Kwass, M. (2000), *Privilege and the Politics of Taxation in Eighteenth-Century France*, Cambridge University Press.

La Bruyère, J. de (1881), *The Characters*, London: John C. Nimmo.*

La Roque, G. de (1678), *Traité de la Noblesse*, Paris.*

Lavergne, L. (1879), *Les assemblées provinciales en France sous Louis XVI*, Paris: Calmann Lévy.*

Lavisse, E. (1989), *Louis XIV*, Paris: Robert Laffont.*

Lebow, R. (1996), "Thomas Schelling and Strategic Bargaining," *International Journal* 51, 551–576.

Lecestre, L. (1925), "Le procès du duc de la Force en 1721," *Revue des Questions Historiques* 53, 322–60.*

Lecuyer, B.-P. (1981), "Une quasi-expérimentation sur les rumeurs au XVIIIe siècle," in R. Boudon, F. Bourricaud, and A. Girard (eds.), *Science et théorie de l'opinion*, Paris: Retz, pp. 170–187.

Le Duc, C. (1881), "La fortune du clergé sous l'ancien régime," *Journal des Economistes* 15, 217–40.*

Lefebvre, G. (1924), *Les paysans du Nord pendant la Révolution Française*, Paris: Armand Colin.

Lefebvre, G. (1963), *Etudes sur la Révolution Française*, Paris: Presses Universitaires de France.

Lefebvre, G. (1988), *La grande peur de 1789*, Paris: Armand Colin. [There is an English translation, but it is unreliable.]

Legay, M.-C. (2001), *Les états provinciaux dans la construction de la France moderne*, Paris: Droz.

Lerner, J. and Keltner, D. (2001), "Fear, Anger, and Risk," *Journal of Personality and Social Psychology* 81, 146–159.

Le Roy Ladurie, E. (1966), *Les paysans de Languedoc*, Paris: S.E.V. P. E. N.

Levillain-Hubert, I. (2001), *Le colombier, monument d'élevage dans la Normandie de l'Ancien Régime*, Thèse Présentée et soutenue publiquement en 2001 devant l'Université Paul-Sabatier de Toulouse.*

Lhéritier, M. (1920), *Tourny: Intendant de Bordeaux*, Paris: Felix Alcan.*

Lipsey, R., and Lancaster, K. (1956), "The General Theory of Second-Best," *Review of Economic Studies* 24, 11–32.

Locke, J. (1953), *Travels in France 1675–1679*, Cambridge and New York: Cambridge University Press.

Locke. J. (1979), *An Essay Concerning Human Understanding*, Oxford: Oxford University Press.

Loewenstein, G. (1996), "Out of Control: Visceral Influences on Behavior," *Organizational Behavior and Human Decision Processes* 65, 272–292.

Loewenstein, G. (2000), "Emotions in Economic Theory and Economic Behavior," *American Economic Review: Papers and Proceedings* 90, 426–32.

Lüthy, H. (1998), *La banque protestante en France*, vol. 1, Paris: Editions de l'Ecole des Hautes Etudes.

Lüthy, H. (2005), *La banque protestante en France*, vol. II, Zürich: Verlag Neue Züricher Zeitung.

Luynes, Duc de (1860–1865), *Mémoires*, vols. 1–17, Paris: Firmin.*

MacCormack, J. and Lindquist, K. 2019), "Feeling Hangry? When Hunger Is Conceptualized as an Emotion," *Emotion* 19, 301–319.

Madison, J. (1983), *Papers*, vol. 14, Charlottesville: University of Virginia Press.

Major, J. (1960), *The Deputies to the Estates General in Renaissance France*, Madison: University of Wisconsin Press.

Malesherbes, G.-L. de (1809), *Mémoire sur la librairie*, Paris.*

Malesherbes, G.-L. de (1964), *Malesherbes et son temps: Nouveaux documents inédits*, Paris: Fischbacher.

Malesherbes, G.-L. de (2008), *Les "remontrances" de Malesherbes*, E. Badinter (ed.), Paris: Tallandier.

Malouet, P.-V. (1874), *Mémoires*, Paris: Plon.*

Marais, M. (1859–1867), *Journal et Mémoires*, Paris: Firmin Didot.*

Marie-Thérèse et Mercy-d'Argenteau, Comte de (1974), *Correspondance secrète*, Paris: Firmin Didot.*

Marion, M. (1891), *Machault d'Arnouville*, Paris: Hachette.*

Marion, M. (1898), *La Bretagne et le duc d'Aiguillon*, Paris: Fontémoing.*

Marion, M. (1901), *L'impôt sur le revenu au dix-huitième siècle*, Toulouse: Privat.*

Marion, M. (1910), *Les impôts directs sous l'ancien régime*, Paris: Cornely.*

Marion, M. (1923), *Dictionnaire des institutions de la France aux XVIIe et XVIIIe siècles*, Paris: Picard.*

Marion, M. (1927), *Histoire financière de la France depuis 1715*, vol.1, Paris: Rousseau.

Markoff, J. (1996), *Revolutionary Demands*, University Park: Pennsylvania State University Press.

Mason, G. (1970), *Papers*, vol. 1, Chapel Hill: University of North Carolina Press.

Marx, K. (1849), "Wage Labor and Capital," *Neue Rheinische Zeitung*, April 5–8 and 11.

Masselin, J. (1835), *Journal des Etats Généraux de Tours*, Paris: Imprimerie Royale.*

Maury, A. (1879), "Les assemblées du clergé sous l'ancien régime," *Revue des Deux Mondes* 31, 754–96.*

Maury, A. (1880), "Les assemblées du clergé sous l'ancien régime," *Revue des Deux Mondes* 40, 621–667.*

McManners, J. (1998), *Church and Society in Eighteenth-Century France*. Vols. 1 and 2. Oxford: Oxford University Press.

Meilhan, G. de (1795), *Du gouvernement, des moeurs, et des conditions en France avant la Révolution*, Hamburg*

Mercier, L.-S. (1879), *Tableau de Paris*, vol. 12, Amsterdam.*

Mercy-Argenteau, Comte de (1874), *Correspondance Secrète*, Paris: Firmin Didot.*

Meuvret, J. (1988), *Le problème de subsistance à l'époque Louis XIV: Le commerce des grains et la conjoncture* (texte), Paris: Editions de l'Ecole des Hautes Etudes en Sciences Sociales.

Meyer, J. (1981), *Colbert*, Paris: Hachette.

Milanovic, M., Lindert, P., and Williamson, J. (2011), "Pre-Industrial Inequality," *Economic Journal* 121, 255–72.

Mill, J. S. (1846), *A System of Logic*, New York: Harper.*

Mill, J. S. (2007), *On Liberty and the Subjection of Women*, London: Penguin.

Montaigne, M. de (1991), *The Complete Essays*, Harmondsworth: Penguin.

Montesquieu, Baron de (1748), *L'esprit des lois*.

Montmort, R. de (1713), *Essay d'analyse sur les jeux de hazard*, 2nd ed., Montpellier.*

Montyon, J. (1812), *Particularités et observations sur les ministres des finances de la France*, Paris*

Moote, A. (1972), *The Revolt of the Judges*, Princeton: Princeton University Press.

Morgan, E. (1975) *American Slavery, American Freedom*, New York: Norton.

Mornet, D. (2010), *Les origines intellectuelles de la Révolution Française*, Paris: Tallandier.

Morris, G. (1939), *A Diary of the French Revolution*, vol. 1, Boston: Houghton Mifflin.*

Mousnier. R. (2005), *Les institutions de la France sous la monarchie absolue*, Paris: Presses Universitaires de France.

Mullhainathan, S., and Shafir, E. (2014), *Scarcity*, London: Picador.

Musset, V.–D. (1828), *Nouveaux mémoires secrets pour servir à l'histoire de notre temps*, Paris.*

Narbonne, P. (1866), *Journal des règnes de Louis XIV et Louis XV*, Paris.*

Necker, J. (1773), *Eloge de Jean-Baptiste Colbert*, Paris.*

Necker, J. (1778), *Mémoire donné au Roi*, Paris.*

Necker, J. (1784–1785), *De l'administration des finances de la France*, Paris*

Necker, J. (1797), *De la Révolution françoise*, Paris.*

Nemours, P. du Pont de (1844), Editorial introduction to Turgot (1844), vol 1.*

Nicolas, J. (2008), *La rébellion française*, Paris: Gallimard.

Ogle, A. (1893), *The Marquis d'Argenson: A Study in Criticism*, London: T. Fisher Unwin.*

Olivier-Martin, F. (1997), *L'absolutisme français suivi de Les parlements contre l'absolutisme traditionnel au XVIIIe siècle*, Paris: L.G.D.J.

Olivier-Martin, F. (2010), *Histoire du droit français*, Paris: CNRS.

Olson, M. (1991), "Autocracy, Democracy, and Prosperity," in R. Zeckhauser (ed.), *Strategy and Choice*, Cambridge MA: MIT Press, pp. 131–157.

Ormesson, O. de (1860–1861), *Journal et mémoires*, Paris.*

Palatine, Madame (1857), *Correspondance Complète de Madame, Duchesse d'Orléans*, Paris.*

Palatine, Madame (1985), *Lettres de la Princesse Palatine 1672–1722*, Paris: Mercure de France.

Palatine, Madame (1989), *Lettres Françaises*, Paris: Fayard.

Pascal, B. (2011), *Pensées*, éd. Sellier, Paris: Garnier.

Peake, T. (2005), "Eavesdropping in Communication Networks," in P. McGregor (ed.), *Animal Communication Networks*, Cambridge University Press, pp. 13–37.

Pélaquier, E. (2014a), "L'assemblée des Etats," in S. Durand, A. Jouanna and E. Pélaquier (eds.), *Des Etats dans l'Etat: Les Etats de Languedoc de la Fronde à la Révolution*, Geneva: Droz, pp. 31–66.

Pélaquier, E. (2014b), "Les relations avec les cours souveraines," ibid., pp. 317–343.

Pélaquier, E. (2014c), "Le crédit des Etats," ibid., pp. 235–266.

Perez, S. (2004), "Les brouillons de l'absolutisme: Les 'Mémoires' de Louis XIV en question," *Dix-septième Siècle* No. 222, 225–250.

Pernot, M. (2012), *La Fronde: 1648-1653*, Paris: Tallandier.

Petitfils, J.-C. (2005a), *Louis XVI*, Paris: Perrin.

Petitfils, J.-C. (2005b), *Fouquet*, Paris: Perrin.

Petitfils, J.-C. (2008), *Louis XIII*, Paris: Perrin.

Petitfils, J.-C. (2013), *Le régent*, Paris: Fayard.

Petitfils, J.-C. (2014a), *Louis XIV*, Paris: Perrin.

Petitfils, J.-C. (2014b), *Louis XV*, Paris: Perrin.

Phillips, K. (1999), *The Cousins' War*, New York: Basic Books.

Picard, R. (1912), "Les mutations économiques et les doctrines économiques en France," *Revue d'histoire des doctrines économiques et sociales* 5, 343–367.*

Picot, G. (1888), *Histoire des Etats Généraux*, Paris.

Pillorget, R. (1975), *Les mouvements insurrectionnels de Provence entre 1596 et 1715*, Paris: Pedone.

Pillorget, R., and Pillorget, S. (1995), *France Baroque, France Classique 1589-1715*, vol. 1: *Récit*, Paris: Bouquins.

Plongeron, B. (1964), *La vie quotidienne du clergé français*, Paris: Hachette.

Ploux F. (2003), *De bouche à oreille*. Paris: Aubier.

Poirier, J.-P. (1999), *Turgot*, Paris: Perrin.

Potegal, M., Stemmler, G., and Spielberger, C. (eds.) (2010), *International Handbook of Anger*, New York: Springer.

Quétel, C. (2011), *Les lettres de cachet*, Paris: Perrin.

Ramsay, D. (1789), *The American Revolution*, cited after the reprint by Indianapolis, IN: Liberty Fund, 1990.*

Rapine, F. (1651), *Recueil très exact et curieux de tout ce qui s'est passé de singulier & memorable en l'Assemblée generale des Etats tenus à Paris en l'année 1614 & particulierement en chacune séance du tiers ordre*, Paris.*

Ravallion, M. (1987), *Markets and Famines*, Oxford University Press.

Réaux, T. de (1960), *Historiettes*, Paris: Gallimard (Editions de la Pléiade).

Rébillon, A. (1932), *Les Etats de Bretagne de 1661 à 1789*, Paris: Picard.

Reddy, W. (2001), *The Navigation of Feeling*, Cambridge University Press.

Reymond, Abbé (1776), *Droits des curés et des paroisses* (cited after the 1780 edition*).

Roche, D. (1981), *Le peuple de Paris*, Paris: Aubier-Montaigne.

Rocquain, F. (1878), *L'esprit révolutionnaire avant la Révolution 1715-1789*, Paris: Plon.*

Root, H. (1987), *Peasants and King in Burgundy*, Berkeley: University of California Press.*

Rousseau, J.-J. (1973), *Confessions*, Paris: Gallimard.

Rozental, A. (1956), "The Enclosure Movement in France," *American Journal of Economics and Sociology* 16, 55–71

Rudé, G. (1964), *The Crowd in History*, New York: Wiley.

Rule, J. (1989), *Theories of Civil Violence*, Berkeley: University of California Press.

Saint-Jacob, Pierre de (1960), *Les paysans de la Bourgogne du Nord au dernier siècle de l'Ancien Régime*, Paris: Les Belles Lettres.

Saint-Simon, Duc de (1879–1924), *Mémoires* (ed. Boislisle), Paris: Hachette.*

Saint-Simon, Duc de (1994), *Mémoires* (extraits) *et œuvres diverses*, Paris, Gallimard.

Saint-Simon, Duc de (1996), *Traités politiques et autres écrit*, Paris: Gallimard (Editions de la Pléaide).

Schelling, T. (1966), *Arms and Influence*, New Haven, CT: Yale University Press.

Ségur, Comte de (1859), *Mémoires*, Paris: Firmin-Didot.*

Sévigné, Madame de (1955–1957), *Lettres*, Paris: Gallimard (Editions de la Pléiade).

Shackle, G. L. S. (1967), *The Years of High Theory*, Paris: Cambridge University Press.

Shapiro, G., and Markoff, J. (1998), *Revolutionary Demands*, Palo Alto, CA: Stanford University Press 1998.

Shibutani, T. (1966), *Improvised News*, New York: Bobbs-Merrill.

Sieyès, Abbé de (1789), *Qu'est-ce que le Tiers Etat*, 3rd ed., cited after the translation in M. Sonenscher (ed.), *Sieyès: Political Writings*, Indianapolis: Hackett, 2003.

Simmel, G. (1908), *Soziologie*, Berlin: Duncker & Humblot.

Skinner, G. W. (1975), "Cities and the Hierarchy of Local Systems," in G. W. Skinner (ed.), *The City in Late Imperial China*, pp. 275–364, Stanford, CA: Stanford University Press.

Slater, M. (2018), *The National Debt*, London: Hurst.

Slaughter, W. (1988), *The Whiskey Rebellion*, Oxford: Oxford University Press.

Smith, A. (1976), *The Wealth of Nations*, Oxford: Oxford University Press.

Smith, J. (1997), "No More Language Games: Words, Beliefs, and the Political Culture of Early Modern France," *American Historical Review* 102, 1413–1440.

Soule, C. (1968), *Les Etats Généraux de France, 1302-1789*, Paris: UGA.

Spanheim, E. (1973), *Relation de la Cour de France*, Paris: Mercure de France.

Spiegelhalter, D. (2019), *The Art of Statistics*, London: Penguin Books.

Spykman, G. (1955), *Attrition and Contrition at the Council of Trent*, Kampen, Holland: J. H. Kok N.V.

Staël, Madame de (2000), *Considérations sur la Révolution Française*, Paris: Tallandier.

Stendhal (1952), *Le rouge et le noir*, in *Œuvres: Romans et Nouvelles* (édition Pléiade), vol. 1, Paris: Gallimard.

Stendhal (2006), *Vie de Napoléon*, Paris: Fayard.

Storez-Brancourt, I. (2007), "Vers la punition," in Daubresse, Morgat-Bonnet, and Storez-Brancourt (2007), pp. 537–731.

Swann, J. (1995), *Politics and the Parlement of Paris under Louis XV, 1754-1774*, Cambridge: Cambridge University Press.

Swann, J. (1997), "Le Parlement de Paris et la réforme financière au XVIIIe siècle, 1749-1789," *Extrait de l'administration des finances sous l'ancien régime*, Paris: Comité pour l'histoire économique et financière, pp. 325–46

Swann, J. (2003), *Provincial Power and Absolute Monarchy: The Estates General of Burgundy, 1661–1789*, Cambridge: Cambridge University Press.

Swann, J. (2010), "Coopération, opposition ou autonomie? Le parlement de Dijon, les états de Bourgogne et Louis XIV, 1689–1715," in G. Aubert and O. Chaline (eds.) *Les parlements de Louis XIV: opposition, coopération, autonomisation?* Rennes: Presses Universitaires de Rennes, pp. 117–132.

Swann, J. (2017), *Exile, Imprisonment, or Death*, Oxford: Oxford University Press.

Swanson, D., and Trout, A. (1992), "Alexander Hamilton's Hidden Sinking Fund," *William and Mary Quarterly* 49, 108–116.

Tackett, T. (1977), *Priest & Parish in Eighteenth-Century France*, Princeton: Princeton University Press.

Tanchoux, P. (2004), *Les procedures et pratiques electorales en France*, Paris: Comité des travaux historiques et scientifiques.

Taylor, G. (1972), "Revolutionary and Nonrevolutionary Content in the Cahiers of 1789," *French Historical Studies* 7, 479–502.

Tellier, L.-N. (1987), *Face aux Colbert*, Quebec: Presses de l'Université du Québec.

Testu, F. X. (2014), *Le dictionnaire des méchancetés*, Paris: Robert Laffont.

Thagard, P. and Nussbaum, D. (2014), "Fear-driven Inference," in L. Magnani (ed.), *Model-Based Reasoning in Science and Technology*, Berlin: Springer, pp. 43–53.

Thireau, J.-L. (1973), *Les idées politiques de Louis XIV*, Paris: Presses Universitaires de France.

Thomas, A. (1844), *Une province sous Louis XIV*, Paris.*

Thompson., E. P. (1971), "The Moral Economy of the English Crowd in the 18th Century," *Past and Present* 80, 76–136.

Tocqueville. A. de (1987), *Recollections*, New Brunswick, NJ: Transaction Books.

Tocqueville. A. de (1992), *De la démocratie en Amérique*, Paris: Gallimard (éd. de la Pléiade).

Tocqueville. A. de (1998), *Œuvres Complètes*, vol. 14: *Correspondance Familiale*, Paris: Gallimard.

Tocqueville, A. de (2001), *The Old Regime and the Revolution*, vol. 2, Chicago: University of Chicago Press.

Tocqueville, A. de (2003), *Lettres choisies*, Paris: Gallimard.

Tocqueville, A. de (2004a), *On Democracy in America*, New York: Library of America.

Tocqueville, A. de (2004b), *Oeuvres Complètes* (Pléiade), vol. III, Paris: Gallimard.

Tocqueville, A. de (2010), *De la démocratie en Amérique / Democracy in America* (bilingual ed.), Indianapolis: Liberty Fund Press, vols. 1–4.

Tocqueville, A. de (2011), *The Ancien Régime and the French Revolution*, Cambridge: Cambridge University Press

Touzery, M. (2007), Introduction to Vauban (2007).

Turgot, A.-R.-J. (1844), *Œuvres*, ed. Daire, Paris: Guillaumin.*

Ulph, O. (1947), "Jean Bodin and the Estates General of 1576," *Journal of Modern History* 19, 289–96

Vaillé, E. (1950), *Le Cabinet Noir*, Paris: Presses Universitaires de France.

Vaillot, R. (1974), *Madame de Tencin . . . et le Cardinal*, Paris: Roger Maria.

Valfons, Marquis de (1860). *Souvenirs*, Paris: Pillet fils ainé.*

Vauban, Maréchal de (1882), "De la conduite à tenir par les gouvernements envers les peuples nouvellements soumis à leur domination," *Journal des Economistes* (May), 334–337.*

Vauban, Maréchal de (2007), *Projet de dîme royale*, in M. Virol (ed.), *Les oisivetés de Monsieur Vauban*, Paris: Champ Vallon 2007.*

Veillé, E. (1950), *Le cabinet noir*, Paris: Presses Universitaires de France.

Velde, F., and Weir, D. (1992), "The Financial Market and Government Debt Policy in France, 1746–17983," *Journal of Economic History* 52 (1–39).

Vergne, A. (2006), *La notion de constitution d'après les cours et assemblées à la fin de l'ancien régime (1750–1789)*, Paris: De Boccard.

Véri, Abbé de (1928), *Journal*, vol. 1, Paris: Tallander.*

Véri, Abbé de (1930), *Journal*, vol. 2, Paris: Tallander.*

Vermeule, A. (2011), "Intermittent Institutions," *Politics, Philosophy, and Economics* 10, 420–444.

Vermeule, A. (2012), "Contra Nemo Iudex in Sua Causa," *Yale Law Journal* 122, 384–420.

Veyne, P. (1976), *Le pain et le cirque*, Paris: Seuil.

Veyne, P. (2005), *L'empire gréco-romain*, Paris: Seuil

Vovelle, M. (1987), "La représentation populaire de la monarchie," in K. Baker (ed.), *The Political Culture of the Old Regime*, Oxford: Pergamon Press, vol. 1, pp. 77–86.

Walcot, P. (1978), *Envy and the Greeks*, Warminster: Aris and Phillips

Walpole, H. (1913), *Letters on France*, London: Blackie and Son.

Walpole, H. (2000), *Memoirs of the Reign of King George III*, vol. 1, New Haven, CT: Yale University Press.

Walpole, H. (2017), *Selected Letters*, New York: Knopf.

Walter, G. (1963), *Histoire des paysans français*, Paris: Flammarion

Warvick, E. (1974), "The Character of Louis XIII: The Role of His Physician," *Journal of Interdisciplinary History* 4, 347–74.

White, E. (2001), "France and the Failure to Modernize Macroeconomic Institutions," in M. Bordo and R. Cortés-Conde (eds.), *Transferring Wealth and Power from the Old to the New World*, Cambridge: Cambridge University Press, pp. 59–99.

Wood, G. (2009), *Empire of Liberty*, Oxford: Oxford University Press.

Young, A. (1794), *Travels During the Years of 1787, 1788, and 1789 with a view of ascertaining the Cultivation, Wealth, Resources, and National Prosperity of the Kingdom of France*, London.*

Zeller, G. (1957), "Une notion de caractère historico-social: La dérogeance," *Cahiers Internationaux de Sociologie*, Nouvelle Série 22, 40–74.

Zinoviev, A. (1981), *The Radiant Future*, New York: Random House.

Adams, John, 136
Aiguillon, Emmanuel-Armand de
    Richelieu, Duc d', 58, 187
amour-propre, 18–19, 37, 43, 59n138,
    148–149, 193
anger,13–16, 26–27, 19–20, 22, 26–27,
    66n170, 67n172, 86–87, 93, 136–137,
    220–221, 232. *See also* indignation
Aristotle, 16, 18

Badinter, Elisabeth, 122
bankruptcy of the kingdom, 129, 140, 152,
    153n67, 170, 171, 230
Barbier, Edmond Jean François, 92–93,
    128–129, 185, 221, 243–244
bargaining, 29, 30, 184n220, 185, 198,
    205–206
Bercé, Yves-Marie, 23, 33, 65–67, 72, 73,
    118–119, 131–133, 135–136, 158, 209n87,
    226, 237–238
Bernis, Cardinal François-Joachim de
    Pierre de, 50, 55
Bertin, Henri Léonard Jean Baptiste, 27,
    37, 59n138, 126, 151, 187
bias, 12–13; agency, 67, 221–223
Bodin, Jean, 196
Bois, Paul, 83
Boisguilbert, Pierre de, 70, 77n220, 120,
    130, 243
Bretonne, Rétif de la. *See* Rétif,
    Nicolas-Edme
Bruyère, Jean de la. *See* La Bruyère,
    Jean de
Bussy-Rabutin, Roger de, Comte, 55

cadasters, 59n138, 60, 71, 74, 103, 129,
    172
Calonne, Charles-Alexandre de, 34, 36,
    169, 202n54
cabinet noir, 106–111
cens (seigneurial rent), 62n146, 82
censorship, 168–169
Chambres de Justice, 33, 162
choice, 8–20

Choiseul, Étienne François, Duc de,
    109–110, 155, 173n168, 180
class consciousness, 43, 58, 164n127.
    See also solidarity
clergy, 1n1, 95–102; assembly of, 27, 39,
    96–98, 199; *congruistes*, 99–101; divi-
    sion of, 98–99; nepotism in, 98n318;
    parish priests, 99–101; solidarity with
    the peasantry, 101
Colbert, Jean-Baptiste, 13, 33, 50, 70–71,
    77, 107, 114, 142, 150, 155
collective action, 20–24, 30, 83n251,
    163n127, 185n230, 194n28; Assurance
    Game, 45; Battle of the Sexes, 30;
    Prisoner's Dilemma, 45; snowball
    model of, 22–24
compellence, 116–117, 161, 167, 182
conspiracy theories, 134–135, 221–223;
    two-layered, 222
contempt, 16, 19, 52, 54–55, 231–232, 233
Continental Congress, 28
corvée (forced labor on the roads), 76,
    78–79, 88, 152, 221
Cosandey, Fanny, 45

debt, public, 106
debt, royal, 106
Descartes, René, 15, 326n153
divide and conquer, 166, 179, 185, 198,
    207n81, 209n89, 217, 221. See also
    tertius gaudens
Donne, John, 77
dragonnades, 162
Droz, Joseph, 54–55, 232–33
Dupont de Nemours, Pierre Samuel, 109,
    111

Edict of Nantes, 162; revocation of, 115,
    162, 223
Egret, Jean, 38, 182
émotion (riot) 67, 131, 218. *See also* Flour
    War; Great Fear
emotions, 13–16, 18–20, 86–87, 218; inde-
    terminacy of, 19–20; intensity of, 19;

emotions (*continued*)
  short half-life of, 18, 24, 168; triggered
    by beliefs, 15; triggering action tenden-
    cies, 18, 87. *See also* anger; contempt;
    enthusiasm; envy; fear; hatred; hope;
    hubris; indignation; shame; sympathy
Enlightenment, the, 9, 211
enthusiasm, 13, 17
envy, 6n14, 19–20, 231, 232
Esmonin, Edmond, 35, 59n138, 236–237
Estates-General, 188–200; demands by,
    192; elections to, 194–195; of 1302,
    189–190, 191; of 1355, 190; of 1484,
    192n14, 193, 195–196, 198; of 1560/61,
    28, 191n10, 198; of 1576, 190–191, 196,
    199; of 1614, 52, 191n10, 193; voting
    in, 195–198
Estates, provincial, 200–213; of Artois,
    199, 201, 205; of Brittany 27, 58, 65,
    201, 203n59; of Burgundy, 35n19, 45,
    58, 65, 125n107, 159, 202–203, 206;
    composition of, 201; of Languedoc,
    65, 201, 206; of Provence, 46, 58,
    200; relations among, 204–205;
    relations to the *parlements*, 207–211;
    relations to the royal government,
    200, 203–206; voting rules in, 201
évocation, 131n130, 209n87
exile, 30, 48, 162–168

Faure, Edgar, 79, 88, 108–109, 131, 133,
    135, 149
fear, 23, 26–27, 63, 68n176, 87, 116, 134,
    153, 169, 204–205; of hell, 145n27;
    prudential, 232; of ridicule 53;
    visceral 232
Fehr, Ernst, 15
Félix, Joël, 37, 155, 236
Fénelon, François de Salignac de la
    Mothe, 120–121
Festinger, Leon, 87
finance ministers, tenure of, 155
Fleury, Cardinal André-Hercule de, 55, 165
Fleury, Jean-François Joly de, 126
Flour War, 86, 93, 131, 133
forains (absentee owners), 73, 74, 85
Fouquet, Nicolas, 148
Fronde, 96n315, 126n108, 182, 208
fundamental laws of the kingdom, 139–145,
    181, 228

game theory, 11–12. *See also* bargaining
Goubert, Pierre, 43, 137, 160
Granovetter, Mark, 23–24
Great Fear, 26, 132n133, 134
grievance books, 1, 62, 64, 69n182, 111,
    213n98

half-measures, 169, 233
Hamilton, Alexander, 288
Hardy (bookseller), 9, 88, 93, 112, 127–128,
    135, 244
hatred, 16, 20, 116, 231–232
Heckscher, Eli, 113–114, 160
hope, 26–27, 119
hubris, 55
Hume, David, 17, 163n127, 221, 229n42
hunger, 13n24, 22, 66, 67n171, 93; trans-
    muted into anger, 16, 220–222

indignation, 15–16, 221. *See also* anger
injustice, peasant conceptions, of, 69–91,
    219–221; horizontal, 69–76, 219; ver-
    tical, 76–9, 219
inflation, 176–177
intendant (royal official in the provinces),
    35–37, 157–160
interest. *See* self-interest
irrationality, 12–13, 115, 176–177, 240n13.
    See also emotions.

Jansenism, 94, 115n64, 165
John Paul II, 182
Jouanna, Arlette, 50, 191

Kant, Immanuel, 17n31
Kaplan, Steven, 67n172, 115, 117n73
Kaunitz, Madame Maria Ernestine de, 109
Keynes, John Maynard, 114n58

La Bruyère, Jean de, 40, 54, 243
La Fontaine, Jean de, 13, 134
Lamoignon, Guillaume de, 59
La Rochefoucauld, François, Duc de, 18–19,
    242–243
L'Averdy, François de, 116, 151, 153n68, 187,
    209n85
Lavisse, Ernest, 67n176, 132–133, 147
Lefebvre, Georges, 191n11, 225–226
Legay, Marie-Laure, 205
Le Nain, Jean, 204–206

Lerner, Jennifer, 13n26
Locke, John, 29, 65n166, 73, 239
Loewenstein, George, 13, 95
Louis XIII, 145
Louis XIV, 49n91, 115–116, 118, 121n87, 144, 146–148, 164; obsession with glory of, 121, 146, 148, 175, 202, 218, 229
Louis XV, 27n61, 124–125; alleged hoarding by, 127–128; flagellation speech of, 125–126
Louis XVI, 108–109, 112, 122–123, 149, 164, 174n169
Louvois, François Michel le Tellier de, 116–117, 147
Lüthy, Herbert, 150, 153, 173–174

Machault, Jean-Baptiste de, 128, 142n12, 151, 154, 164–165, 172–173, 199–200
Madison, James, 8–9, 229
mainmorte, 35
Maintenon, Madame de (Françoise d'Aubigné), 121, 140
Malesherbes, Guillaume-Chrétien de Lamoignon de, 38, 122, 131, 141, 168, 169, 180, 227, 244
Marie-Antoinette, 54n104, 57, 94, 112, 142, 239n11
Marion, Marcel, 152–153, 159, 161, 171, 172–173, 201, 230n43, 131n130, 151
Markoff, John, 69n182, 133
Masselin, Jean, 195–196
Maupeou, René Nicolas, Comte de, 166
Maurepas, Jean-Frédéric Phélypeaux, Comte de, 122–123, 164
McManners, John, 74–75
mercantilism, 13, 113–114
methodological individualism, 8
militia, 60n142, 75–76, 93, 221
Mill, John Stuart, 13, 98n325
monitoire, 224–225
banalités (monopolies of the seigneur), 84
Montaigne, Michel de, 26, 51, 148, 228
Montespan, Madame de (Françoise-Athénaïs de Rochechouart), 110n36, 144
Montmort, Nicolas de, 11–12

Necker, Jacques, 1, 100, 110, 142, 158, 173–177, 229–230, 241; preferred loans over taxes, 176–177, 241; vanity of, 175

Nicolas, Jean, 66, 75, 82–84, 91, 224, 237–238
Noailles, Adrien Maurice de, Duc de, 70–72
nobility, 19, 47–60, 163n127, 191, 217, 233; ancestry cult of, 50–52; Court, 47–57; derogation from, 47n80, 52; elevation into, 47–48; exclusion from power of, 49n91; incompetence of, 49n90; legal, 159–160; provincial, 57–59

officials, venal, 155–157
Olivier-Martin, François, 158
Ormesson. Olivier de, 107
ostracism of norm-violators, 22, 23n47, 184, 226, 227

Palatine, Madame (Elisabeth Charlotte, Duchesse d'Orléans), 56–57, 110, 124, 142–143, 241
parlements (high courts), 8, 27–28, 30–31, 37–39, 44, 46, 52–53, 93–94, 112–113, 144, 166–168, 178–179; magistrates in, 59–60, 113n50, 152, 163n123, 166, 179–181, 182–184; Premier Président of, 16, 30, 178; relations to the royal government, 124–127, 143–144, 184–187, 222–223, 227–229; relations to the provincial Estates, 206–211; union of, 30, 44, 178, 204, 222–223
Pascal, Blaise, 143, 162
pays d'élection, 69n181, 71n188,
pays d'état, 71n188, 74, 181, 185
peasantry, 60–88; exploitation of, 63–69; feudal burdens of, 83–84; living standard of, 60–64; taxation of, 69–74; tithe payments by, 65–66. See also injustice, peasant conceptions of
persecution of heretics, 20, 115
Philippe, Duc d'Orléans, 140–141, 144, 182
Philippe le Bel (Philip IV), 190–191
Picot, Georges, 28, 190–191, 193
Pillorget, René and Suzanne, 66n170, 86–87
pluralistic ignorance, 24–25
Pompadour, Madame de (Jeanne Antoinette Poisson), 94, 108, 154
préséance, 30, 40–47, 55, 180–181, 192–193, 217
Protestants, 115, 162, 223

publicity, 103–104, 122, 125–130

public good/public interest, 17, 22, 35, 37n28, 63n150, 211, 215, 228

quartering of soldiers, 77n222, 161–162, 217

Rapine, Florimond, 196–198

rationality, 10–12. *See also* irrationality

reactance, 149

Rébillon, Armand, 207

Regent. *See* Philippe, Duc d'Orléans

remonstrances, 30, 37–39, 122, 125–126, 144, 152, 179, 182, 210, 223, 228; publication of, 30, 37, 125–126

rentes sur l'hôtel de ville (government bonds), 152, 180

reputation, 35, 55–56, 104, 244

Rétif, Nicolas-Edme (Rétif de la Bretonne), 80, 81–82

Retz, Cardinal de (Jean François Paul de Gondi), 55, 117

Reymond, Henri, 100, 105n11

Richelieu, Cardinal de (Armand Jean du Plessis), 48n80, 98, 145

Richelieu, Armand de Vignerot du Plessis, Duc de, 109

risk-assessment, 13

risk-aversion 13, 22, 24, 50

Rochefoucauld, Duc de la. *See* La Rochefoucauld, François, Duc de

Rousseau, Jean-Jacques, 80

rumors, 13, 25–27, 60, 66n170, 87, 92, 129, 133–135, 182n215, 222

safety valve, 8; Estates-General as, 189; remonstrances as, 182n214

Saint-Jacob, Pierre de, 62, 64, 72n195, 79, 83–84, 85, 88, 137, 237–238

Saint-Priest, François-Emmanuel Guignard, Comte de, 205

Saint-Simon, Louis de Rouvroy, Duc de, 49–50, 52–53, 104, 121, 140–141, 152, 182n215, 242–243

Salic law of succession, 143–145

salt tax, 80–81, 142, 224–225

Sauvigny, Louis Bénigne François Bertier de, 95

Schelling, Thomas, 23, 167n144

seigneurial justice, 88–91

self-interest, 17–18, 32–34, 37n28, 65, 215

Seneca, Lucius Annaeus (the younger), 14, 18, 25, 116n67

Seven Years' War (1756–1763), 117, 155, 173, 210

Sévigné, Madame de (Marie de Rabutin-Chantal), 51, 56, 57n123, 110, 217

shame, 59n138, 111–112, 127, 232

Shiller, Robert, 111

Sieyès, Abbé Emmanuel Joseph, 65n167

Smith, Adam, 67n176

solidarity, 23, 101, 225. *See also* class consciousness

Spanheim, Ezéchiel, 123n97, 148, 239

Staël, Madame de (Anne Louise Germaine de Staël-Holstein), 175, 232–233

Stalin, Joseph, 182

Stendhal (Henri Beyle), 51, 56n118, 99

strike, judicial, 164, 182, 183

sympathy, 57n122, 233

Swann, Julian, 45, 163, 164–165

Tackett, Timothy, 99–100

taille, 77, 80, 170; objections to, 77–80; *taille personnelle*, 59n138, 73–74, 238n5; *taille réelle*, 59n138, 73–74, 238n5

taxes, 69, 170–171; *capitation*, 69n179, 99, 170; checks on, 73; collector of, 18, 72n194, 105, 137–138, 212, 224, 225, 226; *dixième*, 104, 225; exemptions from, 216; indirect, 81n240, 170–171 (*see also* salt tax); proposals to reform, 70; *taxation populaire*, 93n302, 135n148; *vingtième*, 69n179, 105, 152, 170n158, 199–200, 225. *See also taille*

Tencin. Cardinal Pierre Guérin de, 109

Tencin, Madame Claudine Guérin de, 109

tertius gaudens, 181, 186. *See also* divide and conquer

third estate, 190–191, 193

tithe, 84–86; tithe-holder, 65n167, 85

Tocqueville, Alexis de, ix–x, 5–7, 8, 19, 22, 25, 34n14, 44–45, 55, 57, 68–69, 75–76, 87–88, 89n278, 131n130, 136, 157n94, 163–164, 169, 179n202, 189, 201, 212–213, 227, 231–233; on emotions, 231–232; predictions by, 7; Tocqueville effect, 6

tolls, internal, 142, 160

Tourny, Louis-Urbain-Aubert, 158, 159

Turgot, Anne Robert Jacques, 11, 35n19, 36n20, 73, 88, 101, 105, 108–110, 122–123, 127, 135, 138, 149, 170n158, 173, 180, 244

uncertainty, 12, 106, 111, 130, 131, 218–219

Unigenitus (papal bull), 27, 37n28, 39, 94, 126n108, 140n1, 183

urgency, 14, 18n35, 33, 218

Varenne, Jacques, 210

Vauban, Maréchal Sébastien Le Prestre de, 48n80, 70, 78, 120, 243

Veyne, Paul, x, 143

village assemblies, 211–213

Walpole, Horace, 54, 240

war, 171; civil, 2, 80, 117, 143, 208; defensive, 77n221, 229; funding of, 229–230; against Holland, 117, 121, 148n34; of independence, American, 77n221, 173–174; offensive, 77n221, 202, 218, 229; Thirty Years, 145; two-front, 233. *See also* Flour War, Seven Years' War

wit (*esprit*), 2–3, 55–56

Young, Arthur, 56, 67n176, 79, 240